T0198273

SPICE

The Theory and Practice of Software Process Improvement and Capability Determination

IEEE Computer Society Press

Mohamed E. Fayad
Editor-in-Chief, Practices for Computer Science and Engineering

---

SELECTED TITLES

Distributed Objects: Methodologies for Customizing Operating Systems
Nayeem Islam

Software Engineering Risk Management
Dale Karolak

Digital Design and Modeling with VHDL and Synthesis
K.C. Chang

Industrial Strength Software: Effective Management Using Measurement
Lawrence Putnam and Ware Myers

Unified Objects: Object-Oriented Programming Using C++
Babak Sadr

Interconnection Networks: An Engineering Approach
José Duato, Sudhakar Yalamanchili, and Lionel Ni

SPICE: The Theory and Practice of Software Process Improvement and Capability Determination
Khaled El Emam, Jean-Normand Drouin, and Walcélio Melo

Meeting Deadlines in Real-Time Systems: The Rate Monotonic Analysis
Daniel Roy and Loic Briand

Executive Briefings

Controlling Software Development
Lawrence Putnam and Ware Myers

SPICE

The Theory and Practice of Software Process Improvement and Capability Determination

edited by Khaled El Emam, Jean-Normand Drouin, and Walcélio Melo

IEEE
COMPUTER
SOCIETY

Los Alamitos, California

Washington • Brussels • Tokyo

Library of Congress Cataloging-in-Publication Data

SPICE: the theory and practice of software process improvement
and capability determination / edited by Khaled El Emam, Jean-Normand Drouin,
and Walcélio Melo.

     p.   cm.

    Includes bibliographical references and index.

    ISBN 0-8186-7798-8

    1. Computer software—Standards.   2. Computer Software—
Evaluation.   I. El Emam, Khaled.   II. Drouin, Jean–Normand.
III. Melo, Walcélio.

QA76.76.S73S65 1998

005.1 ' 068—dc21

                            97-29226
                             CIP

IEEE Computer Society Order Number BP07798
Library of Congress Number 97-29226
ISBN 0-8186-7798-8

Additional copies may be ordered from:

IEEE Computer Society Press	IEEE Service Center	IEEE Computer Society	IEEE Computer Society
Customer Service Center	445 Hoes Lane	13, Avenue de l'Aquilon	Ooshima Building
10662 Los Vaqueros Circle	P.O. Box 1331	B-1200 Brussels	2-19-1 Minami-Aoyama
P.O. Box 3014	Piscataway, NJ 08855-1331	BELGIUM	Minato-ku, Tokyo 107
Los Alamitos, CA 90720-1314	Tel: +1-908-981-1393	Tel: +32-2-770-2198	JAPAN
Tel: +1-714-821-8380	Fax: +1-908-981-9667	Fax: +32-2-770-8505	Tel: +81-3-3408-3118
Fax: +1-714-821-4641	mis.custserv@computer.org	euro.ofc@computer.org	Fax: +81-3-3408-3553
Email: cs.books@computer.org			tokyo.ofc@computer.org

Editor-in-Chief: Mohamed Fayad
Publisher: Matt Loeb
Developmental Editor: Cheryl Baltes
Advertising/Promotions: Tom Fink
Production Editor: Lisa O'Conner
Cover art: Studio Productions
Printed in the United States of America by Edwards Brothers, Incorporated

Contents

Part 1

Part 2

Foreword

Alec Dorling

IVF Centre for Software Engineering, Sweden

The SPICE Project, in comparison to many other international collaborative efforts, has been an unprecedented success. This book is a tribute to all those SPICE resources from over twenty-five countries who have contributed to the project.

The first notion of a standard for process assessment began during a visit to the Software Engineering Institute in Pittsburgh in 1988. In 1992 such a notion became a reality when the international standardization community approved a new work item to develop an International Standard for Software Process Assessment following a study period that would gather the needs and requirements of the user community.

SPICE owes its origins to the existence of other assessment methods and models, most notably the Capability Maturity Model developed by the SEI, Bootstrap developed by the Bootstrap Institute, Trillium developed by Bell Canada, Northern Telecom, and Bell Northern Research, and SPQA developed for internal use within Hewlett Packard.

Creating a climate within the SPICE Project whereby all the major players could come together has been as much a political feat as a technical one. Notable events in the study phase leading to the launch of the project included a 24-hour whistle-stop visit to New York at the invitation of the US TAG to ensure that the US requirements were addressed, the visit by Mark Paulk of the SEI to the UK and the SEI's subsequent commitment to the project, Bootstrap coming on board at the EOQ Software Quality Conference in Madrid, and the visit to the European Commission in Brussels where the UK Ministry of Defence, at the time the main sponsor of the activity, proposed that the new European Software Institute (ESI) become the focus for the SPICE Project activity in Europe.

It is significant that the major method and model developers have been allocated key roles as project editors, allowing them to exert influence over the technical aspects of the project. The major sponsors and key software engineering centers, such as the SEI (US), ESI (Spain), ASQI (Australia), and

CRIM (Canada), are represented on the SPICE Management Board and manage and control the SPICE Project by setting its overall direction. Within the project, however, all countries have an equal vote, much to the frustration of some of the larger software-producing countries. Maintaining a fine balance of the many factors of the project has required the skill, determination, overall respect, and confidence of each and every member that has participated.

A key feature of the SPICE Project has been the conduct of user trials to ensure the emerging standard meets the needs of its users. Such an activity is unprecedented in the software engineering community. The completion of the first phase of user trials was a great achievement for the SPICE Project. Now entering its second phase of user trials, it is anticipated that there will be over 200 organizations participating in this phase of trials.

There is no doubt that the SPICE Project is having a worldwide impact: a whole new industry has developed around the SPICE Project. It has captured the imagination of users, developers, consultants, trainers, tool developers, and the like. The SPICE Project is already embarking upon its fifth International Conference. The list of publications and papers in learned journals is considerable and growing all the time. The emerging standard has already become standard curriculum in many undergraduate programs in software engineering and has been the subject of research in many post-graduate research programs. Hundreds of people have been trained in SPICE training courses. A Certified SPICE Assessor program exists to meet the demand for the qualification of assessors. Several SPICE software tools have been developed to support assessments and are freely available in the public domain.

Looking forward to the near future there are exciting prospects at hand. SPICE *plug-ins* (to the reference model) is one concept that has gained momentum: plug-ins can be envisaged in systems engineering, data centers, and computer operations. Another concept that is gaining ground is the offering of an *ISO 9001 Plus* certificate, combining a traditional ISO 9001 certificate with a SPICE certificate denoting objective evidence of a SPICE conformant self-assessment having been performed and resultant improvement actions undertaken. No doubt you will hear more about these developments in the future.

I hope that by reading this book you will gain useful insight into the emerging standard and will be encouraged to participate in the SPICE Project. I look forward to welcoming you personally aboard!

Preface

This book is intended for current and potential users of the emerging International Standard on Software Process Assessment (SPA). Users may include organizations wanting to conduct process assessments internally or as a service to their customers, providers of models, methods, and tools compliant with the requirements of the emerging standard, educators wanting to teach the principles of SPA as part of a university course, and researchers developing technology to support process assessments and then empirically evaluating them.

This book provides the first comprehensive coverage of the theory and practice of SPA as embodied in the current version of the ISO/IEC documents. The official title of these documents is ISO/IEC PDTR 15504, although they are also commonly known as the SPICE Version 2.00 documents. The main focus of the book is twofold: to help the reader understand the evolution of the SPA ideas that were developed between 1993 and 1997 and to provide guidance for interpreting and using the documents for assessment and subsequent improvement and/or capability determination.

Initial thoughts about writing this book began to emerge in March 1996, primarily to address the needs of the software engineering community:

- There was little technical information about the SPICE document set available to the general software engineering community when we started to write this book. We wanted to fill this gap by providing up-to-date information.

- Early and potential users of the emerging standard asked such questions as "Why does the emerging standard do X this way and not that way?" By describing the rationale for the design decisions that were made during the development of the SPICE document set, these questions could be answered. Different perspectives and issues about how a Software Process Assessment framework could and would be used were considered carefully throughout the documents' development and these views are described in the following chapters.

- While potential users can obtain the ISO/IEC documents—instructions for doing so are included below—the practical experiences and empirical evaluations of those who have used them are not available just by reading the emerging standard. To provide insights into the practice and empirical evaluations that have been gained, both key elements of the SPICE Project, half of this book has been devoted to reporting the results of experienced users of the emerging standard.

In short, much of the content of this book is not and will not be available elsewhere and contained in a single package. The information is complementary to that which is available in the ISO/IEC documents and provides a contextual frame of reference to those readers who want to understand the rationale behind its development.

The name SPICE—Software Process Improvement and Capability dEtermination—was given to this project as the development vehicle for the initial version of the SPA documents and as the management of the trials. The ISO/IEC/SC7 Working Group mandated to develop the SPA standard is WG10. While each of the two entities has a different objective, they consist of mainly the same people. Therefore, the document set is commonly referred to as the SPICE documents or the ISO/IEC documents. We have retained the use of the term *SPICE documents* because, within the software engineering community, it has become synonymous with the ISO/IEC emerging standard document set.

The set of documents comprising ISO/IEC PDTR 15504 is available freely under certain conditions. For example, organizations participating in the SPICE Trials can request access to the documents by sending an email to "sugar@qai.u-net.com" and including in the subject field "DOCUMENT REQUEST."

This book is divided into three parts, a paper appendix, and an electronic appendix on a CD-ROM.

Part 1 describes software engineering standardization efforts mainly from the perspective of ISO and the place of WG10 and the SPICE Project within that context.

Chapter 1 *Introduction to Software Engineering Standards* describes the structure, goals, and projects in ISO/JTC1/SC7 and places the SPA effort within the context of other software engineering projects within ISO.

Chapter 2 *Introduction to SPICE* provides the history of the project to date as it tries to help the reader understand the multiple parts of the emerging standard. It describes how the project started, how the teams were formed, how the precedent-setting use of the Internet facilitated worldwide communication and the relatively-fast development of the emerging standard. It also describes why user trials—the first such formalized trials within the software engineering standards community—were introduced. It chapter also explains the difference between the SPICE Project and WG10, which in the past has been a constant source of confusion.

Part 2 provides a complete description of the ISO/IEC PDTR 15504 (or SPICE Version 2.00) documents. This part gives the reader an insight into the technical aspects of SPICE through the SPICE reference model and its rating framework. The reader will also gain an understanding of how to perform a SPICE-conformant assessment. The emphasis in this part of the book is on the principles of the emerging standard and how to interpret its contents.

Chapter 3 *Introduction to the SPICE Documents and Architecture* describes the basic SPA architecture and its evolution. It provides insight into how the architecture has evolved to where it is today, presents its basic principles and the two-dimensional process model, introduces the current nine parts, and describes how the parts were derived from their requirements. An addendum to this chapter explains ongoing work to further harmonize the emerging SPA standard with the existing ISO/IEC 12207 standard on Software Life Cycle Processes.

Chapter 4 *The Reference Model* presents the first of two normative components of the emerging standard. The reference model is one of the key documents that provides a framework for process assessment.

Chapter 5 *Process Assessment Using SPICE: The Assessment Activities* provides comprehensive guidance on how to conduct an assessment and how to select a compatible model, method, and tool to conduct the assessment.

Chapter 6 *Process Assessment using SPICE: The Rating Framework* explains the measurement framework and its evolution. The measurement framework is one of the key elements for ensuring the repeatability of assessment results and for clearly presenting and interpreting assessment scores.

Chapter 7 *The Assessment Model* describes the exemplar model that is part of the document set. The exemplar model is compliant with the requirements of the emerging standard and can be used for conducting an assessment.

Chapter 8 *Guidelines for Process Improvement* provides information on what needs to be done to ensure successful process improvement following an assessment.

Chapter 9 *Guidelines for Determining Supplier Process Capability* explains how the results of an assessment can be used in the context of capability determination, such as, for example, during supplier selection.

Chapter 10 *Qualification and Training of Assessors* provides information about a recommended process for the qualification of assessors as well as the outline of a course for training assessors. Assessor qualification is one of, if not the most, critical element to ensure the repeatability of assessments.

Chapter 11 *A Comparison of ISO 9001 and the SPICE Framework* discusses how the SPICE framework is suitable for use as a prerequisite process management model when considering registration to ISO 9001. It presents the SPICE framework as a path toward achieving compliance with the Quality System standard as well as for maintaining its process improvement objectives post-registration. It also provides a table showing a SPICE-ISO 9001 mapping.

Part 3 discusses experiences in using the SPICE document set. The reader will find a discussion about the background of the SPICE Trials' activity, a summary of the results, and a detailed analysis of the findings. Through a case study, the reader will be walked through a typical SPICE Trial assessment and thereby gain an insight into the whole process.

Chapter 12 *Introduction to the SPICE Trials* gives an overview of the trials, the hypothesis upon which the Phase 1 Trials were based, their objectives, the structure of the program, and an overview of the empirical research methods used.

Chapter 13 *Empirical Evaluation of SPICE* presents the results of evaluating Version 1.00 of the SPICE document set during the Phase 1 Trials.

Chapter 14 *Analysis of Assessment Ratings from the Trials* provides a summary of the ratings from the Phase 1 Trials as well as an analysis of the ratings and how they were defined. It also identifies clusters of similar organizations that can be useful for doing benchmarking.

Chapter 15 *Analysis of Observation and Problem Reports* describes the structured feedback that was collected from the Phase 1 Trials and discusses the analysis based on the data provided by the assessors. The discussion includes the problems they faced, the classification systems used to group the problems, and action items derived for input into the new version of the emerging standard.

Chapter 16 *Interrater Agreement in Assessment Ratings* describes a case study to evaluate the repeatability of ratings within the context of a single assessment.

Chapter 17 *Using SPICE as Framework for Software Engineering Education: A Case Study* describes an application of SPICE in teaching a software engineering course at university, lessons learned, and speculations about how such applications could be used in the future.

Chapter 18 *Assessment Using SPICE: A Case Study* describes an assessment using Version 2.00 of SPICE documents, the methods, templates, assessment plans used, as well as discussions of the assessment report.

Chapter 19 *The Future of the SPICE Trials* describes the ongoing Phase 2 Trials and how readers can find out more about participating in them.

Version 2.00 of the document set is the version that will be used in the official SPICE Trials until Version 4.00 of the document set is baselined. (Version 3.00

will be an interim developmental version only.) Early experience with Version 4.00 of the document set is expected to be available during the SPICE Trials toward the end of 1998 at the earliest.

There are two appendices that provide information on how to install the automated tools included with the CD-ROM. Contact information about the developers of these tools is also provided for readers with questions or who want to obtain upgrades.

The CD-ROM contains two automated tools that can help to improve the efficiency of conducting assessments. The first tool is useful mainly for conducting assessments, and the second was developed for visualizing and manipulating assessment ratings data. These tools should help the reader get started with conducting assessments. We also included the full Version 1.00 document set as well as a program to read and print the document files.

We hope this book will shed a clear and insightful light on the emerging standard for SPA and on the SPICE Project, as well as provide you with additional incentive to embark on the long and never-ending journey that is Software Process Improvement and Capability dEtermination.

Acknowledgments

This book could not have been realized without the support of a large number of people. Of course, first we have to thank all the participants of the SPICE Project who actively worked either within the core document groups or as reviewers of the documents, several of whom participated in the drafting of parts of this book. They are acknowledged in the relevant chapters.

Victoria A. Hailey was the Technical Editor for this book. Her involvement in the book project started after our contract with the publisher was signed. Her contribution, however, was as one of the main editors of this book.

Others who have made a significant contribution to the book are:

- Innocent Nungentwali of the Fraunhofer—Institute for Experimental Software Engineering, Germany, who worked on typesetting the chapters
- Jyrki Kontio of the University of Maryland, US, and Dietmar Pfahl of the Fraunhofer—Institute for Experimental Software Engineering, Germany, for acting as external reviewers for chapters.

Finally, thanks must be extended to the Fraunhofer—Institute for Experimental Software Engineering for supporting the typesetting of the book, to the Applied Software Engineering Center (ASEC—a division of Centre de recherché informatique de Montreal) and CRIM of Montreal for sponsoring the publicity for the book and for providing the ftp site, a service that proved to be extremely useful to the team of writers scattered all over the world, and to the European Software Institute (ESI) for sponsoring the publicity for this book.

Khaled El Emam
Jean-Normand Drouin
Walcelio Melo

Introduction to Software Engineering Standards

François Coallier

ISO/IEC JTC1/SC7 Secretary, Bell Canada, Canada[*]

Prof. Motoei Azuma

ISO/IEC JTC1/SC7/WG6 Convenor, Waseda University, Japan[*]

The SPICE Project is an activity of Working Group (WG) 10 of Subcommittee (SC) 7 of the Joint Technical Committee (JTC) 1 of the International Organization for Standards (ISO) and the International Electrotechnical Commission (IEC).

The purpose of this chapter is to describe the context of international standardization activities in which the SPICE documents are being developed.

International standardization

Types of standardization activities

Standards are developed by groups of individuals or organizations to harmonize product specifications, interfaces, processes, terminology, and so on. Standards

---

[*]The opinions expressed in this paper are those of the authors.

cover a wide range of topics and are recognized by various groups of individuals and countries.

Standards are—and should—be developed in response to a user, organization, or market need. Some standards are developed in a formal fashion by organizations that are mandated to do so, while others impose themselves on the market.

There are five basic types of standards:

1. Organization standards: internal company standards (for example)

2. Market standards: standards that become such because of the market preponderance of a product (for example, the Microsoft Windows* Application Programming Interface and the VHS videotape standards)

3. Professional standards: standards developed by professional organizations, such as the IEEE, based on professional consensus

4. Industrial standards: standards developed by industrial associations, where the consensus is at the level of each industrial member (for example, the CD-V videodisk and the CDIF CASE tool interface standards)

5. International standards: standards developed by international standards bodies, based on international consensus, where the membership consists of national organizations (such as ISO, IEC, ITU)

Standards, in general, represent a *consensus*. This representation means that, for standards' types 3, 4, and 5 above, a substantial majority of individuals, organizations, and/or countries have reached an agreement, usually by compromising on their initial positions. As a result, standards are generally less than technically perfect or optimal from an idealistic perspective.

The value of standards does not decrease, however. On the contrary, standards are an ideal medium to communicate:

Microsoft and *Windows* are registered trademarks of Microsoft Corporation.

- terminology
- procedures
- models
- benchmarks

The last item is rather significant: a standard can also be a benchmark since it represents the lowest common denominator to which consensus could be attained.

International standardization activities

There are many international standards organizations. Some are focused on *regional* groupings of countries or trade groups, such as the European Union (for example, CEN), while others have a wider international scope. This latter category either has organizations linked to the United Nations or are self-standing organizations, such as the International Telecommunication Union (ITU). Of particular interest to the reader are two of these organizations: ISO and IEC.

The *International Organization for Standardization* (ISO) was founded on 23rd February 1947. The *International Electrotechnical Commission* (IEC) was founded in 1906. Both these organizations had mandates from their respective members to put into place an international standardization framework to facilitate commerce and international exchanges of goods and services. While IEC was initially concentrating on, as its name suggests, standards in the electrical and electronic engineering fields, ISO was founded to address other topics.

In 1987, ISO and IEC decided to establish a *Joint Technical Committee* (JTC), with the mandate of elaborating *Information Technology* (IT) standards.

This Joint Technical Committee, still unique and known as Joint Technical Committee 1 (JTC1), has presently 19 active Subcommittees (SCs). They are listed in Appendix A, along with their areas of responsibilities.

Software engineering standards

The first standard to be published in the area of *software engineering* was a US military standard on software quality assurance in 1972. The publication of this standard was followed in 1976 by an Institute of Electrical and Electronics Engineers (IEEE) standard on Software Quality Assurance Plans. After that, the

IEEE initiated a systematic program of software engineering standards development. This program was, and still is, managed by a Subcommittee.

The IEEE is the organization that currently has published the most comprehensive set of software engineering standards. Twenty-nine standards have been published as of April, 1996, and 13 additional standards were being developed.

In a recent study, T. Matsubara inventoried 550 standards from 76 organizations, pertinent to the software engineering area.[1] There is a considerable overlap between these standards, either because of work duplication between professional, national, and international organizations or because of domain or organization-specific instantiations of standardization on a given software engineering topic: for example, software development, documentation, and testing policies for Navy Mission Critical Systems.

Interestingly enough, as international standards become available in software engineering, many national and transnational organizations are adopting these standards instead of developing their own. This adoption is driven by two factors:

1. the high costs associated with the development of standards
2. the globalization of the world economy.

Types of software engineering standards

Software engineering standards are focused on the following:

TYPE	EXAMPLE	PURPOSE
Process	life-cycle processes, verification, validation, configuration management, measurement, CASE tool selection	describe mechanisms and a set of tasks related to the engineering of software products
Work Products	requirements, design descriptions, documentation	focused on deliverables generated by a given, or a given set of, software processes or tasks
Methods	unit testing, software quality metrics methodology	specify a procedure for performing a given task or process

Measurements	functional size, software process assessment	define software engineering metrics used in measuring processes as well as work products
Formalisms	CASE tool data interchange, diagrams, Petri-Net	define notations and representations that are usually human as well as machine readable
Terminology	standard vocabularies	define the natural language terms used by practitioners and standards writers

While the above taxonomy represents one way of looking at standards, it illustrates the diversity of types of software engineering standards. Not all software engineering standards fall into a specific category. Some could fall into two or more.

Subcommittee 7

The history of ISO/IEC JTC1/SC7

The roots of SC7 go back to ISO/TC97 (Technical Committee 97), established in 1960 for international standardization in the field of *information processing*.

What is now JTC1/SC7 was put into place as one of the Subcommittees of TC97 (Technical Committee 97) in 1963. Its area of work was *Problem definition and analysis* and its first project was to address the standardization of flowcharting techniques and representations. From this work, ISO 1028 *Flowchart symbols for information processing* and ISO 2636 *Information processing—Convention for incorporating flowchart symbols in flowcharts* became standards, with both being published in 1973.

When JTC1 was established in 1987, ISO/TC97 was combined with IEC/TC83 into a JTC1 Subcommittee as the 7th (SC7). The title SC7 was changed to *Software Engineering*. SC7 proposed the title *Information System Technology*, but this title was rejected by JTC1 on the grounds that the title itself could be interpreted extensively, and it might include the entire field in which JTC1 intended to work.

The first SC7 plenary was held in Paris, France in 1987. At the 1996 plenary in Prague, Czechoslovakia, 156 delegates from 17 countries attended.

SC7 organization and program of work

SC7 is presently split into nine active working groups that are mandated to carry on its program of work (see Figure 1.1).

This program of work is a set of standardization projects that are defined by the SC7 Terms of Reference as follows:

Development of guidelines for the management techniques and standardization of supporting methods and tools necessary for the development and testing of software.

These Terms of Reference are being considered for update to:

Standardization of processes, supporting tools and supporting technologies for the engineering of software products and systems.

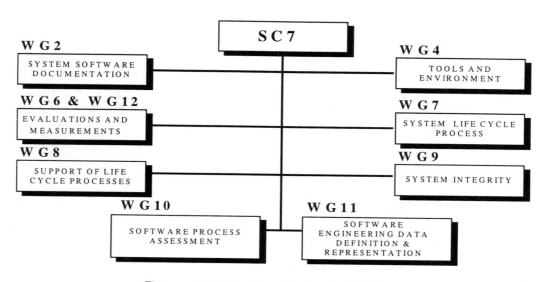

Figure 1.1: Working Groups of SC7.

The key word in these Terms of Reference is *process*. SC7 is a standardization organization that is focused on processes, specifically the processes required for the engineering of software products and systems. These Terms of Reference translate into the projects shown in Figure 1.2.

A more comprehensive list of the projects that constitute the SC7 Program of Work is given, on a Working Group basis, in Appendix B.

The SPICE Project

The SPICE Project is project 07.29 in the SC7 Program of Work. It is a multipart document—nine parts—that at the time of printing is going through its first formal review as a Proposed Draft Technical Report (PDTR). The next stages of the standardization process are Draft Technical Report and then publication as a Technical Report.

The project will not end there. Since the SPICE documents will be what are called Technical Reports Type 2—Technical Reports that are published when there is doubt that sufficient consensus can be attained—these documents will have to be reballoted after two years to become full International Standards.

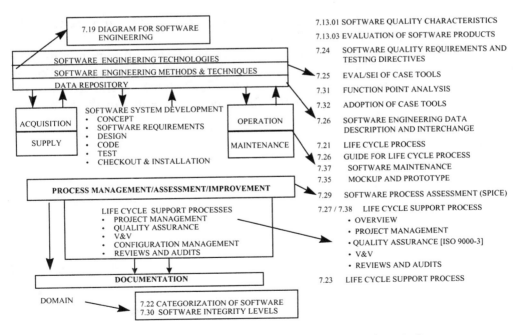

Figure 1.2: SC7 framework and projects.[2]

Conclusions

The Program of Work of SC7 has evolved considerably in the past five years. Participation in its meetings has increased, as well as its production of standards. It is expected that more than 30 software engineering standards will be published by SC7 within the next two years.

SC7 has made considerable efforts to ensure its standards and Program of Work meet customer needs. For instance, SC7 and its Working Groups have put into place a comprehensive set of formal liaisons with professional and industrial associations, including:

- IEEE Computer Society (WG4)
- NATO (WG7)
- European Software Institute (WG10)
- CDIF (WG11)
- International Function Point User Group—IFPUG and European Function Point User Group—EFPUG (WG12).

Members from these organizations can participate as technical experts in the Program of Work of these Working Groups.

As SC7 publishes more standards, their influence on the software engineering profession and industry will increase. Already, standards ISO/IEC 9126 on software product quality characteristics and ISO/IEC 12207 on the software life cycle have made their marks. The SPICE documents will surely contribute greatly to this future influence.

Appendix A: JTC1 Subcommittees and their area of responsibilities

SC	Title	Areas of Responsibilities
1	**Vocabulary**	Standardization of terminology for information technology and related fields.
2	**Coded Character Sets**	Standardization of graphic character sets and their characteristics, associated control functions, their coded representation for information interchange, and code extension techniques.
6	**Telecommunications and Information Exchange Between Systems**	Standardization in the field of telecommunications and Open Systems Interconnection, of system function, procedures and parameters, as well as the conditions for their use, for the four OSI layers that support the Transport Service, to facilitate the transport of both OSI and non-OSI application protocols and multimedia and hypermedia information.
7	*Software Engineering*	***Standardization of processes, supporting tools, and supporting technologies for the engineering of software products and systems.***
8	**Flexible Magnetic Media for Digital Data Interchange**	Standardization for the purpose of digital data interchange of flexible magnetic media, such as tapes, tape cassettes, tape cartridges, and flexible disk cartridges, the recording of data on these media, and algorithms for the lossless compression of data.
14	**Data Element Principles**	Standardization of data elements (including general rules and guidelines for their definition, description, classification, representation, and registration) that are interchanged among information processing systems, and the syntax by which these data elements are associated.
17	**Identification Cards and Related Devices**	Standardization in the area of identification cards and related devices for use in inter-industry applications and international interchange.
18	**Document Processing and Related Communication**	Standardization of document processing and communication and the user-system interface as applied to the fields of publishing and office systems. The term "document" used above describes any representation of information intended for human perception. A document can consist of component objects of different types, textual and nontextual, linked in a linear or nonlinear fashion.
21	**Open Systems Interconnection, Data Management, and Open Distributed Processing**	Standardization of protocols, services, interfaces, and information objects, and of related reference models covering the areas of Open Systems Interconnection, management of data and information resources in both a local and distributed processing environment, Open Distributed Processing, security and management aspects related to the above, and the relationships among these areas. Standardization of related conformance-testing methodologies, description languages and techniques, and registration procedures.
22	**Programming Languages, their Environments and System Software Interfaces**	Standardization of programming languages, their environments, and systems software interfaces, such as specification techniques, and common facilities and interfaces.

23	**Optical Disk Cartridges for Information Interchange**	Standardization of Optical Disk Cartridges for Media and Information Interchange between Information Processing Systems.
24	**Computer Graphics and Image Processing**	Standardization of interfaces, in windowed and nonwindowed environments, for computer graphics, image processing, and interaction with and visual presentation of information.
25	**Interconnection of Information Technology Equipment**	Standardization of interfaces, protocols, and associated interconnecting media for information technology equipment, generally for commercial and residential environments
26	**Microprocessor Systems**	To prepare international standards for microprocessor systems, where the term "microprocessor systems" includes but is not limited to microprocessor assemblies, and the related hardware and software for controlling the flow of signals at the terminals of microprocessor assemblies.
27	**IT Security Techniques**	Standardization of generic methods and techniques for IT security
28	**Office Equipment**	Standardization of Basic Characteristics, performance, test methods, and other related aspects of office equipment and products.
29	**Coding of Audio, Picture, Multimedia, and Hypermedia Information**	Standardization of coded representation of audio, picture, multimedia, and hypermedia information, and sets of compression and control functions for use with such information.
30	**Open EDI**	Standardization in the field of generic information technology standards for open electronic data interchange needed to attain global interoperability among the systems used by organizations. Such interoperability is viewed from both business and information technology perspectives.
31	**Automatic Data Capture**	Standardization of common coding; data format, syntax, and structure; and enabling technologies for individually and uniquely-identifying items and entities without human intervention.

Appendix B: SC7 Program of Work

WG2   System Software Documentation

        Scope   Development of standards for the documentation of software systems.

Projects	07.03.01	User Documentation and Cover Information for Consumer Software Packages [ISO 9127]
	07.03.02	Guidelines for Software Documentation (Revision) [ISO 6592]
	07.18	Guidelines for the Management of Software Documentation [ISO 9294]
	07.39	Software Life Cycle Process— Guidelines for the Content of Software Life Cycle Process Information Products
	07.40	Software User Documentation Process

WG4   Tools and Environment

        Scope   Development of standards and technical reports for tools and Computer Aided Software/System Engineering (CASE) environments.

Projects	07.25	Evaluation and Selection of CASE Tools
	07.32	Adoption of CASE Tools

WG6   Evaluation and Metrics

        Scope   Development of standards and technical reports for software products evaluation and metrics for software products and processes.

        Projects   07.13.01.01   9126-1, Software Quality Characteristics and Metrics—Part 1: Quality Characteristics and Subcharacteristics

                        07.13.02.02   9126-2, Software Quality Characteristics and Metrics—Part 2: External Metrics

                        07.13.03.03   9126-3, Software Quality Characteristics and Metrics—Part 3: Internal Metrics

                        07.13.02.01   14598-1, Software Product Evaluation—Part 1: General Overview

                        07.13.02.02   14598-2, Software Product Evaluation—Part 2: Planning and Management

                        07.13.02.03   14598-3, Software Product Evaluation—Part 3: Process for Developers

                        07.13.02.04   14598-4, Software Product Evaluation—Part 4: Process for Acquirers

                        07.13.02.05   14598-5, Software Product Evaluation—Part 5: Process for Evaluators

                        07.13.05.06   14598-6, Software Product Evaluation—Part 6: Evaluation Modules

                        07.13.03.07   Software Product Evaluation— Indicators and Metrics

                        07.24   Software Quality Requirements and Testing [ISO 12229]

	07.36	[14756] Measurement and Rating of Performance of Computer-based Software Systems.

WG7 Life Cycle Management

Scope Development of standards and technical reports on Life Cycle Management.

Projects	07.21	Life Cycle Process
	07.26	Guidebook for Life Cycle Process
	07.35	Mock-Up and Prototype
	07.37	Software Maintenance
	07.38	System Life Cycle Process

WG8 Support of Life Cycle Processes

Scope Development of standards and technical reports on Life Cycle Management processes.

Projects	07.23	12220-2, Life Cycle Process— Software Configuration Management
	07.27	Support of Life Cycle Processes
	07.27.02	12220-3, Life Cycle Process—Project Management
	07.27.03	12220-4, Life Cycle Process— Quality Assurance
	07.27.04	12220-5, Life Cycle Process— Verification & Validation
	07.27.05	12220-6, Life Cycle Process—Formal Review and Audits

WG9 Software Integrity

Scope Preparation of standards, technical reports, and guidance documents related to software integrity at the system and system interface level.

In this context, software integrity is defined as ensuring the containment of risk or confining the risk exposure in software.

Projects 07.20.03.01 Mapping of Standards Pertinent to Software Engineering

07.22 Categorization of Software

07.30 System and Software Integrity Levels

WG10 Process Assessment

Scope Development of standards and guidelines covering methods, practices, and application of process assessment in software product procurement, development, delivery, operation, evolution, and related service support.

Organization: SG1 Concepts and Introductory Guide

SG2 Model for Process Management

SG3 Rating Processes

SG4 Guide to Conducting Assessments

SG5 Construction, Selection, and Use of Assessment Instruments and Tools

SG6 Qualification and Training of Assessors

SG7 Guide for Use in Process Improvement

	SG8	Guide for Use in Determining Supplier Process Capability
	SG9	Vocabulary

Projects	07.29	Software Process Assessment
	07.29.01	Concepts and Introductory Guide
	07.29.02	A Model for Process Management
	07.29.03	Rating Processes
	07.29.04	Guide to Conducting Assessments
	07.29.05	Construction, Selection, and Use of Assessment Instruments and Tools
	07.29.06	Qualification and Training of Assessors
	07.29.07	Guide for Use in Process Improvement
	07.29.08	Guide for Use in Determining Supplier Process Capability
	07.29.09	Vocabulary

WG11 Software Engineering Data Definition and Representation

Scope	Development of standards and technical reports to define the data used and produced by software engineering processes, establish representations for communication by both humans and machines, and define data interchange formats.

Projects	07.01	Conventions for Incorporating Flowchart Symbols in Flowcharts [ISO 2636]
	07.07	Single Hit Decision Logic Tables [ISO 5806]

07.28.02.02	Syntax
07.28.02.03	Encoding
07.28.03	Abstract Model
07.28.03.01	Presentation Location
07.28.03.02	Presentation Global
07.28.03.03	Presentation Shapes
07.28.03.04	Foundation Subject Area
07.28.03.05	Common Subject Area
07.28.03.06	Data Definition Subject Area
07.28.03.07	Data Flow Model Subject Area
07.28.03.08	Data Modeling Subject Area
07.28.03.09	State / Event Model Subject Area
07.28.03.10	Physical Relational Data Base Subject Area
07.28.03.11	Project Planning and Scheduling Subject Area
07.28.04	PCTE Schema Definition Sets
07.28.05	IRDS Content Modules

WG12 Functional size measurements

Scope To establish a set of practical standards for functional size measurement. Functional size measurement is a general term for methods of sizing software from an external viewpoint and encompasses methods such as Function Point Analysis.

Projects	07.31	Function Point Analysis
	07.31.01	Definition of Functional Size Measurement

07.31.02	Compliance Assessment of Software Sizing Methods
07.31.03	Verification of a Functional Size Measurement Method
07.31.04	Functional Size Measurement Reference Model
07.31.05	Determination of Functional Domains for use with Functional Size Measurement.

References

1. Matsubara, T., ed., *DTR 14399, Information Technology Reference List of Standards Relevant to ISO/IEC JTC1/SC7—Software Engineering,* 1996.

2. Tripp, L., *Presentation on SC7 Product Planning*, 1995.

2

Introduction to SPICE

Jean-Normand Drouin
Bell Canada, Canada

Harry Barker
Defence Evaluation Research Agency, UK

The intent of this introduction is to help the reader understand the history behind the SPICE Project, why the project was created, its objectives, how it is managed, and its relationship with the standardization effort lead by ISO/IEC JTC1/SC7 WG10.

History of SPICE

Software Process Assessment (SPA) and the SPICE Project find their roots both in the needs of thousands of organizations worldwide that have been increasing their use of—and dependence on—Information Technology (IT) to automate their operations and in the growing frustration and different expectations that both developers and users have when it comes to software.

Starting in the 1980's, two key initiatives were undertaken by the military in the US and in the UK. Both initiatives had as their objective the improvement of the selection mechanism for software contractors in an attempt to contain the growing cost associated with software so as to both reduce the risks associated with software projects and improve the quality of the software being delivered.

In the US, the Department of Defense mandated the Software Engineering Institute to develop a software-supplier selection approach. That mandate and its outcomes are well-documented history[5] and so will not be discussed again here. The UK initiative, however, will be covered since it had a direct impact on and relationship with the SPICE Project.

Improve-IT Study

In the UK, a joint Government and Defense Industry Trade Association committee, the Computing Policy Consultative Committee (CPCC), recognized the need for a more rigorous approach to the selection of suppliers of Software Intensive Systems. The task of investigating how to select a competent supplier of software-intensive projects was given to one of the authors (Harry Barker of the Defence Evaluation Research Agency (DERA)) who considered two possible approaches to this problem:

- a *defense-specific* solution for use in the evaluation of prospective suppliers

- an industry-wide solution involving the methods adopted by other large-system procurers and developers to resolve similar problems.

DERA opted for the latter approach and hired Alec Dorling, then of Admiral Management Services Ltd. (AMS), and Peter Simms of Cranfield IT Institute (CITI) to look at methods used by industry to assess the capability of software suppliers and the approaches adopted by software developers for the improvement of their own software processes.

The study report, called Improve-IT,[1] identified a number of both mature and fledgling methods used by the industry. Figure 2.1 shows a partial list of models and methods covered by the report and their application domain(s).

The Improve-IT study report concluded by stating that:

- Major procurers have similar needs.

- Most software developers are interested in self-improvement.

- There is a range of methods already in existence today.

- There is a desire for a common approach to SPA.

- Emphasis should be placed on self assessment.

ORIGIN	METHOD NAME	FOCUS	PROJECT SIZE	PUBLIC DOMAIN	STANDARDS
SEI	CMM	PCD & PI	Large	Yes & No	
BT	SAM	PCD & PI	Large	No	
BT/DVP	Healthcheck	PI	Small/ medium	No	
Bell, Nortel	TRILLIUM	PCD & PI	Large	Yes	ISO9000, IEEE, IEC, Malcolm Baldrige, SEI
HP	SQPA	PI	Medium	No	ISO9000
COMPITA	STD	PI	Small	License	ISO9000
ESPRIT	Bootstrap	PI	Medium	No	ISO9000

PI = Process Improvement   PCD = Process Capability Determination

Figure 2.1: Models/methods covered by the Improve-IT study.

With many large organizations equipped with their own individual-supplier selection approach and tools, large software suppliers were subjected to and often asked to comply with a growing number of SPA approaches, thus significantly increasing their operational costs, with few additional benefits other than to please their customers.

ISO/IEC JTC1/SC7 study period

The DERA decided to adapt slightly its Improve-IT Study Report and to table it at the 4th Plenary Meeting of ISO/IEC JTC1/SC7 in Stockholm in June 1991. The modified report included the following conclusions and recommendations:

1. There is international consensus on the needs and requirements for a standard for SPA.

2. There is international consensus on the need for a rapid route to development and trialling to provide usable output within an acceptable timeframe and to ensure the emerging standard fully meets the needs of its users.

3. The standard should initially be published as a Technical Report Type 2 (TR-2) to enable the emerging standard to stabilize during a period of the user trials, prior to its issuing as a full International Standard (the TR-2 designation is described later in this chapter).

The report was so well received that SC7 approved a study period (to be described in the next section) to be lead by Alec Dorling and Peter Simms to investigate the needs and requirements for a standard for SPA.

In the UK, a group of SPA and improvement experts set themselves the task of creating the first set of requirements that met the principles of the Improve-IT report. The development of these requirements were completed by November 1991 and finalized at a meeting with the IEEE Technical Advisory Group in the USA the same month. A study report called *The Need and Requirements for a Software Process Assessment Standard*[2] that captures the final requirements and the resulting New Work Item Proposal (NP) were tabled and approved at the 5th ISO/IEC JTC1/SC7 Plenary Meeting in London in June 1992. Later that same year, ISO approved the new project and the creation of Working Group 10 (WG10) with the mandate to develop an International Standard for Software Process Assessment.

WG10 started its work in January 1993 headed by Alec Dorling as Convenor with Peter Simms as Project Editor.

The ISO route to an International Standard

This section provides readers not familiar with ISO with an overview of how ISO projects work and are managed. It will also provide the background of the relationship between the ISO group and the SPICE Project explained later in this chapter.

The exact rules governing these ISO standardization projects can be found in the ISO Directives and the JTC1 directives and the reader should refer to the exact text of these directives where necessary.

Normal ISO Standardization Route

The following sections describe the normal route for standardization:

Stage 0:   A study period is underway

This stage is optional to be used by the group to clarify what would be the exact content and subject of the New Work Item Proposal (NP). Once clear and properly documented, the NP is prepared or the subject is abandoned altogether.

Stage 1: A New Work Item Proposal (NP) is under consideration

A NP is submitted to all P-member (Participating member) countries for formal approval. If more than half of the members accept the proposal, and if more than five countries commit to participate in the new project, the proposal is accepted, a new project is created, and it is assigned to a Working Group (WG).

Stage 2: A Working Draft (WD) is under consideration

A WG captures the progression of its efforts by writing Working Drafts. It is likely that a WG will produce several versions of a WD before it is deemed ready to proceed to the next stage. Usually WDs are reviewed by the WG experts who vote on a given version of the WD and provide comments aimed at improving the draft. When mature enough, a WD is progressed to the next stage by holding a formal Committee Draft (CD) registration ballot where each P-member country is asked to vote. If accepted by a majority of countries, the WD becomes a CD, is assigned an ISO number, and is registered at ISO.

Stage 3: A Committee Draft (CD) is under consideration

Committee Drafts are progressed in a much more formal way. Every version of a CD is subjected to a formal CD ballot where each country is asked to vote and provide comments where applicable. If accepted by a substantial majority of countries, the CD progresses to the next stage and becomes a Draft International Standard (DIS).

Stage 4: A Draft International Standard (DIS) is under consideration

At this stage, only formal ballots are used to progress DIS into IS. The vote is successful if at least 2/3 of the P-members voting approve and not more than ¼ of the total number of votes cast are negative.

Stage 5: An International Standard (IS) is being prepared for publication

The document is produced in its final form and published in English, French, and Russian. International Standards are reviewed after five years.

Alternate standardization route

The route described above leads to the publication of an ISO standard, such as ISO 9001 and ISO/IEC 12207. JTC1 in its directives allows for an alternate route that leads to what is called a Technical Report Type Two (TR-2). This route is usually selected by a WG when it is not sure that it can achieve the degree of consensus required by an IS. A TR-2 is expected to be revised within two to three years of its publication as opposed to five years for International Standards. In a way, a TR-2 may be viewed as a standard under trial.

The stages followed by TR-2 projects are very similar to the normal route, as shown below:

- Stage 0: identical
- Stage 1: identical
- Stage 2: identical
- Stage 3: A *Proposed Draft Technical Report* (PDTR) is under consideration
- Stage 4: A *Draft Technical Report* (DTR) is under consideration
- Stage 5: A *Technical Report* (TR) is being prepared for publication.

This alternate route was selected by the WG10 for two reasons:

1. to deliver the final documents to the marketplace as quickly as possible since it felt this route would help
2. the final documents would need to be tested in the marketplace to ensure the needs of the industry were addressed.

The JTC1 Directives state that after a period of no more than three years—and usually of at least one year—the WG will have to decide on the fate of the TR-2 using the following alternatives:

- If the trial is positive in all respects, the WG may decide to convert the TR-2 *as is* to an International Standard.
- If the trial is conclusive, but some changes are required, the documents will be revised and progressed following the normal ISO stages leading to an IS.
- If the trial is inconclusive, the TR-2 status may be kept for another three years.

- If the trial shows that there is no need for the emerging standard in the marketplace, the project will be canceled altogether.

Why create the SPICE Project?

Normally, ISO WGs progress their work by holding meetings twice a year. Over the past few years, this route has proven to be quite lengthy. An example is ISO/IEC 12207, which took seven years to develop. The Study Report N944R[2] tabled to SC7 in June 1992 clearly indicated the need for a *fast route to standardization*.

Another significant point considered by WG10 when the project was started was the limitations imposed by the framework of ISO. One such limitation is the need for participants to be official delegates from an ISO P-member country. At present, there are only 28 such P-member countries in JTC1/SC7. Furthermore, many companies that might want to participate in the SC7 program of work just do not have the financial means to support such a participation (by attending both the national and the international meetings). As a result, the number of "experts" that develop the standards is limited and may not always represent well the views of those who cannot afford to be present.

Finally, the ISO framework does not allow a WG to trial draft standards while they are in the development stages to verify early on whether the ideas put forward in the drafts address the needs of the industry.

For these reasons, WG10 decided to create a project called SPICE with the mandates to develop the first draft SPA standards and to conduct early trials.

As for the name SPICE, it was created in London right after the June plenary meeting of 1992 where SC7 approved the project. After several unsuccessful attempts, Software Process Improvement and Capability Evaluation was selected, to be rejected later because the term "Capability Evaluation" could be translated differently in French. Therefore, the group decided to replace "Evaluation" with "Determination" and to play with the letters to form today's acronym—SPICE: **S**oftware **P**rocess **I**mprovement and **C**apability d**E**termination.

SPICE Project management

It is important for the reader to understand that the management of the SPICE Project was now outside the control of ISO. This freedom allowed the project to define its own rules of participation and management.

One such rule was that *any experts* from around the world would be allowed to participate either by their direct attendance to SPICE meetings or via electronic mail (email). When considering that the team members were scattered around the world, it became apparent very quickly that the only viable way to progress the work would be through the use of email. An FTP site was set up initially so that drafts ready for review could be available for team members to retrieve. This approach allowed the SPICE Project to reduce the draft review period to a mere *three weeks* as opposed to several months when paper-based. As a result, the work progressed more rapidly while allowing a very wide group of experts to participate.

Another decision taken by the project was to hold meetings four times a year, twice as many as is the case at the ISO level. Just how those decisions were made and how the project was managed is explained below.

Project management structure

The SPICE Project gave itself a management structure composed of a Project Manager supported by a number of Technical Center Managers (TCM). Initially there were four TCMs responsible for four geographic regions: Canada, US and Latin America, Europe and Africa, and the Pacific Rim. At the time the project started, Japan was not involved but their presence was deemed highly desirable. So a fifth Technical Center was set aside for when Japan would be ready to join the project, which they did in 1996. Today, the five regions are somewhat different as shown in Figure 2.2.

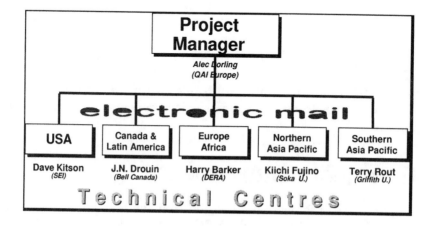

Figure 2.2: The SPICE Project management structure.

This group of six people is called the *SPICE Executive Management Board*. It is a key management body that makes decisions for the project in specific cases as documented in the *SPICE Project Organization, Management, and Control Procedures*. Another key management body is the *SPICE Management Board* that includes the SPICE Executive Board, three industry representatives from each of the five regions, the International SPICE Trials Coordinator, and the five Regional Trials Coordinators (the Regional Trials Coordinator role is described in chapter 12). The SPICE Management Board was created to allow key project sponsors to participate in the management of the project. The SPICE Management Board's role is to lay down the policies and procedures needed to manage the project.

Development team management

As will be explained in the next chapter, the SPICE Project set out to develop seven products in parallel. At the onset of the project, seven teams were created to manage each of the seven products. Each team had a team leader to coordinate the activities of the team and two types of resources:

- *core* team members who would attend the meetings and be responsible for developing and reviewing the drafts
- *extended-core* team members who would participate in the electronic review of drafts.

Team leaders were responsible to resource their project, prepare and maintain a project plan, plan the meetings and conference calls as necessary, manage the meetings, and prepare project status reports at fixed intervals.

Each team started its work by developing a *Product Description* (PD) to capture the design specifications of their products, document the requirements for which they were responsible, draft the table of contents of the actual product, and document the plans they were to follow during the development phase. It may seem overzealous to have decided to write such a document but this time was well spent since it allowed the team members to harmonize their sometimes-diverging views on the product. It also allowed them to capture early ideas that were then discussed and resolved at the meetings.

Project Architect

It became apparent early on in the project that there were multiple dependencies between the various products. A Project Architect (PA) was appointed to ensure that each team respected the dependencies they had or that other teams had on them.

Over time, the PA became the technical arbitrator between the various teams as well as a technical advisor where necessary. Whenever a key issue could not be resolved within a team, the team leader would bring it to the attention of the PA who would step in and try to help find a solution. When no consensus could be reached by the team, the issue would be documented and brought to the attention of the entire SPICE Project for resolution. Consensus would eventually be reached by project-wide vote where each expert would have a vote. This process is somewhat different from the ISO process where consensus is reached at the national member body level (each country has one vote).

Finally, the PA acted as the project-wide editor responsible for harmonizing all seven parts prior to delivering them to WG10.

Internet coordination

At the time the project was started, Internet was little known or used. It is fair to say that the SPICE Project pioneered the widespread use of Internet as a means with which to speed up document exchange and day-to-day project management at the ISO level. Because very few tools were available to support the use of Internet, an Internet Coordinator (IC) was appointed. The role of the IC was to develop the Internet infrastructure (an FTP server and several email distribution lists) necessary to support the project's objectives.

The IC also developed a set of standard tools to be used by all project resources to exchange documents over Internet. The tools were selected for their ability to support a transparent exchange of documents over Internet between different platforms.

SPICE Web site

The SPICE Project has created an official Web site where project information can be found. The Web site has a *public* region for all to access and a *private* region that is accessible only to SPICE resources. As time goes by, more and more use will be made of the Web for document storage and transfer.

The use of the Web has forced the project to take a long, hard look at its own document distribution policies (or lack thereof). Several new policies were created and are enacted by the Project Manager to ensure that the Web is used in a fair and neutral way. An obvious danger that came about with the Web was the endorsement of SPA tools, methods, training courses, or individuals that would have led to an unfair advantage. The SPICE Management Board has therefore decided to stay away from any form of endorsement. Instead, the SPICE Web site simply provides a list of tools, methods, courses, and assessors in the form of hyperlinks only with a nonendorsement statement clearly visible.

At the time of going to press, the IC was about to publish a set of *mirroring* practices to help those interested in mirroring the official Web site.*

Relationship between the SPICE Project and WG10

The relationship between the SPICE Project and WG10 has been somewhat nebulous in the past. One of the key reasons for this confusion was the fact that the SPICE Project and WG10 held meetings together and, not surprisingly, most resources attending the SPICE meetings also happened to be official WG10 delegates attending the WG10 meetings. In reality, the SPICE Project has been acting as and remains a subcontractor to WG10. During the first three years of the project, it developed and delivered to WG10 the SPICE Version 1.00 document set. It has also conducted the SPICE Phase 1 Trials in parallel.

This relationship has been clearly documented in a document called WG10/N002 *Modus Operandi*[3] and has been approved by WG10. Today, the SPICE Project's major activity is to conduct more trials on the emerging standard, to provide feedback to WG10, and to promote SPICE in industry by organizing symposiums around the world and maintaining a SPICE Web site.

SPICE Trials

As mentioned earlier, one of the key roles of the SPICE Project was to conduct early trials of the emerging standard. This role is unique to international standardization efforts. The intention is to gain early experience on the emerging standard and to empirically evaluate its basic premises. Evidence collected from the trials will then be used to shape the evolution of the SPICE documents and to provide guidance on how they should be used.

While the emerging standard evolves, new trials are being conducted to evaluate the new versions of the document set and to compare them with previous versions. As the project progressed, technical discussions came to rely more on the empirical evidence provided by the trials.

---

*The URL for the official SPICE Web site is not included in this text since it may become outdated with time. Any decent search engine on the Web should be able to help readers locate the official SPICE Web site.

A detailed description of the organizational structure implemented to support the trials, their objectives, and results from the Phase 1 Trials is given in Part 3 of this book.

Current status

The current status of the SPA documents is Proposed Draft Technical Report (stage 3). This status is referred to throughout this book as SPICE Version 2.00. The first version, developed by the SPICE Project, is referred to as SPICE Version 1.00.

Version 2.00 will remain the document set that is under evaluation in the official SPICE Trials until Version 4.00 of the document set emerges. This is expected to happen in 1998. Some of the important expected architectural changes to Version 2.00 are reviewed in Chapter 3.

References

1. Dorling, A. and P. Simms, Study Report: ImproveIT, 1992.

2. Dorling, A. and P. Simms, Study Report: The Need and Requirements for a Software Process Assessment Standard, ISO/IEC JTC1/SC7/WG7/WG7/SG1 N944R Issue 2.0, 11 June 1992, Admiral plc, Cranfield IT Institute and UK Ministry of Defence.

3. ISO/IEC/JTC1/SC7/WG10, Modus Operandi, Document WG10/N066, Version 1.00 2, Mar. 1995.

4. ISO IEC, ISO IEC Directives, Procedures for the technical work of ISO/IEC JTC1 on Information Technology, Third Ed., 1995.

5. Carnegie Mellon University, Software Engineering Institute, *The Capability Maturity Model*, Addison Wesley, Reading, Mass., 1995.

Introduction to the SPICE Documents and Architecture

Terry P. Rout[*]

Australian Software Quality Research Institute, Australia

Peter G. Simms

CITI Limited, UK

The techniques described generically as Software Process Assessment (SPA) derive from the basic premise that the quality of manufactured products is largely determined by the quality of the processes that produce them.[2] As Humphrey[5] points out, the first step in any program to improve software process capability is to understand the current status of the development process. Process assessment is the means of achieving this understanding. The technique is defined as:

> The disciplined examination of the processes used by an organization against a set of criteria to determine the capability of those processes to perform within quality, cost, and schedule goals. The aim is to characterize current practice, identifying strengths and weaknesses and the

*When this chapter was in preparation, Rout was a Visiting Fellow at the European Software Institute. Their support is gratefully acknowledged.

ability of the process to control or avoid significant causes of poor quality, cost, and schedule performance.[7]

The primary impetus for the use of assessments has come not from the mainstream of the software development industry, but from acquirers of large, critical, software-intensive systems—notably in the defense and telecommunications sectors. Thus, the Capability Maturity Model (CMM),[13] was developed by the Software Engineering Institute (SEI) as a response to the needs of the US Department of Defense (DoD) for better techniques in the selection of contractors. Process assessment methods have also been developed by several of the major players in the telecommunications field, including British Telecom, Bell Canada/Northern Telecom, and Bellcore and are applied to the management of risk in acquisition. There were also many others in widespread use, and all used different assessment models and methods.

However, by the early 1990s, many software development organizations were facing the prospect of frequent, costly, and disruptive capability evaluations by potential customers. Multinational companies were also facing the prospect of international customers employing a wide variety of evaluation, audit, and assessment methods. Staff were finding themselves facing an internal assessment one week, an external audit the next, and a customer evaluation the following week—and they were being asked similar questions during all three.

At the same time, there has always been a recognition that software process assessment can be a strong and effective driver for process improvement. Most acquirers use assessment approaches as part of a partnership approach with their suppliers, focusing on the supplier's improvement. A major focus of use of the SEI's Software-CMM has been on improvement.[6] Other assessment methods have been developed with a specific focus on improvement.[1] Yet, each method tends to vary slightly in its focus: for example, the SW-CMM on large, software suppliers to the US DoD and the Software Technology Diagnostic on small business. As experience with the technique has grown, empirical evidence has accumulated, demonstrating the potential benefits that can be derived from an assessment-based improvement program.[4]

A strong international consensus began to emerge on the urgent need for an international standard for SPA to somehow unify and harmonize these diverse approaches. The SPICE Project was conceived to fast-track the development of such a standard. (The requirements for the standard are detailed in Appendix A of this chapter.)

The SPICE vision was on process assessments that would be repeatable, comparable, and verifiable. Under SPICE, different assessments of a single organization, irrespective of the approach used, would result in similar outcomes. In addition, the results of assessments of different organizations would allow meaningful comparisons of process capability across those organizations, permitting comparative evaluations of the risks associated with process performance.

The potential payoff would be great: reusing the same assessment results—in some suitable form—for both internal process improvement and external customer evaluation could dramatically reduce both the disruption to suppliers and the cost to customers. Furthermore, by building on previous experiences with assessment-based process improvement, the SPICE documents would combine the best-available process improvement expertise. The development of an international standard provided the opportunity for process experts to advance the state-of-the-art, building upon the best attributes of each existing method to produce a public, shared model and framework for assessment and a route for the harmonization of existing assessment schemes.

This chapter describes the evolution of the architecture underlying the emerging standard for SPA. It starts off with an outline of the basic concepts of process assessment and the goals of the standardization effort. It then describes, at a high level, the initial framework for assessment defined in Version 1.00 of the documents developed by the SPICE Project and then outlines the key problems identified in the initial validation of this framework. The revised architecture, documented in the second release of the emerging standard, is then presented. This chapter concludes by examining some of the potential strengths and weaknesses of the new framework and discusses some of the issues yet to be explored in the next phase of the SPICE Trials. An addendum to this chapter covers last minute information about the future direction of the SPICE documents.

Concepts of a SPICE process assessment

General applicability

The design goals of the SPICE Project were to develop an assessment standard that would:

- be applicable to both process improvement and capability determination
- be applicable to different application domains, business needs, and sizes of organizations

- not presume specific organizational structures, management philosophies, software life cycle models, software technologies, or software development methods
- use objective and, where possible, quantitative criteria
- produce output in the form of profiles, rather than a single number or pass/fail result and support comparisons with outputs from other, similar assessments.

In other words, it was important that the emerging standard could be used in a wide variety of environments rather than be restricted to a particular type of industry, business sector, or size of organization.

Basing measurement on objective and quantitative criteria is essential if an assessment is to produce consistent and repeatable results which, in turn, are essential characteristics if the results from different assessments are to be compared.

One of the axioms underpinning the design of the emerging standard was the recognition that individual businesses have individual business goals and that to be effective, the software processes used by that organization must contribute to and support those business goals. For some businesses, for example, the goal might be speed to market, while other organizations might place more emphasis on efficiency, cost of development, or dependability of the software product. The software processes employed in these situations may be different in many respects. There would be little point or validity in comparing a supplier of nuclear reactor protection systems with a supplier of games software. Both may have excellent processes suited to their own business needs and be best-of-class within their own industry, but the processes of one may be totally inappropriate to the needs of the other.

Nevertheless, for the purposes of a standard, particularly if one of the goals is comparability (at least of similar entities), there would need to be a definition of *universal good practice*—a yardstick by which to measure. The aim, therefore, was to define such an *assessment model*, for processes and the capability of processes, at a relatively abstract level so as not to constrain the ways in which the implementations of processes could be realized.

Basic concepts for an assessment

Within the SPICE context, the scope of assessment is an *organizational unit* (OU): all or part of an organization with a coherent sphere of activity and a coherent set of business goals. The characteristics that determine the coherent scope of activity—the *process context*—include the application domain, the size, the criticality, the complexity, and the quality characteristics of its products or services. These factors, together with the business goals, are important since they influence the judgment, comprehension, and comparability of ratings.

Ratings during an assessment are of *process instances*. Process instances are important because they are the fundamental units of assessment. A process instance is a singular instantiation of a process that is uniquely identifiable and about which information can be gathered in a repeatable manner. Process instances often correspond to projects. A particular project will instantiate, for example, a set of management, support, and engineering processes. The key output of the assessment is a set of *process profiles*, one for each instance of each process assessed.

Stages of an assessment

An assessment process typically consists of four broad phases:

1. preparing for the assessment
2. gathering the data
3. analyzing the data, assigning the ratings, and preparing the output
4. feeding back the results.

In *preparing for the assessment*, one of the key tasks is to prepare the input to the assessment. This task includes defining the scope of the assessment: the OU, its business goals and process context, the set of processes to be assessed, and the process instances to be assessed. Typically, the OU's processes do not align directly with the processes in the assessment model and therefore need to be mapped to the model. The scope of the assessment does not need to be of *all* the processes within the organization and typically will be of only a subset. Hence, the scope is likely to be a subset of the model.

In the *data gathering* phase, the process instances are investigated against the assessment model. Data gathering is often performed by a qualified assessor or assessment team, through interviews and/or discussions with the people concerned with the process, and through the examination of relevant documents. Other forms of data gathering, however, may include the use of automated tools taking the place of the assessor, or collecting data in a (semi-) continuous fashion. Qualified assessors are guided by indicators—in questionnaires, checklists, or other instruments, paper-based or automated—of what to look for and as an aid to organizing and recording data. The data gathering activities probe on two broad fronts: *what* is done (for example, activities, work products) and *how well* is it done. The former deals primarily with the execution of the process, while the latter is concerned with the effectiveness or capability of the process.

In the *analysis* phase, the qualified assessor uses the data that has been gathered to assign ratings to the process instances. The rating scale defines what to rate and the scale of values. In the SPICE model, attributes of the process are rated on a four-point ordinal scale of purpose achievement: **N**ot adequate, **P**artially, **L**argely, **F**ully.

The assignment of ratings is not simply a mechanical process, but demands the skilled judgment of the qualified assessor. In making the judgments, the data collected is reviewed and analyzed against the definitions of the attributes in the model. The judgments are moderated by the qualified assessor's understanding of the business goals of the organization and the factors of the process context. Although the ratings are based on judgment, they are not "gut reaction," subjective opinions, but are skilled judgments based on objective criteria. Furthermore, an essential part of the rating process is to record the evidence and justification for the ratings that were assigned.

The formal *output* of a SPICE assessment is a set of process profiles, together with a record of the assessment containing information pertinent to the assessment. The assessment record is important to the understanding and interpretation of the process profiles since it includes the assessment scope and, therefore, the information about the OU and the process context. The information recorded and retained also plays an important role in demonstrating that the assessment has been conducted in accordance with the emerging standard.

Process profiles are typically recorded in a spreadsheet, or in a database. For presentation purposes, however, graphical techniques generally are used as an aid to understanding and to create the desired impact. To simplify and summarize the results of larger assessments, particularly for management understanding, process profiles can be aggregated in a number of ways.

For process improvement, the output is used to identify the current state of the OU, highlighting its strengths, weaknesses, risks, and opportunities for improvement. This breakdown feeds the improvement cycle of planning and prioritizing improvement actions, implementing the improvement plans, monitoring the results, and taking further improvement actions.

For capability determination, for example in supplier selection, the assessed profiles are compared to *target*, or desired, *profiles* to identify the gaps and to assess the potential risks resulting from any gaps. In supplier selection, in particular, comparability of the results of the assessment is a key issue.

The level of *feedback* from an assessment may vary depending on the nature and purpose of the assessment and on any agreements reached about the dissemination and use of the results. Feedback and reporting may be through formal written reports, presentations to one or more groups, or simply informal, verbal communications.

The initial approach to assessment

The initial version of the SPICE documents[15] put forth a draft standard that defined a framework for conducting assessments, together with guidance for using the framework in process improvement and process capability determination. The framework, in turn, depends on a model of process capability that defines processes and their attributes in a way that allows the capability of the processes to be reliably assessed.

The intent of the framework is to maximize the objectivity of the assessment process, thereby ensuring the repeatability and comparability of the results of the assessment. The intent is achieved by using a clearly-defined process, by ensuring that assessors and team members, through training and qualification, have the necessary skills and competence to apply the rules consistently, and by requiring that judgments of process adequacy be justified by reference to a defined set of objective indicators. The achievement of consistency and comparability of results is further ensured by requiring the use of an assessment instrument that meets specified requirements as an aid in the conduct of assessments. This requirement reflects the aims of the initial study group report,[7] that envisaged that the emerging standard would define "how an assessment will be carried out using the assessment instrument as a sensor to probe specific areas."[7] Such instruments are based on the use of objective *process indicators* as justification for the assignment of ratings. The contributors to the framework, and their relationships, are shown in Figure 3.1.

SPICE conformance

The intent of the SPICE Project is that the results of a conformant assessment can be applied equally to either internal process improvement or to the demonstration of capability by a supplier to a prospective purchaser. It should be possible, within the framework defined by the SPICE documents, for parties to have sufficient confidence in the results of assessments when performed in accordance with the emerging standard and that the results of self-assessment can be provided to a purchaser as a demonstration of the required capability.

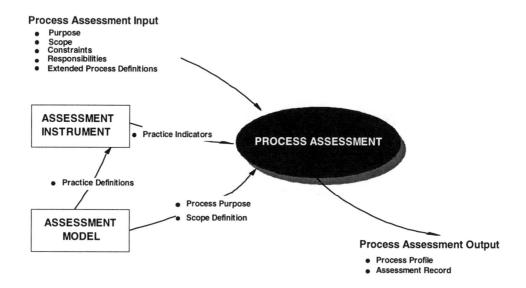

Figure 3.1: The initial framework for process assessment.

It is not envisaged, therefore, that the emerging standard will establish a new infrastructure of certification bodies and independent assessment authorities. Demonstration of conformance to the requirements of the emerging standard should be sufficient to establish the desired level of confidence in the results.

Rather than prescribe a common assessment method, or provide for the issue of "certified assessment results" by third parties, the intent of the SPICE Project is that the emerging standard should document a standard *framework*, so that bodies undertaking an assessment—including a self-assessment—can demonstrate conformance to the emerging standard and therefore provide the necessary degree of confidence in the results of the assessment to any other interested parties. This confidence is achieved by clearly prescribing the (minimum) inputs to and outputs from the assessment and requiring that these inputs and outputs are properly documented.

The emerging standard, therefore, does not prescribe a method for performing assessments, nor does it embody requirements for conformant methods. *It is the individual assessment that must meet the requirements.* Methods may support the achievement of meeting the requirements, but there is no certainty that a given (conformant) method would always be applied in a conformant manner. Hence, the concept of a *conformant assessment* is central to the effective use of the SPICE framework.

A conformant assessment, meeting all the following criteria, is defined as one that:

- is conducted by a qualified SPICE assessor or a team containing a qualified SPICE assessor, as defined in the emerging standard
- uses an assessment process that, at a minimum, meets the requirements specified in the emerging standard
- is based on a set of practices that, at a minimum, include those practices defined in the emerging standard
- uses an assessment instrument meeting the requirements defined in the emerging standard
- utilizes the process rating scheme defined in the emerging standard
- has retained objective evidence demonstrating the above conditions have been met.

The assessment model

The initial study group report recognized the importance of using a consistent software process model to perform the assessments and placed this model at the core of the architecture. The model was designed to facilitate the assessment of an organization's software processes and to make judgments and recommendations regarding their improvements.

In the initial version of the SPICE documents, the model defined two dimensions of organizational performance in the software domain: (1) a *functional* dimension, comprising processes organized into process categories and (2) a dimension of *process capability*, comprising six capability levels. The relationship of the model to the assessment process requirements is shown in Figure 3.1. In this model, the baseline practices of software engineering formed the lowest level of the architecture.

Two different types of practices were distinguished. One type of practice—called *base practice*—describes the essential activities of a specific process. Base practices were grouped, by type of activity, into processes and process categories. This grouping formed the *process* (or functional) *dimension* of the model, encompassing the software development and management aspects of the process.

The second type of practice—called *generic practices*—are the management practices that implement or institutionalize a process in a general way. Generic practices can be applied potentially to any process and were grouped into *common features* and *capability levels*, according to the aspects of implementation and institutionalization they address. These practices form the *capability di-*

mension of six capability levels (from Level 0 to Level 5). It is the generic practices that have the greatest influence on process capability—the ability to predict performance. This architecture is shown in Figure 3.2.

This initial model formed the basis for Version 1.00 of the SPICE documents and was released in June 1995.

The process profile

The SPICE ratings can be expressed as a two-dimensional array of values, each of which is either **N**ot adequate, **P**artially, **L**argely, or **F**ully. This array is illustrated in Figure 3.3. Listed down the left side of the array are the *processes* that comprise the Customer-Supplier *process category* (the processes are shown as CUS.1, CUS.2, and so on).

Along the bottom of the array are the *generic practices* that are applicable to any process. Generic practice ratings can be combined to derive ratings for the common features and capability levels to which they belong. In determining the rating for a capability level, the generic practice ratings are combined. In Figure 3.3, a single row of the array represents the ratings for a single *process instance* of the process.

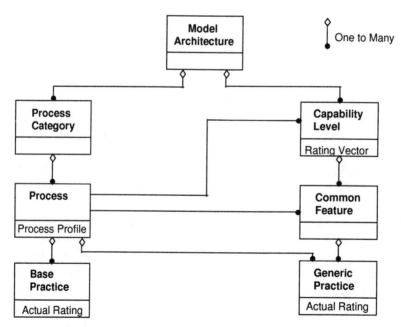

Figure 3.2: The initial process architecture.

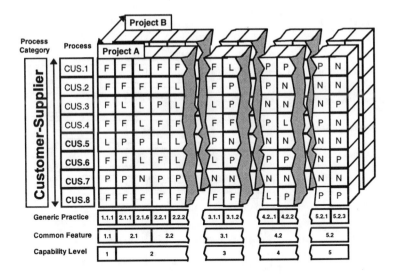

Figure 3.3: Generic practice ratings.[17]

Before assessing the capability of individual processes, the extent to which the processes are *actually performed* must be determined. To make this determination, the base practices can be rated using either the same four-point ordinal scale for adequacy as the generic practices or a binary scale for existence (or otherwise). By examining the base practices of a process, the extent to which the process is actually implemented is assessed. If a process is barely implemented, applying the concepts embodied by the generic practices will have little effect.

To produce a capability profile, a rating for adequacy is assigned first to a particular generic practice in the context of a particular process. For example, in Figure 3.3, generic practice 2.1.1 *Allocate Resources* is deemed to be **L**argely adequate for process CUS.3 *Identify Customer Needs*. That is, when identifying customer needs, the project allocation of resources was largely adequate.

An assessed capability profile would show, for each process assessed and for each capability level, the proportions of practices that had been assessed as **N**ot adequate, **P**artially, **L**argely, or **F**ully. Figure 3.4 shows how an example assessed capability might be illustrated as a profile. This profile may apply to a single process instance (for example, Project A in Figure 3.3), or it may apply to all process instances, depending on whether one or all process instances are included in calculating the proportions.

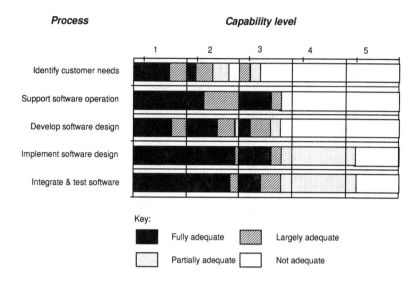

Figure 3.4: Example of a capability profile using the initial version of the architecture.

Evolution of the document set

The initial study group report envisaged a standard that would contain six components. At an early stage in its development, however, it was recognised that material relating to the qualification of assessors was also required and the original Product Specification[8] provided for seven documents. The relationship between these documents is shown in Figure 3.5. The purpose of each of these documents and their interrelationships is described below.[8]

The *Introductory Guide* (IG) was the top-level, umbrella document that described how the other parts of the emerging standard fit together and provided guidance for their selection and use. It defined criteria for conformance to the emerging standard. All other products in the emerging standard suite depended on this document.

The *Process Assessment Guide* (PAG) specified the assessment method that defined how to conduct an assessment using the AI and the BPG and set out the basis for analysing, profiling, rating, and scoring. The AI and BPG were required for the application of the method described in the PAG. The use of the PIG and PCDG depended on the results of applying this method.

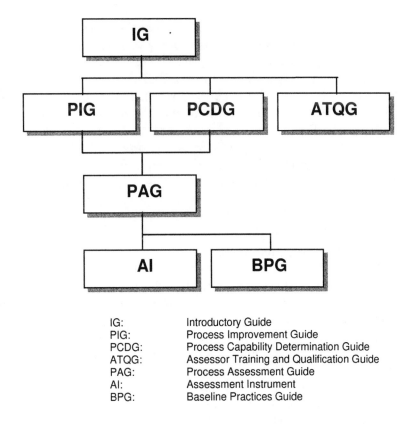

IG: Introductory Guide
PIG: Process Improvement Guide
PCDG: Process Capability Determination Guide
ATQG: Assessor Training and Qualification Guide
PAG: Process Assessment Guide
AI: Assessment Instrument
BPG: Baseline Practices Guide

Figure 3.5: The relationship between the original SPICE documents.

The *Process Improvement Guide* (PIG) provided guidance on how to prepare for and use the results of an assessment for the purposes of process improvement. Embedded within, or as a companion to, the PIG were a number of guidance models that were applicable to particular situations. The PIG specified one of the starting points for process assessment. As such, the PAG was dependent on actions defined in the PIG. Conversely, the completion of activities conceived in the PIG required results from the PAG. The BPG was necessary for the application of the method contained therein. This guide was complementary to the PCDG.

The *Process Capability Determination Guide* (PCDG) provided generic guidance on how to prepare for and use the results of an assessment for the purposes of process capability determination. Embedded within the PCDG, or as a companion to it, were a number of guidance models applicable to particular situations. The PCDG specifically addressed capability determination within two different scenarios: (1) for use within an organization (first party) and (2) by a purchaser for supplier assessment (two-party contractual). This document specified one of the starting points for process assessment. As such, use of the PAG was dependent on actions defined in the PCDG. Conversely, the completion of activities conceived in the PCDG required results from the PAG. The BPG was necessary for application of the method contained therein. The PCDG was complementary to the PIG.

The *Assessor Training and Qualification Guide* (ATQG) provided generic guidance for the development of training programs for training people to act as assessors when using the emerging standard. The ATQG also defined procedures for the qualification of assessors who intended to act in third-party situations. The ATQG referenced the PAG, BPG, and AI for curricular requirements. The PIG and PCDG referenced the ATQG in relation to the composition of improvement and determination teams.

The *Baseline Practices Guide* (BPG) defined, at a high level, the goals and fundamental activities that were essential to software engineering, structured according to increasing levels of process capability. The baseline practices may have been extended through the generation of application or sector-specific practice guides to take into account specific industry, sector, or other requirements. The BPG stood alone as a definition of the goals and fundamental activities that are essential to software engineering. It was needed for the use and complete understanding of any of the other documents in the standard suite. A rigorous method was specified for registering the application or sector-specific variants of the BPG as compliant with the emerging standards' suite.

The *Assessment Instrument* (AI) was a generic tool for extracting data related to the process(es) undergoing assessment. It was to be used in conjunction with the BPG and provided assistance in confirming the presence of the set of baseline practices. This document provided instructions for constructing alternative assessment instruments in specific situations. Conformant instruments may have served as sensors or probes into an area to open and invite discussion and further investigation. Any conformant assessment instrument must have been able to provide complete coverage of the baseline practices, although an individual assessment may have covered only a selection of such practices. This document specified how the coverage was to be demonstrated. The AI was necessary for application of the PAG. It required the use of the BPG for its application.

Appendix B of this chapter shows how the initial allocation of the functional requirements were defined with respect to each of the above documents.

As the different documents were developed, it became apparent that changes were needed to meet the prescribed criteria for standards, as contained in the

JTC1 Directives. The wording was edited to clarify the differences between the normative and informative elements of the documents. The names were redrafted to conform to the normal format for standards' nomenclature. It became necessary to split the *Introductory Guide* and the *Process Assessment Guide* into two components each. A separate vocabulary document became necessary because of the number of specific terms being referenced.

The result was a final set of nine documents. The core set of the SPICE Project documents had been assembled under the general title *Software Process Assessment*. It now consisted of the following parts:

- The Introductory Guide (IG) (excluding the Vocabulary section) became *Part 1: Concepts and Introductory Guide.*

- The Baseline Practices Guide (BPG) became *Part 2: A Model for Process Management*

- The normative elements of the Process Assessment Guide (PAG), defining the requirements for process rating, became *Part 3: Rating Processes.*

- The remainder of the PAG became *Part 4: Guide to Conducting Assessment.*

- The Assessment Instrument (AI) became *Part 5: Construction, selection, and use of assessment instruments and tools.*

- The Assessor Training and Qualification Guide (ATQG) became *Part 6: Qualification and Training of Assessors.*

- The Process Improvement Guide (PIG) became *Part 7: Guide for use in Process Improvement.*

- The Process Capability Determination Guide (PCDG) became *Part 8: Guide for use in determining supplier capability.*

- The vocabulary section of the IG became *Part 9: Vocabulary.*

Following the release of the document set to the standards community for ballot and subsequent development, the SPICE Project Management Board decided that Version 1.00 of the documents—comprising the nine parts listed above—should be made freely available to the public. Electronic copies of these documents are included with this book.

Evaluation of the initial assessment framework

Evaluations of Version 1.00 of the assessment model and framework came from two principal sources: (1) from the initial phase of the SPICE Trials and (2) from the ISO ballot comments. Both of these sources culminated in what has become known as the *Kwa Maritane Accord*.

Sources of evaluation

The core elements of the initial baseline documents (the BPG, PAG, and AI) were trialled by participants during Phase 1 of the SPICE Trials in the early part of 1995.[10] Overall, the trials provided an encouraging view of the principal aims of the model. Many participating organizations reported on the overall usefulness of the results and confirmed the validity of the two-dimensional approach to modeling processes and process capability.[16] For example, one organization, experienced in process improvement, reported that the results from the SPICE assessment confirmed their priorities for improvement. They believed that the results accurately profiled the areas assessed.[3] (Further details of the trials are presented in Part 3 of this book.)

The main purpose of the trials, however, was to report on problem areas to enable the framework to be refined: the intent was to gain benefit from the experience of the trials organizations using it. The *SPICE Phase 1 Trials Report* contained a detailed analysis of 238 problem reports raised.[11] The single largest category of reports was related to problems with the clarity of the process and practice descriptions. The next largest category related to the structure of the model: the accuracy and appropriateness of the process descriptions were examined and questioned. Feedback was also collected from assessors and participants in the trials organizations in the form of a detailed set of questionnaires. (The analysis of the trials data is presented in detail in Part 3 of this book.)

The second source of criticisms came from an official ISO document review[*]. The Version 1.00 baseline of the nine-part document suite was submitted to ISO for balloting in June 1995. Several significant areas of concern were raised, many of which had also been noted during the trials. Three primary themes were identified from the most substantive comments:

---

[*]Note that some of the comments were based directly on the results of the trials.

1. The assessment model was not related strongly enough to ISO/IEC 12207, the International Standard for *Software life cycle processes*.

2. The assessment model was seen as too prescriptive and detailed. It was perceived that the model might be misunderstood to be saying *how* software development should be performed. The emerging standard's objectives were targeted toward assessing *how well* software processes were implemented, not at prescribing a specific approach. The SPICE model, as it had been defined, was highly complex, containing 35 processes with over 200 base practices and 26 generic practices. The total number of individual ratings for a complete assessment was too high, with over 1,000 individual judgments.

3. The path for recognition of existing models and frameworks was too restrictive. This restriction resulted in problems, with the possible loss of investment by users of existing models. It was proposed that:

    - A compliant assessment should be based on any model (commercial or not), as long as the model and its associated assessment methodology met criteria that should be defined in the Technical Report.

    - The current model for assessment (set out partly in Part 2 and developed in Part 5) should be informative.

    - The documents should specify the requirements that existing models must meet to be conformant.

This proposal meant that for companies already using other approaches (for example, SW-CMM,[13] Bootstrap,[12] STD[1]) the SPICE Project would not be proposing that they change their approach as long as they could prove that it was conformant with the requirements to be set out in the Technical Report. In addition, keeping the existing SPICE architecture, but providing a more flexible interface for existing approaches, would mean companies without an existing software process improvement program would have a well-defined example on which to build their process improvement strategies.

The Kwa Maritane Accord

The Kwa Maritane* Accord involved compromise, negotiation between nations, and consensus before finally being approved by a full session of WG10 members. Each national body in the WG10 membership has only one vote to ensure that a level playing field is kept. Approximately 20 nations were present at the Kwa Maritane meeting.

The Accord addressed four fundamental and pervasive issues that were repeatedly mentioned in the preliminary national body comments:

1. **The need to closely align with the recently-approved ISO/IEC 12207[9] International Standard for *Software life cycle processes*:** It did not make sense to have two ISO documents calling the same thing by two different names. On the other hand, it is recognized that ISO/IEC 12207 is not sufficiently rich in detail to support an assessment or improvement program. However, there needs to be a consistent vocabulary used by both documents, as well as a mapping that shows the coverage of the processes in the Software Process Assessment (SPA) model.

2. **The need to make the emerging standard less prescriptive:** The detail in Part 2, and the Part 5 indicator lists in particular, were targets of numerous comments. The way the SPA documents had been structured meant that in order to be compliant, an organization had to use Part 2, the Part 5 indicators, the measurement scheme defined in Part 3, and so on. This prescriptiveness would be viewed as punitive to companies that had already initiated software process improvement programs based on other approaches. The expense of changing models or methods in midstream, for even a moderate size company, is high. The reeducation for assessors, managers, and software practitioners, as well as the purchase or development of the processes and their supporting tools, had to be taken into consideration.

3. **The need to provide a clear route for migration /harmonization of existing, commercially-available approaches:** If the emerging standard was going to be adopted by industry, it would have to provide a way for existing software process

---

*Kwa Maritane is the name of the place in South Africa where a milestone SPICE meeting took place in November 1995.

improvement investments to become compliant. It didn't seem sensible to ask companies to make significant investments in realigning their existing programs.

4. **The need to simplify the architecture to address problems that were identified during the SPICE Trials, particularly those related to the capability dimension:** As anticipated, assessments were collecting a lot of data and taking a long time.

WG10 created an other working group (OWG) specifically to work out these changes. This smaller group was chosen to speed the changes through. This effort led to the revision and restructuring of the framework during the early part of 1996.

The revised model for assessment

A comprehensive restructuring of the architecture took place, resulting in a new structure based upon a different concept of the assessment model—one based on the concept of a *reference model*.

The reference model concept

The concept of a reference model is one that is used widely within the standards community, particularly where there is a need for harmonization of different approaches to a problem or group of problems. There are at least five reference models defined in standards in the area of Information Technology, in fields ranging from Open Systems Interconnection to Computer Graphics. The adoption of a reference-model approach to the standardization of process assessment directly addressed two of the primary concerns raised in the document review: (1) it would remove the prescriptive nature of the model and (2) it would allow for much easier harmonization of existing models.

The overall framework of the emerging standard was thus changed from one using a prescriptive model to one using an assessment model compatible with the reference model defined in the emerging standard. The new framework is shown in Figure 3.6. Comparison with Figure 3.1 illustrates the change in approach.

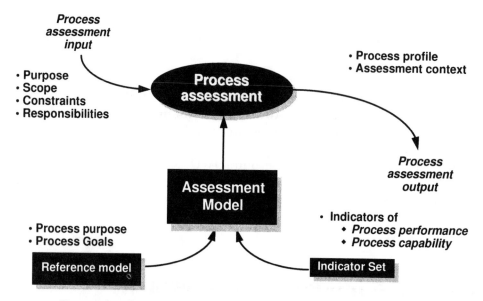

Figure 3.6 Revised framework for process assessment.

Within the new framework, the concept of a conformant assessment is modified to be one that encompasses all of the following. It:

- is overseen by an assessor qualified according to the guidance in the emerging standard

- uses an assessment process that meets the requirements set out in the emerging standard

- is based on an assessment model that is compatible with the reference model in the emerging standard

- uses a comprehensive set of indicators of process performance and process capability

- utilizes the process attribute rating scheme defined in the emerging standard

- has objective evidence retained to demonstrate that the conditions have been met.

The principal change, therefore, is a change in the concept of the emerging standard, from being an outline of a comprehensive model for assessment to a framework of which the primary focus is on the comparability of results derived from using different models.

The reference model contains the set of requirements that clearly define the compatibility rules for assessment models. A *compatible* model then must:

- be one that has been developed for the purpose of process assessment
- have a clear and unambiguous mapping from the elements in a compatible model to the basic elements of the reference model—the *processes* and *process attributes*
- contain a comprehensive set of indicators of process *performance* and *capability* that explicitly address the purpose(s) of the processes in the reference model and the achievement of the process attributes
- be a mechanism for translating the results of assessments performed with the model to the form defined in the emerging standard.

Structure of the reference model—the process dimension

In designing the SPICE reference model, consideration was given to using ISO/IEC 12207 directly as its basis, but this idea was rejected in favor of a separate and richer set of process definitions compatible with ISO/IEC 12207. The reason for this change of consideration is the strong emphasis placed on two-party contractual use which makes ISO/IEC 12207 less suitable for process assessment, especially self-assessment. Furthermore, some of the processes in ISO/IEC 12207 lack the detail necessary to provide for detailed assessment. Finally, there are a number of processes important for assessment that are not within the scope of ISO/IEC 12207.

The reference model retains the two-dimensional architecture that characterized the initial version. The *process* dimension of the model has been restructured in such a way as to provide for a strong mapping to ISO/IEC 12207, the International Standard for *Software life cycle processes*.

The process dimension of the reference model consists, at a high level, of five *process categories*:

1. **Customer-Supplier (CUS)**—consists of processes that directly impact the customer, support development and transition of the software to the customer, and provide for its correct operation and use

2. **Engineering (ENG)**—consists of processes that directly specify, implement, or maintain a system and software product and its user documentation

3. **Support (SUP)**—consists of processes that may be used by any of the other processes (including other supporting processes) at various points within the software life cycle

4. **Management (MAN)**—consists of processes that contain practices of a generic nature that may be used by anyone who manages any type of project within a software life cycle

5. **Organization (ORG)**—consists of processes that establish the business goals of the organization and provides for the development of process, product, and resource assets that, when used by projects in the organization, may help the organization achieve its business goals.

However, the process dimension relates to the ISO/IEC 12207 framework closely. There are three types of processes in the reference model:

1. those that are identical to ISO/IEC 12207 processes
2. those that are subcomponents of ISO/IEC 12207 processes
3. those that are outside the scope of ISO/IEC 12207.

ISO/IEC 12207 defines the range of, and establishes a common framework and architecture for, 18 software life cycle processes. In ISO/IEC 12207, the processes are classified into three principal life cycle categories and map to the reference model as follows:

ISO/IEC 12207 Life Cycle Processes		Reference Model Process Categories
Primary	*are covered by*	Customer-Supplier and Engineering
Supporting	*map directly to*	Support
Organizational	*are covered by*	Management and Organization

In the process dimension of the reference model, the processes are characterized in terms of their purpose, which describes at a high level the overall objectives of performing the process and the likely outcomes of an effective implementation of the process.

Structure of the reference model—the capability dimension

The second dimension of the reference model—the capability dimension—effectively defines a measurement scale for the assessment of process capability. This scale is based on a set of process attributes, arranged into a six-level ordinal capability scale. This arrangement enables capability to be assessed from the bottom of the scale, the *Incomplete* process (Level 0), through to the top of the scale, the *Optimizing* process (Level 5). The scale represents increasing capability of the Incomplete process, from performance that is not capable of fulfilling its purpose(s), through to performance that is capable of meeting its purpose(s) and sustaining continuous process improvement. The levels, therefore, constitute a rational way of progressing through improvement of the capability of any process.

Process capability is defined as "the range of expected results that can be achieved by following a process."[14] Thus, a process with higher capability will have a narrower distribution of outcomes about a mean than one of lower capability. It is more difficult to predict the outcome of less capable processes and estimates tend to be less accurate.

Process capability is expressed in the architecture in terms of nine *process attributes*. Process attributes are characteristics of a process that can be evaluated on a scale of purpose achievement, providing a measure of the capability of the process.

The process attributes are the basic elements of the assessment scheme. In an assessment, each is rated on a four-point scale of purpose achievement (**N**ot adequate, **P**artially, **L**argely, **F**ully). The task in performing a process assessment is to determine the extent to which the purpose of each of these attributes is achieved in the processes being assessed. The results of a full assessment, therefore, are the set of ratings of the nine attributes for each instance of every process assessed. The set of nine attribute ratings for a process instance is the *process profile*.

Revised process profile

The four-point rating scheme was retained, but has become a fundamental component of the *capability* dimension: each process instance is now rated on the extent to which each process attribute is achieved. Compatible assessment models have to provide a mapping to each element of the reference model and a translation from whatever rating mechanism they use during an assessment to the four-point rating scheme of the reference model.

Assessment results mapped to the reference model now show, for each process assessed, the proportions of process instances that are rated at each point on the scale for each process attribute, as illustrated in Figure 3.7. Although this presentation is superficially similar to Figure 3.4, the important distinction is that now *process attributes*—and not generic practices—*are the units for presenting the ratings*.

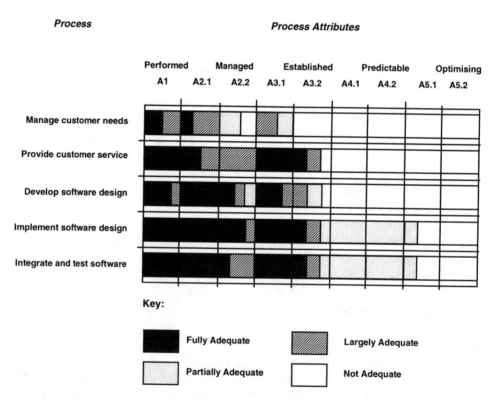

Figure 3.7: Example of a capability profile using the second version of the architecture.

The current document set

At the time this book was written, the current version, Version 2.00 of the SPICE documents, is comprised of nine parts. Figure 3.8 shows the nine parts of the document set and indicates the relationships between them. All the requirements relating to the assessment framework are contained in two parts of the set—Parts 2 and 3—with the remaining parts containing guidance on conducting assessments and applying the results.

Part 1: Concepts and Introductory Guide is an entry point into the document set. It describes how the parts of the suite fit together and provides guidance for their selection and use. It explains the requirements contained within the documents and their applicability to the performance of an assessment.

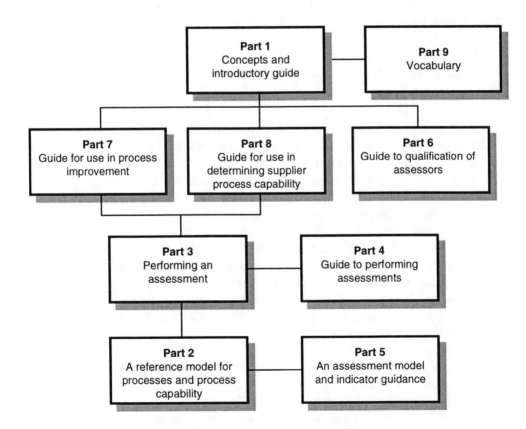

Figure 3.8: Components of the Version 2.00 document set.

Part 2: A Reference Model for Processes and Process Capability defines a two-dimensional reference model for describing the outcomes of process assessment. The reference model defines a set of processes, defined in terms of their purpose, and a framework for evaluating the capability of the processes through the assessment of process attributes, structured into capability levels. Requirements for establishing the compatibility of different assessment models with the reference model are defined. This part is a normative part of the standard. (Part 2 is described in Chapter 4.)

Part 3: Performing an Assessment defines the requirements for performing a conformant assessment in a manner such that the outcomes will be repeatable, reliable, and consistent. This part is also normative. (Part 3 is described in Chapter 5.)

Part 4: Guide to Performing Assessments provides guidance on performing Software Process Assessments and on interpreting the requirements of Part 3 for different assessment contexts. The guidance covers:

- the selection and use of a compatible assessment model
- a supportive method for assessment
- an appropriate assessment instrument or tool.

This guidance is generic enough to be applicable to all organizations, to perform assessments using a variety of different methods and techniques, and to be supported by a range of tools. (Part 4 is described in Chapter 5.)

Part 5: An Assessment Model and Indicator Guidance provides an exemplar model for performing process assessments that is based upon, and is directly compatible with, the reference model in Part 2. The assessment model extends the reference model through the inclusion of a comprehensive set of indicators of process performance and capability. (Part 5 is described in Chapter 7.)

Part 6: Guide to Qualification of Assessors describes the competence, education, training, and experience of qualified assessors, relevant to conducting process assessments. It describes mechanisms that may be used to demonstrate competence and to validate education, training, and experience. (Part 6 is described in Chapter 10.)

Part 7: Guide for Use in Process Improvement describes how to define the inputs to, and use the results of, an assessment for the purposes of process improvement. It includes examples of the application of process improvement in a variety of situations. (Part 7 is described in Chapter 8.)

Part 8: Guide for Use in Determining Supplier Process Capability describes how to define the inputs to, and use the results of, an assessment for the purpose of process capability determination. It addresses process capability determination in both straightforward situations and in more complex situations involving, for example, future capability. The guidance on conducting process capability determination is applicable for use within either an organization to determine its own capability or by a acquirer to determine the capability of a potential supplier or a potential supplier. (Part 8 is described in Chapter 9.)

Part 9: Vocabulary is a consolidated vocabulary of all terms specifically defined for the purposes of the document set.

Conclusion

At the time of writing, Version 2.00 of the architecture, in the form of an ISO/IEC Proposed Draft Technical Report, had been circulated throughout the standards community for comment. Within the SPICE Project, Phase 2 Trials have begun to use the new set of documents. As a result of these activities, it is likely that further revision, at the editorial level at least, will be required in 1997. It is the hope of the development team that the forthcoming ballot—and subsequent ones, as required—will not result in further, substantive changes to the assessment framework, that is, to the concept of the reference model and to the general status of the requirements.

From many perspectives, the revised architecture is a substantial improvement upon the original release. The revision provided the opportunity to incorporate several areas of new thinking that were beginning to crystallize during the latter phases of the development of the initial version. With the benefit of hindsight, it is now easy to see that the initial version was flawed in terms of its complexity, particularly in the capability dimension. It is also encouraging, however, that in spite of the criticisms, the early trials substantiated the value of the two-dimensional nature of the architecture.

The revised version of the architecture is perhaps closer to the ideals of the initial concepts set out in the initial study group report.[7] The reference model concept is a cleaner way of expressing the envisioned, high-level descriptions of the goals and fundamental activities that are essential to good software engineering practices and their assessment criteria. The reference model also establishes a mechanism that enables other, more detailed assessment models, catering to the needs of particular industries, sectors, or communities, to exist while still being related to the emerging standard. This same concept also provides the route by which existing assessment models can demonstrate conformance to the emerging standard or can be evolved or migrated to become conformant. In this way, the substantial investments in process improvement made by companies using existing models is protected.

In the capability dimension, the more abstract nature of the process attributes, compared with the generic practices of the initial version, links them more closely with a substantial gain in process capability. Each process attribute expresses a particular capability in the management of a process, but without being too prescriptive in the way that it might be achieved. The benefit of implementing that particular capability (in illustrating what it could buy the organization) is much clearer, and hence has substantial advantages in "selling" an improvement path to the management of an organization.

There are, inevitably, a number of unanswered questions that the trials may begin to address. It remains to be demonstrated from the experience of use that each process attribute really does represent a significant gain in capability. Some of the issues that need to be answered are:

- Are the process attributes that were chosen the characteristics that tend to make a process more capable?

- Do the process attributes cover all the relevant capabilities defined at each level?

- Are the process attributes defined so as to be independent of each other?

- Is this set sufficient to characterize the range of capabilities?

- Do the process attributes cover all the relevant capabilities defined for each level and are they defined so as not to overlap?

- Do the process attributes represent the "universal truths" of process capability?

- Are the process attributes genuinely applicable to any process?

At a more abstract level is the question of whether the model may still contain a recursive element. Each of the process attributes could be supported by one or more of the processes from the process dimension. For example, the process attributes at capability Level 2 (the *Performance Management* and *Work Product Management* attributes) are clearly related to processes in the Management and Support process categories. Others are related to processes in the Organization process category.

The situation becomes relatively straightforward when assessing the Customer-Supplier and Engineering categories. But what happens when assessing the capability of processes from the Management process category? In practice, there is a strong argument that suggests that the greatest benefits are to be gained from increasing the capability of the processes in the Customer-Supplier and Engineering categories since these processes are the primary ones that are directly within the value chain that creates the products and/or services. The Management, Support, and Organization categories contain those processes that assist the primary processes in some way.

The further these processes are from the primary processes, the less apparent the value is of them having a high level of capability. An organization would benefit greatly from having an improvement process that fully achieves at the Performed level (Level 1), but what additional gain would there be from improving the improvement process itself until it reaches the Optimizing level (Level 5)? If this case can be made, it begs the question of what value there is of even assessing some of the Management, Support, and Organization process at levels above the Performed level.

In addition to the issues related to the reference model, there are other key matters that remain to be confirmed through practical application. In particular, while the general set of requirements for a conformant assessment have remained unchanged from those successfully evaluated in the Phase 1 Trials, the changed perspective relating to the assessment instrument represents a fundamental change in approach that needs careful evaluation. Specific issues that must be addressed include:

- Is it possible to meet the requirement of documenting evidence, sufficient to justify ratings, with reasonable economy?
- Can conformance to this requirement be effectively demonstrated and validated?
- Is the concept of *indicators* one that can be effectively applied in different assessment methods?
- Can a complete and unambiguous set of indicators be generated that are useable for assessing capability across the entire defined scale?
- To what extent can assessments using different sets of indicators— but the same basic measurement scale—be compared?

The path to the development of an international standard is not straightforward. It is strewn with pitfalls, rocks, and barriers to be overcome. These challenges come in the form of not only technical problems to be solved, but in the shape of political problems, the specific interests of each of the National Bodies participating in the development and the voting, through competing commercial pressures, and through some of the administrative steps required. As a consequence, the resulting product will often involve compromise. So far, in the development of this emerging standard, it has been possible to maintain a reasonable degree of consensus on the movement forward, although at times there have been major differences of opinion. The results of the SPICE Phase 2 Trials and the next series of ballots may help to show whether the right decisions have been made.

Appendix A: Requirements for a process assessment standard

The original requirements for a Software Process Assessment standard are grouped into three categories:

1. **goals:** those requirements that address the rationale for the emerging standard
2. **functional:** those requirements that apply to the way the emerging standard operates or define the purpose of the emerging standard
3. **nonfunctional:** those requirements that define the characteristics of the emerging standard.

Goals

The process assessment standard shall:

Requirement A: Encourage predictable quality products

Requirement B: Encourage optimum productivity

Requirement C: Promote a repeatable software process

Requirement M2:   Not be used for trade restraint

Requirement W: Be subject to continuous improvement through periodic reviews to maintain consistency with current good practice

Functional requirements

The process assessment standard shall:

Requirement B2:   Ensure the organization's ability to "set and realize defined, achievable goals for productivity and/or development cycle time, linked to business needs and project requirements" is made visible in the assessment results

Requirement C3: Ensure the organization's ability to *"manage the process to achieve a repeatable software process"* is made visible in the assessment results

Requirement D: Provide guidance for improving software processes aligned to business goals, including its starting point and target

Requirement D1: When used for process improvement, process assessment must include an activity to elicit business goals and align the assessment criteria to them

> **Requirement D1.1:** An organization or project will not be adversely affected by the absence of processes specified in the standard that are not applicable

Requirement D2: When used for process improvement, process assessment must include:

> **Requirement D2.1:** Guidance to include full results of the assessment

> **Requirement D2.2:** Guidance to include desired capability

> **Requirement D2.3:** Guidance to include changes needed in processes, to move from actual to desired processes, activities, or tasks

> > **Requirement D2.4.1:** Assessment concepts to be explained to those being assessed during the assessment phase

> > **Requirement D2.4.2:** Those being assessed have opportunity to clarify their understanding during assessment

Requirement E: Support process capability determination for risk identification and analysis within an organization

Requirement E1: When used for process capability determination within an organization, assessment must include activities to establish success factors for the subsequent phases, including:

> **Requirement E1.1:** How capability will be determined

> **Requirement E1.2:** The criteria to be used for assessment

Requirement E1.3: Appropriate steps to ensure nonconcealment during process assessment

Requirement E2: Process capability determination must include activities to identify and analyze risks and to draw out strengths and weaknesses

Requirement F: Support process capability determination for risk identification and analysis within a two-party contractual situation

Requirement F1: When used for process capability determination in a two-party contractual situation, assessment must include activities to establish success factors for the subsequent phases, including:

Requirement F1.1: How capability will be determined

Requirement F1.2: The criteria to be used for assessment

Requirement F1.3: Appropriate steps to ensure non-concealment during process assessment

Requirement F2: Process capability determination must include activities to identify and analyze risks and may also draw out strengths and weaknesses

Requirement G1: Process assessment must ensure that the project/work areas selected for assessment are sufficiently representative for the results of the assessment, not to be unduly dependent on their selection

Requirement K2: The standard will allow for variants to be developed to suit the special needs of:

Requirement K2.1: Different application domains

Requirement K2.2: Different business needs

Requirement K2.3: Different sizes of organizations

Requirement L: For each process, define baseline practices that are appropriate across all application domains, business needs, and sizes of organization. The baseline practices should be extensible to allow for industry or business variants

Requirement L1:   Variants developed to suit the needs of special circumstances may add baseline practices within a process but may not remove them

Requirement L2:   Variants may delete processes

Requirement M: Define standard requirements for the development of industry or business variants of the baseline practices

Requirement M1:   Define standard requirements for the development of variants to suit the special needs of the following circumstances: different application domains, business needs, and sizes of organizations

    Requirement M1.1:   Variants must comply with these requirements to comply with the standard

Requirement N: Be applicable at the project and organizational levels, with connectivity between the two

Requirement O: Focus on process, but also address people and the application of technology

    Requirement O1:   Deal with those people issues that significantly influence process effectiveness

    Requirement O2:   Deal with technology application issues that significantly influence process effectiveness

Requirement Q1:   The standard must define quantitative measures of:

    Requirement Q1.1:   Degree of conformity (actual and target)

Requirement Q2:   The standard will provide guidance on how an organization can define and use quantitative measures of effectiveness, the effectiveness being related to its business needs

Requirement R: Support output as process profiles that allow views at different levels of detail. The profiling method should support comparisons against other similar entities or industry "norms"

Requirement R1:   The standard must define profiling methods. In particular, it must:

    Requirement R1.1:   Define the process profiles that may be used.

Requirement R1.2: Define how the process profiles are to be generated

Requirement R1.4: Define the circumstances in which comparison between process profiles are valid

Requirement S: Require that agreement is reached over ownership and confidentiality of assessment results prior to assessment

Requirement T: Define the initial and ongoing qualification of assessors

Requirement T1: The standard must give guidance on the selection of assessors and the makeup of the assessment team. Such guidance should include:

Requirement T1.1: The skills and experience required by the assessment team as a whole

Requirement T1.2: The general structure of an assessment team and the distribution of those skills and experiences across team members

Nonfunctional requirements

The process assessment standard shall:

Requirement G: Be capable of being employed reliably and consistently

Requirement H: Be simple to use and understand

Requirement H1: Be based on clear elementary concepts

Requirement H3: Use clear, unambiguous language

Requirement H4: Use well-defined terms

Requirement H5: Be governed in its use by executable procedures

Requirement I: Be culturally independent

Requirement I1: Be independent of national and linguistic cultures

Requirement J: Not presume specific organizational structures, management philosophies, software life cycle models, software technologies, or software development methods

Requirement K: Recognize different application domains, business needs and sizes of organizations

Requirement P: Be objective

Requirement Q: Be quantitative wherever possible

Requirement U: Be supportive of and consistent with other ISO/JTC1/SC7 standards and projects

Requirement V: Be supportive of and consistent with the ISO 9000 series of standards

Appendix B: Allocation of functional requirements

The matrix below (Table 3.1) shows an allocation of the functional requirements for the emerging standard to the identified components of the emerging standard. It indicates which component(s) is seen to be *chiefly* contributing to the satisfaction of each of the requirements. Where there are differences in allocation of individual subrequirements, this difference is shown. This table reflects the original requirements allocation in the product specification document.

Table 3.1: Mapping of documents to requirements.

	IG	PAG	AI	BPG	PIG	PCDG	ATQG
B2		X	X	X			
C3		X	X	X			
D		D1			X		
E		E1			E2	X	
F		F1				X	
G1	X	X					
K2	X	X	X	X			X
L	X			X			
M	X			X			
N		X	X		X	X	
O		X	X	X	X	X	
Q1		X	X		X		
Q2		X			X		
R		X	X			X	
S		X					
T	X						X
T1		X					X

Addendum to Chapter 3: Further evolution of the reference model architecture

The document set described in this book was distributed within ISO/IEC JTC1/SC7 for ballot as Preliminary Draft Technical Report 15504.[18] Consideration of the ballot comments has resulted in a further evolution of the reference model architecture. The aim of this brief addendum is to describe the current and ongoing changes and to try to look to the future progression of the emerging Software Process Assessment standard.

ISO/IEC 12207 and the reference model

The principal area of concern was with respect to the process dimension of the reference model. Concerns were raised that the level of mapping to ISO/IEC 12207 was not at a sufficiently high level of detail. The general view was that there should be a single overall model for software life cycle processes.

It was acknowledged that different levels of detail within a model for life cycle processes were required, depending on whether the primary purpose was for assessment (the objective of the SPICE documents) or implementation (the objective of ISO/IEC 12207). However, it was thought that these differences could and should be expressed within the context of a single process model. ISO/IEC 12207 was seen as the primary source for this model.

Following WG10 discussions, the following policy was agreed upon for progressing the issue:

- The reference model will use the same process framework as ISO/IEC 12207. The model will use the same process groupings, processes, and terminology as in ISO/IEC 12207.
- The process definitions in the reference model will comprise *process purpose* and *process outcome* statements, adding to the process definitions of ISO/IEC 12207.
- Where it is deemed necessary, the reference model will provide new processes or extend the scope of existing processes and/or activities defined in ISO/IEC 12207.
- To provide adequate assessment granularity, the reference model will define the term *component process* as a group of one or more defined activities from the same process within ISO/IEC 12207.

- Lessons learned during the development and trialling of the reference model will be provided as input during the revision of ISO/IEC 12207 after the DTR ballot for ISO/IEC PDTR 15504.

The structure of the revised process dimension will therefore be *similar* to that shown in Figure 3.9. It should be noted that this revision is an indicative draft only, based on preliminary discussions within WG10. Using ISO/IEC 12207

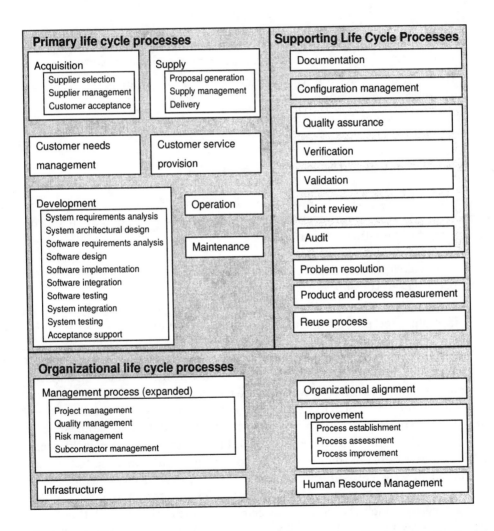

Figure 3.9: ISO/IEC 15504—Structure of the process dimension (indicative draft)

as the model for life cycle processes, there would be, for example, ten component processes within the Development Process. At the present time, it is also the intent to preserve the process categories within ISO/IEC 15504, since these categories may provide significant added value in terms of the usability of the model.

Several aspects of the revised model remain uncertain and will not be finalized before the next WG10 meeting in June 1997. These uncertainties include:

- the level of granularity within the Development Process
- the status of processes within the Management Process Category
- the placement within the model of the new process, Process and Product Measurement
- the reintroduced Reuse Process.

Initial evaluation of the proposed changes

The revision introduces both benefits and problems. The use of a consistent, single process model for both implementation and assessment of software processes is a substantial benefit for two reasons:

1. It encourages a common frame of reference for discussing the key processes of the software life cycle.
2. It provides a mechanism for unambiguous assessment of processes implemented pursuant to a contractual agreement.

However, problems likely will arise with the declaration of a one-to-one relationship between the ISO/IEC 15504 assessment and ISO/IEC 12207 implementation models for software processes. Perhaps the key issue is that the processes defined in ISO/IEC 12207 do not—by design—conform to the basic (Performed) level of capability of the reference model. The general intent of ISO/IEC 12207 is that most processes should possess substantial achievement of the Level 2 attributes of the reference model: they should be close to the status of a Managed Process. This intent can be clearly identified with respect to all the Primary processes. Consequently, although the same terms are used to describe the processes—in fact, the process descriptions in ISO/IEC PDTR 15504 in many instances represent a lower level of capability than those defined in ISO/IEC 12207—*the processes are not the same.*

There is no easy solution to this problem. The processes in the ISO/IEC 12207 model are not all defined with equivalent levels of capability. In general, the Primary Processes are defined so as to be performed at a Managed level, while most of the Support and Organizational processes are defined for implementation only at the Performed level. Consequently, an attempt to use the complete process definitions from ISO/IEC 12207 as the basic process definitions in the SPICE documents will fail, since the processes themselves are not defined to be of equivalent capability. The only solution may be to establish an awareness of this problem and to use the same terminology in the knowledge that the processes so defined are not exactly equivalent in performance, but in fact are so only in scope.

For a good example of the problem, compare the Maintenance Process in ISO/IEC 12207 with the Maintain System and Software process in Version 2.00 of ISO/IEC 15504. The process as defined in ISO/IEC 12207 contains the following activities that represent achievement of the Performance Management attribute and for this reason are not identifiable in the equivalent ISO/IEC 15504 Version 2.00 definition:

5.5.1.1 The maintainer shall develop, document, and execute plans and procedures for conducting the activities and tasks of the Maintenance Process.

5.5.4.1 The maintainer shall conduct review(s) with the organization authorizing the modification to determine the integrity of the modified system.

5.5.5.2 A migration plan shall be developed, documented, and executed. The planning activities shall include users. Items included in the plan shall include the following:
   a) Requirements analysis and definition of migration
   b) Development of migration tools
   c) Conversion of software product and data
   d) Migration execution
   e) Migration verification
   f) Support for the old environment in the future.

5.5.5.6 A post-operation review shall be performed to assess the impact of changing to the new environment. The results of the review shall be sent to the appropriate authorities for information, guidance, and action.

5.5.6.1 A retirement plan to remove active support by the operation and maintenance organizations shall be developed and documented.

The planning activities shall include users. The plan shall address the items listed below. The plan shall be executed.

    a) Cessation of full or partial support after a certain period of time

    b) Archiving of the software product and its associated documentation

    c) Responsibility for any future residual support issues

    d) Transition to the new software product, if applicable

    e) Accessibility of archive copies of data.[19]

All these activities are concerned with "(managing the execution of the process) to produce work products within stated time and resource requirements"—the definition of the Performance Management attribute—through the production and execution of plans and the review of progress or achievements against the plans, usually jointly with the users.

Similar examples can be found in the activities and tasks that describe the achievement of the Work Product Management attribute. In total, these elements actually comprise the major part of the definition in ISO/IEC 12207.

Based on this logic, the incorporation of identical process definitions into the ISO/IEC 12207 standard and the emerging ISO/IEC 15504 standard is not possible without abandoning the basic principles of process assessment—the evaluation of capability using a defined and common scale of measurement. Providing that this fact is recognized, the benefits of utilizing common terminology and of basing both ISO/IEC 12207 and ISO/IEC 15504 on a common vocabulary and terminology can be achieved. Ultimately, it appears to be, on balance, worth striving for.

The adoption of such a policy, however, must have a flow-on effect in the further evolution of the standards and in the development of related standards. An example of the problems that may arise can be seen in the early drafts of a new standard for System Life Cycle Processes,[20] where the defined model does not allow for the unambiguous mapping of the processes from ISO/IEC 12207 onto the new model. The implications of the policy, and the restrictions it implies for future standardization efforts, will need to be explored in depth by the standards community.

From the perspective of the SPICE Project, the major impact of the policy will be to delay the official publication of the document set as Technical Reports Type 2. It would seem almost certain that a further round of ballots will be required. With good faith on the part of all participants, the delay should not be more than a further six months, and we may see the release of an interim standard in this critical area before the end of 1998.

References

1. Craigmyle, M. and I. Fletcher, "Improving IT Effectiveness Through Software Process Assessment," *Software Quality J.*, Vol. 2, 1993, pp. 257–264.

2. Deming, W.E., *Out of the Crisis*, MIT Center for Advanced Engineering Study, 1982.

3. European Software Institute, "First Feedback from SPICE Trials Gives Encouraging Results," *Improve—The Newsletter of the European Software Institute*, Issue 3, 1995, pp. 4–5.

4. Herbsleb, J., et al., *Benefits of CMM Based Software Process Improvement: Initial Results*, Technical Report, CMU/SEI-94-TR-13, Software Engineering Institute, Aug. 1994.

5. Humphrey, W., *Managing the Software Process*, Addison-Wesley, Reading, Mass., 1989.

6. Humphrey, W., T. Snyder, and R. Willis, "Software Process Improvement at Hughes Aircraft," *IEEE Software*, Vol. 8, No. 4, July 1991, pp. 11–23.

7. ISO/IEC, *The Need and Requirements for a Software Process Assessment Standard*, Study Report, Issue 2.0, JTC1/SC7 N944R, 11 June 1992.

8. ISO/IEC, *Product Specification for a Software Process Assessment Standard*, Version 1.00, JTC1/SC7/WG10, 22 June 1993.

9. ISO/IEC 12207, *Information Technology—Software life cycle processes*, 22 Feb. 1995.

10. Maclennan, F. and G. Ostrolenk, "The SPICE Trials: Validating the Framework," *Proc 2nd Int'l SPICE Symp.*, Australian Software Quality Research Institute, Brisbane, Australia, 1995.

11. Marshall, P., F. Maclennan, and M. Tobin, "Analysis of Observation and Problem Reports from Phase 1 of the SPICE Trials," *IEEE TCSE Software Process Newsletter*, No. 6, Spring 1996.

12. Kuvaja, P. et al., *Software Process Assessment and Improvement: The BOOTSTRAP Approach*. Blackwell Publishers, 1994.

13. Paulk, M., et al., *Capability Maturity Model for Software*, Version 1.1. Technical Report CMU/SEI-93-TR-24, Software Engineering Institute, Pittsburgh, Feb. 1993.

14. Paulk, M. et al., *Key Practices of the Capability Maturity Model, Version 1.1*. Technical Report CMU/SEI-93-TR-25, Software Engineering Institute, Feb. 1993.

15. SPICE Project, *Software Process Assessment*, Parts 1—9, June 1995.

16. SPICE Project, "SPICE Phase 1 Trials Report", Oct. 1995.

17. Woodman, I. and R. Hunter, "Analysis of Assessment Data from Phase 1 of the SPICE Trials," *IEEE TCSE Software Process Newsletter*, No. 6, Spring 1996.

18. ISO/IEC JTC1/SC7 PDTR 15504. *Parts 1—9: Information Technology—Software Process Assessment*, PDTR, November 1996.

19. ISO/IEC 12207. *Information Technology: Software Life Cycle Processes,* 1995.

20. ISO/IEC JTC1/SC7/WG7. *Information Technology: System Life Cycle Processes*, unpublished working draft, Feb. 1997.

4

The Reference Model

Alan W. Graydon
Nortel, Canada

Risto Nevalainen
European Software Institute, Spain

Jean-Normand Drouin
Bell Canada, Canada

This chapter describes in detail the development of what is now ISO/IEC *PDTR 15504-2: Software Process Assessment, Part 2: A Reference Model for Processes and Process Capability.*[5] The previous versions of this document were developed by the SPICE Project team between 1993 and 1995. At that time, and until Version 1.00, it was called the *Baseline Practices Guide* (BPG).

This *reference model* embodies the set of core software engineering practices around which an organization can be assessed. As such, it is a pivotal component of the SPICE document set. Three key versions of the reference model are discussed in this chapter:

- the product specification
- the *Baseline Practices Guide*[4] (also known as SPICE Version 1.00 Part 2)
- *Part 2: A reference model for processes and process capability*, Version 2.00.[5]

To gain a first-hand understanding behind the thinking of the BPG team during the development of each key stage of the reference model, passages from these documents are included in the text of this chapter. Where appropriate, commentaries are provided to highlight the ideas that may not be apparent from reading the text. Finally, the important versions of the document are introduced to explain its evolution.

Product specification

The initial work on the *Baseline Practices Guide* (BPG) started with the drafting of the Product Description (PD). The purpose of this document was to provide the BPG development team with a description of the design, structure, and content requirements of the BPG itself. The work performed during that early phase was of a planning and preparatory nature.

The initial BPG team included representatives from all the major process assessment model and method providers in existence at that time—for example, there was representation from the Software Engineering Institute's (SEI) Capability Maturity Model (CMM), Trillium, Bootstrap, Software Technology Diagnostic (STD), and HealthCheck among others. This core team of experts took advantage of the opportunity to create the PD to capture their initial ideas. Some of these ideas were captured in the PD Version 0.01[1] and are included below verbatim to illustrate how several have endured to become part of Version 2.00:

> *Software process management* means the disciplined application of good software engineering practices, which in turn implies the need for a management system that empowers the implementation of these practices.

> A *software process* can be defined as a set of activities, methods, practices, and transformations that people use to develop and maintain software and their associated products (for example, project plans, design documents, code, test cases, and user manuals). As an organization matures, the software process becomes better defined and more consistently implemented throughout the organization.

> *Software process capability* describes the range of expected results that can be achieved by following a software process.

> Software *process performance* represents the actual results achieved by following a software process.

As a software organization gains in software process maturity, it institutionalizes its software process via policies, standards, and organizational structures. *Institutionalization* entails building an infrastructure and a corporate culture that supports the methods, practices, and procedures of the business so that they endure after those who originally defined them have gone.[1]

Each process within the BPG is performed to achieve certain *goals*. These goals can be stated from both a compliance and an effectiveness perspective. *Effectiveness* can only be judged from within the context of the business environment in which an organization is operating. *Compliance*, however, can be judged against a standard of what is commonly believed to be good software engineering practice. Those good engineering practices, and the goals they should achieve, are described in the BPG.

The goals summarize the practices, which in turn describe a reasonable software process. Compliance with a reasonable process, however, does not mean that the process is efficient in achieving its purpose. Effectiveness attributes can be applied only within the context of the business environment and the specific circumstances of the project and the organization. Such effectiveness judgments can be made only by the organization as a part of its continuous process improvement cycle. Perfection is never achieved, and continuous process improvement never ends. The activities fundamental to continually improving the process capability are shown in Figure 4.1.

The BPG practices are organized into a framework that supports the fundamental activities shown in Figure 4.1. This framework is straightforward because the fundamental activities anticipate the framework (their process capability areas, goals, and so on). An additional perspective of organizational maturity levels is introduced, as envisioned in Trillium,[6] which was strongly based on the notion of the maturity levels presented in the CMM,[10] which in turn were first introduced by Crosby.[11]

Product requirements

The major source of input to the project came from the process management study report *The Need and Requirements for a Software Process Assessment Standard*,[14] completed in June, 1992. The study document included a number of conclusions that were meant to summarize the findings of the study. Two of these conclusions are worth mentioning here since they had a profound effect on the reference model. The first conclusion stated:

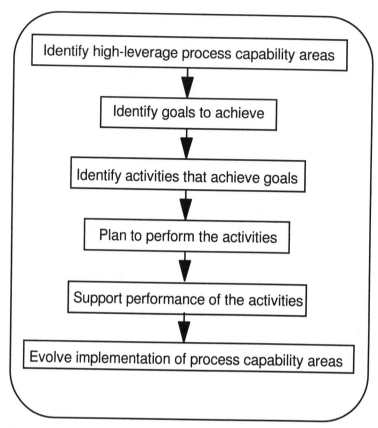

Figure 4.1: Fundamental process capability improvement activities.

A standard for Software Process Assessment should be concerned with the processes used in the procurement, development, delivery, operation, evolution, and related service support of software and software-dependent systems.[14]

This conclusion essentially mandated the BPG team to include all the major phases of the software development life cycle in their model definition. The life cycle, beginning with the procurement of a software product by a customer or its representative, throughout the software's development, delivery, and post-development operation and support, was now within the scope of the BPG. In the case of support, not only was the typical software product field support to be included in the model, but the perspective of how ongoing enhancements or improvements to the software product would be made now had to be considered. This full life-cycle scope meant that the BPG team needed to research and integrate a number of different input sources to ensure that this high-level requirement for the scope of all the processes would be included in the model.

The second conclusion stated:

> The development of the standard should aim to utilize the proven and best features of existing assessment methods and to draw on existing material wherever relevant.[14]

During the course of the process management study, a number of existing methods and models were researched as a means of identifying candidate assessment and evaluation methods. The methods researched included the CMM, the STD, the British Telecom Software Assessment Method (SAM), the Bootstrap Assessment Method, and the Bell Canada/Nortel Trillium Software Process Self-assessment model. The methods researched represented the existing *de facto* standards for SPA. They provided a representative sample of the existing models, some of which could not be fully researched because they were not in the public domain.

The first conclusion drawn by the study indicated that industry—by the mere fact that a large number of methods had been developed, some at great expense—had recognized the value of performing assessments. The second fact uncovered by the study was that most of the methods had specific industry sectors for which they were developed. For example, the CMM was developed for the sole purpose of assuring the capability of software contractors to the US military.

The Trillium model, as developed by Bell Canada and Nortel, was focused solely on enhancing the capability of software developed for telecommunications products and services. The telecommunications industry had certain reliability and quality criteria that had to be met in their products—for example, less than two hours of downtime in 40 years—and it was deemed necessary to develop an assessment method to ensure compliance to these criteria. The same could be said of the majority of the other methods researched during the study. The conclusions of the study led the BPG team to use these existing methods since they represented the *state-of-the-art* practice for software engineering.

From this study, the product requirements were developed.[13] These consisted of goals and functional/non-functional requirements. See Appendix A in Chapter 3 for a complete list of functional requirements—nonfunctional requirements were not applicable to the BPG—and for the allocation of functional requirements to the BPG.

Context of the product

The objectives of the BPG were to encourage predictable quality products and optimum productivity and to promote a repeatable software process. There were many standards and software practices that had already been defined by national and international bodies such as IEEE and ISO. Only those that addressed methods for *improving the quality of the software process* were used by the BPG team.

The Baseline Practices Guide

Chapter 3 presented the basic architecture of the BPG, which is similar to Part 2, Version 1.0. In this section we explain this architecture in more detail.

The process dimension

The process dimension of the architecture illustrates grouping by *type of activity*. The processes and activities characterize the *performance* of a process, even if that performance is not systematic. Performance of the base practices may be *ad hoc*, unpredictable, inconsistent, poorly planned, and/or result in poor quality products, but those work products are at least marginally usable in achieving the purpose of the process.

The team considered that implementing only the base practices of a process would be of minimal value and may represent only the first step in building the organization's process capability, but the base practices represented the unique, functional activities of the process. (For a list of the processes covered in the BPG, see Part 2, Version 1.00 on the CD-ROM. The list is organized as a hierarchy with the processes grouped by process category. A summary of each process category and associated processes is also provided.)

Process categories and processes

Each *process category* was defined as a set of processes that addressed the same general area of activity. The process categories covered in the BPG addressed five general areas of activity: customer-supplier activities, software engineering, project management, support, and organization-infrastructure building activities. These are summarized below:

PROCESS CATEGORY	DESCRIPTION
Customer-Supplier	Consists of processes that directly impact the customer, supporting development and transition of the software to the customer, and provide for its correct operation and use.
Engineering	Consists of processes that directly specify, implement, or maintain a system and software product and its user documentation.
Project	Consists of processes that establish the project and coordinate and manage its resources to produce a product or provide services that satisfy the customer.
Support	Consists of processes that enable and support the performance of the other processes on a project.
Organization	Consists of processes that establish the business goals of the organization and develop process, product, and resource assets that will help the organization achieve its business goals.

A *process* is a set of activities that achieves a purpose. Each process in the BPG stated a purpose and consisted of a set of practices that addressed that purpose. The processes in the BPG were not processes in the sense of being complete process models or descriptions. Rather, they contained essential practices, but they did not describe how to perform the process. The BPG was, as is the current reference model, a descriptive, not prescriptive model.

The rationale behind the selection and organization of the process categories was customer-based, placing the focus of software engineering activities where it really should be—on the customer. The Customer-Supplier process category consisted of those processes closest to the customer. Each succeeding process category is *one layer removed* from the customer. The Engineering process category consisted of processes that build the product to be delivered to the customer. The Project process category consisted of processes that manage the development of the product. The Support process category consisted of processes that enable and support the performance of the previous processes, whether management, engineering, or customer-related. Finally, the Organization process category consisted of processes that build organizational infrastructure on which all previous processes could potentially exercise the most benefit to the organization.

Processes and base practices

The type of practices that serve as the essential activities of a specific process were named the *base practices*. They were grouped by type—area and purpose—

of activity. Base practices are software engineering or management activities that address the purpose of a particular process. Consistently performing the base practices associated with a process were intended to help the organization in consistently achieving its purpose.

Thus a *process* consisted of a set of base practices. The base practices in the BPG were also described at an abstract level, identifying *what* should be done without specifying *how*.*

Capability dimension and common features

The BPG development team then grouped the architectural elements by *type of implementation* or *institutionalization* activity. A *capability level* was defined as a set of common features—sets of activities—that work together to provide a major enhancement in the organization's capability to perform a process. For example, to effectively attain conformance to the practices at the Well-defined level (Level 3), for some processes the organization would require support through an effective implementation of another process, namely *Define the process* (ORG.2).

Each of the six capability levels provided a major enhancement in capability to that provided by its predecessors in the performance of a process. Together, they constituted a roadmap for improving a specific process in a logical fashion.

Level suggests sequence, and in fact the capability levels became a rational way of progressing through enhancements to a process as characterized by the practices. This progression may not, however, apply to all software environments. Organization-wide improvement considerations, and taking advantage of what has already been implemented in an organization, may influence progression through the capability levels. Since there are dependencies between processes, the successful satisfaction of a capability level within a process may require support from another process.

A *common feature* was defined as a set of practices that address one aspect of process implementation or institutionalization. For example, the Planned-and-Tracked level contained the Planning performance, Disciplined performance, Verifying performance, and Tracking performance common features. The Tracking performance common feature consisted of practices that track process status using measurements and take corrective actions as appropriate. (For a list of the common features covered in the BPG, see Part 2, Version 1.00 on the CD-ROM).

---

*See other ISO/JTC1/SC7 standards for further information and guidance on implementing these practices.

Ordering common features by capability levels

The BPG team decided that the nature of capability levels permitted more than one way to group aspects into common features and common features into capability levels. The team's rationalization was that the ordering of the common features stems from the observation that some implementation and institutionalization aspects benefit from the presence of others. They felt this to be especially true if institutionalization aspects are well established. For example, providing a well-defined, usable process for an entire organization to tailor and use should follow from some experience in managing the performance of that process at the level of individual projects. For example, prior to institutionalizing a specific estimation process for an entire organization, the organization first attempts to use the estimation process on a project.

When an organization has some, but not all common features implemented at a particular capability level for a particular process, the organization usually is operating at the lowest completed capability level for that process. For example, at capability Level 2, if the Tracking performance common feature is lacking, it will be difficult to track project performance. If a common feature is in place, but not those at the lower capability levels, the organization may not have benefited from having implemented that common feature.

The team still maintained, from early on in the project, that organizing the practices into capability levels would provide an organization with an improvement roadmap with which to enhance its capability for a specific process. It still made sense to keep the practices in the BPG in the groupings of common features ordered by capability levels.

The purpose of an assessment was still to determine the capability levels for all the different processes. While processes would likely always exist at different levels of capability, the organization would be able to use this process-specific information—the results of the assessment—as a means with which to focus on the improvements of their processes. The priority and sequence of the improvement of the organization's software processes, all of which are up to the organization, would have to take into account their own business goals.

Generic practices

The second type of practice was intended to represent the implementation or institutionalization of a process in a general way. These practices—called *generic practices*—could be applied potentially to any process and were grouped according to the aspect of implementation and institutionalization they addressed. A generic practice is an implementation or institutionalization practice that enhances the capability to perform any process. For example, the Disciplined performance common feature contained this generic practice:

> **2.4.1** *Track with measurement.* Track the status of the process against the plan using measurement.

The team believed that recording data on conditions and results while performing a process would increase the understanding of its performance and address the disciplined performance aspect of performing the process. This example demonstrates one of many generic practices that contribute to improved capability to manage the performance of the process: the data conveys status and results to the person tracking the performance of the process. The generic practices were applied to a process as a whole and could be aggregated by common features and by capability levels to describe the capability of a process.

This way of looking at the BPG architecture—by capability level, common feature, and generic practices—depicted the grouping by *type of implementation* or *institutionalization* activity. The generic practices characterize good process management that results in an increasing process capability for any process. A planned, well-defined, measured, and continuously-improving process is consistently performed as the generic practices are implemented for a process. Process capability is built on the foundation of the base practices that describe the unique, functional activities of the process.

When using the generic practices, the team thought it would be helpful to substitute the specific name of the process for the phrase "the process." For example, when judging generic practice 2.1.1 for the process *Perform configuration management*, "allocate adequate resources (including people) for performing the process" became "allocate adequate resources (including people) for performing configuration management."

Numbering for identification during assessment

A numbering scheme was developed to clearly identify each process category, process, capability area, common feature, base practice, and generic practice. This scheme made the BPG usable for the purpose of performing an assessment, an important operational requirement for Phase 1 of the SPICE Trials, the objective of which was to verify the usability of Version 1.00 of the BPG and its two closely-related SPICE documents, the *Process Assessment Guide* and the *Assessment Instrument*.

The team assigned each practice an identifier consisting of a three-character alphanumeric code:

Base practice	PC.PR.PT	
Generic practice	CL.CF.PT	
Codes	PC	process category identifier
	PR	process # (within the process category)
	CL	capability level #
	CR	common feature # (within the capability level)
	PT	practice # (within the process or common feature)

For example, using the above numbering scheme, *ENG.3.1 Develop software architectural design* denotes a base practice in process category ENG (Engineering), process 3 (Develop Software Design), base practice 1.

Version 2.0

In June 1995, Version 1.00 of the SPICE document set was handed over to ISO/IEC JTC1/SC7 for progression through the normal ISO balloting scheme. Version 2.00 was the result of this first balloting. Because the BPG has evolved into what is now owned by ISO, it is not possible to include the current version of the emerging International Standard on the CD-ROM without infringing on copyright. Therefore, this final section describes the changes made to Version 1.0 of the BPG, starting with the name change from *Baseline Practices Guide* to *PDTR ISO/IEC 15504-2: Software Process Assessment, Part 2: A reference model for processes and process capability.*[5]

Process dimension

The high-level architecture of the process model described in the BPG did undergo some change between Versions 1.0 and 2.00. The most significant changes were as follows:

- Modifications were applied to the processes with a resultant reduction from 35 processes to 29.
- The Project process category was renamed to Management to better align with ISO/IEC 12207.
- Base practices were moved from Part 2 to Part 5.
- Processes were aligned to ISO/IEC 12207.
- The process model, and hence the emerging standard, was made less prescriptive.

- Each process is now described in terms of *a purpose statement*.
- A set of measurable objectives for each process, derived from its purpose, have been included.

These changes, as well as additional minor changes incorporated into Version 2.00, are described in the remainder of this section.

Base practices

The most striking architectural change was that *base practices* are no longer part of what was previously the process model. They have been moved to Part 5 where, together with the work products, they act as *process indicators* to help the qualified assessor gather objective evidence that the goal of the processes has been achieved. In essence, Part 2 is now a *reference model of processes and process capability*.

The document's purpose therefore has changed dramatically and now limits itself to provide a reference model of processes. It also includes the concept of *conformant model*: an industrial model that has been shown to adequately map to the reference model. Part 2 includes the guidelines necessary to establish this mapping and demonstrate conformance.

This new approach ensures that the results of assessments performed with different models can be reported within a common context. The use of a conformant model during an assessment will ensure a common context for the reporting of assessment ratings and should help make the results comparable. This last point remains to be demonstrated and is one of the study areas in the SPICE Phase 2 Trials.

The number of base practices and work product indicators has remained about the same. On the other hand, several *processes* differ from the previous version, as will be shown later.

ISO/IEC 12207 alignment

The processes have been aligned further to ISO 12207's software life cycle processes. This recently-approved ISO standard regroups its 18 processes into three main categories: (1) *Primary processes*, (2) *Support processes* and (3) *Organizational processes*.

In the following table, the processes of Version 1.00 are compared with those of Version 2.00 on a one-to-one basis. Where there are blanks in the Version 2.00 column, the processes of Version 1.00 have been either moved elsewhere, integrated within another process, or removed all together.

Version 1.00 processes		Version 2.00 processes	
CUS	**Customer-Supplier process category**	**CUS**	**Customer-Supplier process category**
CUS.1	Acquire software product and/or service	CUS.1	Acquire software
CUS.2	Establish contract		
CUS.3	Identify customer needs	CUS.2	Manage customer needs
CUS.4	Perform joint audits and reviews		
CUS.5	Package, deliver, and install the software	CUS.3	Supply software
CUS.6	Support operation of software	CUS.4	Operate software
CUS.7	Provide customer service	CUS.5	Provide customer service
CUS.8	Assess customer satisfaction		
ENG	**Engineering process category**	**ENG**	**Engineering process category**
ENG.1	Develop system requirements and design	ENG.1	Develop system requirements and design
ENG.2	Develop software requirements	ENG.2	Develop software requirements
ENG.3	Develop software design	ENG.3	Develop software design
ENG.4	Implement software design	ENG.4	Implement software design
ENG.5	Integrate and test software	ENG.5	Integrate and test software
ENG.6	Integrate and test system	ENG.6	Integrate and test system
ENG.7	Maintain system and software	ENG.7	Maintain system and software
PRO	**Project process category**	**MAN**	**Management process category**
PRO.1	Plan project life cycle	MAN.1	Manage the project
PRO.2	Establish project plan		
PRO.3	Build project teams		
PRO.4	Manage requirements		
PRO.5	Manage quality	MAN.2	Manage quality
PRO.6	Manage risks	MAN.3	Manage risks
PRO.7	Manage resources and schedule		
PRO.8	Manage subcontractors	MAN.4	Manage subcontractors
SUP	**Support process category**	**SUP**	**Support process category**
SUP.1	Develop documentation	SUP.1	Develop documentation
SUP.2	Perform configuration management	SUP.2	Perform configuration management
SUP.3	Perform quality assurance	SUP.3	Perform quality assurance
		SUP.4	Perform work product verification
		SUP.5	Perform work product validation
SUP.5	Perform peer reviews	SUP.6	Perform joint reviews
		SUP.7	Perform audits
SUP.4	Perform problem resolution	SUP.8	Perform problem resolution
ORG	**Organization process category**	**ORG**	**Organization process category**
ORG.1	Engineer the business	ORG.1	Engineer the business
ORG.2	Define the process	ORG.2	Define the process
ORG.3	Improve the process	ORG.3	Improve the process
ORG.4	Perform training	ORG.4	Provide skilled human resources
ORG.5	Enable reuse		
ORG.6	Provide software engineering environment	ORG.5	Provide software engineering infrastructure
ORG.7	Provide work facilities		

After the balloting period for Version 1.00, two important comments were raised:

1. a better alignment of Part 2 with ISO/IEC 12207 was needed

2. the need to make the emerging standard and the process model itself less prescriptive.

In developing Version 2.00, the developers went to great lengths to address both comments. For instance, MAN.1 *Manage the project* is the result of compressing four different Version 1.00 processes: PRO.1, .2, .3, and .7. Also, SUP.5 in Version 1.00 was split into SUP.4, .5, and .6 in Version 2.00 because *Peer review* was considered to be too prescriptive. Although Version 1.00 was inspired by the various existing process assessment models, Part 2 made this experience more consistent with the ISO/IEC 12207 standard.

Part 2 includes eleven processes more than ISO/IEC 12207. The main reasons for this difference are:

*   The scope of SPICE is larger than the ISO/IEC 12207 standard. Several processes such as *Manage the project* and *Manage subcontractors* have been added because they are important in a software engineering context.

*   Some of the ISO/IEC 12207 processes are based on the premise of a two-party contractual situation. This scope does not require many of the management and organizational processes that have been included in Part 2.

*   There is a higher degree of granularity of the processes included in Part 2, especially in the Engineering process category. Many tasks (or subprocesses) of ISO/IEC 12207 are presented as processes in the emerging standard (for example MAN.3 *Manage risks*).

The following table shows the mapping of ISO/IEC 12207 to the processes of Part 2.

ISO/IEC 12207 Process	ISO/IEC 15504-2
Acquisition	Acquire software products/service
	Establish contract
Supply	Establish contract
	Perform joint audits and reviews
	Package, deliver, and install the software
	Support operation of software
	Plan project life cycle
	Establish project plan
	Manage project resources
	Manage quality
Development	Develop software requirements
	Develop software design
	Integrate and test software
	Integrate and test system
	Package, deliver, and install software
	Perform audits and reviews
	Plan project life cycle
	Establish project plan
Operation	Support operation of software
Maintenance	Maintain system and software
Documentation	Develop documentation
Configuration management	Perform configuration management
Quality assurance	Perform quality assurance
Verification	Level 2 generic practices
	Perform peer reviews
Validation	Perform work product validation
	Integrate and test software
	Integrate and test system
Joint review	Perform audits and reviews
	Manage project resources
Audit	Perform quality assurance
	Perform joint audits and reviews
Problem resolution	Problem resolution
Management	Level 2 generic practices
	Establish project plan
	Manage project resources
Infrastructure	Level 3 generic practices
	Define the process
	Provide development environment
	Provide work facilities
Improvement	Levels 3, 4, 5 generic practices
	Define the process
	Improve the process
Training	Level 2 generic practices on training
Tailoring	Other SPICE document(s)
	Level 3 generic practices

Process categories

The process categories of Part 2, Version 2.00 are still very similar to those of Version 1.00. Minor changes were made to SUP, MAN, and ORG as shown below:

Process Category	Description of process category
Customer-Supplier (CUS)	Consists of processes that directly impact the customer, support development and transition of the software to the customer, and provide for its correct operation and use.
Engineering (ENG)	Consists of processes that directly specify, implement, or maintain a system and software product and its user documentation.
Support (SUP)	Consists of processes that may be employed by any of the other processes (including other supporting processes) at various points in the software life cycle.
Management (MAN)	Consists of processes that contain practices of a generic nature which may be used by anyone who manages any sort of project within a software life cycle.
Organization (ORG)	Consists of processes that establish the business goals of the organization and develop process, product, and resource assets that, when used by the projects in the organization, will help the organization achieve its business goals.

Process purpose statements

Each process in Part 2 is now described in terms of *a purpose statement*. These statements capture the unique functional objectives of the process when instantiated in a particular environment. Satisfying the purpose statement of a process represents the first step in building process capability—capability Level 1.

Part 2 does not define how, or in what order, the elements of the process purpose statements are to be achieved. The process purposes will be achieved in an organization through the implementation of various lower-level activities, tasks, and practices being carried out to produce work products. These performed tasks, activities, practices, and characteristics of the work products produced are the indicators that demonstrate whether or not the specific process purpose is being achieved. Every time a particular process is assessed, the ratings and interpretations should be checked against the purpose statement of process.

Part 2 also includes a set of measurable objectives for each process, derived from its purpose. The measurable objectives are formulated to express the required achievements. They have been refined further into base practices and work products and put into ISO/IEC 15504-5 (Part 5) of the emerging standard. For instance, process ENG.3 *Develop software design* has the following measurable objectives:

- An architectural design will be developed that describes major software components that accommodate the software requirements.
- Internal and external interfaces of each software component will be defined.
- A detailed design will be developed that describes software units that can be built and tested.
- Traceability will be established between software requirements and software designs.

The base practices associated with ENG.3 are:

ENG.3.1 Develop software architectural design. Transform the software requirements into a software architecture that describes the top-level structure and identifies its major components.

ENG.3.2 Design interfaces. Develop and document a design for the external and internal interfaces.

ENG.3.3 Develop detailed design. Transform the top level design into a detailed design for each software component. The software components are refined into lower levels containing software units. The result of this base practice is a documented software design document that describes the position of each software unit in the software architecture.

Note 1: The detailed design includes the specification of interfaces between the software units.

ENG.3.4 Establish Traceability. Establish traceability between the software requirements and the software designs.[5]

Finally, the work products[5] associated with ENG.3 are:

Input		Output	
52)	*Software* requirements	54)	High-level software design
53)	System design / architecture	55)	Low-level software design
		58)	Traceability record/mapping
		101)	Database design

The *process purpose statements* have been included below[5] for the benefit of the reader. They have been formulated so that each model and/or method developer can easily develop a mapping between their model elements and Part 2 to demonstrate their model's conformance to Part 2.

Process	Process Purpose Statement
CUS.1 Acquire software	To obtain the product and/or service that will satisfy the need expressed by the customer. The acquisition process is enacted by the acquirer. The process begins with the identification of a customer need and ends with the acceptance of the product and/or service needed by the customer.
CUS.2 Manage customer needs	To manage the gathering, processing, and tracking of ongoing customer needs and requirements throughout the operational life of the software; to establish a software requirements baseline that serves as the basis for the project's software work products and activities, and to manage changes to this baseline.
CUS.3 Supply software	To package, deliver, and install the software at the customer site and to ensure that quality software is delivered as defined by the requirements.
CUS.4 Operate software	To support the correct and efficient operation of the software for the duration of its intended usage in its installed environment.
CUS.5 Provide customer service	To establish and maintain an acceptable level of service to the customer to support effective use of the software.
ENG.1 Develop system requirements and design	To establish the system requirements (functional and nonfunctional) and architecture, identifying which system requirements should be allocated to which elements of the system and to which releases.
ENG.2 Develop software requirements	To establish the requirements of the software component of the system.
ENG.3 Develop software design	To define a design for the software that accommodates the requirements and can be tested against them.
ENG.4 Implement software design	To produce executable software units and to verify that they properly reflect the software design.
ENG.5 Integrate and test software	To integrate the software units with each other, producing software that will satisfy the software requirements.
ENG.6 Integrate and test system	To integrate the software component with other components, such as manual operations or hardware, producing a complete system that will satisfy the users expectations expressed in the system requirements.
ENG.7 Maintain system and software	To manage modification, migration, and retirement of system components (such as hardware, software, manual operations, and network if any) in response to user requests.
SUP.1 Develop documentation	To develop and maintain documents, recording information produced by a process or activity within a process.
SUP.2 Perform configuration management	To establish and maintain the integrity of all the work products of a process or project.

Process	Process Purpose Statement
SUP.3 Perform quality assurance	To ensure that work products and activities of a process or project comply with all applicable standards, procedures, and requirements.
SUP.4 Perform work product verification	To confirm that each work product of a process or project properly reflects the requirements for its construction.
SUP.5 Perform work product validation	To confirm that the specific requirements for a particular intended use of the work product are fulfilled.
SUP.6 Perform joint reviews	To maintain a common understanding with the customer of the progress against the objectives of the contract and what should be done to help ensure development of a product to satisfy the customer.
SUP.7 Perform audits	To confirm independently that the products and processes employed conform with the specific requirements defined.
SUP.8 Perform problem resolution	To ensure that all discovered problems are analyzed and removed, and that trends are identified.
MAN.1 Manage the project	To define the processes necessary to establish, coordinate, and manage a project and the resources necessary to produce a product.
MAN.2 Manage quality	To manage the quality of the project's products and services and to ensure that they satisfy the customer.
MAN.3 Manage risks	To continuously identify and mitigate the project risks throughout the life cycle of a project.
MAN.4 Manage subcontractors	To select qualified subcontractor(s) and manage their performance.
ORG.1 Engineer the business	To provide the individuals in the organization and projects with a vision and culture that empowers them to function effectively.
ORG.2 Define the process	To build a reusable library of process definitions (including standards, procedures, and models) that will support stable and repeatable performance of the software engineering and management process.
ORG.3 Improve the process	To improve continually the effectiveness and efficiency of the processes used by the organization in line with the business need, as a result of successful implementation of the process.
ORG.4 Provide skilled human resources	To provide the organization and projects with individuals who possess skills and knowledge to perform their roles effectively and to work together as a cohesive group.
ORG.5 Provide software engineering infrastructure	To provide a stable and reliable environment with an integrated set of software development methods and tools for use by the projects in the organization, consistent with and supportive of the defined process.

Capability dimension

In Part 2, the concepts of *common features* and *generic practices* have been simplified greatly. This major change to the architecture was motivated by several observations made in different parts of the world during the SPICE Phase 1 Trials. The application of the generic practices to all the processes that are the focus of an assessment was tedious and cumbersome and needed simplification for the assessment to be manageable. As a result, the 11 *common features* were replaced by a set of nine attributes that characterize the various levels. As for the *generic practices*, they have been moved to Part 5 where they use *process management indicators* as a way for the qualified assessor to provide objective evidence at each level of any process instance.

The measure of capability is now based upon a set of nine process attributes. Process attributes are used to determine whether or not a process has reached a given capability. Each attribute measures a particular aspect of the process capability. The attributes are themselves measured on a four-point ordinal scale and therefore provide a more detailed insight into the specific aspects of process capability required to support process improvement and capability determination.

The definitions of the six capability levels themselves have been restated to take into consideration the changes in the process dimension which now focuses on the *process purpose*, as described in the previous section. The new definitions of the capability levels are:[5]

Level	Level Name	Capability Level Definition
Level 0	*Incomplete*	There is general failure to attain the purpose of the process. There are no easily identifiable work products or outputs of the process.
Level 1	*Performed*	The purpose of the process is generally achieved. The achievement may not be rigorously planned and tracked. Individuals within the organization recognize that an action should be performed, and there is general agreement that this action is performed as and when required. There are identifiable work products for the process, and these testify to the achievement of the purpose.
Level 2	*Managed*	The process delivers work products of acceptable quality within defined time scales. Performance according to specified procedures is planned and tracked. Work products conform to specified standards and requirements.
Level 3	*Established*	The process is performed and managed using a defined process based upon good software engineering principles. Individual implementations of the process use approved, tailored versions of standard, documented processes. The resources necessary to establish the process definition are also in place.

Level	Level Name	Capability Level Definition
Level 4	*Predictable*	The defined process is performed consistently in practice, within defined control limits, to achieve its goals. Detailed measures of performance are collected and analyzed. This practice leads to a quantitative understanding of process capability and an improved ability to predict performance. Performance is objectively managed. The quality of work products is quantitatively known.
Level 5	*Optimizing*	Performance of the process is optimized to meet current and future business needs, and the process achieves repeatability in meeting its defined business goals. Quantitative process effectiveness and efficiency goals (targets) for performance are established, based on the business goals of the organization. Continuous process monitoring against these goals is enabled by obtaining quantitative feedback, and improvement is achieved by analysis of the results. Optimizing a process involves piloting innovative ideas and technologies and changing noneffective processes to meet defined goals or objectives.

Process Attributes

The *capability attributes* are defined as follows.[5]

Level	Process Attributes
Incomplete	*None.* The process is not implemented or fails to achieve its purpose.
Performed	*PA 1.1 Process performance attribute.* The extent to which the execution of the process uses a set of practices that are initiated and followed using identifiable input work products to produce identifiable output work products that are adequate to satisfy the purpose of the process.
Managed	*PA 2.1 Performance management attribute.* The extent to which the execution of the process is managed to produce work products within stated time and resource requirements.
	PA 2.2. Work product management attribute. The extent to which the execution of the process is managed to produce work products that are documented and controlled and that meet their functional and nonfunctional requirements, in line with the work product quality goals of the process.
Established	*PA 3.1 Process definition attribute.* The extent to which the execution of the process uses a process definition based upon a standard process that enables the process to contribute to the defined business goals of the organization.
	PA 3.2 Process resource attribute. The extent to which the execution of the process uses suitable skilled human resources and process infrastructure effectively to contribute to the defined business goals of the organization.

Level	Process Attributes
Predictable	*PA 4.1 Process measurement attribute.* The extent to which the execution of the process is supported by goals and measures that are used to ensure that implementation of the process contributes to the achievement of the goals.
	PA 4.2 Process control attribute. The extent to which the execution of the process is controlled through the collection and analysis of measures to control and correct, where necessary, the performance of the process to reliably achieve the defined process goals.
Optimizing	*PA 5.1 Process change attribute.* The extent to which changes to the definition, management, and performance of the process are controlled better to achieve the business goals of the organization.
	PA 5.2 Continuous improvement attribute. The extent to which changes to the process are identified and implemented to ensure continuous improvement in the fulfillment of the defined business goals of the organization.

Conclusions

Part 2 of the document set has gone through a number of major refinements that the team believes make it a much more usable document for the purpose of an assessment. On the other hand, it has become a poorer document in and of itself since it does not include any practices that could be used to perform an assessment.

The Phase 2 Trials, still in progress at the time of writing this book, should help the teams determine whether these changes have succeeded in making the emerging standard useful to the industry. Of the utmost interest will be the *conformance study* of the trials that will try to establish whether or not the concept of a *conformant model* and, on a larger scale, of a *conformant assessment*, works and yields comparable results. If the SPICE Phase 2 Trials reveal success in this regard, the SPICE team will have met one of the key requirements of this emerging International Standard. Time—and user feedback—will tell.

References

1. SPICE Project, *Baseline Practices Guide Product Description*. Version 0.01, May 1993.

2. SPICE Project, *Baseline Practices Guide Product Description*. Version 1.00, June 1994.

3. SPICE Project, *Baseline Practices Guide*. Version 0.01, Nov. 1993.

4. SPICE Project, *Baseline Practices Guide*. Version 1.01, June 1995.

5. ISO/IEC JTC1/SC7/WG10, *Software Process Assessment—Part 2: A Reference model for processes and process capability*. Version 2.0, Oct. 1996.

6. Coallier, F., N. Gammage, and A.W. Graydon, *Trillium—Software Process Self-assessment Capability Assessment*. Bell Canada, Bell Northern Research, Northern Telecom, PI Q008, Issue 4.0, Mar. 1993.

7. Compita Ltd, *Software Technology Diagnostic Practitioner's Guideline*. Version 2.5, 1993.

8. Esprit Project number 5441, Bootstrap, SPU *Assessment Report, Assessment Questionnaire*. Mar. 1991. BOOT/II-ETNO/RL-AR/3.91/Questionnaire/IE. (not available as a public domain document)

9. British Telecom, *Health check / SAM* in-house assessment methodology (not available as a public domain document)

10. Paulk, M.C. et al., *Key Practices of the Capability Maturity Model, Version 1.1*, Technical Report CMU/SI-93-TR-25, Software Engineering Institute, Pittsburgh Pennsylvania, Feb. 1993.

11. Crosby, Philip B., *Quality Is Free*. McGraw-Hill, New York, N.Y., 1979.

12. WG10/N016R, *Product Specification for a Software Process Assessment Standard*, Version 1.00, June 1993.

13. WG10/N017R, *Requirements Specification for a Software Process Assessment Standard*, Version 1.00, June 1993.

14. Dorling A. and P. Simms, *Study Report: The Need and Requirements for a Software Process Assessment Standard*. ISO/IEC JTC1/SC7/WG7/WG7/SG1 N944R Issue 2.0, 11 June 1992, Admiral plc, Cranfield IT Institute and UK Ministry of Defense.

15. ISO/IEC 12207, *Information Technology—Software Life Cycle Processes*, 1995.

16. ISO 9001:1994, *Quality Systems for Design, Development, Production, Installation and Servicing*.

5

Process Assessment Using SPICE: The Assessment Activities

Antonio Coletta
Tecnopolis, Italy

A successful process assessment must ensure that the resulting outputs are objective, impartial, consistent, repeatable, and representative of the processes assessed. To achieve these objectives, SPICE has defined requirements and guidelines for the activities to be performed during an assessment in Parts 3 and 4 of the emerging international Software Process Assessment (SPA) standard.

Part 3 sets out the basic requirements for performing an assessment, defines the circumstances under which assessment results are comparable, and indicates how to provide evidence of conformance with the emerging standard. Part 4 provides organizations wishing to perform an assessment with guidance for interpreting these requirements through the selection and use of appropriate models, methods, and tools.

The requirements and related guidance are aimed primarily at qualified assessors who have the responsibility for performing the assessment activities in a conformant manner. Developers of assessment models, methods, and tools can also use the requirements and guidance as an aid in understanding how to correctly implement conformant products.

The Product Specification[1]

Initial definition of the emerging standard

In the initial specification of the emerging standard, the intent was to define a general-purpose approach for conducting an assessment, applicable for both process improvement and capability determination. It intended to set out the basis for collecting information, analyzing it, rating it, and presenting the results through process capability profiles.

It soon became clear that the emerging standard could not define a detailed process assessment method with the ambition of covering all contexts. It appeared, however, to be feasible and appropriate to define a framework containing the minimum set of requirements for conducting an SPA that would ensure that the outputs of the assessment would be consistent, repeatable, and representative of the process instances being assessed.

Requirements of the emerging standard

The first significant requirement of the emerging standard was to "recognize different application domains, business needs, and sizes of organization." This meant that the process assessment approach, as defined by the SPICE document set, needs to be flexible enough to be used in different types of contexts but, at the same time, be sensitive to and take into account the specific characteristics of the context while assessing, rating, and profiling the processes' capabilities.

Another, closely-related requirement concerned the applicability of the SPICE document set "at the project and organizational level with connectivity between the two." This requirement emphasized an important aspect of process assessment: some processes are performed at the organizational level (independent of projects), while others are performed within projects. Therefore, the scope of an assessment can vary and can include process instances observed in both specific projects and processes deployed at the organizational level. The output from an assessment must reflect and document the exact scope covered.

Furthermore, these two types of processes are connected by the fact that the organizational processes, when implemented, enhance the capability of all the other processes. This connectivity must be recognized and demonstrated in the results of the assessment. Examples include processes such as "defining and improving the process" or "providing skilled human resources" that provide an effective organizational environment for the execution of all the processes within an organization.

A further requirement relating to the scope of an assessment was to "ensure that the project/work areas selected for assessment are sufficiently representative for the results of the assessment not to be unduly dependent on their selection." Although the SPICE document set cannot provide a complete set of criteria to ensure that this happens, it does require that "the set of process instances selected for assessment be sufficient to meet the assessment purpose and scope" and that "the rationale and justification for the selection of the instances assessed be recorded."

A requirement regarding the comparability of the results was that "the standard must define the circumstances in which comparison between process profiles are valid." Since the SPICE document set must be applicable in different contexts, it is necessary to clearly define when assessment results are comparable, thus avoiding a comparison of different elements. To implement this requirement, the results of an assessment must be recorded, together with the description of the context, and it must be explicitly clear that the comparison is meaningful only between contexts with comparable characteristics.

A specific requirement was placed on the composition of the assessment team, stating that "the standard must give guidance on the selection of assessors and make-up of the assessment team." Part 6 of the emerging standard covers the issue of assessor qualification, while Part 3 requires that a SPICE assessment be conducted by a team that must include at least one qualified assessor responsible for ensuring conformance to the emerging standard.

Further requirements related to the organizational unit (OU) being assessed. During an assessment, the "assessment concepts need to be explained to those being assessed" and they must "have opportunities to clarify their understanding." This meant that the assessment activities should include a preparation phase in which everyone—the assessment team and personnel in charge of the processes being assessed—is briefed on the assessment concepts affecting them and has an opportunity to clarify any misconceptions they may have.

An additional requirement addressed explicitly in Part 4 of the emerging standard was that "an agreement must be reached over ownership and confidentiality of assessment results prior to assessment." Its meaning was straightforward: the SPICE document set specifically requires that such agreement be reached to avoid the improper use of assessment results. On the other hand, the assessment activities must include "appropriate steps to ensure non-concealment" of information and data that could affect the result. The implication is that the ratings must be based on sound evidence (indicators) and that the information gathered must be verified and validated.

Finally, an important requirement concerned the execution of the assessment activities. They must "be governed by executable procedures" and not be left to improvised approaches. The methods claiming conformance to the emerging standard must be well documented and provide written procedures to their users.

First version

Inputs used for the development of the emerging standard

The initial study group report[2] clearly indicated that several assessment methods already existed on the market, yet the need was felt for a common approach that could build upon their best features. Furthermore, the study reported the intent of existing assessment-method providers to support the development of the new emerging international standard, bringing with them the knowledge, experience, and maturity gained by dedicated resources in using these methods.

Many of the method suppliers provided important input to the project and, in many cases, detailed documentation of their method was made available to the SPICE Project. This contribution has been very valuable for the success of the project.

The emerging standard was developed by also maintaining an alignment with existing standards, including the ISO 9000 series on Quality Management Systems and the ISO 10011 standard on Quality Systems Auditing. Since it is not for certification, the SPICE document set does not encompass an audit approach, encouraging instead a self-assessment approach. However, some parts of the ISO 10011 standard (especially *ISO 10011-1 Auditing* and *ISO 10011-3 Management of Audit Programs*) provided valuable input to the definition of the requirements being placed upon the assessment activities.

Context

The basic issue at hand in developing the first version of process assessment guidance was to determine to what extent the emerging standard should provide details on the assessment activities. The more details that were added to the description of the assessment activities, the more the description started to resemble a method, thereby putting unnecessary constraints on users. On the other hand, while keeping the document to a few basic requirements permitted greater freedom of implementation, it ran the risk of becoming trivialized and would not capture the richness and best features of existing methods. Striking the right balance became a real challenge. Some help in solving this problem was identified by the ability to define parts of an emerging standard that are *normative* (the requirements) and *informative* (generally, guidance in interpreting the requirements of the normative parts). Using this mechanism, it became possible to provide a more significant amount of detail, but to provide it as guidance.

In deciding how to solve the problem of comparing the results of assessments, it was clear from the beginning that results could be compared only between similar entities, such as through the classification of assessment contexts.

The issue was whether or not it was feasible and appropriate to define a classification schema for all the different contexts in which an assessment could take place. This idea was considered outside the scope of the emerging standard and was abandoned in favor of a definition of the minimum information that needed to be recorded as the *context description*, together with the assessment results. Those who needed to compare assessment results would then need to be careful to compare only results from entities having similar contexts.

The guidance document that was developed contained two major chapters, providing:

- an overview of process assessment
- guidance on how to conduct a team-based assessment.

Overview of process assessment

The overview of process assessment contained a description of the different types of approaches, including self-assessment, independent, team-based, and continuous assessments. (This part has been refined in Version 2.00 of the emerging standard.) The overview also contained a section (and remained unchanged in Version 2.00) about the factors considered essential for conducting successful process assessments. Before examining these factors, it is important to define the terms used therein:

- **the assessment *sponsor:*** "the individual, internal or external to the organization being assessed, who requires the assessment to be performed, and provides financial or other resources to carry it out"

- **the assessment *owner*:** "the management role that takes ownership of the assessment and the assessment output, and has the authority to make assessment happen"

- ***organizational unit*:** "that part of the organization that is the subject of an assessment. An organizational unit deploys one or more processes that have a coherent process context and operates within a coherent set of business goals." The OU typically is part of a larger organization (for example, a specific project or a set of related projects) or may be the entire organization.

The following sections detail the assessment success factors, as identified by the SPICE Project.

Commitment

Both the sponsor and owner should commit themselves to the objectives they have established for the assessment so as to provide the authority to undertake the assessment within the organization. This commitment requires that the necessary resources, time, and personnel are made available to undertake the assessment. The commitment of the assessment team is fundamentally important to ensuring that the objectives are met.

Motivation

The attitude of the organization's management, and the method by which the information is collected, has a significant influence on the outcome of an assessment. The organization's management, therefore, needs to motivate participants to be open and constructive. The assessment should be focused on the process, not on the OU members implementing the process. The intent is to make the outcome more effective in an effort to support the defined business goals, not to allocate blame to individuals.

Providing feedback and maintaining an atmosphere that encourages open discussion about the preliminary findings uncovered during the assessment helps to ensure that the assessment output is meaningful to the OU. The organization needs to recognize that the participants are a principal source of knowledge and experience about the process and that they are in a good position to identify potential weaknesses.

Confidentiality

Respect for the confidentiality of sources of information and documentation gathered during the assessment is essential to secure that information. If discussion techniques are used to gather information, consideration should be given to ensuring that participants do not feel threatened or have concerns about the confidentiality of their comments. Some of the information provided might be proprietary to the organization. Therefore, it is important that adequate controls be put into place to handle, and protect, such information.

Relevance

The OU members should believe that the assessment will result in benefits that are relevant to their needs.

Credibility

The sponsor, management, and staff of the OU must believe that the assessment will deliver a result that is objective and representative of the assessment scope. It is important that all parties are confident that the team selected to conduct the assessment has adequate experience in performing assessments, an adequate understanding of the OU and its business, and sufficient impartiality.

The stages of a team-based assessment

The other major chapter in the guide was dedicated to illustrating the eight stages of a team-based assessment. Although recognizing that process assessment could be performed using different approaches (continuous, tool-based, and so on), the guide made it clear that the stages were designed for conducting a discrete, team-based assessment. Alternative approaches for conducting an assessment were described. For example an assessment could be performed by an automated tool, gathering and reporting data continuously, rather than in a one-time, discrete manner. The eight stages are described briefly here, since the second version of the SPICE document set dropped this approach, in favor of guidance that would be applicable to all types of assessment approaches. The eight stages are shown in Figure 5.1.

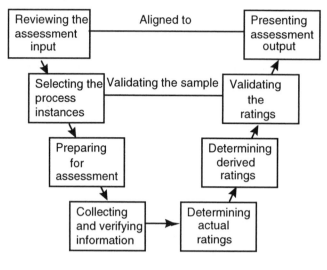

ASSESSMENT STAGES

Figure 5.1. The assessment stages.

1. **Reviewing the assessment input**

   At this stage, the qualified assessor reviews the assessment input to ensure consistency and feasibility with respect to the assessment purpose. The assessment input must include a definition of the purpose and scope of the assessment as well as any constraints. The input also includes the identification of roles and responsibilities within the assessment team, the definition of extended processes, and any additional information that needs to be gathered.

2. **Selecting the process instances**

   If not already identified in the input as part of the assessment scope, the process instances to be assessed and the performing OU both need to be identified, based on the assessment purpose. The sample size should take into account the expected depth and coverage required. Before selecting the process instances, a mapping must be performed between the OU's processes to be assessed and the corresponding processes as defined in the process model being used for the assessment (in Version 1.00 the only model allowed was the one defined by the SPICE document set in Part 2). This step is important because a process, as defined in the model, may not necessarily have a one-to-one mapping to the processes of the organization being assessed.

3. **Preparing for a team-based assessment**

   The purpose of this stage is to ensure the completion of all the preparatory work necessary for performing the assessment effectively. First, the assessment team must be selected and prepared so as to ensure a common understanding of the tasks to be performed in conformance with the requirements in the emerging standard. Roles and responsibilities must be defined for each member of the team. The assessment must be thoroughly planned, in detail, identifying and taking into account any risk factors. Specific assessment techniques (interviews, group discussions) and instruments (checklists, automated tools, and so on.) are identified at this stage. The preparation activities also involve the OU being assessed. A briefing to the OU must be provided as to how the assessment is going to be conducted, who the participants from the OU are, and what the assignment of responsibilities is. All participants should be specifically informed about the confidentiality agreement and how to meet it. Finally this stage includes an activity for gathering any documentation that may be useful for the assessment of the processes.

4. **Collecting and verifying information**

   Assessment techniques and instruments help the assessment team collect all the information necessary to determine whether a process is performed and how its capability is rated. The information may need to be verified by supporting evidence. Although the SPICE document set encourages a self-assessment approach, the more evidence made available for the rating, the more reliable the judgment of the qualified assessors will be.

5. **Determining the actual ratings for process instances**

   During this stage, the selected process instances are assessed individually. For each process instance, a profile is generated. (See Chapter 6 on the rating framework for more details on this activity.)

6. **Determining derived ratings**

   The actual ratings for each process instance determined in the previous stage are aggregated to generate derived ratings for each process type. (See Chapter 6 on the rating framework for more details on meaningful aggregations.)

7. **Validating the ratings**

   The ratings generated in the previous stage are validated to ensure that they are an accurate representation of the assessed process. The validation should ensure that the instances selected and the sample size are sufficient to give reliable results. Different techniques, such as feedback sessions and consistency checks, are suggested for performing the validation.

8. **Presenting the assessment output**
   The final stage includes the preparation and recording of the assessment output, which includes the profiles generated and the assessment record. The assessment record contains the definition of the context for comparability purpose. The output can then be used for process improvement or capability determination as defined in other parts of the emerging standard. The results are documented generally in a report or presentation to be given to the interested parties, the OUs assessed, the owner, and the sponsor. No specific format is required for the presentation of the output.

Evolution to Version 2.00

Changes made to Version 1.00

The parts of the emerging standard regarding the assessment activities were revised to make them compatible with the new model's architecture and to respond to a need for greater harmonization with existing methods. The new version should provide a smoother migration path to the new emerging standard for the current methods in use.

The more significant changes in this part of the emerging standard can be summarized as follows:

- The rating mechanism, previously contained in Part 3, has been moved to Part 2 since it is closely connected to the process capability model.

- Part 3 has been renamed *Performing an assessment*, thus reflecting the emphasis on requirements for performing the assessment activities, and no longer on the rating mechanism.

- The emerging standard now explicitly recognizes the existence of different models, methods, and instruments that can use different approaches to process assessment and yet still be compatible with the requirements of the emerging standard. The compatibility requirements are specified in Part 2, together with the reference model for processes and process capability. The requirement in Part 3 is to use compatible models, methods, and instruments. Guidance is given on how to select the compatible model, method, and instrument most appropriate for the purpose and scope of the assessment.

- The detailed description of the eight stages suggested for a team-based assessment has been dropped. The requirements are now stated in such a way as to be applicable to all different approaches. The guidance given in Part 4 for performing an assessment may be most easily understood in the context of a discrete, team-based assessment, however, it states principles that are the same for a continuous, tool-based assessment.

Overview of Version 2.00

In Version 2.00 of the emerging standard, the requirements for performing an assessment are defined in Part 3. The requirements are grouped into five sections:

1. requirements for defining the assessment input
2. requirements for the assessment responsibilities
3. requirements for the assessment process
4. requirements for recording the assessment output
5. a basis for comparing assessment results.

Part 4 of the emerging standard contains guidance for the interpretation of the requirements stated in Part 3. It is structured into four major sections:

1. overview of process assessment
2. selection and use of a compatible model
3. selection and use of a method
4. selection and use of instruments and tools.

Guidance on selecting and using compatible models and instruments are discussed in the last section of this chapter. The sections that follow describe the assessment activities that should be provided for in a compatible method so as to meet the requirements of the emerging standard.

The assessment activities in a compatible method

The method to be used may be selected by either the sponsor or the qualified assessor. In any case, the method should be suitable for the context and purpose of the assessment and should include the following activities:

Defining the assessment input

Before initiating an assessment, the assessment input must be defined and approved by the sponsor. The input must include, at a minimum, the following information:

1. **the identity of the assessment sponsor and the sponsor's relationship to the OU being assessed**

   The sponsor may be internal to the organization, as is often the case when an assessment is performed for process improvement, or may be external to the organization when a customer wishes to assess the capability of a supplier's processes.

2. **the assessment purpose**

   The purpose may be process improvement or capability determination. Any other specific information may help in effectively meeting the purpose.

3. **the assessment scope**, including:

   a. *the processes to be investigated* within the OU

      The number of processes to be assessed can range from a single process to the entire set of processes

   b. *the highest capability level* to be investigated

      It may not be necessary or useful to investigate the attributes for all five capability levels, especially in an organization where it is clear from the start of the assessment that it lacks the organizational processes necessary for supporting the higher level attributes.

   c. *the organizational unit* that deploys these processes

      Based on the processes chosen, the OU involved may be only part of the entire organization (for example, one or more projects or project areas).

d. *the process context* that, as a minimum, includes:
  - the size of the OU
  - the demographics of the OU
  - the application domain of the products or services of the OU
  - the size, criticality, and complexity of the products or services
  - the quality characteristics of the products or services (for example, see ISO/IEC 9126).

This type of information is necessary to determine the similarities between two entities being assessed and therefore the comparability of the results. Compatible methods should provide guidance on classifying the process context based on this type of data.

4. **the assessment constraints,** which may include:
  a. *availability of key resources*
    It is important to carefully plan the process assessment to secure the availability of key resources, which are often sources of important information. The assessment activity is as important as the normal business activity, however, if not planned correctly, it may be seen as an unnecessary disruption.
  b. the *maximum amount of time* to be used for the assessment
  c. *specific process instances* to be included or excluded from the assessment
    The exclusion of specific process instances may be motivated by the fact that they may be considered *a priori*, not representative of typical process performance. On the other hand, specific instances may be included to gain insight into specific projects or areas of the organization.
  d. *the minimum, maximum, or specific sample size or coverage* that is desired for the assessment
    The sample size is important for the representativeness of the assessment output. If not specified by the sponsor, the sample size chosen should be documented, together with its rationale. Of course, larger sample sizes and more recent information generate more representative results.
  e. *the ownership of the assessment outputs* and any restrictions on their use

Ownership of results and control on their distribution are important aspects of an agreement that should be reached between the parties.

f. *controls on information resulting from a confidentiality agreement*

Confidentiality needs to be guaranteed in order to gather information that is often proprietary.

5. **the identity of the qualified assessor** responsible for the assessment
6. **the identity of any other persons** with specific responsibilities for the assessment
7. **any additional information to be collected** during the assessment to support process improvement or process capability determination.

Any modification to the assessment input that may arise during the execution of the assessment must be negotiated and approved by the sponsor. The entire set of information contained in the assessment input becomes an integral part of the assessment result.

Assigning responsibilities

The most important of the roles and responsibilities in conducting an assessment is assigned to the qualified assessor, who must ensure that the requirements for a conformant assessment have been met. Whatever approach is used, even in an automated, continuous approach, there must always be a qualified assessor overseeing the assessment activities. Guidance on assessor qualification is given in Part 7 of the emerging standard (see chapter 10). The sponsor has the responsibility to verify, on the basis of documentary evidence, the competence and skill of the qualified assessor. The emerging standard does not prescribe a certification schema for qualified assessors, but neither does it exclude the possibility that some sort of register of qualified assessors can be maintained at a national or international level, based on the qualification guidance given in the emerging standard.

In a team-based assessment, in addition to the qualified assessor, the team may include other people in the OU, depending on its size. Precise roles and responsibilities must be assigned and each team member should have access to appropriate guidance on how to conduct the assessment (the emerging standard itself plus any documented procedures supplied by the method provider). All assessors should also have the necessary competence to use the instruments and tools chosen to support the assessment.

The assessment process

After having verified and approved the input, the assessment activities can begin according to agreed-upon plans. The activities should be conducted according to a documented process, capable of meeting the assessment purpose. The documented process should also include supporting activities such as document control, project management, and so on.

The assessment activities must make use of a model that provides the basic definitions of processes and process attributes as a reference point against which the assessed processes can be judged. The model chosen for the assessment can be either the assessment model defined by the SPICE document set in Part 5 or it can be any other compatible model for software engineering practices, as long as it meets the requirements in Part 2. Part 5 of the SPICE document set is an instance of a compatible model.

Once the model has been identified for use, the processes to be assessed need to be mapped to the processes as they are performed in the organization. As already mentioned, the organization can identify and structure the processes differently from the assessment model. *It is important to map the organization's processes to the ones in the model.* The organization's processes must be directly or indirectly (through the compatible model) traceable to the process descriptions in the reference model.

Following the mapping of the processes, the assessment can begin by examining one or more instance of each process. The instances to be examined may already have been identified in the input or may have to be chosen during the assessment. The instances and the sample size must be sufficient to meet the purpose and scope of the assessment. The rationale and justification for the selection of the process instances must be recorded.

The instances are examined one by one and, for each instance, a rating is assigned. The primitive ratings using the compatible model, if not at the attribute level, must be expressed as ratings for each process attribute in each capability level to be examined.

Ratings are heavily dependent upon the qualified assessor's judgment. The skill and competence of the assessor are important factors, but the basis for repeatability across assessments must be provided by more objective mechanisms. The model chosen for the assessment must provide a set of indicators to be used for evaluating the effective performance and management of the process. Indicators may consist of practices being used, job functions, work products, and so on. All the objective evidence collected using the indicators, and supporting the qualified assessors' judgment, must be recorded, together with the assigned ratings. Automated assessment instruments may be useful in prompting and recording this data. The evidence gathered provides the basis for the verification and validation of the ratings.

The set of attribute ratings for each process instance assessed makes up the process instance profile. The ratings can be used to derive the capability level for each process instance and can be aggregated across instances of the same process to show the frequency distribution of each process attribute rating (see Chapter 6, rating framework for more details). Aggregated data may also be recorded together with the profiles.

Recording and presenting the assessment output

The final result of an assessment must be recorded in an assessment record that must include, at a minimum, the following data:

- the date of the assessment
- the assessment input
- the identification and justification of the selected process instances
- the assessment approach used, including the unique identification of the assessment model, method, and any supporting instruments or tools, together with evidence to support claims of compliance
- the names of the team members conducting the assessment, including the qualified assessor responsible for the assessment and the supporting assessors
- the set of process profiles resulting from the assessment—one profile for each process instance assessed
- the location of the records of objective evidence supporting the process attribute ratings in the process profiles
- any additional information collected during the assessment and identified in the assessment input to support process improvement or process capability determination or a reference to the location of the records of the additional information.

The results are usually summarized in a report and presented to the sponsor, owner, and OU assessed. The presentation may include other findings and proposed action plans, depending on the purpose of the assessment. The findings and results are analyzed and form the basis for developing improvement actions or determining the capability for contractual requirements. The guidance on how to perform process improvement and capability determination is contained in Parts 7 and 8 of the emerging standard.

Selecting compatible models, methods, and instruments

As already mentioned earlier in this chapter, the purpose of the emerging standard is to provide the basic requirements necessary for a worldwide harmonization of the SPA activities, together with guidance for users and suppliers of assessment products and services on how to meet the requirements.

It is expected that organizations operating in the open market will make available a variety of models, methods, and instruments that are conformant to the emerging standard, yet are characterized by specific features.

The model, the method, and the instruments to be used in an assessment may be selected by the qualified assessor or may be stipulated by the sponsor of the assessment (in which case, this selection should be documented as a constraint). In either case, there are criteria that may help ensure that the selection is appropriate for the use envisaged.

The first obvious selection criteria, the compatibility with the requirements of the emerging standard, maximizes the reliability of different approaches and helps achieve a greater degree of uniformity and comparability of the results.

Selection of a compatible assessment model

The guidance provided by the SPICE document set on the selection of compatible models, methods, and instruments is summarized in the following paragraphs.

Compatible purpose

There are many different types of modeling techniques available for describing, specifying, and enacting processes, however, using models that have not been specifically developed for the purpose of process assessment (for instance ISO/IEC 12207 used by itself) will not yield reliable results. These models will most likely lack the basic concepts necessary for a mapping to the SPICE reference model. The selected model should, therefore, have been developed for use in process assessments.

Compatible scope

A further aspect to consider regarding compatibility is the scope coverage. The reference model defines 29 processes in five different process categories. Any compatible model must contain, in its process dimension, at least a part of this scope. The model may include only a subset of the reference model. It may be a superset of the reference model, covering all the defined processes, together with additional process descriptions outside the emerging standard scope. A compatible model may also include processes outside the reference model, providing it encompasses at least one process from it. Finally, the scope of the model may be directly equivalent to the reference model.

In selecting a model, the qualified assessors should ensure that the scope of the model covers the intended area of interest for the assessment. It would not be appropriate, for example, to select a model that was restricted to the Engineering processes if the assessment was intended to investigate all aspects of requirements elicitation since it would involve evaluation of some of the Customer-Supplier processes.

For the capability dimension, a model must cover a complete set of capabilities for all the processes in its scope. The set of capabilities must encompass the whole of the capability level scale in the reference model or a subset starting at Level 1. It is permissible, therefore, for a model to claim coverage of Levels 1 to 3 only, but not of only Levels 3 to 5.

Models covering only the lower levels may be suitable for organizations having processes with low capabilities, although this may not be known before performing the assessment. More mature organizations should select models covering the full range of capability levels defined in the emerging standard.

Indicators

A compatible model must be equipped with sets of indicators that can be used to gather data about processes and process attributes during an assessment.

To effectively determine the performance and capability of a process, the model must contain descriptions of the practices to be observed and indicators of the performance of these practices, so that the judgments about the achievement of the various process attributes may be made reliably and consistently. The indicators must be documented and must allow judgments to be based soundly on objective evidence.

There is a clear expectation that the indicators will fall into two categories: (1) factors that indicate the performance of the process and (2) factors that indicate its capability. In selecting a model, clear attention should be paid to the use of indicators in the model, the comprehensiveness of the indicator set, and the applicability of the indicator set for the two defined purposes.

Mapping to the reference model

The model's fundamental elements should be mapped in a complete, clear, and unambiguous way to the process and capability dimension of the reference model. In particular, it should be possible to demonstrate that the model addresses the purposes of the processes as defined in the process dimension of the reference model and that it has mechanisms to demonstrate the achievement of the process attributes in the various capability levels.

The mapping may be simple, as is the case with the model defined in Part 5 of the emerging standard, or it may be quite complex, where the structure of the model is significantly different from the reference model. It is essential to have access to the details of this mapping.

A qualified assessor should attempt to confirm that the mapping is accurate by sampling some of the lowest-level components in the model and by confirming that the mapping declaration permits the components to be located in the reference model, either as elements of a process or as contributors to a process attribute. Mappings that result in elements being identified as components of more than one process attribute may indicate problems with the model structure, which could result in an ambiguous translation of results.

Translation of the results

The output from a process assessment is a set of process profiles; one profile for each instance of every process in the assessment scope. A process profile is a set of nine ratings, one for each process attribute. Assessment results from any compatible model must be able to be converted into this form so that a common basis for comparison exists.

The mechanism for translation may be manual or computer based. It may require the inclusion of additional information collected during the assessment, and may involve further judgment on the part of the qualified assessor. The rules for translating the results, however, should be clear and unambiguous and should be provided by the model developer.

Other criteria for selecting a model

Given that the model to be selected is compatible with the reference model, the other major consideration in performing the selection will be the suitability of the model for the context of the assessment. The principal factors affecting the selection of a model are:

- the planned scope of the assessment
- the industry sector of the organization being assessed
- the application domain of the software components that are the focus of the assessment
- specific requirements for strong comparability with other assessments or organizations.

Where models exist that have been specifically developed for use in particular industry sectors (for example, telecommunications, defense, and aerospace) or for particular application domains (such as high security systems, safety critical systems, and real-time embedded software), these models should be preferred.

Part 5 of the emerging standard provides a generic, compatible model designed to be applicable across all industry sectors and application domains, however it may require tailoring for specific contexts.

Selection of a compatible assessment method

A compatible assessment method should contain descriptions of the activities to be performed, the responsibilities of key individuals, and the documentary evidence that must be recorded. It may also define specific compatible models and tools that are required to be used with the method.

Defining the assessment input

The method should describe how all the information required for the assessment input is collated, reviewed, approved, and documented. It may be appropriate for the method to require tool support to collect and store this information. The assessment input, together with other information and analyses, will form the assessment output. The method should provide support for recording or transferring the assessment input to a suitable form to become part of the assessment output.

The method should provide guidance on:

- defining ownership and distribution of the assessment output
- establishing suitable confidentiality statements and how these are to be fulfilled
- classifying the process context.

The method should also define mechanisms to:

- enable the assessment to be performed effectively within the constraints defined, or indicate how the constraints and/or scope can be renegotiated, if this is not possible
- support the collection of any other information defined by the assessment sponsor.

Responsibilities

The method should define the roles and responsibilities within the assessment activities and what competencies are required for each role. It should also provide mechanisms to ensure that the qualified assessor has the competencies necessary to undertake the assessment as well as mechanisms to validate those competencies.

The method should provide mechanisms to ensure that the assessment is conformant with the requirements of the emerging standard and should define how this conformance is achieved and validated.

Assessment process

The method should define documented processes for undertaking all the activities required to perform the assessment, including supporting activities, such as document control, quality assurance, and project management. This documentation might be in the form of guidance material, procedures, standards, and so on.

The method should define how qualified assessors are to attain the required competencies to use the method correctly, for example through training courses or experience levels.

The method should identify a compatible model or models for use with the method, or provide guidance on selection and use of an alternative compatible model. Guidance should also be provided for the mapping of the model's elements to the processes enacted by the assessed OU, as well as a translation of the ratings and results when the latter differ from the reference model.

To ensure that the set of process instances selected is appropriate to the assessment purpose, the method should provide guidance on sampling and should supply a mechanism to retain the sampling information and rationale.

The method should define mechanisms to validate the ratings assigned and to record them in such a way so as to assure traceability to the process instances assessed and the indicators used. It should also provide mechanisms to represent aggregated ratings and process profiles in forms that allow straightforward interpretation of their meaning and value.

Recording the output

Depending upon the circumstances and instruments used to support the assessment, the method should define how the output is recorded (that is, paper based or electronic) and how and by whom it is retained (for example, the sponsor, the assessor, the assessed organization, or another person or body depending upon the confidentiality agreement reached).

Other criteria for selecting an assessment method

The method should provide support in estimating the resources needed to perform an assessment and ensuring that each defined role can attain the required competencies, for example through training and experience requirements.

The other major consideration in selecting a method will be its suitability for the contexts and scope of the assessment. The principal factors affecting the selection of a method are:

- the planned purpose and scope of the assessment
- the assessment approach selected
- the process context of the selected processes.

Where methods exist that have been specifically developed for specific process contexts, particular assessment approaches, and for specific processes, these methods should be preferred.

Selecting instruments and tools

In general, the method selected for the assessment will indicate the level of support needed and may identify particular instruments to be used. Alternatively, the user may have the choice of selecting tools independent of the method. The following is a list of criteria for selecting appropriate and suitable instruments. A comprehensive instrument or set of instruments and tools selected should:

- be appropriate for the scope and purpose of assessment
- provide assistance in collecting and storing information, including assembling the assessment input and recording it in a suitable form for transfer to the assessment output
- make available the compatible assessment model through the defined set of indicators, at least for the scope of the assessment
- have the ability to capture the data required to be used in the production of ratings, as defined in the rating mechanism of the reference model
- have the ability to capture and maintain supporting information as defined in the assessment input
- support the rating process, according to the defined rating schema
- support the representation of process profiles in forms that allow straightforward interpretation of their meaning and value and the representation of aggregated ratings
- have the ability to load, store, and compare process profiles
- provide appropriate segregation of different classes of information and data to enable the information and/or data to be used or distributed in different ways
- provide the ability to store, retain, and recall information and results for later use with appropriate levels of security.

The selection of the types of instruments and tools will be influenced by:

- the intended mode of use, method of assessment, and the compatible model chosen
- the purpose of the assessment
- facilities for customization and the impact on the tool's performance
- the set of features, functions, and the quality characteristics possessed by the instrument or tool
- supplier-identified limitations or usage requirements
- the availability of support for the instrument or tool (training, hotline, documentation and so on)

- the supplier's past history or other users' experiences in using the instrument or tool

- the evaluation of the potential of the instrument or tool to aid meeting the requirements within this Technical Report.

References

1. ISO/IEC JTC1/SC7/WG10, *Product Specification for a Software Process Assessment Standard*, Version 1.00, 22 June 1993.

2. ISO/IEC JTC1/SC7, *The Need and Requirements for a Software Process Assessment Standard*, Study Report, Issue 2.0, N944R, 11 June 1992.

Process Assessment Using SPICE: The Rating Framework

Mac Craigmyle
Compita Ltd., Scotland

The rating framework defined for the emerging standard represents the foundation for achieving repeatability and reliability of assessment results. As such it is critical to the usability of the resulting standard. This chapter describes the evolution of the rating framework up to its current incarnation.

The rating framework is designed to fulfill two purposes:

1. to produce a set of process measures as *process profiles* that will support the identification of improvement opportunities in processes aligned to the business goals of the organization
2. to determine the process capability of a supplier's processes to identify its suitability in fulfilling a specified requirement.

Initial measurement model

The SPICE requirements specification sets out all the requirements the product set had to fulfill. The subset of requirements for the rating framework were identified in the *Process Assessment Guide* (PAG) Product Description as B2, C3, E1.1, N, Q1.1, Q2, R, and R1.4. (see Chapter 3).

These requirements were analyzed and the following components were required for the rating framework (especially to satisfy requirements Q1.1 and Q2):

1. a measure of conformance to the practices defined in the *Baseline Practices Guide* (BPG)

2. a measure of effectiveness of the processes defined in the BPG.

Process conformance

To assess process conformance, a scale was defined that could be applied to all base and generic practices defined in the BPG. This scale is defined as *practice adequacy*.

A number of possible rating scales were investigated with different end points. Ordinal scales such as Very Poor, Poor, Average, Good, Very Good were looked at, as were continuous scales such as a percentage scale. A continuous scale was discounted because it was not felt that human judgment could be applied accurately on such a scale with any reliability in the context of process assessment. Various ordinal scales were investigated with two, three, four, five, and more points on the scale. A binary scale rapidly was discounted as not providing enough discrimination to be useful as a measurement. The scale was shortlisted to an ordinal scale with three, four, or five points.

The four-point scale was selected on the basis that measurement experiments demonstrate that scales with a midpoint are often misused by selecting the midpoint as an easy option rather than collecting more evidence to support a higher or lower rating. The end-point selection for this scale was also investigated thoroughly. A relative scale from very poor to very good or excellent suffers from the problem that few can agree on excellence. A scale was needed to allow qualified assessors to use the full extent of the scale reliably and repeatedly. A definition of the measured attribute was required that had easily-identified endpoints. The ability of a practice to satisfy the purpose of undertaking it was considered to be straightforward to identify: at one end of the scale, when it does not in any way meet its purpose—most usually when it is not performed at all—through to the opposite end of the scale where it fully meets its purpose. The scale selected was *practice adequacy* which encapsulates this concept.

Practice adequacy is defined as:

Not Adequate	The practice is either not implemented or does not to any degree contribute to satisfying the process purpose.
Partially Adequate	The implemented practice does little to contribute to satisfying the process purpose.
Largely Adequate	The implemented practice largely contributes to satisfying the process purpose.
Fully Adequate	The implemented practice fully contributes to satisfying the process purpose.

Having defined a rating scale to assess practices for each process, it was necessary to understand how this scale could be applied reliably and repeatably to assess processes. A number of key concepts evolved that are believed to be the cornerstone of achieving reliability and repeatability: the organizational unit (OU), the process context, the process instance, and aggregation mechanisms. These concepts are described in more detail below.

Organizational unit (OU)

Processes are deployed by an organizational unit (OU) to achieve a set of goals that may be either explicitly defined or implicitly understood. A process within an OU can only operate effectively if the context within which it operates is coherent. For this reason, a process can be assessed only if it is operating within a coherent context. The OU that deploys a set of processes must have one or more coherent contexts for each of the processes it deploys. Each process assessed with this measurement model must belong to a coherent and definable context.

Process context

An understanding of the context within which a process operates within an OU is critical to accurately assessing whether a practice that has been implemented fulfills its purpose. The implementation of a practice that fully meets its purpose in a small, noncritical development environment may be totally inadequate in a large, critical environment. Therefore, the context within which a process is deployed fundamentally influences judgments of practice adequacy.

Process instance

To assess a given process within an OU, a qualified assessor must find evidence that the process has been deployed. Most processes are deployed many times within an OU to meet its needs. Each deployment is termed an *instance* of the process. The rating framework is based on assessing a specific process instance. A process instance is a *singular instantiation of a process* that is uniquely identifiable and about which information can be gathered in a repeatable manner. The ratings that are determined for the process instance should therefore be repeatable when assessed by different qualified assessors.

Some instances may be well performed and others less so. Therefore, the selection of the process instances that are assessed is critical to the measures that are gathered. Unless every instance undertaken within a given time period is assessed, the selection of a sample will always influence the accuracy with which that sample can represent the true overall capability of the process.

The only possibility for true repeatability of such a measurement is to strive for repeatability at the process instance. If the same process instance is assessed by different qualified assessors at different times, the results should be comparable and repeatable within an acceptable margin of error. One objective of the Phase 1 Trials was to establish early feedback about the level of repeatability (see Chapter 16).

To characterize a process' capability within the context of a given OU, a representative sample of process instances must be selected and assessed. The rating framework requires that the sample size and rationale for the specific instances chosen be documented as part of the assessment output.

Aggregation

Since for many assessments the number of instances assessed will be greater than one, a mechanism is required to aggregate the process instance ratings to provide a meaningful set of ratings for each process assessed. The rating framework defines each instance as having equal weighting when aggregating practice adequacy. This mechanism ensures that the derived ratings are not hiding or obscuring any data by applying low-weighting factors.

Process effectiveness

Having defined a scale that enables a process to be assessed for conformance to a best-practice model, a measure of the process to be assessed was still required that enabled a determination of whether or not the practices were achieving the process' goals. A generic goal-achievement measure was defined in earlier versions of the PAG, but project-wide consensus could not be reached on a standard set of goals for each process. It was therefore decided to withdraw the effectiveness rating from the rating framework. Guidance is still provided in *Part 7: Guide for use in process improvement* on the selection of effectiveness measures for improvement purposes (see Chapter 8).

Version 1.00 rating framework

The BPG has two distinct kinds of practices:

1. *Base practices*

   These practices define the fundamental activities that must be performed by any instance of a given process for the process purpose to be fulfilled, as defined in the BPG. These practices are unique to each process.

2. *Generic Practices*

   A set of practices were identified that do not directly add value to the process, but rather enable the performance of the base practices to be undertaken in a more repeatable, predictable, or efficient manner. These practices are generic to the instantiation of any process.

To address the measurement of the two different types of practices, two distinct adequacy ratings were defined:

1. base practice adequacy
2. generic practice adequacy.

As this architecture for the process model emerged, it started to become clear that the generic practice defined as 1.1.1 *Perform the process* was itself a representation of the adequacy of all the base practices as *performed*. The measure of generic practice adequacy was becoming the fundamental measure, with base practice ratings providing further evidence to support the rating for 1.1.1 for any given process.

Generic practice adequacy determines the adequacy of the implemented practice in meeting the overall process purpose as defined in Part 2. It can therefore be seen as much an assessment of the *effectiveness* of the implemented practice within the process context—the OU characteristics and the product characteristics—as it is an assessment of the *conformance* of the implemented practice to the practice definition in Part 2.

Base practice existence versus adequacy

With a greater understanding of the role of base practices, the project team was concerned that judging adequacy on a four-point scale would be too onerous in terms of time and effort. Since base practice ratings are not fundamental to the generic practice adequacy scale, but rather provide the qualified assessor with supporting evidence, a base practice existence scale was also introduced as an alternative to base practice adequacy as a measure. This measure was a binary scale that provided a Yes/No measure of the existence of work products produced by a practice. An objective of the Phase 1 Trials was to provide feedback on which scales, either one or both, should be retained within the rating framework.

Process capability level rating

It was also found that the generic practices could be grouped according to the contribution they made to the *capability* of any process. The generic practices, 26 in all, were grouped into five capability levels that described the contribution they made to the process' capability.

A rating scale emerged that enabled the overall capability of the process to be assessed in one or more of these *states*. A sixth point was defined for this scale—Not performed—that represents the absence of any other capability. A rating scale was included therefore within the rating framework—called the *process capability level* rating—that defines how these capabilities are to be measured. This measure is not truly a rating scale at all but rather a set of rules that define the aggregation of all the generic practice adequacy ratings for a given process instance into their respective capability levels. Hence, each capability level can be described as a frequency distribution of the generic practice adequacy ratings associated with that level. A greater sense of clarity emerged as to how we could assess *process capability* and fulfill requirement E1.1.

Each process instance has a set of capabilities—one at each level—each of which is achieved by a set of generic practices. Correspondingly, a process instance is characterized by a process profile consisting of a set of five capability level ratings, each of which is an aggregation of the generic practice adequacy ratings. Hence, the generic practice adequacy ratings were the foundation for the rating system.

Summary of rating framework for Version 1.00

Hence four measurement scales were defined within the rating framework in Version 1.00:

1. base practice existence
2. base practice adequacy
3. generic practice adequacy
4. process capability level.

The process rating scheme, illustrated in Figure 6.1, links process instances, capabilities, and practices to the defined process purpose.

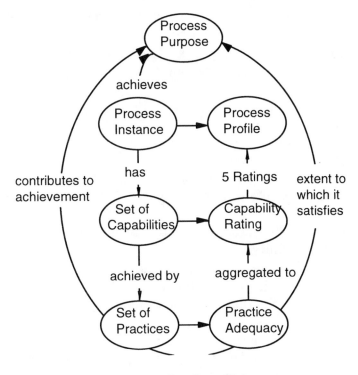

Process Rating Scheme

Figure 6.1: Process rating scheme.

Evolution to Version 2.00

During the Phase 1 Trials, 137 problem reports were raised (see Chapter 15). These problem reports were grouped by the Trials Core Team into six high-level Requests For Change (RFC). One RFC concerned the architecture of Part 2 and the manner in which the artifacts defined in that model were being assessed. These problems were analyzed by a group established under the guidance of the trials team and some of their findings are summarized below:

- There was no explicit guidance as to whether or not the fundamental measure was process capability level or generic practice adequacy. The consensus appeared to be that process capability was the fundamental measure that we were all striving for, but that each *capability level* consisted of a *set of capabilities*. The generic practices did not, however, represent these *capabilities*.

- The common features in the process model seemed to be closer to our understanding of a capability, but no rating component existed for these.

- It was widely believed that there were too many ratings when assessing the generic practices (26 ratings per process) and that assessing at the level of abstraction of the common feature would be more useable (11 ratings).

- There was concern that there were widely different numbers of generic practices at different capability levels that may adversely affect repeatability.

- There was conflicting feedback about which generic practices should be at which capability level.

- There was no justification for the inclusion of *any* generic practice in the model: no justification of why anyone should perform these practices and the benefits that might be obtained.

- The most common representation of the output from an assessment was a graph depicting the frequency distribution of the generic practice adequacy ratings for each capability level. This representation masked the individual adequacy ratings and emphasized capability levels.

- These representations were often used to describe a particular process as being "broadly Planned and Tracked" or "moving into Well Defined," depending on the relative distribution of the ratings at a given level. Whereas there was an intuitive understanding emerging within the project describing how a process could be defined as attaining a particular level, this description was not defined explicitly in Parts 2 or 3.

• There was a strong implication that attaining a Fully Adequate rating for all the generic practices for a particular level would ensure that it was possible to characterize the capability of the process as having attained the capability described by the capability level, such as Planned and tracked. However, there was a concern arising that since each component of that level was being assessed in isolation, the assessor was not making any judgments about the effectiveness of those individual practices in achieving a desirable outcome.

• The capability levels themselves were not well enough defined to ensure a consistent interpretation of their meaning.

The recommendations made by the trials analysis team to resolve these concerns were that the rating framework must define:

• what capabilities *any* process can attain

• what purpose the capability fulfills—what does it buy you?

• how you attain these capabilities

• what aspects of these capabilities are associated with individual instances

• what aspects of these capabilities relate to an organizational capability.

The report went on to define an outline set of capabilities that formed one of the inputs to the Version 2.00 rating framework.

SPICE Version 2.00 rating framework

To define an indirect measure of process capability, a model was defined that relates nine measurable attributes of capability to the six-level capability-level scale. Each attribute is itself measured on a four-point ordinal scale of *achievement*. This scale of achievement is itself derived from the adequacy scale defined in Version 1.00.

Process attribute rating scale

A *process attribute* represents a measurable characteristic of any process. The rating scale defined below can be used to describe the levels of achievement of the defined capability of the process attributes:

N	**N**ot achieved	There is no evidence of achievement of the defined attribute.
P	**P**artially achieved	There is some achievement of the defined attribute.
L	**L**argely achieved	There is significant achievement of the defined attribute.
F	**F**ully achieved	There is full achievement of the defined attribute.

Each attribute in turn can be assessed without predefining what set of practices are required to fulfill the capability. As a result, the model no longer prescribes how outcomes are achieved, but rather defines what outcomes are to be assessed.

The attainment of the attributes associated with capability Levels 2 to 5 is normally associated with the performance of some or all of the processes in the Support, Management, and Organization process categories defined within the process dimension. The Managed level attributes are associated with the processes in the Management and Support process categories, and the Established, Predictable, and Optimizing level attributes with the processes in the Organization process category. Part 5 provides suitable indicators to provide the evidence required to support the attribute ratings.

The model of process capability level that defines how the process attribute ratings are used to derive the capability level was defined to ensure that only one interpretation of capability level could exist. Therefore, any process instance can be rated as belonging to one capability level, as described in Figure 6.2.

The model allows some latitude in the ratings of the process attributes at a particular level—Fully or Largely—as long as the ratings for all the attributes for lower-level attributes (upon which the higher level of capability is based) are rated Fully. This flexibility somewhat reduces the sensitivity of the model to the ratings associated with the particular capability level that a process instance has attained.

Capability Level	Process Attributes	Rating
Level 1	Process performance	Largely or Fully
Level 2	Process performance	Fully
	Performance management	Largely or Fully
	Work product management	Largely or Fully
Level 3	Process performance	Fully
	Performance management	Fully
	Work product management	Fully
	Process definition	Largely or Fully
	Process resource	Largely or Fully
Level 4	Process performance	Fully
	Performance management	Fully
	Work product management	Fully
	Process definition and tailoring	Fully
	Process resource	Fully
	Process measurement	Largely or Fully
	Process control	Largely or Fully
Level 5	Process performance	Fully
	Performance management	Fully
	Work product management	Fully
	Process definition and tailoring	Fully
	Process resource	Fully
	Process measurement	Fully
	Process control	Fully
	Process change	Largely or Fully
	Continuous improvement	Largely or Fully

Figure 6.2: Calculating the capability level rating for a process instance.

Aggregation

Aggregation is now possible for both of the rating components. Aggregating process attribute ratings permits a view of the relative spread of capabilities of the various attributes across a number of process instances for a given process.

Part 2 defines two requirements for aggregation of process attribute ratings:

1. Process attribute ratings within a capability level shall not be aggregated.

2. When aggregating ratings, the representation used shall identify the process, the process attribute, the ordering of the ratings within the distribution, and the number of instances included within the aggregation.

Part 2 goes on to suggest that aggregated ratings could be expressed in the following form:

PC.PR [number of instances]; CL.PA = [% Fully, % Largely, % Partially, % Not]

where PC is the process category, PR is the process within the category, CL is the capability level containing the process attribute, and PA is the process attribute.

Any individual attribute rating can be represented by placing 100 percent at the measured value and 0 percent for all the other values. A single process attribute rating can be represented as:

ENG.1[1];3.1=[0,100,0,0]

This shorthand notation informs us that the process definition attribute for a single instance of the *Develop system requirements and design* process was measured as Largely achieved. Extending this notation to four instances of the same process we might find:

ENG.1[4];3.1=[25,50,25,0]

Upon inspection, one of the instances was rated as Fully, two as Largely, and one as Partially.

Extending this example, the entire process can be characterized as:

ENG.1[4];1.1=[75,25,0,0]
ENG.1[4];2.1=[50,50,0,0]
ENG.1[4];2.2=[50,25,25,0]
ENG.1[4];3.1=[25,50,25,0]
ENG.1[4];3.2=[25,25,25,25]
ENG.1[4];4.1=[0,50,25,25]
ENG.1[4];4.2=[25,25,25,25]
ENG.1[4];5.1=[0,0,25,75]
ENG.1[4];5.2=[0,0,25,75]

This notation in a graphical form appears as in Figure 6.3.

The above examples have focused on process attributes, but each process instance can also be represented as attaining a particular capability level. Once again, Part 2 defines two requirements:

1. Where more than one instance of a process is assessed, the process' capability levels achieved by the process instances may be aggregated to show a frequency distribution of achieved capability levels.

2. When aggregating capability levels, the representation used shall identify the process, the capability levels included in the aggregation, the ordering of the ratings within the distribution, and the number of instances included within the aggregation.

Part 2 goes on to suggest that aggregated capability levels could be expressed in the following form:

$$PC.PR \text{ [number of instances]}; (CL0 \text{ to } CLn) = [\% \text{ } CL0, \% \text{ } CL1, ..., \% CLn]$$

where PC is the process category, PR is the process within the category, and CL0 to CLn is the capability level range that was assessed. This arrangement allows, for example, for the case where an assessment only assessed a process up to capability Level 3.

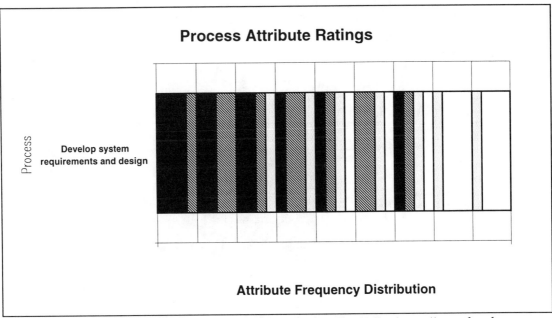

Figure 6.3: Example of graphical presentation of attribute ratings for four process instances.

Once again, any individual capability level rating can be represented by placing 100% at the measured value and 0% for all the other values. A single process capability rating can be represented as:

ENG.1[1];(0—5)=[0,0,100,0,0,0]

This shorthand notation informs us that the capability level attained by a single instance of the *Develop system requirements and design* process was measured as Capability Level 2—Defined. Extending this notation to four instances of the same process depicts:

ENG.1[4];(0—5)=[0,25,50,25,0,0]

Upon inspection, one of the instances attained Level 1, two attained Level 2, and one attained Level 3. This notation in a graphical form appears as in Figure 6.4.

Version 2.00 provides a much more robust set of measures to enable the capability of a process to be accurately assessed and represented. The process capability level gives a good single-value representation of the capability of a process instance and the process attributes enable the detailed composition of that capability to be represented and analyzed. Both measures are useful to depict process capability and can be used in the appropriate the context and for the intended audience.

Process Capability Level - Frequency Distribution

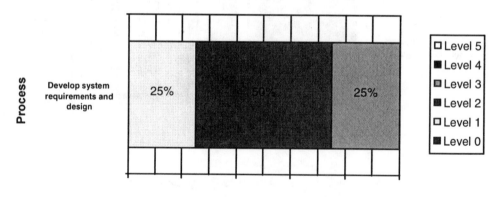

Percentage at each Capability Level

Figure 6.4: Graphical example for representing capability levels.

Conclusion: The new Part 3 and the rating framework

The new Part 3 now places all the requirements for defining the assessment inputs and responsibilities within the assessment process and the recording of assessment output to demonstrate compliance. The key clauses in Part 3 that relate to the rating framework and compatible models are:

- The model used within the assessment shall be a compatible model.

- Correspondence shall be established between an OU's processes specified in the assessment scope through the compatible model to the processes defined in Part 2.

- Each process shall be assessed by examining one or more process instances. The set of process instances assessed shall be sufficient to meet the assessment purpose and scope.

- A rating shall be assigned and validated for each process attribute for each process assessed up to the highest capability level defined in the assessment scope.

- Objective evidence based on the indicators in the model that support the qualified assessors' judgment of process attribute ratings shall be recorded and maintained.

- Comparisons of process profiles shall be valid only if their process contexts are similar.

7

The Assessment Model

Carroline Buchman
AlliedSignal Inc., USA

Helen Thomson
Faxbase Ltd., UK

Each part of the SPICE Project went through a number of evolutionary steps before Version 2.00 was produced. The original concepts supporting an assessment instrument (AI) are described in the *Assessment Instrument Product Description*[1] (AIPD). The AIPD is the design document for Part 5. After further comment ratification, Version 2.00 was consolidated and named *Part 5: An assessment model and indicator guidance.*[6] This chapter describes the evolution of Part 5 of the emerging standard and how the assessment model can be used to support assessments.

Product specification

The AIPD and Versions 1.00 and 2.00 of Part 5 were written to augment the Part 2 *Baseline Practices Guide* (BPG) and to provide *indicators* from which to assess good software engineering practice. A secondary, though equally important, objective for the AIPD and Part 5 Version 1.00 was to define the requirements for the development or selection of a SPICE-conformant AI and is described in Chapter 5.

Initially, the expectation was that Part 5 would provide the necessary detail to make the BPG fully usable in performing an assessment. By Version 2.00 however, the emerging standard was scoped to provide a complete model—but not a method—that could be used to support an assessment. Additional information on how to define indicators was also given.

AI charter

The AI document definition in WG10/N016R[3] is:

> This document provides instructions for the construction of alternative instruments for assessment in specific situations. It is envisaged that conformant instruments will act as sensors or probes into an area to open up discussion and further investigation.

This initial description was very brief. It was felt that there are many ways that a qualified assessor can evaluate an organization's strengths and weaknesses and so we needed to define the following:

- terms, for example, *assessment instrument*
- what constituted a sensor or probe (or indicator)
- the scope of the AI Product Description.

This definition process would allow us to progress the concepts defined in the AIPD to form Part 5 of the emerging standard.

Assigned requirements

There were seven requirements assigned to the AI by WG10/N017R[4] (see Chapter 3). These requirements are very high level and needed interpretation in the context of the AIs. The Product Description (PD) further delineated the assigned requirements and allowed the team to consolidate and specify further their application to AIs. It was found to be also necessary to document additional requirements in the PD. These requirements for a SPICE-conformant AI were consolidated and interpreted in the AIPD as:

- correspond directly to the set of base practices defined in the BPG (Requirement O)
- be of a scope and depth appropriate to the assessment being carried out (Requirements K2 and N)

- assist in the creation of objective and consistent results through the use of the defined indicators (Requirements C3 and N)

- produce results consistent with the measurement framework defined in the Process Assessment Guide (PAG) (Requirements B2 and R)

- analyze and aggregate ratings using the mechanisms defined in the PAG (Requirements B2, Q1 and R)

- capture and present the information necessary to support the format and usage defined in the *Process Improvement Guide* (PIG) and the PCDG (Requirement R)

- make a provision for adaptability to cope with the addition of practices and indicators that may be needed for assessments using SPICE variants as defined in the BPG and PAG (Requirement K2)

- allow for a view of assessment results that shows the relationship between an individual project's results and an entire organization's results (Requirement N)

- have the ability to map the organization's actual processes to the BPG defined processes. This mapping is defined in the PAG.

- record deviation from the base practices in a significant way.

The requirement number following each of the derived requirements indicates its traceability to the high-level requirements in Chapter 3. Several requirements not explicitly assigned to the AI were also addressed indirectly by the clarified and expanded AIPD.

The AI Product Description (AIPD)

The aim of the AIPD was to outline the information that would be contained within the emerging standard. Specifically this document defined:

- the requirements for building conformant AIs
- adequacy and consistency through the use of indicators
- scoping of assessments
- work products, job functions, process indicators, and process management indicators
- the relationship of the AIPD to the other SPICE documents.

Indicators provide the foundation of an assessment in that they are the structural framework by which a qualified assessor judges the adequacy of an organization's practices against the process purposes as described in the BPG. Indicators also provide reasonable assurance of repeatable results. Therefore, the assumption can be made that a second assessment performed by a different qualified assessor would produce similar results when similar indicators are used. The indicator set needs to have sufficient breadth to cover all the practices of the BPG and sufficient depth to promote repeatability across assessment methods and assessors.

The universal requirements that are the most difficult to meet remain that of repeatability and cultural independence. The indicator set needs to be comprehensive and must provide a solid foundation so that different assessors will reach similar conclusions when an organization has multiple independent assessments performed. At the same time, the indicator set must remain culturally independent and be equally applicable to a large range of development methodologies.

The AIPD also made it clear that an AI could take many forms. It was not necessary to be even an online tool—SPICE Trials have been successfully conducted with paper-based AIs. Although an assessment generates a lot of information, a paper-based tool can be used effectively to collect, store, and analyze the data. AIs can be based on paper, relational databases, or expert systems; and all are valid implementations of AIs.

AIPD definitions and development issues

Since the AIPD was the design document for Part 5 Version 1.00, it needed to establish some working definitions for assessment tools and "probes and sensors." The AIPD defined probes and sensors as indicators that were defined as work products and their characteristics providing insight into an organization's implementation of the base practices of the BPG process. Process management indicators would provide the same insight into the generic practices. In this way, both the process and capability dimensions of the architecture would be supported.

Initially, the AI team tried to organize indicators by job function—by those personnel who would be interviewed or otherwise would supply the evidence of the practice. The concept of job function was later dropped in order to maintain cultural independence.

Version 1.00

As mentioned earlier, the AI became known as Part 5 Version 1.00 and defined the requirements of an AI and provided guidance in its use and selection. It provided AI builders with ample information to determine what was sufficient coverage of Part 2 Version 1.00 (BPG) for the scope of the assessment and the basic requirements of any AI.

An AI is a support tool designed to be used in conjunction with the practices defined in Part 2 Version 1.00. Part 5 Version 1.00 augmented the process and practices of Part 2 Version 1.00, with indicators mapped to the base and generic practices of each Part 2 Version 1.00 process. Indicators do not replace qualified assessor judgment, but rather provide a common basis for supporting the assessment of a practice.

Part 5 Version 1.00 provided both the details necessary to meet the requirements of Part 4 Version 1.00 and the ability to capture assessment results in a format to meet the needs of the assessment. It described the context record in further detail and its possible implementation in an AI. The AI supports the qualified assessor in analyzing the data collected and computing the assessment ratings as defined in Part 3 Version 1.00.

Scope

The AI scope for Part 5 Version 1.00 was quite broad. The document had several purposes and identified the audience as:

1. *Qualified assessors who would select an AI for use in an assessment.* They would require an understanding of the tool requirements so that they could be assured that the AI they selected met those requirements. Also, it was deemed to be appropriate to provide some guidance on what makes a tool effective and easy to use. The qualified assessor also needed to understand the indicator set within the scope of the assessment being planned and how to tailor and augment that set.

2. *Organizations being assessed that would want to know which indicators would be used.* In addition, the AI team always hoped that the AI(s) might someday be integrated into the software engineering environment itself so that organizations could automatically collect assessment data at frequent intervals for analysis and use as part of an improvement strategy.

3. ***Tool providers who would supply tools to qualified assessors.***
Tool developers would need to know the requirements of the tools so
that they could ensure their tool was compliant with the SPICE standard. Tool providers probably also would make use of the selection
guidance that would be used by the qualified assessor or organization.

Definitions

The definitions of the fundamental concepts of AIs and assessment indicators
that appeared in Part 5 Version 1.00 are:

- **AI:** a tool or set of tools that is used throughout an assessment to
support the evaluation of the existence or adequacy of practices
within the scope of the assessment. It may provide assistance in collecting, recording, formalizing, processing, using, storing, or retriev-
ing information gathered during an assessment.

- **assessment indicator:** a keyword or phrase that guides a qualified
assessor in recognizing characteristics of practice adequacy.

Development issues

Existence and adequacy ratings

Many of the issues revolved around whether adequacy ratings should be made at
the practice or process level and whether or not a specific set of indicators should
be a required component of a conformant assessment. Initially, a definition was:

> Practice adequacy is a judgment of the extent to which the deployed
> practice contributes to meeting the purpose of the process as stated in
> the BPG, judged in the context of the size, complexity and criticality of
> the software product.

Rating adequacy at the practice versus the process levels is a fundamental
concept that has a profound effect on the quantity of data that needs to be
collected and managed by an assessment instrument. Part 2 (the BPG) had 201
base practices and 26 generic practices. The orthogonal nature of the SPICE
architecture and the base practice rating scheme required that 5226 ratings be
collected per process instance if all Part 2 processes were to be assessed. There
seemed to be a clear indication that an automatic AI would be needed to track
and roll up this quantity of information.

The AI team recognized early that the Part 2 model, although nominally orthogonal, had some overlap in it, and examination of a particular practice in one process would contribute to a rating for another. Several of the generic practices, such as those relating to peer reviews and configuration management, were also incorporated into specific support processes.

For Part 5 Version 1.00, the issue of having a compulsory set of indicators was resolved by requiring the set of indicators to be present, but since the qualified assessor only used them as memory joggers, probes, and so on, the assessors would still base the practice rating on their best judgment. The indicator set would be a common set of probes, sensors, and memory joggers to assist an assessor with more reliable and consistent judgments of practice adequacy. The indicator set was never intended to be all inclusive, but rather was meant to provide guidance on what to consider when making a judgment about existence and adequacy of an organization's implementation of a process practice. This requirement would change almost two years later at Kwa Maritane.

Developing indicators

The result of a process assessment is a *process profile* (Figure 7.1). The premise is that the profile is based on indicator-based observations of the organization's process instantiations. Indicators are the objective evidence that a practice is being performed or managed.

The AI team initially proposed existence indicators and adequacy indicators that were characterized by the type of software and size of the development effort and that were sortable by job function, meaning those who in an organization would be responsible for the indicator. The software types were classified as risk (critical, average, noncritical), size (large, medium, small), and complexity (complex, simple).

In theory, this sort of classification is possible, even desirable, as indicators are identifiable for each of these categories and all the combinations. To build a single set of indicators however, and to classify them for all categories while retaining cultural and organizational independence, was just too monumental a task. Imagine trying to have noncultural, nonorganizational specific job classifications!

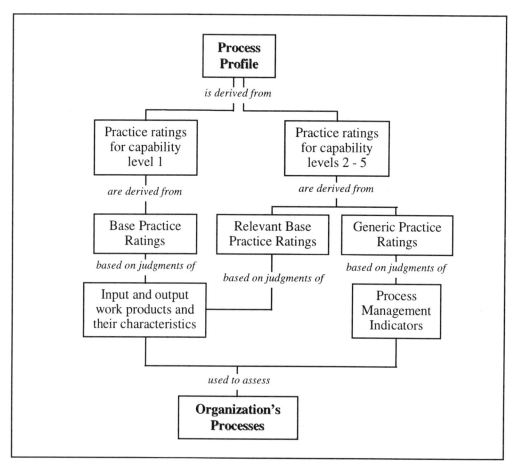

Figure 7.1: Process profile development from an organization's process instantiations.

After many attempts, the AI team agreed that the best and most universally-acceptable indicators of a practice adequacy were the existence and characteristics of the artifact produced by the practice, namely the work product (Figure 7.2). The work products and their characteristics, however, needed to be presented in a culturally-independent and unbiased way. They could not imply a level of competence since that is the domain of the model. The indicator set had to be thorough, but could not presume that any work product exists in a specific format or media. The indicators are not requirements, but are memory joggers. A specific characteristic assigned to a work product may actually be found elsewhere. The key was to judge the adequacy of the practice within the context of the organization's business domain.

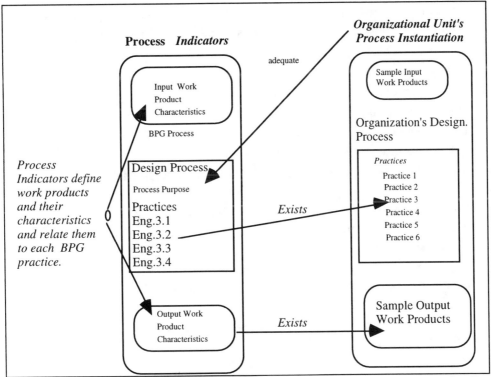

Figure 7.2: Relationship of the model and indicators to the organization's processes.

An example of a work product is a software test plan. Just choosing the words "software test plan" may immediately bring to mind a specific standard's requirements such as Mil-STD-2167A. Clearly, to be culturally and methodology-independent, that cannot be the intent.

Notice that the words "software test plan" are not capitalized, making them appear generic. The software test plan is not required to be in any specific format or even required to be a formal document. The software test plan may have much information contained within it that could be used to evaluate multiple practices across processes. Obviously, it is desirable to examine the document once and record all the information needed to support ratings of all the relevant practices. The software test plan characteristics listed below are cross-referenced to specific processes and practices from Part 2 Version 1.00.

For the most part, work products address most of the practices within a process. For example, software test plan is traced to all six practices in the Engineering Process (ENG.5), Integrate and Test Software, of Part 2 Version 1.00.

The characteristics listed to jog the qualified assessor's memory are extensive; but these are not requirements. The characteristics of the test strategy and plan are:

- the test purpose
- the responsible test plan owner
- the approach to performing the test
- the components to be tested
- test aggregates and sequence for testing
- any required system configurations (software, hardware, interface components)
- the developer of the components to be tested
- associated test scripts/test cases
- sequence ordering of how testing will be executed
- requirements that will be validated by tests: customer requirements, regulatory requirements, and system requirements
- the problem-reporting mechanism
- the test tools and resources required: test channels, analyzers, test emulators, and so on
- the test schedule
- the test completion criteria
- the official source libraries and versions of software defined.

The above list shows just the work product and characteristics indicators. Process management indicators were also developed to facilitate the judgment of each generic practice. As the generic practices were applied to each base practice, the process management indicators were written generically to allow for the application to the process and practice under evaluation.

The AI team also looked at the work products already considered in order to facilitate the evaluation of the generic practices. Qualified assessors would want to look at the results of evaluating the related base practice work products as well as the process management indicators listed in evaluating the generic practice. For *Defining a standard process*, other base practices are associated and the results of their evaluation would have a bearing on the resulting capability level of the practice under consideration. For Part 5 Version 1.00, the tables contained a considerable amount of information to provide a basis for a paper instrument that would support the SPICE Trials. In addition, the Part 2 base and generic practice descriptions were repeated to make the document more usable (Figure 7.3).

3.1.1 Standardize the process	Document a standard process or family of processes for the organization that describes how to implement the base practices for the process.
Associated processes/practices:	**ORG.2** Define the process **SUP.1** Develop documentation **PRO.1.3** Describe activities and tasks **ORG.2.10** Document the standard process * *(*duplicate base practice)*
Potential sources for existence evidence	• Process description • Job practices, procedure • Work breakdown structure • Standards • Software development methodology • Quality criteria

Process management Indicators	• The standard process documented provides coverage for the associated base practices
	• The organization's standard process documentation exists and includes:
	  – The expected input and output work products
	  – The work breakdown structure for the process, such as:
	    ◊ Tasks to be performed
	    ◊ Task ownership
	    ◊ Objective criteria to demonstrate the task completeness
	    ◊ Objective criteria to demonstrate the sufficiency of input and output work products
	  – A definition of any internal and external interfaces
	  – Quality controls, such as:
	    ◊ Process entry and exit criteria
	    ◊ Process decision control points
	    ◊ Process measures
	    ◊ Process performance characteristics and expectations
	  – Performance characteristics for the standard or tailored process that consider things like:
	    ◊ productivity expectations
	    ◊ quality expectations
	    ◊ process adherence objectives
	    ◊ development resource estimates, such as time, cost, and personnel

Figure 7.3: Sample process management indicators.

Of course all indicators have to support the generation of a process profile. Process profiles encompass the assessment results and are a mechanism by which organizations can be compared when assessed for capability determination or process improvement.

Evolution to Version 2.00

The Version 1.00 document was revised based on the evaluations described in Chapter 3. These revisions addressed the issues that were raised and are described below.

Aligning with ISO/IEC 12207

Part 2 Version 1.00 was abstracted into a reference model and Part 5 Version 1.00 into an assessment model. The reference model documented the essential elements of a conformant model and therefore provided the interface for other approaches. Both the reference and assessment models would now align with the processes described in ISO/IEC 12207, where appropriate, and would maintain a mapping to the ISO/IEC 12207 processes. Reference model processes and assessment model practices, outside the scope of ISO/IEC 12207, were also identified.

Reducing the prescriptiveness of the emerging standard

The prescriptiveness issue raised during the evaluations of Version 1.00 were addressed by both:

- moving the practices defined in Part 2 Version 1.00 into Part 5 and making the new Part 5 Version 2.00 informative
- allowing models, methods, and approaches that could document conformance (rules for which would be defined in Part 2) to be used in a conformant assessment.

WG10 also agreed to assess processes against the process purpose, not each individual practice. This change has a significant impact on the quantity of data collected during an assessment. WG10 hoped that this change would drive down considerably the amount of required data to be collected.

Migration and harmonization with existing methods

Part 2 Version 2.00 would now describe the mechanisms by which existing models (including the informative model in Part 5 Version 2.00) could show conformance to the emerging standard. Part 5 would need to include conformance documentation for the assessment model described in the new Part 5.

Changes indicated by the Phase 1 Trials

A complete mapping from the old to the new approach needed to be maintained so that practice information would not be lost. In addition, the Phase 1 Trials data could be translated to the new model: the old approach had to be shown to be conformant to the new.

The assessment model had to be kept identical in structure to the reference model. However, Part 5 had to absorb the base and generic practices and their mapping to the reference model had to be accurately documented. This structure served two purposes:

- **Trials validity:** The Phase 1 Trials had to remain valid so that the data could be manipulated and used for comparison with the Phase 2 Trials data. The Version 1.00 architecture had to be proved conformant to that defined in Version 2.00 of the emerging standard.
- **Proof of conformance:** The assessment model had to be shown to be based on and compatible with the reference model defined in Part 2 Version 2.00.

Part 5 Version 2.00: an assessment model and indicator guidance

The reference model alone cannot be used as the basis for conducting reliable and consistent assessments of process capability since the level of detail provided is not sufficient. The descriptions of process purpose and process attributes in the reference model need to be supported with comprehensive sets of indicators of process performance and capability. Any model meeting the requirements of Part 2 Version 2.00 can be used for assessment. Different models may be needed to address differing business needs. The assessment model in Part 5 Version 2.00 is therefore provided as an example of a compatible model.

Part 5 Version 2.00 provides a complete assessment model for the purpose of supporting the assessment process. It provides guidance both in the form and content of a conformant model and on defining and using process indicators. The assessment model is directly compatible with the reference model defined in Part 2 in that it encompasses all the processes and capability levels in the reference model. As a result, in the process dimension the model provides full coverage of each of the processes in the Customer-Supplier, Engineering, Support, Management, and Organization process categories.

The assessment model is derived directly from Parts 2 and 5 of Version 1.00. Many of the base practices of the original model, representing examples of good software engineering practice, have been retained in this model and reorganized to fit with the arrangement of processes within the reference model. Where necessary, new base practices have been created. The management practices of the assessment model are a refinement of the generic practices of the old model. The difference in scope from Part 5 Version 1.00 is summarized in Table 7.1.

Table 7.1: Change summary for Part 5 Version 2.00.

Part 5 Version 1.00 *Construction, selection and use of assessment instruments and tools*	**Part 5 Version 2.00** *An assessment model and indicator guidance*
	Is aligned with ISO/IEC 12207.
Defines indicators to augment the practices in Part 2 Version 1.00.	Defines a complete example assessment model that encapsulates the reference model in Part 2 Version 2.00.
Assumes the use of the practices defined in Part 2 Version 1.00 in any conformant assessment.	Absorbs the Part 2 Version 1.00 practices. Provides documentation of conformance of the assessment model in Part 5 Version 2.00 to the reference model in Part 2 Version 2.00.
Provides guidance on the use of indicators in judging *practice* adequacy.	Provides guidance on the use of indicators (including practices) in judging *process* adequacy.
Specifies requirements for AIs.	AI requirements simplified and moved to Part 3.
Provides guidance in the selection and use of AIs.	Guidance on selection and use of AIs moved to Part 4.

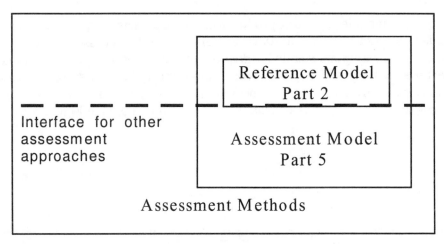

Figure 7.4: The relationship between the reference model, assessment model, and other assessment approaches.

The indicators are used to gather the evidence to enable a qualified assessor to assign ratings to process attributes. The set of indicators is not intended to be an all-inclusive set nor is it intended to be applicable in its entirety. Subsets that are appropriate to the context and scope of the assessment should be selected and possibly augmented with additional indicators.

Definitions

Conceptually, the definitions of an assessment indicator and AI did not change. However, since processes are now rated instead of practices, the practices are now part of the indicator set. The definitions in Part 9 Version 2.00 were changed accordingly.

- **assessment indicator**: An objective attribute or characteristic of a practice or work product that supports the judgment of the performance of, or capability of, an implemented process.
- **assessment instrument**: A tool or set of tools that is used throughout an assessment to assist the qualified assessor in evaluating the performance or capability of processes and in handling assessment data and recording the assessment results.

Assessment indicators are now more comprehensive than in Version 1.00 (Figure 7.1). The process dimension indicators, now called *indicators of process performance*, include the work products and characteristics as before, as well as the base practices from the Part 2 Version 1.00 processes. The capability dimension indicators, now called *indicators of process capability*, include not only characteristics of practice performance, characteristics of associated resources and infrastructure and their associated processes, but also the management practices (the generic practices from Part 2 Version 1.00) (see Figure 7.5).

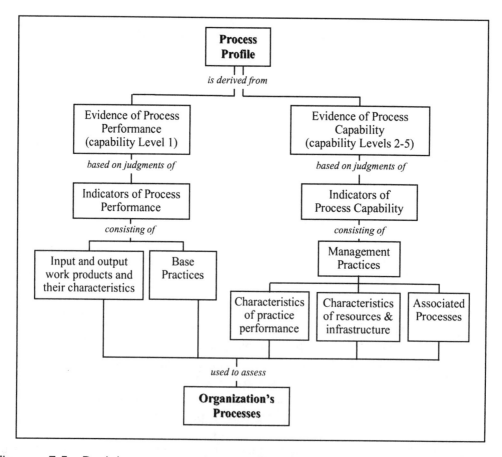

Figure 7.5: Deriving a process profile for an organization's process instance.

The structure of the assessment model

The basic structure of the assessment model defined in Part 5 Version 2.00 is identical to that of the reference model defined in Part 2 Version 2.00. There is a one-to-one correspondence between the process categories, processes, process purposes, process capability levels, and process attributes of the reference model and the assessment model.

The assessment model expands the reference model by adding the definition and use of assessment indicators (Figure 7.6). *Assessment indicators* are objective attributes or characteristics of a practice or work product that support a qualified assessor's judgment of the performance or capability of an implemented process.

Base practices, work products, and their characteristics relate to the processes defined in the process dimension of the reference model and are chosen to address explicitly the achievement of the defined process purpose. The base practices and work products are the indicators of process performance. Base practices are the operational decomposition of a process and demonstrate the performance of the processes.

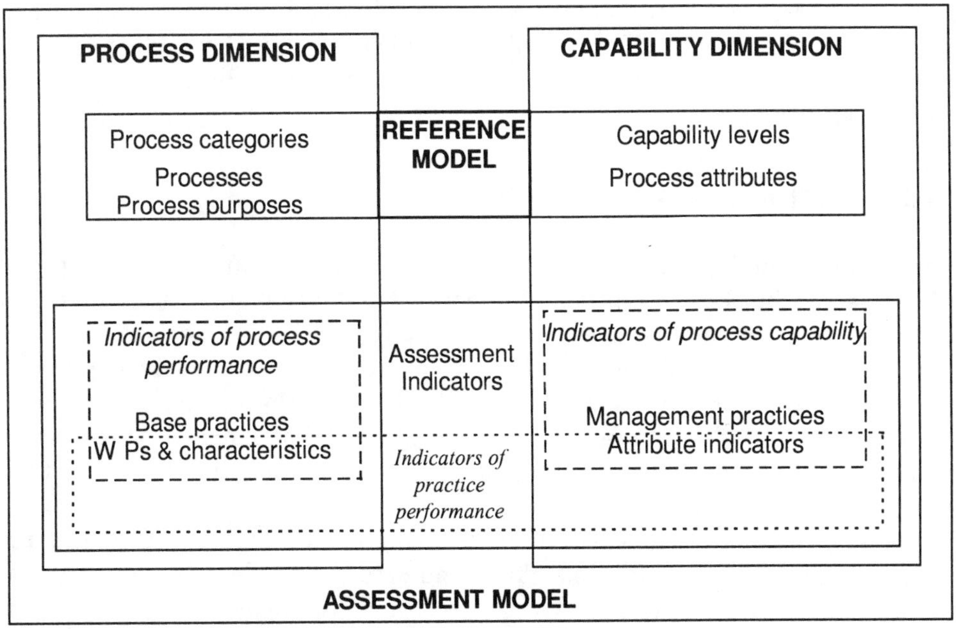

PROCESS DIMENSION		CAPABILITY DIMENSION
Process categories Processes Process purposes	**REFERENCE MODEL**	Capability levels Process attributes
Indicators of process performance Base practices W Ps & characteristics	Assessment Indicators *Indicators of practice performance*	*Indicators of process capability* Management practices Attribute indicators
	ASSESSMENT MODEL	

Figure 7.6: Relationship between the reference model (Part 2) and assessment model (Part 5).

Base practices are defined to support the judgment of the achievement of the process purpose and outcomes. Processes also use and produce (input and output) work products with specific characteristics.

Management practices relate to the process attributes defined in the process capability dimension of the reference model, and evidence of their performance supports the judgment of the degree of achievement of the attribute.

Management practices, with their associated attribute indicators, are the indicators of process capability. Management practices are the means of achieving the capabilities addressed by process attributes. Management practices are linked with attribute indicators:

- practice performance characteristics that provide guidance on the implementation of the practice
- resource and infrastructure characteristics that provide mechanisms for assisting in the management of the process
- associated processes from the process dimension that support the management practice.

Specific management practices are linked to each process attribute. The set of management practices is intended to be applicable to all processes in the process dimension of the model. The attribute indicators help establish objective evidence that the management practices associated with the process attribute are being performed.

Principles of the assessment model

The assessment model is based on the principle that the capability of a process can be assessed by demonstrating the achievement of process attributes. Each process in the process dimension has a set of associated base practices, the performance of which provide an indication of the extent of achievement of the process purpose. Similarly, each process attribute in the capability dimension has a set of associated management practices, the performance of which provide an indication of the extent of achievement of the attribute in the instantiated process.

The assessment indicators in the assessment model are the criteria against which an assessment is performed. These indicators provide an example of good software engineering practice. To make them applicable to all software applications and domains they are defined as abstract, high-level concepts without constraining the ways in which they may be implemented. The indicators are a set of attributes that might be found in an instantiation of a process.

The assessment model includes many indicators but it is not an all-inclusive set. The absence of some indicators in an organization being assessed may not be significant. Qualified assessors should examine the assessment model and indicators for applicability to the organizational context.

Indicators help identify what is present or missing from a process or work product and provide guidance to the qualified assessor when assigning a rating to a process. The information provides an *indication* of the extent to which the purpose of the process is met. The detailed information captured during the assessment about the presence or absence of specific indicators provides the valuable input into analysis and process improvement planning.

Defining and using indicators

The assessment model defines base practices, input and output work products, and their characteristics as indicators of process performance. It also defines management practices, process characteristics and related work products, and their characteristics as indicators of process capability (see Figure 7.6). Indicators are not requirements but provide a set of detailed discriminators used to assess whether a particular instantiation of a practice meets the purpose of the process.

Additional indicators can and should be defined to support specific industry domains and/or regulatory standards. The set of indicators and the form of the AI should be tailored to meet the needs of the assessment team or sponsor in the following respects:

- the modification of indicator format to accommodate presentation style preferences—questions, sentences, tables, online input screens, and so on—the choice being dictated only by preference
- the modification of indicator wording to accommodate synonym names or meaning for cultural differences. The emerging standard specifically lists indicators in the most culturally-neutral way possible. Instrument providers need to adapt the indicators for use within their particular cultural and application domains. Translation tables may be necessary to ensure that the organizational work products' names are matched with the characteristics of the work products against which the qualified assessor is evaluating.

- the addition of scoping characteristics to help select the set of indicators used by process area, user, job function, application domain, software product, or other predefined organizational unit or tool characteristics. This use of characteristics can help tremendously during an assessment by presenting the indicators to the qualified assessor in a way that complements the assessment method.
- the addition of new indicators to support new work products, new technology, and specific extended processes.

Typically, the chosen AI will have predetermined some of these choices. Indicator tailoring and presentation can make a difference in the ease with which the assessment is performed and as a result, its cost. Indicators are used by qualified assessors during an assessment to provide a foundation for the ratings of process attributes. They are critical for achieving repeatability. Qualified assessors are required to record the indicator set used for assessment and the actual practices and work products examined and used in judging process capability. Indicators should be defined for each process within the assessment scope.

Document organization

Part 5 Version 2.00 is entirely informative. The normative section on AI requirements has been moved to Part 3. The main body of the document consists of an overview of the assessment model that includes information on the reference model architecture, the assessment model structure, principles of the assessment model, the views of process performance and process capability, and guidance on using indicators in rating processes. The contents of Part 5 Version 2.00 are described briefly in Table 7.2.

Use of indicators in rating processes

Each process in the process dimension has a set of associated base practices, the performance of which provides an indication of the extent of achievement of the process purpose. Similarly, each process attribute in the capability dimension has a set of associated management practices, the performance of which provides an indication of the extent of achievement of the attribute in the instantiated process.

Table 7.2: Summary of the contents of Part 5 Version 2.00.

Introduction	The introduction describes what is in the document Part 5 Version 2.00.
Clause 1	Scope. The scope statement provides a context for the remainder of the document.
Clause 2	Normative References. There are no normative references.
Clause 3	Definitions. This section is a pointer to Part 9 of the emerging standard where the vocabulary used by all parts is defined. Additional definitions specific to Part 5 are also defined here.
Clause 4	Overview of the assessment model. This section provides a detailed description of the structure and key components of the exemplar assessment model defined in Part 5.
Clause 5	The process dimension. Each process category and process of the reference model in Part 2 is described and expanded to include base practices. .Annexes A and C would normally be used in conjunction with this clause.
Clause 6	The capability dimension. Each capability level is described in terms of detailed process attributes and management practices. Annex B would normally be used in conjunction with this clause.
Clause 7	Compatibility with the reference model. This clause provides a compatibility statement that fully meets the requirement of Part 2 of the emerging standard. It not only provides users of the assessment model with the necessary conformance documentation, but also serves as an example of *proof of conformance* for other model providers.
Annex A	Processes and associated work products. This annex contains the input and output work products associated with each process defined in clause 5.
Annex B	Indicators of process capability. This annex contains the process performance, resource and infrastructure characteristics and related processes associated with each management practice defined in clause 6.
Annex C	Work products and their characteristics. This annex contains the work product characteristics for each work product used in Annex A. This annex is intended to be used in conjunction with Annex A as a cross reference. The work product characteristics are in an Annex to provide a single point of reference. Many of the work products are listed multiple times in Annex A. By cross-referencing the work product to the characteristics in Annex C, the characteristics need only be described once.
Annex D	Style guide for defining base practices. This informative annex provides guidance to those who wish to define their own base practices to either expand those already defined or to support additional processes. If the model is tailored or extended, this information will help identify the indicators needed to support assessment against the tailored or extended model.
Annex E	Style guide for defining management practices. Similarly to Annex D, this informative annex provides guidance on developing management practices to support expanding the capability dimension. If the model is tailored or extended, this information will help identify the indicators needed to support assessment against the tailored or extended model.
Annex F	References. References are given for documents used as input in creating Part 5 or that may prove useful to those creating their own indicators, practices, or processes.

The output from a process assessment is a set of ratings of the process attributes for all process instances within the scope of the assessment. Each attribute rating represents a judgment by the qualified assessor of the extent to which the attribute is achieved. To maximize the objectivity of these judgments, thereby improving the reliability and repeatability of the assessment, the judgments of the qualified assessor must be based on a coherent set of documented, objective evidence.

This assessment model provides a set of indicators to form the basis of such a set of documented evidence. Two different classes of indicators can be identified: *indicators of process performance* and *indicators of process capability*. Within the context of this model, these indicator types relate respectively to the base practices defined for the process dimension and the management practices for the capability dimension. The classes and types of indicators, and their relationship to the assessment output, is shown in Figure 7.7.

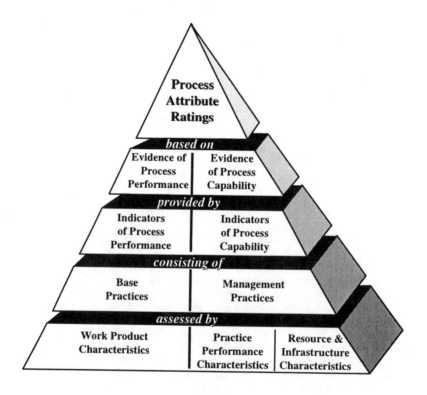

Figure 7.7: The relationship between indicators and process attribute ratings.

Indicators are attributes or characteristics, the existence of which confirms that certain practices are performed and for which it is possible to collect objective evidence during an assessment. Objective evidence may come either from the examination of work products of the processes assessed or from statements made by the performers and managers of the processes. The existence of the work products and their characteristics provide evidence of the performance of the practices associated with them. Similarly, the evidence obtained from performers of the process provides evidence regarding the performance of the practices and the manner in which they are performed.

The indicators in this model comprise lists of suggested evidence that a qualified assessor might obtain or observe during the course of an assessment. They are not intended to be regarded as a mandatory set of checklists to be followed but rather as guidance for a qualified assessor in accumulating the necessary objective evidence to support their judgments of capability. The evidence obtained should be recorded in a form that clearly identifies the indicator types and classes so that the support for the qualified assessor's judgment can be readily confirmed or verified.

Two brief examples taken from Part 5 Version 2.00, of the process dimension (with indicators of process performance) and the capability dimension (with indicators of process capability), are given below.

The process dimension—indicators of process performance

The process dimension is directly mapped to that of the reference model and adopts the same process categories, processes, and process purpose definitions that are defined for use by the reference model. The process categories and processes are strongly aligned to those defined in ISO/IEC 12207.

In the assessment model, the description of each process comprises:

1. From the reference model defined in Part 2, both:

    - the process purpose definition, taken from the reference model
    - explanatory notes amplifying this definition, where necessary.

2. From the exemplar assessment model defined in Part 5:

    - a set of base practices for the process, representing a definition of the tasks and activities needed to accomplish the process purpose (defined in clause 5)

- a number of input and output work products associated with each process (defined in Annex A)

- the characteristics associated with each work product (defined in Annex C).

The example process used here is *CUS.2 Manage customer needs*, one of the five processes of the Customer-Supplier process category (CUS). Figure 7.8 shows the information given in Part 5 Version 2.00 clause 5. This clause lists the process and its process purpose taken from Part 2 and then defines the associated base practices.

A *base practice* is a software engineering or project management activity that addresses the purpose of a particular process. Consistently performing the base practices associated with a process helps in consistently achieving its purpose. A coherent set of base practices is associated with each process in the process dimension.

The base practices are described at an abstract level, identifying *what* should be done without specifying *how*. The base practices characterize performance of a process, even if that performance is not systematic. Performance of the base practices may be *ad hoc*, unpredictable, inconsistent, poorly planned, and/or result in poor quality products, but those work products must be at least marginally usable in achieving the purpose of the process. Implementing only the base practices of a process may be of minimal value and represents only the first step in building process capability, but the base practices represent the unique, functional activities of the process.

The performance of a process typically produces work products. In turn, every work product has a defined set of characteristics that can be used to assess the effective implementation of a process. The processes with their related work products are found in Part 5 Annex A. For example, Figure 7.9 continues with the work products associated with the CUS.2 process *Manage customer needs*.

The work product characteristics listed in Part 5 Version 2.00 Annex C can be used when reviewing the potential inputs and outputs of an organization's process implementation. The characteristics are provided as guidance for the attributes to look for in a particular sample work product to help assess if the process that created the work product is adequate. Qualified assessor judgment is needed to use this information to ensure that the application domain, business purpose, development methodology, size of the organization, and so on are taken into consideration as well as the characteristics of the work products. An example of the characteristics of work product 83) Customer Request (taken from Annex C) is shown in Figure 7.10.

CUS.2   Manage customer needs

The purpose of the *Manage customer needs* process is to manage the gathering, processing, and tracking of ongoing customer needs and requirements throughout the operational life of the software; to establish a software requirements baseline which serves as the basis for the project's software work products, and activities; and to manage changes to this baseline. As a result of successful implementation of the process:

- clear and ongoing communication with the customer will be established
- documented and agreed customer requirements will be defined, with managed changes
- customer requirements will be established as a baseline for project use
- a mechanism will be established for ongoing monitoring of customer needs
- a mechanism will be established for ensuring that customers are easily able to determine the status and disposition of their requests.

Base practices:

CUS.2.1   Obtain customer requirements and requests. Obtain customer requirements and requests through direct solicitation of customer and user input and through review of customer business proposals, target hardware environment, and other documents bearing on customer requirements.

CUS.2.2   Agree on requirements. Obtain agreement across teams on the customer's requirements, obtaining the appropriate sign-offs by representatives of all teams and other parties contractually bound to work to these requirements.

CUS.2.3   Establish customer requirements baseline. Document the customer's requirements and establish as a baseline for project use.

CUS.2.4   Manage customer requirements changes. Manage all changes made to the customer requirements to ensure those who are affected by the changes are able to assess the impact and risks, and initiate appropriate change control and mitigation actions.

CUS.2.5   Understand customer expectations. Review with customers and users their requirements and requests to better understand their needs and expectations.

CUS.2.6   Keep customers informed. Keep customers informed about the status of and disposition of their requirements and requests.

  Note: This may include joint meetings with the customer or formal communication to review the status for their requirements and requests; refer SUP.6, *Perform Joint Reviews*.

Figure 7.8: Part 5 Version 2.00 clause 5—the process, process purpose, and associated base practices.

CUS.2 Manage customer needs	
Associated Work Products:	
Input	Output
83) Customer Request 52) Customer Requirements 21) Analysis Results 22) Risk Analysis record 51) Contract 96) Change History 6) Work breakdown structure	83) Customer Request 46) Market Analysis 87) Communication Mechanism 31) Review Records 44) Product Needs Assessment 82) Customer Support Procedures 50) Commitment / Agreements / Agreements 52) Customer Requirements 51) Contract 95) Change Control 96) Change History 17) Project Plan 87) Communication Mechanism 58) Traceability record/mapping 97) Corrective Actions

Figure 7.9: The work products associated with the CUS.2 process.

83)	Customer request record (internal or external)	– Identifies request purpose, such as:
		  – new development
		  – enhancement
		  – internal customer
		  – operations
		  – documentation
		  – informational
		– Identifies request status information, such as:
		  – date opened
		  – current status
		  – date assigned and responsible owner
		  – date verified
		  – date closed
		....

Figure 7.10: Work product 83 characteristics.

The capability dimension—indicators of process capability

The capability dimension is directly mapped to that of the reference model and adopts the same capability levels and process attributes. Evolving process capability is expressed in the assessment model in terms of process attributes grouped into capability levels. The attributes and capability levels are identical to those defined in the reference model.

Process attributes are features of a process that can be evaluated on a scale of achievement, providing a measure of the capability of the process. They are applicable to all processes. Each process attribute describes a facet of the overall capability of managing and improving the effectiveness of a process in achieving its purpose and contributing to the business goals of the organization.

A capability level is a set of attribute(s) that work together to provide a major enhancement in the capability to perform a process. The levels constitute a rational way of progressing through improvement of the capability of any process and are defined in Part 2.

Within the assessment model, the measure of capability is based upon the set of nine process attributes. Process attributes are used to determine whether a process has reached a given capability. Each attribute measures a particular aspect of the process capability.

The attributes are evaluated on a four-point ordinal scale of achievement, as defined in Part 2 Version 2.00. They therefore provide a more detailed insight into the specific aspects of process capability required to support process improvement and capability determination.

Following the definition of each process attribute, the assessment model provides a set of management practices that, if adequately performed in the process instantiation, achieve the characteristics of the attribute. The practices are management activities of a generic type and are intended to be applicable to all processes. They are designed around the achievement of the principal management functions of Planning, Organizing, Resourcing, and Controlling. There are usually, but not necessarily, four practices for each attribute. The example given here (Figure 7.11) is from Part 5 Version 2.00 clause 6 and shows the capability Level 1 Performed process with its associated process attribute and management practice.

The management practices (defined in clause 6) are related to the process attributes and capability levels defined in the process capability dimension of the reference model (Part 2 Version 2.00). Evidence of management practice performance supports the judgment of the degree of achievement of the process attribute. Management practices with their associated attribute indicators are the indicators of process capability. Management practices are the means of

---

6.2 Level 1: Performed process

The implemented process achieves its defined purpose.

The following attributes of the process demonstrate the achievement of this level:

> **PA 1.1   Process performance attribute.**
> The extent to which the execution of the process uses a set of practices that are initiated and followed using identifiable input work products to produce identifiable output work products that are adequate to satisfy the purpose of the process.

- In order to achieve this capability, a process needs to have base practices of the process implemented and work products produced that satisfy the process purpose.
  The related **Management Practice** to achieve this process attribute is:

ID	Management practices
1.1.1	**Ensure that base practices are performed** to satisfy the purpose of the process.

Figure 7.11: Part 5 Version 2.00 clause 6.

---

achieving the capabilities addressed by process attributes. Management practices are linked with their attribute indicators:

1. practice performance characteristics that provide guidance on the implementation of the practice
2. resource and infrastructure characteristics that provide mechanisms for assisting in the management of the process
3. associated processes from the process dimension that support the management practice.

Specific management practices are linked to each process attribute as shown in clause 6. The set of management practices is intended to be applicable to all processes in the process dimension of the model.

The attribute indicators help to establish objective evidence that the management practices associated with the process attribute are being performed (see Annex B).

The example shown here (Figure 7.12) is of process attribute 1.1 and its associated indicators of process capability.

Process Attribute 1.1	Process performance attribute. The extent to which the execution of the process uses a set of practices that are initiated and followed using identifiable input work products to produce identifiable output work products that are adequate to satisfy the purpose of the process.
MP 1.1.1	Perform base practices to provide work products and required support to a customer.
Practice performance characteristics for MP 1.1.	The process representatives can demonstrate that the base practices for process are used (even though the process may not be documented) to achieve the purpose of the process. In each organizational unit assessed, evidence exists that each base practice is actually performed. Samples of the input and output work products similar to those specified in the process in Part 2 of this International Standard exist and have the characteristics to indicate an adequate implementation (see Annex C). A mechanism exists to distribute the work products associated with the process.
Resource and infrastructure characteristics for MP 1.1.	See Process dimension.
Associated Processes	This practice applies to each process within the scope of the assessment. Note To help evaluate this management practice, use the Indicators of process performance defined in Clause 5 and Annexes A and C.

Figure 7.12: Process attribute 1.1 and its associated indicators of process capability.

Conformance issues

The model conformance requirements are defined in Part 2. Each of the elements defined for compatibility is defined in clause 7 of Part 2 and addressed in clause 7 of Part 5. The assessment model can be used in the performance of assessments that meet the requirements set down in Part 2 and it may also be used as an example for other model developers. Since this model has been explicitly constructed to be an elaboration of the reference model, the conformance claim is relatively trivial. For other models, particularly ones with a different architecture, the demonstration of conformance may be more difficult, requiring more detail in the mapping. The requirements for compatibility enable comparison of outputs from assessments using different, but compatible, models and methods. The assessment model in Part 5 Version 2.00 is a fully-conformant model.

Supporting assessments

The assessment model and its indicator set are designed to support assessments. The assessment model however, does not provide a method and such provision is outside the scope of Part 5 Version 2.00. Embedding the model in an AI supports the assessment and the recording of the qualified assessors' judgments about indicators and judgments of process capability. Instruments can be paper-based or online tools.

The AI chosen should support the scope and purpose of the assessment and should be based on a conformant model.

An AI can be a valuable tool in organizing the assessment inputs and outputs. It is helpful to have the actual conformant model itself embedded in the tool to help the qualified assessors collect and attribute the information they collect to the processes and capability levels. As a repository for assessment information, an AI provides the basis for software process improvement, capability determination and, measuring improvement from one assessment to the next.

AIs should facilitate:

- adapting of the AI to accommodate extended processes, limited scope modularity, or intended distribution of tools to collect the assessment data incrementally
- customizing the user interface—format for data input, method of recording data, and so on
- customizing the format of the results—presentation format, output record format, and so on
- meeting the assessment requirements defined in Part 3 Version 2.00.

Guidance on the selection and use of AI is in Part 4 Version 2.00 and has been elaborated on in Chapter 5.

Acknowledgments

This chapter has briefly described the development of Part 5 of the SPICE Project. This Part has been the largest and most complex part of the emerging standard and has evolved at a considerable pace over three years. This task has involved recognized software professionals from all over the world, each of whom has contributed a wealth of knowledge and experience in the production of the assessment model. Since large sections of this chapter use their words, it is only appropriate that they should share the recognition. The core AI team was lead by Mary Campbell (US/Bellcore), Peter Hitchcock (Canada/TUNS University), and Arnoldo Diaz (Mexico/Servios en Informática) and consisted of Kazuyuki Aoyama (Japan/Hitachi Limited), Dave Banister (UK/ British Aerospace), Carrie Buchman (US/AlliedSignal), Anthony Coletta (Italy/Tecnopolis), Janne Järvinen (Finland/CCC Software professionals Oy), Paul Madden (Ireland/Mari Group), Jeff Perry (UK/Nortel Technology), Helen Thomson (UK/ Faxbase Ltd. and University of East Anglia), and John Vernon (Ireland/Mari Group). There are many, many others who contributed their time and expertise in reviewing and commenting on the AI drafts. Many thanks to the core and extended core teams and to all those who contributed in making this such an exceptional standard.

References

1. *Assessment Instrument Product Description*, Version 1.00, 24 June 1994.

2. *Assessment Instrument Guide*, Version 1.00, 21 May 1995.

3. WG10/N016R, *Product Specification for a Software Process Assessment Standard*, Version 0.05, 3 June 1993.

4. WG10/N017R, *Requirements Specification for a Software Process Assessment Standard*, Version 1.00 June 1993.

5. *Software Process Assessment—Part 5: Construction, Selection and Use of Assessment Instruments and Tools*, Version 1.00, June 1995

6. *Software Process Assessment—Part 5: An Assessment Model and Indicator Guidance*, Version 2.00, Oct. 1996.

7. ISO/IEC 12207, *Information Technology—Software Life Cycle Processes*, 22 Feb. 1995.

8

Guidelines for Process Improvement

Pascal Jansen
Finsiel, Italy

Joc Sanders
Center for Software Engineering, Ireland

Part 7[1] of the SPICE product set has the crucial scope of helping users of the emerging standard understand the *spirit* with which it is being developed. In particular, users will find that one of the fundamental values of the SPICE document set will be the stimulation of improvement efforts triggered by the results of *self-assessments*.

This chapter emphasizes the lessons learned in putting together the text of the guide. In this chapter, readers will find:

- a definition of the product and a presentation, discussion, and interpretation of the requirements the product must meet, as initially set out during the requirements definition phase
- Part 7 put into context: its position in both the functional and the conceptual architecture of the complete product suite and key relationships with other products are described
- the key ideas behind the first draft of the product captured and the evolution of these ideas and new concepts
- in closing, a synopsis of Version 2.00 of the product as it stands today.

Product specification

Interpreting the requirements

A number of functional requirements for the emerging standard were explicitly allocated to Part 7 prior to its development. The current allocation differs slightly, however, from the preliminary allocation indicated in the "Allocation Matrix" contained in N016R.[2] The reason for this change is due to a combination of factors:

- partly because some requirements, originally allocated only to other SPICE products, were felt to be, to some extent, within the scope of Part 7 as well
- partly because some requirements were believed to be not necessarily being met by Part 7 at all.

The result is that *Part 7: Guide for Use in Process Improvement* was expected to contribute chiefly to the following functional requirements[*]:

1. Provide guidance for improving software processes aligned to business goals including its starting point and target (D).

   The requirements dictate Part 7's main reasons for being. Requirement 1 clearly indicates the spirit with which assessment results should be obtained and used: *to improve with a view to finding better ways to satisfy the organization's business goals.* It is Part 7's role to ensure that users of the emerging standard will understand that the value of SPICE-conformant assessments resides not only in knowing to what extent the organization's practices conform to a reference model, but primarily in using process assessment as a tool to express the current and desired state of the practices so that changes will allow for better alignment to known business goals.

2. Be applicable at the project and organizational levels with connectivity between the two (N).

   Requirement 2 calls for guidance for process improvement in which improvements are dealt with at different levels in the organization.

---

[*]Note that the requirements have been renumbered for convenience to the reader, leaving the original N017R requirement references in parentheses. See Chapter 3, Appendix A for the full listing of requirements.

In fact, the *coherent improvement program* in N944R³ already promotes the idea of senior management involvement at the organizational level, while changes themselves are most likely to occur at the project level.

3. Focus on process but also address people and the application of technology (O) and the emerging standard will provide guidance on how an organization can define and use quantitative measures of effectiveness, the effectiveness being related to its business needs (Q2).

   These requirements focus on other substantial aspects for which Part 7 is responsible. People issues are the soft elements that can play a significant role in eliminating natural barriers to change and therefore typically are to be considered in a product such as Part 7. Technology-application issues are believed to have more *indirect* impacts on software process improvement in the sense that technological innovation can often be related to people issues, such as training and motivation.

   These requirements, however, also bring to the surface the issue of *measurement of effectiveness*. The debate on effectiveness is a central issue and is most probably the most controversial and difficult requirement to deal with for various reasons. One reason is that it is desirable for a standard method that assesses the goodness of processes to be based on the degree to which the processes are effective. Any specific measure of effectiveness would only make sense in a particular situation, making this measurement immediately a very subjective and context-dependent judgment.

4. Ensure the organization's ability to both "set and realize defined, achievable goals for productivity and/or development cycle time, linked to business needs and project requirements" (B2) and "manage the process to achieve a repeatable software process" (C3) are made visible in the assessments results.

   The requirements in 4 were seen as important information that Part 7 simply would make use of in framing its advice for improvement. In fact, the two requirements point to the value an assessment ideally will give the organization and therefore to what information it may want to look for when analyzing assessment results.

5. Support process capability determination for risk identification and analysis within an organization (E).

Requirement 5 was considered to be partially met by Part 7 since it is required to point to the possibility of carrying out a process capability determination when risk identification and analysis is useful.

6. Support output as process profiles that allow views at different levels of detail. The profiling method should support comparisons against other similar entities or industry norms (R).

    Even though it was recognized that Part 7 would not play a major role in meeting requirement 6, it was felt that the profiles and their use would be extensively mentioned in its guidance.

7. Require that agreement is reached over ownership and confidentiality of assessment results prior to assessment (S) and give guidance on the selection of qualified assessors and the makeup of the assessment team (T1).

    Similarly, the two requirements in requirement 7 would see Part 7 involved in a supporting role as well. This support would come in the form of specific references to Parts 3 and 4, within the guidance on how to prepare for an assessment.

Finally Part 7 was felt to contribute to all *nonfunctional* requirements as well. This contribution has a significant impact when considering that nonfunctional requirements must *"be culturally independent"* (I) and *"not presume specific organizational structures, management philosophies, software life cycle models, software technologies, or software methods"* (J). These requirements practically leave out a number of solution-oriented practices for software process improvement that in and of themselves may be good ideas, but that do not deserve a place in an emerging standard that should be applicable to all technical environments and cultures.

The language to be used in this part had to be necessarily restricted to general principles and criteria or simply common sense. This approach would enable us to show the reasoning behind the use of assessment results for process improvement. It would not preclude any specific method or technique, while at the same time, it would leave the details of the improvement to these techniques.

Another nonfunctional requirement stating the need to *"harmonize with ISO 9000 series of standards"* (V) had a strong influence in deciding to use a similar type of guidance document, ISO 9004-4,[6] to help us further in finding the right tradeoffs for the contents of the product.

Inputs used for the development of the product

With respect to inputs to the product, a number of contributions were used. From the beginning, views on process improvement were presented from the Bootstrap experience,[7] the SEI in carrying out the IDEAL model for process improvement,[8] and the Dublin-based Center for Software Engineering's *Framework for Success* methodology for process improvement.[9]

Articles on process effectiveness were also helpful,[10] as were the guidebook from the Software Productivity Consortium[11] and the ami handbook.[12] Finally, ISO 9004-4[6] was another main source for the development of Part 7.

First version

The scope of the Process Improvement Guide

Process improvement essentially means a number of different things to different people. It may involve management issues (for example, management style, strategy, competitive advantage, and business plans), people issues (motivation, barriers to change, and the role of middle management), culture (organizational values, communication channels, and information hiding), quality improvement techniques (TQM, root-cause analysis, and Plan-Do-Check-Act), change management techniques (business process reengineering, and cost-benefit analysis), all of which are aspects that may be perceived as more or less essential to process improvement in general. *A resolution was taken to make the SPICE model of improvement consistent with the outside world and improvement processes in other disciplines.*

The issue of how *software* specific the guidance should and can be had to be considered:

- Should there be a description of how to avoid major risks when deciding to proceed with software process improvement?
- Is software process improvement in itself substantially different from generic process improvement and in what ways?

The discussion of this issue focused on the need to understand what makes it different or harder to improve software processes. In the end, it was not clear as to the extent to which business improvement should be kept separate from software process improvement, especially if alignment to business goals is a crucial success factor.

In synthesis, the question to be addressed was more one of understanding where to *stop*, than of where to *start*. This question was not simple. A decision as to whether or not to include a more generic improvement model had to be made.

The need for a generic process improvement model

A strong reason in favor of a generic model in addition to the specific one is that most organizations will be using the SPICE document set as a tool within a broader concept of process improvement. People using the SPICE document set will need to see the context in which the more specific model is applied in order to relate it to the real world in their organization. The need therefore exists to provide Part 7 users with a simple generic approach or model for process improvement as the *context* in which the SPICE-specific model for applying process assessment for process improvement is applied.

This generic model is also the place where some high level guidance about process improvement could be given, to make sure that people using the SPICE document set for process improvement are at least jogged into considering some of the wider issues outside the proper scope of Part 7, such as culture and the management of process improvement.

The idea of describing a generic process improvement model in Part 7 existed nearly from the beginning. The SEI IDEAL model[8] was an excellent example of one possible way to do it. The issue that came up immediately, however, was how detailed the description of such a model should be.

It was felt that there is a limit to the amount of detail the emerging standard *can* cover, partly to satisfy nonfunctional requirements such as J—not to presume specific organizational structures, management philosophies, and so on—and partly to allow for consultants to use specific techniques that may be useful only in specific circumstances or within specific sectors.

These arguments were reflected in the criteria that was used to select a generic model. ISO 9004-4 would satisfy the criteria and therefore could be selected as the basis for a generic process improvement model, provided that a number of minor changes were made, such as the replacement of the term *quality improvement* by *process improvement*. The main advantage of reusing ISO 9004-4 concepts resides in the fact that every sentence in it is already the result of careful wording and international consensus on what such a guide should or shouldn't contain.

The decisions that were finally made were:

1. Adopt ISO 9004-4 as the structure of the *Process Improvement Guide*.
2. Selectively extract ISO 9004-4 text considered relevant for Part 7.

3. Merge it with the appropriate *software* and/or *SPICE*-specific guidance at hand.

Considering the initial questions raised about the scope of the *Process Improvement Guide* it is neither restricted to process improvement only in the context of process assessment nor is it exclusively focused on process improvement of software. However, it does contain elements that are considered to be important for software process improvement to happen effectively.

The way with which effectiveness measures are dealt

From a technical perspective, perhaps one of the most important issues in Part 7 issue is how to deal with *effectiveness measures*. As was anticipated, the issue is a controversial one (involving not only Part 7). One of the goals of the SPICE document set was to provide an "assessment of effectiveness."[3] Initial drafts of Part 3 considered effectiveness measures to be part of the results of a SPICE-conformant assessment. It was quickly recognized, however, that a true measure of effectiveness can come only from organizations with Level 4 or 5 processes: from those organizations that are setting goals and devising metrics to measure those goals. Moreover, requirement 3—*"the standard will provide guidance on how an organization can define and use quantitative measures of effectiveness, the effectiveness being related to business needs"*—implicitly states that it is not possible currently to define standard measures of effectiveness since such measures are a function of the organization's specific business needs.

The decision was taken to drop effectiveness measures as part of the results of a SPICE-conformant assessment and to introduce the concept of *practice adequacy* instead, with a small element of effectiveness built into it. This small element was related to how well a deployed practice supports the Part 2 purpose of the process to be judged in the context of size, complexity, and criticality of the software product. Part 7 would then provide guidance on how to deal with the *true* measures of effectiveness.

Part of the spirit behind the SPICE Project initiative has been to recognize, from the beginning of the project, that there may not always be sufficient cost-benefit to the organization to fully implement every process—addressing every base and management practice of Part 5—in its attempt to increase its capability level. However, instead it should always make sense to consider improving process capability in the light of the organization's specific business needs and circumstances.

What will guide an organization in choosing the increases in capability that are considered to be beneficial are indeed effectiveness measures. It is those measures, together with the process-adequacy measures, that will tell an organization how much more can be invested into the sophistication of a process to enable it to give positive returns—to increase its contribution in achieving defined business goals—and to find those *improvement opportunities*. In extreme cases, it could be thought that processes with a capability level should be decreased to be more cost-effective. The guidance that therefore needs to be provided by Part 7 is related to how effectiveness measures can be used to evaluate improvement opportunities.

A substantial amount of text was included on what process attribute and capability level ratings (part of the assessment output) mean in the context of improvement, what effectiveness measures mean in the context of process improvement, and how to use both of them in an integrated way to support process improvement.

To enforce the view that the two types of measures indeed serve the same purpose, but in a complementary manner, a framework was established that covers both business goals and improvement actions and uses either process attribute and capability level ratings or effectiveness measures as a link between the two. The decision was made to restructure the document to incorporate examples of how the measurement framework could be applied in concrete terms.

Adding risk management concepts

A new concept was identified that had to be introduced into the product: *risk management*. This concept was covered by including guidance in two ways:

- when to consider the risk of not achieving improvement goals— typically useful to understand the urgency and to set the priority of improvement initiatives
- when to consider the risk of an improvement action failure— principally to assure the proper commitment and organizational support needed to carry out the action.

In fact, the issue of risk management was a crucial one in many respects. First, it helps convince executives of the need to improve, since high risk means probability to incur some serious loss. Second, process improvement is often depicted as being of low risk and high return, but only if adequately managed. If not, a number of barriers to change may not be understood and may cause failure of the program.

The solution adopted in Part 7 was to point to the need to consider risks and to add some guidance on how to do it throughout the text.

Refining management of process improvement

Significant effort was devoted to the issue of streamlining the planning terminology related to the different *levels* of planning used in the PIG. There was a need to refer consistently to the same *process improvement program plan* in different stages of its life cycle, completing it in one stage with the action plan derived from analysis of assessment results. It was seen as important to use that plan as the basis for establishing a level of confidence within a process capability determination activity to ensure alignment of that plan with the more general *business plan* of the organization. It was also important to distinguish a separate, more detailed and operational *process improvement project plan* when needed.

Some specific management issues had to be given particular attention:

- The change in the role of middle management as teamwork principles of process improvement are put into place was believed to be very crucial to the software sector. This change in role is partly because technical middle management may want to refuse the transition from enforcer to facilitator and partly because software production pro- vides better results in a cooperative environment, especially since co- operation is dependent upon educated staff and high intellectual engagement.
- There is a need to emphasize the fact that if an organization is really serious about supplying a quality product with reasonable business returns, that organization must be serious about continuous process improvement and acknowledge the schedule and cost impacts to every project that is part of the process improvement effort. If these costs cannot be aligned with current business goals, either the business goals need to be modified or the organization should not attempt to compete in its product area: finding difficulty with releasing re- sources is counterproductive to process improvement.

The general consensus was to point out possible problems that could arise with managing process improvement, without giving solutions that always tend to be culturally dependent (nonfunctional requirement I: *be culturally independent*). Part 7 therefore refers to responsibilities more than to explicit functions to assign. This approach also allows small organizations, for example, to have the same person handle more responsibilities and still being able to use the guidance in the product.

Evolution to Version 2.00

This section describes in more detail the actual contents of Part 7, Version 2.00, with the *Process Improvement Guide* as it stands today. Note that the concepts that underlie the product did not evolve significantly after Version 1.00. Only minor and straightforward changes had to be incorporated in Version 2.00: some changes were due to comments from the ballot that had to be addressed, while others were needed to maintain the product alignment with those parts that underwent major architectural changes.

Scope of the product

The product essentially provides guidance on using Software Process Assessment as the primary means of understanding the current state of an organization's software processes and on using the results of the assessment to formulate and prioritize improvement plans.

This guidance is embodied within a general framework for performing software process improvement in a continuous cycle that is built on the framework for quality improvement contained in ISO 9004-4. It is therefore assumed that the reader is familiar with the concepts in ISO 9000-4.

Additional guidance is provided in Part 7 on how to:

- measure software process effectiveness, which is embodied in a second, general framework for the use of process metrics in software process improvement
- deal with management issues for software process improvement
- recognize cultural issues in the context of software process improvement.

The guidance is aimed primarily at the management of an organization considering or undertaking a software process improvement program, possibly as a result of a process capability determination, as well as at members of improvement teams, particularly leaders and facilitators, software engineers, and external consultants helping organizations to undertake software process improvement.

The guidance provided does not presume specific organizational structures, management philosophies, software life-cycle models, or software development methods. The concepts and principles are appropriate for the full range of different business needs, application domains, and sizes of organization so that they can be used by all types of software organizations to guide their improvement activities.

An organization can select all or any subset of the software processes from the reference model (as defined in Part 2) for assessment and improvement in the light of its particular circumstances and needs. The guidance provided in Part 7 can also be used with other compatible process models.

The guidance provides a framework for implementing improvements as a continuous cycle, but there is no reason why the organization could not employ the guidance for a single cycle of improvement activity.

Outline of the topics addressed by the product

The main topics addressed by Part 7 are organized according to the following main headings:

- an overview of process improvement—the factors that drive software process improvement and the general principles that underpin it
- a methodology for process improvement—an eight-step model for improving software processes within a continuous improvement cycle
- cultural issues—aspects of organizational culture that are critical for successful process improvement
- management—software process improvement from a management perspective, including an overall framework for process measurement.

The guide also contains annexes that provide supplementary information, including examples of the use of the process measurement framework, a very instructive case study of the application of the process improvement guidelines, and a cross-reference to ISO 9004-4.

An overview of process improvement

The key aspects to be considered when determining whether or not to implement a process improvement program are:

- **What are the main drivers for process improvement?**

  The needs and business goals of an organization are often centered around achieving enhanced customer satisfaction and greater competitiveness. For organizations with a dependence on software, these key management concerns become drivers that initiate software process improvement throughout the organization. Its goals may be higher software quality, lower development and maintenance costs, shorter time to market, and increased predictability and controllability of software products and processes.

- **What is the context within which process improvement takes place?**

  The inputs and outputs of a generic process improvement program are shown in Figure 8.1.

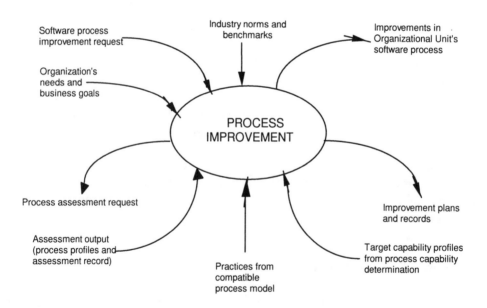

Figure 8.1: Process improvement context.

- *What are the general principles behind software process improvements?*

  Management must set a target for improvement based on the organization's needs and business goals. Software process improvement is best considered as a continuous process, where an organization moves continually within an improvement cycle. Within this cycle improvement is accomplished in a planned series of steps or specific improvement actions, such as introducing new or changed practices into software processes or removing old ones. An important step in the improvement cycle, however, is the execution of some form of data gathering to establish the initial state and subsequently to confirm the improvements. Capability profiles, combined with process effectiveness data, are used to compare current process performance against the target. Software process improvement plans and records can be used to support process capability determination.

- *Who is usually involved in process improvement?*

  Successful changes to the software process start at any level in the organization. However, senior management leadership is required to launch and sustain a change effort and to provide continuing resources and impetus, although ultimately, everyone in the organization is involved.

Guidelines for software process improvement

The key aspects to be considered using the eight-step model, shown in Figure 8.2, are:

1. *How does an improvement program usually start?*

   Step 1 of the improvement cycle, *Examine organization's needs*, starts with a recognition of the organization's needs and business goals, usually based on one of the main drivers for process improvement. This recognition can be derived from any of the forces driving the organization: a mission statement or a long-term vision, a declining market share, feedback from customers, competitiveness changes in the market, and so on. From that information, objectives and priorities for the process improvement initiative are identified, then clearly stated and understood. Executive awareness is developed and managerial and financial commitments are obtained. The process improvement program should form a part of the organization's overall strategic business plan.

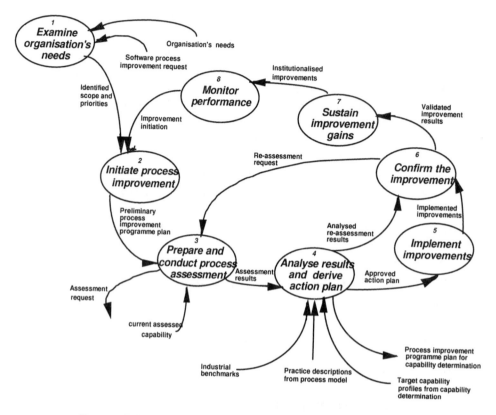

Figure 8.2: Software process improvement steps.

2. Once the objectives are known, what has to be done?

Step 2, *Initiate process improvement*, emphasizes the need to consider a process improvement program as a project in its own right that is planned and managed accordingly. A *process improvement program plan* should be produced, including the improvement goals, a preliminary identification of the improvement scope in terms of processes to be improved and the organizational boundaries affected by it, an outline of all improvement steps, the identification of key roles, the allocation of adequate resources, and the establishment of appropriate milestones and review points.

3. What has to be done to conduct an assessment?

Step 3, *Prepare for and conduct a process assessment*, provides all the necessary guidance to define the assessment inputs associated with a

SPICE-conformant assessment being carried out for improvement purposes. In particular, the choice of a qualified assessor, the definition of a detailed purpose statement, and the identification of an appropriate assessment scope that leads to the selection of the process instances to be assessed are all important issues to be considered. In addition to the required assessment outputs, more specific information can be collected that may help determine improvement priorities afterward.

4. *How is an action plan established?*

In step 4, *Analyze assessment output and derive action plan*, information collected during the assessment is analyzed in the light of the organization's needs. Improvement areas are identified and prioritized, based on the risks related either to not improving an area or to incurring in a failure of specific improvement actions. Effectiveness measures and industry norms or benchmarks, if available, are other possible sources of information that may help in identifying priorities. Targets for improvement should be quantified for each priority area, including either target values for process effectiveness, target capability profiles, or combinations of the two. Specific actions should be developed to meet the quantified targets. The set of agreed actions should be documented as the *process improvement action plan* and should be integrated with the process improvement program plan.

5. *How are improvements implemented?*

Step 5, *Implement improvements*, illustrates the issue of choosing an operational approach to implement improvement actions. In general, specific process improvement projects should be initiated, each concerned with implementing one or more process improvement actions.

A detailed *implementation plan* should be developed for each project. Personnel implementing the actions and affected by them should be involved or consulted while developing the plan and evaluating alternatives, both to draw on their expertise and to enlist their cooperation. The plan should include arrangements to capture cost and resource usage data, especially if it is desirable to carry out a cost-benefit analysis. It is critical while carrying out an improvement project that due account is taken of human and cultural factors. The process improvement project should be monitored by the organization's management against the process improvement project plan.

6. *How are improvements confirmed?*

Step 6, *Confirm improvements*, says that management should be involved both to approve the results and to evaluate whether or not the organization's needs have been met. If, after improvement actions have been taken, measurements show that process goals and improvement targets have not been achieved, it may be desirable to redefine the process improvement project or activity by returning to an appropriate earlier step. Risks of the improvements can be reevaluated to confirm that they remain acceptable.

7. *How are improvements sustained at the new level of performance?*

Within step 7, *Sustain improvement gains*, the improved software process should be used by all those to whom it is applicable, especially if an improved process has been piloted in a restricted area or on a specific group of projects. Management is required to monitor the institutionalization of the improved process and to give encouragement when necessary. Responsibilities for monitoring should be defined, as well as how the monitoring will be done, for example by using appropriate effectiveness measurements.

8. *What happens next?*

Step 8, *Monitor performance*, is the final step of the model, but not of the improvement effort. In this step, the performance of the organization's software processes should be continuously monitored and new process improvement projects should be selected and implemented as part of a continuing process improvement program, especially since additional improvements are always possible.

Further process assessments can be an important component of the continuing improvement program, especially when changing organizational needs indicate a requirement to achieve higher capability levels or when there is a need to give a fresh impetus to improvement.

Cultural issues

The key aspects of cultural issues to be considered are:

- *What impact on management responsibility and leadership does software process improvement usually have?*

The responsibility for leadership and for creating the environment for continuous process improvement belongs to all levels of management, but particularly to the highest. Senior management should be aware of how the success of the organization depends on quality software and its ability to improve software processes. Middle management, often largely concerned with meeting project commitments in the short term, may pay little attention to process improvement benefits that tend to be medium to long term and often resent diverting scarce project resources to process improvement projects. One solution is to ensure senior management is committed to the impact of process improvement actions on the projects to which they are applied. Furthermore, analysis may suggest the need to change the role of middle management: instilling teamwork principles and placing the emphasis on communication could change the relationship between middle management and development teams from enforcement to facilitation, and from imposing ideas to helping teams develop their own ideas. In fact, software production that requires educated staff and high intellectual engagement provides better results in a cooperative environment.

- *How are specific values, attitudes and behaviors affected by software process improvement?*

  Process assessment can help an organization understand which changes are necessary in values, attitudes, and behaviors. If current values, attitudes, and behaviors do not contribute to meeting the organization's needs, the process improvement program should include appropriate cultural change. Effective process improvement often implies a new set of shared values, attitudes, and behaviors, that may include, for example, involving the entire software supply chain in the process improvement program, from suppliers to customers. The recognition process and individual-reward system may help to encourage the attitudes and behavior necessary for successful process improvement.

- *How can staff motivation be ensured in achieving process improvement goals?*

  Staff motivation to achieve goals for improving the software process, whether they are set in terms of using of good software engineering practice that increase process capability levels, or of the effectiveness with which the process meets the organization's needs, will be strengthened if progress is made visible through regular measurement. Furthermore, the goals have to be understandable, challenging, and pertinent.

- *How do communication and teamwork affect software process improvement?*

  When analyzing assessment results it is important to look for the organizational and personal barriers that cause a lack of communication and teamwork. These barriers interfere with the effectiveness and efficiency of the software process. Communication and teamwork require trust and skills. Good teamwork skills improve the ability to perform activities with the high degree of parallel work typical of software projects.

- *How do education and training work within the context of software process improvement?*

  Education and training programs are important in creating and maintaining an environment where process improvement can flourish. Training specifically in process improvement concepts will increase the organization's readiness for process improvement. Training should also be considered as a means of improving the quality and effectiveness of teamwork skills.

Management

The key aspects to be considered in managing software process improvement are:

- *What is the best way to organize for software process improvement?*

  The organizational principles for quality improvement described in ISO 9004-4 apply to software process improvement. Part 7 explicitly addresses responsibilities for process improvement activities that are divided amongst senior management, the process improvement program, process improvement projects, process owners, and the organizational units.

- *How can process improvement be measured?*

  The role of measurements is crucial in software process improvement.

Measurements are needed to show quantitatively the current status of processes and practices against a general understanding of software engineering best practices—process capability level ratings— and to show to what extent software processes are effective in achieving the organization's needs and business goals—effectiveness measures. Process capability level ratings and effectiveness measures can be used together to support software process improvement and to ensure that investment in process improvement is as cost-effective as possible. Figure 8.3 illustrates a framework for measuring processes that can be applied with both process capability level/process attribute ratings and effectiveness measures, integrating them to fulfill the improvement purpose.

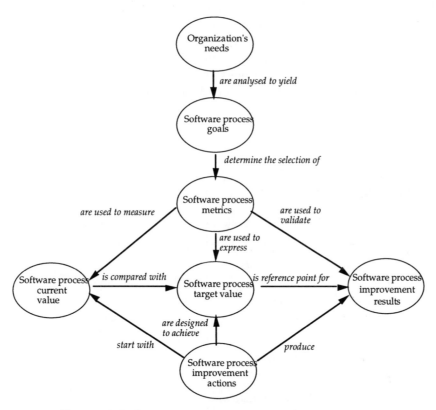

Figure 8.3: Process measurement framework.

- **What examples are there that show how the application of the framework can be** *performed?*

  The following table illustrates that the goal of obtaining a large market share for an innovative product might be achieved by reducing the time to market, improving product quality, or both. Reducing time to market can be achieved by establishing reuse in the software organization and reinforcing configuration management and project management. Improving product quality can be achieved by improved testing and quality control, but possibly also by establishing a proper reuse strategy.

- **What are the relationships between the different levels of process improvement plans?**

  The planning of a software process improvement program is an iterative activity, continuing through all phases of the improvement cycle. Three main levels of planning should be performed resulting in a business plan, a process improvement program plan, and process improvement project plans. The organization's business plan should include software process improvement goals that are aligned with the organization's needs and business goals, as well as resource forecasts and time constraints for the implementation of process improvement.

Organizational needs	Software process goals	Software process capability metrics	Software process effectiveness metrics	Software process targets	Software process improvement results
Obtain a large market share for an innovative product to secure additional financing	1. Short software process time to market 2. High software quality (high reliability); 3. Good Engineering and Support processes and reuse strategy	Capability levels of all processes in the ENG and SUP process categories and the ORG.5 (Provide software engineering infrastructure) process	Calendar time from requirements to delivery	Raise Level 1 ENG, SUP and ORG.5 processes to Level 2	All processes at desired capability level

The process improvement program plan is an evolving document that first exists in a preliminary form when initiating the program, then is completed after the process assessment with the detailed action plan, and is subsequently used and updated during the monitoring of the improvement actions' implementation. Finally when the improvement actions are complex and involve more organizational units, they might need to be implemented as several separate improvement projects, each with its own improvement project plan. Since process improvement projects often involve higher risks than projects that are repetitive in nature, a careful and detailed risk analysis should be performed at each step of each project.

Acknowledgments

The authors of this chapter wish to thank all of the experts and practitioners in the field who contributed their valuable views during the development phase of the guide. Our gratefulness goes in particular to the Part 7 editors Adriana Bicego (Etnoteam, Italy) and Pasi Kuvaja (University of OULU, Finland), to all the other members of the core team, and of course to the many reviewers who did not hesitate to make us aware of sometimes very conflicting ideas. All had impact on the contents of the final product.

Some of these contributions were referenced specifically in this chapter:

- initial inputs to the product came from Adriana Bicego and Pasi Kuvaja (Bootstrap experience), Marylin Bush (SEI's IDEAL model), and Joc Sanders (experience in helping SME's heading for ISO 9000 and "Framework for Success")

- the position paper on the minimal scope of the PIG was provided by Pascal Jansen

- the position paper that discusses the rationale for a generic process improvement model came from Joc and Marty Sanders, and it was Jean-Normand Drouin who first proposed the reuse of ISO 9004-4 concepts

- the fortunate circumstance of having Annie Combelles contributing (known for her experience with the European "ami" method for applying metrics in software organizations) greatly helped in the discussions and in the decisions made in the way effectiveness measures are dealt with, and Marty Sanders provided the first list of sample effectiveness measures (in the sense of metric) for different levels of process sophistication to be integrated with ami

- the comments on Version 0.03 that helped us understand how to introduce risk management concepts came from Linda Ibrahim of the SEI.

References

1. ISO/IEC JTC1/SC7/WG10, *Software Process Assessment Part 7: Guide for Use in Process Improvement*, Document WG10/N117, PDTR, Oct. 1996.

2. ISO/IEC, *Product Specification for a Software Process Assessment Standard*, Version 1.000, JTC1/SC7/WG10, 22 June 1993.

3. ISO/IEC, *The Need and Requirements for a Software Process Assessment Standard*, Study Report, Issue 2.0, JTC1/SC7 N944R, 11 June 1992.

4. ISO/IEC JTC1/SC7/WG10, *Software Process Assessment Standard: Requirements Specification*, Document WG10/N017R, Version 1.000, June 1993.

5. SPICE/PIG_PD/N005, *Process Improvement Guide—Product Description*.

6. ISO 9004-4, *Quality Management and Quality System Elements—Part 4, Guidelines for Quality Improvement*, Reference number ISO 9004-4:1993(E).

7. Kuvaja, P. et al., *Software process Assessment and Improvement: The BOOTSTRAP Approach*, Blackwell Business, 1994.

8. Peterson, B. and R. Radice, "IDEAL: An Integrated Approach to Software Process Improvement (SPI)," SEI Symposium, 1994.

9. Sanders, J. and E. Curran, *Software Quality—A Framework for Success in Software Development and Support*, Addison Wesley, Reading, Mass., 1994.

10. Craigmyle, M. and I. Fletcher, "Improving IT Effectiveness Through Software Process Assessment," *Software Quality J.*, Vol. 2, 1993, pp. 257–264.

11. Software Productivity Consortium, *Managing Process Improvement—A Guidebook for Implementing Change*, SPC-93105-CMC, Version 01.00.06, December 1993.

12. ami, *A Quantitative Approach to Software Management*, The ami consortium, South Bank University, London, 1992.

9

Guidelines for Determining Supplier Process Capability

John Hamilton

Defence Evaluation Research Agency, UK

The SPICE vision was of process assessments that would be repeatable, comparable, and verifiable. Under SPICE, different assessments of a single organizational unit (OU), whether internal or independent, team-based or continuous, would lead to similar results. Customers would have to satisfy only themselves on the validity of a self-assessment rather than carry out a complete, independent evaluation for every new procurement.

The *Process Capability Determination Guide* (PCDG) provides guidance on how to use process assessment to identify and analyze the strengths, weaknesses, and risks associated with using a particular organization's software process to meet a particular specified requirement (SR). A process capability determination (PCD) might be sponsored by either:

- a customer with the objective of determining the suitability of a potential supplier's processes to meet a particular specified requirement

- an organization with the objective of determining the suitability of its own processes to meet a particular specified requirement.

The audience of the PCDG is primarily:

- the PCD sponsor requiring the process capability determination to be carried out and his staff
- the OU staff involved in the PCD
- any independent assessment team
- any process improvement team
- tool and method developers.

Given that changes to the PCDG document were minimal (for example, terminology changes) between Version 1.0 and Version 2.0, this chapter focuses on the concepts and process of implementing PCD in general, with reference to Version 2.0.

Key concepts

This chapter's discussion of process capability determination is based on an understanding of the following key concepts:

- that the process capability determination would be carried out by a PCD sponsor or his agent with respect to a specified requirement
- that the specified requirement might involve a new or existing task, a contract or an internal undertaking, a product or a service, or any other requirement that would be met by deploying the OU's processes. The specified requirement could be a requirement or *class of* requirements, or a contract or *class of* contracts.
- that the specified requirement would be translated into a *process assessment input* and a *target profile* that together represent a *target capability*
- that process assessment outputs would be reusable—possibly in modified or summary form—for either process improvement or process capability determination
- that the process capability determination would be carried out with respect to a future requirement. The OU that would undertake the work might not yet exist. It might have to be constructed from existing organizational elements plus subcontractors, consultants, partners, and so on.

- that although the process capability determination would be firmly based on a current or recent process assessment, the OU might wish to—or have to—offer a capability that had not yet been constructed. Further, the OU might wish to propose a capability in advance of current achievement, supported by a credible *Process Improvement Plan*. The PCDG would acknowledge both of these situations by defining the *proposed profile* (representing a proposed capability) as a set of process-by-process capability level ratings proposed by the OU that they would undertake to achieve in meeting the specified requirement.

- that a proposed profile, in order to be credible, would have to be backed up by a recent, relevant current profile, that represents current capability

- that the OU would provide a current profile to the PCD sponsor that would:

    1. be the output of a SPICE-conformant process assessment
    2. reflect the process assessment input
    3. be put forward as being a true and fair representation of the OU's current process capability
    4. be owned by the OU
    5. be likely to be the product of an internal *process improvement program*, but that could also have been produced during an assisted self-assessment, an independent assessment, or a previous process capability determination.[*]

- that the OU might also wish to submit a *Risk Plan*, showing how they would assess and deal with any shortfall between *proposed capability* and the *required capability* as represented in the target profile

- that the PCD sponsor would review the current profile to establish how much confidence it merited, and then possibly take further action to establish further confidence in it

- that the further action might involve an *independent revalidation* of the current process profile. This action might involve repeating the validation activities already carried out during process assessment with the aim of establishing confidence

---

[*]The PCD sponsor might wish to assist the OU in providing a current process profile if they had not undertaken a process assessment previously.

- that the further action might alternatively involve an independent process assessment of some or all of the OU's processes. This action might involve a verification assessment being carried out by the PCD sponsor or his agent, or alternatively the PCD sponsor might conceivably ask the OU to repeat part or all of the process assessment and resubmit the results, although this does not seem very likely.

- that the PCD sponsor would review the proposed profile to establish how much confidence it merited, taking into account the credibility of the current profile and the credibility of the Process Improvement Plan.

Scenarios of use

The two main scenarios described below illustrate the different application contexts of the PCDG document.

Scenario 1 — PCD in a small organization utilizing self-assessment

This example describes a small organization whose product domain centers on several different types of office automation and business applications. The products are for sale through the organization's own marketing department. The products require initial customer service as well as extensive customer support in customizing the applications.

The current situation has arisen because the marketing department has identified a good opportunity to enter into a very different market segment. The marketing department has placed a high emphasis on the need to quickly take advantage of a window of opportunity and enter the market before the competition can gain any advantage. It wishes to allocate significant budget to the new venture. The Chief Executive Officer (CEO) will not support the new venture until the software risks have been identified and discussed. The software manager has been asked to lay out a process to respond to the marketing department's request and answer the CEO's concerns.

The marketing department has generated a specified requirement (SR) that it feels will meet the success criteria for product sales. The SR has undergone an iterative marketing review process that has now been completed. The software management department was consulted during this process, but has not formally commented on the proposed project. While some of the requirements may imply a solution, the SR does not impose a technical solution. There would be wide latitude for the design of the application architecture and software.

The software manager has just received the SR. The managers must now recommend to the organization's senior management whether or not the company would be capable of developing the desired product and present an assessment of risk associated with the recommendation.

Scenario 2 — PCD in a large organization entering a two-party contract

This scenario involves a very large software development project managed by a large systems integration contractor. It is a two-party scenario that involves significant contract activities and controls. A government agency has developed a specified requirement that evolves a current Air Traffic Control System over a period of several years. The request for proposal describes significant enhancements to the current large system of two million lines of code (MLOC). The agency's estimate of the final application would be approximately 4 MLOC. The enhancements are complex, state-of-the-art, and require a very high degree of quality control processes. The proposal requires significant testing of both the hardware and software as a system. High software reliability, maintainability, and response efficiency are very important aspects of the specification.

Other areas emphasized are the degree of simplicity for the user or aspects of usability. The contract will be a firm fixed-price contract with both incentives and penalties for performance, cost, and schedule goals. The government agency has specified the following process categories as significant:

- integration and test of the systems
- requirements and design of the software
- management of quality assurance
- management of risk
- software reuse management.

The executive that was responsible for developing the proposal works for a company that was primarily a systems integrator. The company has extensive experience in establishing and managing strong subcontractor development teams. Its in-house software development expertise was primarily in the engineering design area for the preliminary design. It then manages the subcontracted work of the subsequent critical design, software development, and life cycle processes. The executive expects strong competition in the areas of design, cost, and quality from other companies.

The executive has received a budget from the marketing department to develop a proposal for the system. The executive must recommend a course of action for the marketing department to consider if it wants to submit a formal proposal to the government agency. The executive selects the SPICE methodology to initiate his proposal process.

Target capability

The *target capability* is chosen by the PCD sponsor to be the capability that will represent a minimal process risk to the successful implementation of the specified requirement.

Target capability is expressed within a *target capability statement* that lists the processes that are key to meeting the specified requirements. It states, for each key process, the required achievement of each process attribute. Only process attribute achievement targets of *Fully*, *Largely*, or *Not required* should be set.

For each key process, PCD sponsors should identify which process attributes are required and set the degree of achievement for each. Process attribute achievement may be set in several ways. For example, the same degree of achievement may be allocated to:

- all the process attributes up to a certain capability level
- individually-selected process attributes.

An example of a target capability statement is shown in Figure 9.1.

Process oriented risk

The scope for considering process-oriented risk in the context of PCD is outlined in Figure 9.2.

Process-oriented risk would be assessed based first on the *probability* of a particular problem occurring, and second on its potential *impact*, should the problem occur.

For a particular process, individual gaps are identified by comparing the individual process attribute ratings awarded to process instances with the corresponding achievement targets specified in the target capability statement. Gaps are designated as shown in Figure 9.3. Gaps within a capability level are designated as shown in Figure 9.4.

Key Process	Process Attributes	Rating Required
CUS.1 Manage customer needs	PA1.1, PA2.1, PA2.2 (that is, all up to and including the *Managed* capability level)	Fully Achieved
CUS.5 Provide customer service	PA1.1, PA2.1, PA2.2, PA3.1, PA3.2 (that is, all up to and including the *Established* capability level)	Fully Achieved
ENG.3 Develop software design	PA1.1, PA2.1, PA2.2, PA3.1, PA3.2	Fully Achieved
ENG.4 Implement software design	PA1.1, PA2.1, PA2.2, PA3.1, PA3.2 PA4.1, PA4.2	Fully Achieved Largely Achieved
ENG.5 Integrate and test software	PA1.1, PA2.1, PA2.2, PA3.1, PA3.2 PA4.1, PA4.2	Fully Achieved Largely Achieved
MAN.1 Manage the project	PA1.1, PA2.1, PA2.2 PA3.1, PA3.2	Fully Achieved Largely Achieved
MAN.2 Manage quality	PA1.1, PA2.1, PA2.2 PA3.1, PA3.2	Fully Achieved Largely Achieved
SUP.2 Perform configuration management	PA1.1, PA2.1, PA2.2 PA3.1, PA3.2	Fully Achieved Largely Achieved

Figure 9.1: Example of a target capability statement.

1. The PCDG would address the capability of an organization's processes to perform within the scope for which they have been designed and implemented.

2. It does not address the wider analysis of all the risk arising from an organization's capability to develop a particular product that would encompass strategic, organizational, financial, social, and many other issues.

3. The output from a SPICE PCD would feed into this wider-risk analysis, but would be confined to the *process-oriented risk associated with any shortfall between required process capability and current or proposed process capability* — that is, the risk associated with using a particular organization's processes to meet a particular specified requirement, assuming that the scope of the organization's current activities encompasses the specified requirement.

4. So, although the PCDG would provide guidance on ensuring that this was so *(meeting a particular specified requirement)*, it would not address the issues that arise when an organization proposes to address a specified requirement that is outside the scope of its current activities.

Figure 9.2: Scope of process-oriented risk.

Target	Assessed	Gap
Fully Achieved	Fully Achieved	None
	Largely Achieved	Minor
	Partially Achieved	Major
	Not Achieved	Major
Largely Achieved	Fully Achieved	None
	Largely Achieved	None
	Partially Achieved	Major
	Not Achieved	Major

Figure 9.3: Gaps associated with process attributes within process instances.

Number of Individual Gaps within a Capability Level	Capability Level Gap
No major or minor gaps	None
Minor gaps only	Slight
A single major gap at Levels 2 - 5 within any of the process instances assessed.	Significant
A single major gap at Level 1 within any of the process instances assessed, or more than one major gap at Levels 2 - 5 within any of the process instances assessed.	Substantial

Figure 9.4: Gaps associated with capability levels.

The nature of the potential *impact* of a particular problem depends only upon the *capability level* within which it occurs, as shown in Figure 9.5. With this approach, the overall process-oriented risk associated with a single process may be summarized as shown in Figure 9.6.

To use the above tables, consider each key process in turn, and then, for each process, consider each capability level in turn. Categorize individual gaps— within any process instance assessed—at the process attribute level using Figure 9.3, and then determine the capability level gap and probability of a problem occurring using Figure 9.4. The potential impact of the problem is then obtained from Figure 9.5. For example, a substantial gap within the Managed level implies a high probability of problems occurring, that, should they occur, will have potentially a medium impact on product quality and a high impact on budget and schedule. According to Figure 9.6, this gap constitutes a high risk.

If gaps exist at more than one capability level, then the overall risk is determined from whichever row of Figure 9.6 shows the greater risk.

It should be emphasized that Figure 9.6 is merely a guide to overall risk. Nominal risk levels should always be confirmed by a critical review against experience and reality.

Capability Level where problem occurs	Nature of Impact				
	Missing work products, un-acceptable product quality	Cost or time overruns	Reduced cost effectiveness, reduced spatial and temporal uniformity of performance	Inability to predict performance or timely detect problems	Reduced cost/time optimization - reduced ability to cope with changes in technology.
Optimizing	**No identifiable Impact**	**No identifiable Impact**	**Low Impact**	**Medium Impact**	**High Impact**
Predictable	**No identifiable Impact**	**Low Impact**	**Medium Impact**	**High Impact**	**High Impact**
Established	**Low Impact**	**Medium Impact**	**High Impact**	**High Impact**	**High Impact**
Managed	**Medium Impact**	**High Impact**	**High Impact**	**High Impact**	**High Impact**
Performed	**High Impact**	**High Impact**	**High Impact**	**High Impact**	**High Impact**

Figure 9.5: Nature of potential impact of problems at each capability level.

Extent of Capability Level Gap

Capability Level	None	Slight	Significant	Substantial
Optimizing	**No Identifiable Risk**	**Low Risk**	**Low Risk**	**Low Risk**
Predictable	**No Identifiable Risk**	**Low Risk**	**Low Risk**	**Medium Risk**
Established	**No Identifiable Risk**	**Low risk**	**Medium risk**	**Medium Risk**
Managed	**No Identifiable Risk**	**Medium Risk**	**Medium Risk**	**High Risk**
Performed	**No Identifiable Risk**	**Medium Risk**	**High Risk**	**High Risk**

Figure 9.6: Overall process-oriented risk.

The capability determination process

The net inputs and outputs of the PCD process are illustrated in Figure 9.7.

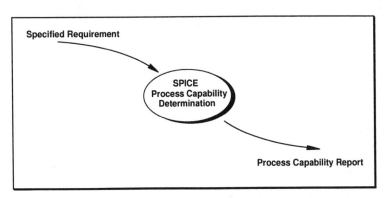

Figure 9.7: Context diagram for process capability determination.

The *Process Capability Report* would be the final output of the PCD process. It would set out an assessment of the overall risk of using the OU's software process to meet the specified requirement. This overall risk would derive from two factors:

1. any shortfall between the OU's proposed profile and the PCD sponsor's target profile
2. the degree of confidence that can be placed in the OU's current profile and proposed profile.

Stages of capability determination

The overall PCD process is expressed as the three principle subprocesses shown in Figure 9.8.

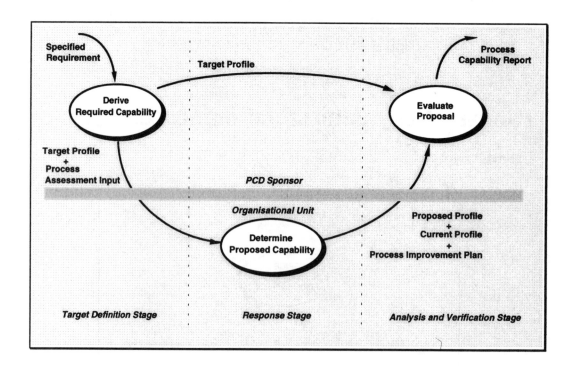

Figure 9.8: First level decomposition.

During the target definition stage, the PCD sponsor's staff would transform the *specified requirement* into a *target profile* that would represent a **required process capability**, as well as a *process assessment input* that would be used to scope the OU's process assessment. The required process capability and process assessment input would be passed to the OU.

As suggested by the gray area in Figure 9.8 between the PCD sponsor and the OU, there might be a process of clarification required in passing the target profile.

During the response stage, the OU would develop a proposed capability—the *proposed profile*—that they would achieve when meeting the specified requirement, plus a process assessment output—the *current profile*—representing current capability. A suitable current profile might already exist, but if not then a process assessment would need to be carried out. The OU's current profile might meet or exceed the PCD sponsor's target, but if not, then the OU might wish to develop a proposed profile that lies somewhere between the current profile and the target profile, as illustrated in Figure 9.9. In addition, the OU might also wish to submit a Risk Plan, addressing each area in which an individual process fell short of the required target capability, setting out the OU's assessment of the seriousness of the associated risk and proposing measures to mitigate the risk.

During the analysis and verification stage, the PCD sponsor's staff would analyze any gaps between the required and proposed capability, and verify the credibility of the OU's response. The *Process Capability Report* would reflect the overall risk of using the OU's processes to meet the specified requirement, arising first from any shortfall between current and required capability, and second from the degree of confidence placed in the OU's response. The Process Capability Report would be the final output of the PCD process.

Verifying the credibility of the proposed profile would involve first verifying the credibility of the current profile and then the credibility of any Process Improvement Plan submitted:

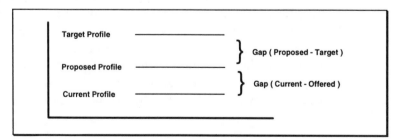

Figure 9.9: Target, proposed, and current profiles.

- Verifying the current profile might involve:

    1. checking that the current profile was SPICE-conformant
    2. carrying out an independent revalidation of the assessment
    3. carrying out an independent verification assessment—a SPICE-conformant assessment of one or more processes.

- Verifying the Process Improvement Plan will involve considering how well it addresses the gap between current and proposed profiles, and how likely it was that the OU would succeed in achieving the planned improvements, taking into account any process improvement records submitted as evidence of an effective ongoing process improvement program.

Consider the following three sample scenarios to see exactly how this might work in practice. These scenarios illustrate examples of:

- a mature customer-supplier relationship
- an internal PCD
- a customer carrying out a PCD on a supplier new to the ideas of process assessment.

Scenario 1 — Procurement within mature customer-supplier relationship

In this scenario, an acquirer wants to analyze a known, potential supplier's process capability to provide a new software product. The acquirer and supplier have established a constructive customer-supplier relationship, and have previously been involved in a process capability determination involving a similar product. The acquirer includes in his invitation to tender a *requirement* that a SPICE process profile be included with bids and an *invitation* to submit evidence of ongoing process improvement. The supplier has in place an established process improvement initiative and submits a process profile that reflects a recent modest improvement trend. This scenario is summarized in Figure 9.10.

1.	Acquirer generates the required scope for the proposed process profile and also generates a target profile that reflects the needs of the new software product. Acquirer includes this information in the invitation to tender.
2.	Acquirer sponsors PCD and reviews process profile submitted by potential supplier. Determines that minimum revalidation involving a single process will be sufficient to establish confidence in profile. Records scope for revalidation and tasks agent.
3.	Acquirer's agent visits supplier and revalidates process profile in accordance with scope and validation guidance in PAG. Validation Report shows process profile is valid.
4.	Acquirer reviews Validation Report and determines that proposed process profile can be deemed a trusted process profile.
5.	Acquirer conducts gap analysis of trusted process profile against target profile to produce SWOR Report.
6.	Acquirer analyses SWOR Report against supplier's process improvement information and produces Capability Report. He may then go on to compare this with his analysis of competing suppliers.

Figure 9.10: Procurement within a mature customer-supplier relationship.

Scenario 2 — Supplier assessment of risk involved in a new contract

In this scenario, a supplier's management wants to analyze the risk involved in undertaking a major new software development contract. Their process improvement program has been in place for some time, but the management must consider carefully how much confidence they can place in the process profiles produced. They cannot afford to take on an excessive degree of risk and so they initiate a PCD to help decide whether or not to accept the contract. This scenario is summarized in Figure 9.11.

1.	Supplier's management generates the required scope and a target profile for the new software development contract.
2.	Supplier's management sponsors the PCD.
	OU proffers recent process profile, generated as part of process improvement program, to PCD sponsor.
3.	PCD sponsor reviews profile and decides that risk assessment of new contract justifies independent reassessment of limited scope. Arranges for independent assessment to reassess just 2 processes using a limited sample size.
4.	Independent assessment carried out in accordance with given scope. Does not see OU's process profile, but awards own practice adequacy scores and generates independent process profile.
5.	PCD sponsor reconciles OU's process profile and independent process profile. Results correlate well. PCD sponsor generates trusted process profile.
6.	PCD sponsor conducts gap analysis of trusted process profile against target profile to produce SWOR Report. This gap analysis provides raw risk analysis.
	PCD sponsor analyses SWOR Report against OU's process improvement plans and produces refined risk analysis within Process Capability Report. This report then supports the decision on whether to accept the contract.
7.	

Figure 9.11: supplier assessment of risk involved in a new contract.

Scenario 3 — Procurement involving new supplier who is also new to process assessment

In this scenario, an acquirer wants to determine the process capability of a small, unknown potential supplier to develop a software product. The supplier has no experience of process assessment or process improvement but does have expertise in the product area that the acquirer requires. The acquirer includes in his invitation to tender the *requirement* that a SPICE process profile must be included with bids. The supplier must therefore arrange for a process assessment to be carried out if he wishes to bid for the contract. The supplier responds that they do not have the expertise to do so. The acquirer nevertheless believes that the supplier may have the process capability he needs and states that an independent process assessment must be carried out if the supplier wishes to be considered further for the contract. The supplier agrees and the acquirer's own assessment team carry out a full process assessment. This scenario is summarized in Figure 9.12.

1.	Acquirer generates the required scope for the proposed process profile and also generates a target profile that reflects the needs of the new software product. Acquirer includes this information in the invitation to tender.
2.	Supplier responds that they cannot undertake the assessment themselves but are willing to be assessed by the acquirer.
3.	Acquirer's assessment team carries out full process assessment of potential supplier and returns process assessment output to both acquirer and supplier.
4.	Acquirer has full confidence in assessment results and deems it to be trusted process profile.
5.	PCD sponsor conducts gap analysis of trusted process profile against target profile to produce SWOR Report.
6.	PCD sponsor analyses SWOR Report against supplier's lack of any process improvement program and produces Process Capability Report.

Figure 9.12: Procurement involving a new supplier who is new to process assessment.

Derive required capability subprocesses

The purpose of the *Derive Required Capability* process is to determine the required capability of a set of processes to enable the successful implementation of a specified requirement.

The Derive Required Capability process is decomposed into the subprocesses illustrated in Figure 9.13.

Determine proposed capability subprocesses

The purpose of the *Determine Proposed Capability* process is to determine the capability of a set of processes that can be offered to enable the successful implementation of a specified requirement. This proposed capability may need to be supported by a Risk Plan when it does not meet the required capability.

The Determine Proposed Capability process is decomposed into the subprocesses illustrated in Figure 9.14.

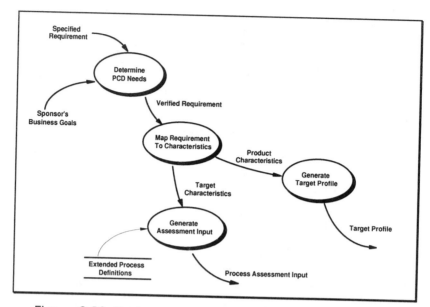

Figure 9.13: Derive required capability subprocesses.

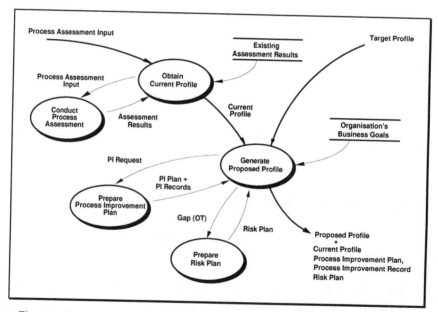

Figure 9.14: Determine proposed capability subprocesses.

Obtain current profile

If an assessment profile with an appropriate scope already existed, then it is used as the current profile. If not, then a process assessment would be invoked.

Conduct process assessment

The whole of this subprocess comprises merely a reference to Part 3 *Performing an Assessment*.

Prepare Process Improvement Plan

A Process Improvement Plan would be produced to show how the gap between Current and proposed profiles can be closed.

Prepare Risk Plan

A Risk Plan would be produced showing how the gap between proposed and target profiles can be managed.

Generate proposed profile

Many OUs will have sophisticated arrangements in place for responding to invitations to tender for contracts. Generating an proposed capability profile parallels such arrangements.

One possible way of generating the proposed profile is illustrated in Figure 9.15 and described below.

Analyze GAP (Current → Target)

REPEAT until Cost of Improvements v Risk is acceptable

    IN SEQUENCE

        Determine where to pitch proposed profile

        IN PARALLEL

            Analyze GAP (proposed → Target); Prepare Risk Plan

            Analyze GAP (Current → proposed); Prepare PI Plan

        Assess Cost of Improvements v Risk

Figure 9.15: Generate proposed profile.

If there is a gap between current capability and target capability for some processes, then the OU must decide where to pitch its proposed profile. Pitching the proposed profile high may involve greater cost. Pitching it low may involve greater risk.

The process of generating the proposed profile is likely therefore to be iterative, with the cost and risk implications of a proposed positioning being traded off until an acceptable balance is achieved. Having determined where to pitch the proposed profile initially, then the gap between current and proposed can be analyzed and a Process Improvement Plan drawn up accordingly, while at the same time the gap between proposed and target can be analyzed and a Risk Plan prepared accordingly. The cost of the improvement, and the risk of not meeting the target, can then be weighed and if necessary the proposed profile adjusted. This process then continues until a balance acceptable with respect to the OU's business goals is found.

Evaluate proposal subprocesses

The purpose of the *Evaluate Proposal* process is to determine whether the proposed capability of a set of processes, together with any associated Risk Plan, will enable the successful implementation of a specified requirement.

The Evaluate Proposal process is decomposed into the subprocesses illustrated in Figure 9.16. For conducting a gap analysis, the proposed and target profiles are compared. For verifying the current profile, the following are considered:

- Confirm Current Process Profile Was SPICE-Conformant

- Determine Need for Re-validation or Verification

- Re-Validate Current Process Assessment

- Prepare Verification Assessment Input

- Conduct Independent Verification Assessment

- Compare Verification Assessment Output and Current Process Profile

The analysis of overall capability takes into account the gap analysis and the verification of the offered profile. Issues related to this analysis have been broached earlier in this chapter.

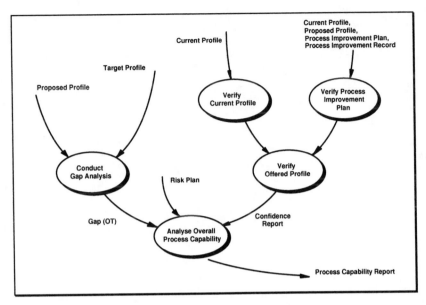

Figure 9.16: Evaluate proposal subprocesses.

10

Qualification and Training of Assessors

Alan Davies
Avocet, UK

Alastair Walker
University of Witwatersrand, South Africa

Process ratings depend on the skilled judgment of qualified assessors. To achieve an acceptable level of consistency, repeatability, and reliability of results qualified assessors must have the appropriate skills, experience, and knowledge of the software process, the reference model, and experience in performing assessments.

Conducting a Software Process Assessment based on the SPICE framework assumes that the assessment team includes at least one qualified assessor. The qualified assessor on the team has the responsibility to ensure that collectively the rest of the team has the right blend of specialized knowledge and assessment skills. The qualified assessor provides the necessary guidance to the team members and helps to moderate their judgments and ratings to ensure consistency of interpretation.

The *Assessor Training and Qualification Guide* (Part 6 of the SPICE document set) details the philosophy used to ensure the right balance is obtained for the qualified assessor conducting a SPICE-compliant assessment. This chapter provides an overview of the requirements for qualification as a SPICE assessor and provides the details of a curriculum that can be used as a basis for training.

Philosophy behind assessor qualification and training

Figure 10.1 maps the route an assessor needs to follow to be able to conduct assessments. It illustrates the need to demonstrate competence as a balance between education, training, and experience. The mix will be different for each person. The route allows for full flexibility: competence can be confirmed either by validation or by an employer accepting the capability of an individual. The qualified assessor also should be familiar with the processes being assessed, however assessments conducted with mixed teams, one team member from the organizational unit (OU) and another familiar with the SPICE documents, ensures a reasonable balance between the teams. It is worth noting that a number of Phase 1 Trials were conducted this way and proved to be highly successful.

Having obtained the necessary qualifications, there is a need to keep it current. Records of assessments performed and the processes addressed would need to be kept to demonstrate continued qualification. These records would then be reviewed after a period of time.

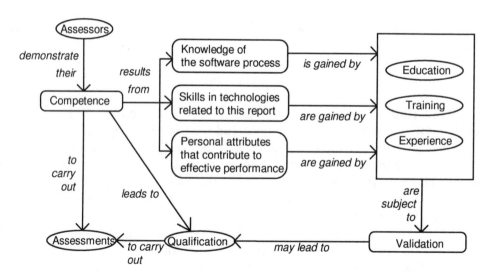

Figure 10.1: The qualification path for assessors.

Figure 10.1 shows the key entities and their relationships and are articulated as follows:

- Assessors demonstrate their competence to carry out assessments.
- It is this competence that leads to assessor qualification.
- Competence results from:

  1. knowledge of the software process
  2. skills in the principle technologies of the emerging standard, including: the reference model, rating processes, and assessment models, methods, and tools
  3. personal attributes that contribute to effective performance.

- The knowledge, skills, and personal attributes are gained by a combination of education, training, and experience.
- An alternative to demonstrable competence is to validate an intending assessor's education, training, and experience.

Assessor competence

The following sections describe the specifics of training, knowledge, and experience requirements.

Knowledge of SPICE processes

The emerging standard is divided into five process areas with which the qualified assessor needs to ensure familiarity in addition to the software development process as a whole. A working understanding of the processes in the lower capability levels is critical. However, when working with Level 3 processes and above, an in-depth understanding of the processes is critical because of the heightened level of complexity introduced by the more mature processes. When the qualified assessor examines these areas, the requirement for the right balance of training, experience, and education is essential. It is important to recognize that many of the processes being assessed are not directly related to software production, but often form part of the infrastructure of the organization to which not much attention had been paid in the past.

In a SPICE-conformant assessment, two critical elements are addressed: *process profiles* and *process improvement*. Once the process profile has been obtained, the qualified assessor can highlight opportunities for improvement. Consideration must be paid to the OU's business goals, its competitors' profiles, and the industry norms before determining which processes should be prioritized for improvement. Once a course of action has been identified, the qualified assessor can draw on expertise to identify potential improvement paths. The depth of experience/competence of the qualified assessor directly affects how the particular improvement path is derived.

A good understanding of Parts 2 ,3, and 4 is required to ensure that the requirements for conducting a SPICE-conformant assessment are known and understood. This understanding can be supplemented by a review of Part 5 to illustrate the contents of a typical assessment instrument.

Other relevant standards, such as ISO/IEC 12207, are beneficial to the qualified assessor's understanding of the approach to use. (See Chapters 3 and 4 for more information on ISO 12207 as well as the models on which SPICE was based.)

Assessor personal attributes

In addition to the technical knowledge and experienced required, the assessor should have the personal attributes and skills described in the next sections.

Effective written and verbal communication

When performing assessments, qualified assessors will interact with a variety of OU representatives. The results of the assessment may be communicated to the OU in written reports and/or presentations. Qualified assessors should be able to communicate the findings of the assessments in a clear, nonjudgmental style. Assessment findings should be documented in clear and unambiguous language.

Diplomacy

Assessors should act with professionalism and decorum at all times. Independent assessors are guests of the OU being assessed and their conduct should be above reproach at all times.

Discretion

Qualified assessors should develop and maintain the confidence of the assessment participants. In particular, qualified assessors should preserve the confidentiality of the results of the assessment and of the information received during an assessment in accordance with the terms of any confidentiality agreement included in the assessment constraints.

Persistence and resistance-handling ability

Qualified assessors should be persistent in carrying out their responsibilities. They should be able to resolve any conflicts and handle any resistance they may encounter from assessment participants.

Judgment and leadership

It is critical that the OU being assessed has confidence in, and respect for, the assessment team leader, the team coordinator, and the team members. If the team is not seen to be credible by the OU, the assessment findings may not be accepted.

Integrity

The assessment team leader, team coordinator, and team members should have no conflict of interest in performing the assessment. For example, none of the assessment team members should be individuals whose performance is being measured by the improvements enacted within the OU. If any team member's individual performances is being measured by the outcome of the assessment, that team member cannot be considered objective.

Rapport

Individuals, who because of their organizational position or personality could stifle the open and honest flow of information, should not participate in the assessment. For example, managers who evaluate the performance of individuals involved in the projects being assessed should not be assessment team members. Project personnel might be reluctant to disclose problem areas to their own management if their individual performance measurements may be affected.

The assessor qualification process

Qualified assessors obtain their qualification by following the path shown in Figure 10.2. The qualification process is twofold: (1) the first step is to become a provisional assessor followed by (2) becoming a qualified assessor.

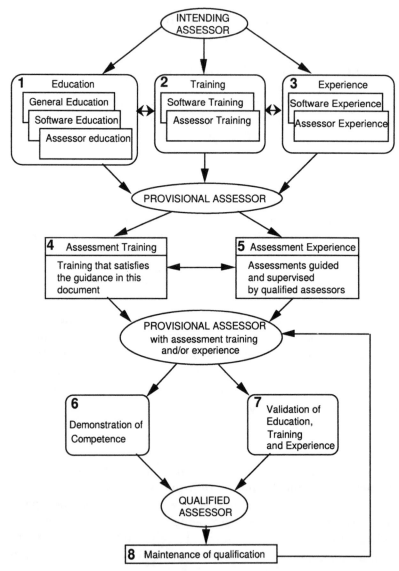

Figure 10.2: Path to becoming a qualified assessor.

Becoming a provisional assessor

A *provisional assessor* is a person competent to carry out assessments under the guidance and supervision of a qualified assessor. A provisional assessor has reached the required levels of education, training, and experience but has not yet participated in a sufficient number of assessments conducted according to the provisions of the SPICE documents.

A provisional assessor should be competent to carry out software audits or assessments. The assessor should be trained and experienced in the software process as well as in SPA or software quality assessment. In addition, a provisional assessor should have an acceptable level of formal education. Formal education is a combination of general education, software education, and assessor education.

Acceptable levels of education may comprise:

- formal courses offered by a college or university
- professional courses organized by recognized local or international bodies
- vendor-sponsored courses
- employer-sponsored courses

Acceptable levels of training may comprise:

- training provided by recognized local or international bodies
- training provided by vendors and trainers, based on the guidance provided later in this chapter.

Acceptable levels of experience may comprise:

- direct hands-on experience in specialist areas, such as software engineering, software development/maintenance, software quality, or quality assurance
- management experience overseeing software specialist areas such as software engineering, software development/maintenance, software quality, or quality assurance.

Becoming a qualified assessor

To become a qualified assessor, an assessor should already be a competent software development/maintenance professional or a software audit/assessment professional (as described above). In addition, the assessor should have completed formal training (based on the guidance provided in the next section of this chapter). In addition, the assessor should have participated in assessments conducted according to the provisions of the SPICE documents.

Qualified assessors should maintain a record of ongoing professional activities to demonstrate their continuing competencies of skills, knowledge, and training. Assessors' professional activities should also be recorded to demonstrate industry experience.

Assessor training curriculum

This section is intended for training providers who will be designing, developing, and/or delivering SPICE assessor training. An assessor training syllabus is provided here to help ensure that courses developed and delivered by training providers cover the minimum set of required competencies. The goal is to provide a common framework for the training offered by various providers and to assure that training adequately addresses the SPICE product suite.

The competency-based approach focuses on the desired participant outcomes of the training. One benefit to be derived from such an approach is that it emphasizes the results participants should expect to achieve, not just the content to be covered. This section also gives guidance for the design of the training program.

While there is no formal mechanism to qualify courses or their providers, both may at some future time be subject to a qualification process. Adherence to the contents of this chapter will provide one means with which to evaluate and qualify SPICE assessor training courses. In addition, it is recommended that course developers and instructors qualify as *qualified assessors*.

Course requirements

An assessor training course comprises, at a minimum, the following topic areas:

1. Overview of the SPICE documents (see Chapter 3)
    *   Background
    *   Architecture and principles
    *   The component parts of the Technical Report
    *   Vocabulary and definitions
    *   Comparison of the SPICE documents with other standards/ methodologies
    *   Assessment versus auditing
    *   How to use the parts of the SPICE document set

2. The process assessment architecture (see Chapter 4)
   - Process categories
   - Processes and process purposes
   - Process attributes and capability levels
   - Rating processes and the process capability level model
   - Requirements for compatible models
   - How to use Part 2 of the SPICE documents.

3. Process Assessment (see Chapters 6 and 7)
   - Defining the assessment input
   - Responsibilities
   - Performing an assessment
   - Recording the assessment output
   - Determining ratings
   - Validation of ratings
   - Presentation of assessment results
   - Selection and use of assessment models, methods, and tools
   - How to use Parts 3 and 4 of the SPICE documents

4. Compatible models for assessment (see Chapter 7)
   - The purpose of an assessment model
   - Model elements, indicators, and mapping
   - Using indicators
   - Translating assessment results into process profiles
   - How to use Part 5 of the SPICE documents.

Competency-based approach

Assessor competencies

Competencies are the skills, knowledge, and personal attributes that enable effective performance. Where possible, competencies are expressed as observable, actionable goals, and hence can be seen as a basic set of learning goals. A competency can complete the following statement: "After completion of this course, an assessor will be able to...". The competencies in this syllabus represent the minimum set that course participants should be able to achieve. Training providers may add to the minimum set.

Assessor training course

Training providers are expected to specify how a qualified assessor will achieve each of the competencies in this syllabus. At a minimum, the vendor will specify actions and performance criteria for each competency. Ideally, the vendor should address who, what, when, why, and how for each competency.

Course design

Target population

The target population for the training activities are individuals familiar with assessment and who desire to become qualified as assessors.

Course prerequisites

The competencies that course participants already possess will influence their future performance and needs as qualified assessors. The emphasis of SPICE assessor-training requirements is to prepare course participants to perform *SPICE-conformant assessments*, not assessments in general. Therefore, participants in the training course should possess *prerequisite* competencies in:

- total quality management principles, tools, and techniques, including quality assurance and quality improvement
- familiarity with an assessment model.

Course organization

The training requirements identify the required competencies, but do not specify how the competencies are to be achieved. It will be up to the individual vendors to select the course design that will best achieve the training goals. For example, the vendor may choose to present the competencies in a series of courses or modules, rather than in a single course.

Course sequence

Training providers can address competencies and topic areas in any sequence, with one exception: the course should introduce the process dimension *before* it introduces the capability dimension. It should also provide examples of both.

Course methods

It is up to the training provider to select the appropriate instructional methods based on professional judgment. An appropriate combination of experiential, lecture, group, and individual work should be used to support the course goals. The course must take participants through at least one process assessment using examples, hands-on exercises, or other experiential methods.

Case study or other experiential methods should be supported by an instructor-facilitated discussion session. This session should give participants the opportunity to seek information beyond what is contained in the case study and to raise and debate various points of view about the case study issues. Participants should be encouraged to defend their opinions with evidence and reason. The discussion session should permit the instructor to check participant skills in inquiry, analysis, and decision making.

The course also should contain guidance for evaluating practice adequacy at the Performed level.

Course assessment

Training providers are advised to include a mechanism for soliciting participant course evaluations and for recording, analyzing, and acting on any participant feedback that is received. Such assessment mechanisms may include both daily and end-of-course assessments to provide evidence that the course offers an appropriate learning opportunity to the participants.

Assessor training syllabus

Overview of SPICE

1. Introduction to the Course
   - Relate the course to the qualification process for assessors. Identify other, non-training actions needed for initial and ongoing qualification as an assessor.
   - Identify the competencies included in this course.

2. Background
   - Outline the background and antecedents of the SPICE product suite.

3. Architecture and Principles
   - Explain and draw the SPICE architecture.
   - Explain the principles that underpin the SPICE product suite.

4. Product Suite
   - Explain the SPICE product suite.

5. Definitions
   - Explain key terms in SPICE terminology.

6. Assessment versus Auditing
   - Compare and contrast SPICE assessment and conformance auditing.

7. Comparison of SPICE with other standards and methodologies
   - Compare and contrast SPICE with other standards and methodologies, including* Software Capability Maturity Model, Trillium, Bootstrap, ISO/IEC 12207, ISO 9000, and ISO 9000-3. Distinguish software process assessment standards from other quality standards.

8. How to use the SPICE Products
   - Identify and describe the factors that determine whether or not an assessment is SPICE-conformant.
   - Identify and explain the contexts in which the SPICE products may be used.

9. Summary
   - Summarize key points and lessons learned.

The reference and assessment models

1. Introduction
   - Describe the field of application (its intended audience and use).
   - Define the purpose.
   - Define the objectives.
   - Identify the advantages and limitations of reference model use.
   - Explain the structure of the reference model document (Part 2).

---

*Other relevant standards may be substituted or added for comparison, based on local needs. Only a high-level comparison of concepts is required.

2. Definitions
   - Define the key terms upon which the process model concepts are based.

3. Components of the reference model
   - Explain the architecture.
   - Describe the components and give examples of each.
   - Draw a diagram showing the relationships between the components.
   - Explain the notation to be used in identifying practices.

4. Detailed Architecture
   - Explain the concept of capability levels and process attributes.
   - Describe each of the process categories.
   - Demonstrate an understanding of the processes.
   - Demonstrate a mapping of OU processes to the reference model.

5. Components of An Assessment Model

   either: The Part 5 Assessment Model
   - Explain and define the base practices.
   - Explain the use and scope of the base practices.
   - From a given scenario (for example, case study, examples, videos, playlets) exercise judgment to identify the set of base practices operating in an Organizational Unit.
   - Explain the management practices.
   - Explain the interrelationships between management practices, process attributes and capability levels.

   Or: A Compatible Assessment Model Structure

6. Application
   - Complete practice exercises in the application of the assessment model to assessment tasks.

7. Summary
   - Summarize key points and lessons learned.

Process assessment

1. Introduction

- Explain the rationale for process assessment. Justify the need and explain the outcomes of process assessment.
- Explain the critical success factors (facilitators/inhibitors) for a process assessment.
- Explain and give examples of assessment context.

2. Assessment Preparation
   - Identify assessment inputs (purpose, scope, constraints, characteristics).
   - Explain and demonstrate how assessment inputs can be reviewed.
   - Perform process instance selection.
   - Identify and explain criteria for the selection of an assessment team.
   - Allocate team roles.
   - Prepare and conduct a team briefing.
   - Explain how risk factors are identified and to whom they are reported.
   - Select a suite of appropriate assessment techniques (interviews, questionnaires, documentation reviews, and so on).
   - Select an appropriate assessment instrument.
   - Develop an assessment schedule.
   - Prepare a complete assessment plan.
   - Explain the duties of OU coordinators.
   - Prepare and conduct OU briefing.
   - Explain how participants are selected.
   - Explain confidentiality issues.
   - Identify criteria for the support documentation and records.

3. Conduct of Assessments (using a conformant assessment instrument)
   - Explain how information is collected.
   - Explain and demonstrate how information is categorized.
   - Explain how information is verified and how compliance is assessed.
   - Guide the assessment and promote discussion.

4. Determination of Actual Ratings
   - Explain the rating reference.

- Describe fully the process dimension.
- Describe fully the capability dimension.
- Explain and demonstrate a process profile.
- Complete a practice exercise on ratings.

5. Determination of Derived Ratings
   - Explain the method by which derived ratings are determined.
   - Explain and demonstrate how process instances are aggregated.
   - Explain and demonstrate how aggregation across process instances is performed.

6. Validation of Ratings
   - Explain and demonstrate the mechanisms by which ratings can be validated.

7. Presentation of Assessment Results
   - Explain and demonstrate how assessment outputs can be presented.

8. Assessment Conformance
   - Explain and demonstrate how an assessment can be checked for conformance and nonconformance to the emerging standard.

9. Application of Parts 3 and 4
   - Guide a review of the assessment after its completion. Review the effectiveness of the assessment—what worked, what didn't, what value was added, the critical success factors.

10. Summary
    - Summarize key points and lessons learned.

Assessment instruments

1. Introduction
   - Define the purpose of an assessment instrument (AI).
   - Describe how the AI supports process assessment.
   - Describe how the AI or a SPICE-compliant model supports the requirements defined in each of the SPICE products.
   - List the inputs to and outputs from an AI.
   - Identify the types of AI assessment indicators.

- Describe how the process indicators relate to the organization's process.
- Identify the advantages and limitations of AI assessment indicators.
- Identify misuses of AI assessment indicators.
- Identify and associate AI indicators with the SPICE processes to which they relate.

2. Selecting Instruments
   - Identify the elements necessary to select a SPICE-conformant assessment instrument.
   - Identify, construct, and review assessment objectives in different environments.
   - Select an AI that matches the assessment objectives.

3. Planning and Use of Instruments
   - Develop a plan for use of the instrument (include schedule, what to see, when to see, checklist, and so on.)

4. Using Instruments
   - Apply AI's scoping characteristics to define the scope and context of an assessment.
   - Map an OU's actual work products to those listed in the AI standard.
   - Apply AI's scoping characteristics to select the appropriate indicators for a given scope and type of assessment.
   - Use the indicators to make guided judgments about process existence and process capability.
   - Use the AI to score, record, and present assessment results.
   - Use the AI to produce ratings.
   - Store other information captured during an assessment.

5. Assessment Instrument Debriefing
   - Guide a review as the project progresses and after project completion (review the effectiveness of the application of the assessment instrument—what worked, what didn't, what value was added, critical success factors)

6. Summary
   - Summarize key points and lessons learned.

Auxiliary competencies

The assessor training syllabus represents the minimum set of competencies a qualified assessor must possess to perform an assessment effectively. These competencies do not make up the total set of competencies that a SPICE-qualified assessor will need. Many of the skills needed for SPICE assessment are not unique to SPICE or to assessment, such as meeting with and reporting to management or problem-solving skills. Additionally, the total set of competencies will depend on the qualified assessor's role, the assessment mode, the organization's needs, and business objectives.

Acknowledgments

The ATQG team was lead by Dr Ron Megoda, a senior lecturer of UTS, Sydney, who was appointed as product editor in November 1996. Core members of the team included Alan Davies, an experienced lead assessor with TickIT and British Aerospace; John Phippen, an independent quality systems management consultant and an experienced ISO 9000 assessor and active in Standards Australia; Professor Alastair Walker, an academic from the Software Engineering Applications Laboratory, University of the Witwatersrand in South Africa, a registered ISO 9000 quality systems assessor and member of the South African Council of Quality Systems Auditors. Mrs. Carrie Buchman, an experienced CMM assessor of AlliedSignal (USA) frequently provided insights to the development of the documents. Mr. Jean-Pierre Legras of SNECMA was the French contingent member of that group. Ms Sue Lightig of Bellcore (USA) joined the team at the Helsinki meeting and was appointed product editor of the Assessor Training Curriculum in Pittsburgh.

11

A Comparison of ISO 9001 and the SPICE Framework

Victoria A. Hailey

The Victoria Hailey Group Corporation, Canada

As the preceding chapters in this book have illustrated, the SPICE document set has been developed to fill a critical need in the software engineering industry. By providing a flexible framework for discerning the strengths and weaknesses of a software organization's processes, both for its own objectives as well as for potential customers, the SPICE framework charts a path toward continually improving those processes once their capability becomes known.

The SPICE framework can provide an important advantage, beneficial to both ISO 9001-registered software organizations as well as those considering registration. One of ISO 9001's requirements is to continually improve the quality system.[2,3] However, the standard does not explicitly provide the software organization with a clear and directed path toward such improvement other than through refinement of its own practices. As a result of the SPICE Project's initiatives, software organizations can use the SPICE model to meet both ISO 9001's requirement of continuous improvement as well as their own objectives since the path to mature and capable processes is built into the emerging standard's framework. An organization can pursue improvement *without* having to use a *trial-and-error* approach.

This chapter discusses how ISO/IEC PDTR 15504[4]—the emerging International Standard for Software Process Assessment—can be used to complement ISO 9001. It compares the two models from the perspective of an organization that wants to obtain a clear definition of how to implement a software process improvement program and that is considering or has already gained registration[*] to ISO 9001.

This chapter assumes that the reader already has a good understanding of the 20 clauses (called elements in this chapter) of ISO 9001. Except where a *requirement* of the ISO 9001 standard is referred to, all discussions of ISO 9001 are in the context of ISO/DIS 9000-3,[5] used as an interpretive guideline for software organizations. References to ISO 9001 in this chapter, therefore, are meant to include references to the specific guidance contained in ISO/DIS 9000-3[**].

The chapter starts with an overview of ISO 9001 from a business and software perspective. It discusses some of the issues surrounding continuous process improvement for ISO 9001-registered software organizations. The SPICE framework is presented at a conceptual level to show how it can be used to complement ISO 9001 through the software process model found in ISO/IEC PDTR 15504-5[6]—Part 5, an exemplar model—as a guide to charting an improvement path. The chapter concludes with an interpretative mapping of the ISO 9001 elements to the processes and base practices of Part 5.

Overview of ISO 9001

Many excellent books have already been written describing how to implement ISO 9001 within a software organization. These books provide excellent descriptions of the purpose of the standard, discussions of how management's commitment and responsibilities are paramount to the achievement of a successful quality system, and element-by-element tutorials of how to achieve compliance as simply and effectively as possible.

---

[*]Registration is typically the term used for having the quality system assessed by an independent, accredited, third party to demonstrate conformance to ISO 9000 in North America. Certification has the same meaning in the United Kingdom and Europe.[3] This chapter uses the term registration throughout.

[**]At the time of writing this chapter, ISO/DIS 9000-3, the software guidance of ISO 9001, voting was about to close (May 1997) and hopefully would be advanced to the Final Draft International Standard stage at the TC176/SC2 Plenary in Copenhagen. Key changes to the guideline include a realignment of its clauses to match the 20 elements of ISO 9001. The purpose of this realignment was to make the guideline more usable for software organizations applying it in their ISO 9001 compliance efforts. In addition, 4.9 Process control was clarified to be applicable to the "replication, delivery, and installation of software" only since the development and maintenance of software is not considered to have a manufacturing phase that requires process control.

Many publications describe ISO 9001's philosophy of "say what you do and do what you say" as the basis of the quality system. As a quality assurance model, ISO 9001's tenet is sound and, if implemented with a focus on improvement of practices, it can yield tremendous benefits to the organization that designs its quality system to meet the needs of its customers.[7]

A software organization may establish as its business goals the objective of becoming registered to ISO 9001, depending on its drivers for developing a structured quality system. There are a variety of reasons why there is a worldwide trend for organizations to become registered, and ultimately it is up to each organization to determine its relative importance to the business.

Organizations that pursue registration to ISO 9001 do so for a variety of reasons:[8,9,10]

- in response to customer demands
- for greater discipline of processes
- to establish a consistent mode of operation
- to secure a marketing advantage
- to introduce a quality system into the organization
- to maintain pace with competitors.

The response to customer demands[8,9,10] is one of the most common reasons for registration. Customers want to ensure they receive "...conformance to requirements...Requirements [that are] clearly stated so that they cannot be misunderstood. Measurements [can then be taken] continually to determine conformance to those requirements. The nonconformance detected is the absence of quality. Quality problems become nonconformance problems, and quality becomes definable."[11] ISO 9001, and the registration system that supports the demonstration of compliance, provide a system through which customers can be assured of their suppliers meeting a minimum set of requirements.

ISO 9001 as the basis of a two-party contractual relationship

ISO 9001 was designed to serve as an end-to-end quality assurance model in which the activities involved in the assurance—and management—of products or services occur in the context of the customer-supplier relationship, for the benefit of the customer. Through the ongoing use and implementation of the quality system, verified through internal and third-party audits, indicators of the consistency with which products or services are produced become a measure of the effectiveness of the quality system.

ISO 9001's requirements for the quality system include any activities that the organization determines may affect the quality of its products or services. Those activities are documented to meet the standard's requirements, then once a documentation set has been created to demonstrate compliance, the audit may be performed—if registration is the objective—to ensure that the organization's procedures are performed as documented.

In the context of registration, the mandate of the ISO 9001 audit is to assess the organization's practices for compliance with both the standard and the organization's own interpretation of ISO 9001, as defined and documented in its operating procedures. The audit is performed by a third-party ISO 9000 Registrar,* reporting a binary finding: compliance/ noncompliance. Since ISO 9001 registration can support a two-party, customer-supplier relationship via an independent third-party audit, the circumstances of the audit require an arms-length relationship between the Registrar and the organization. To prevent a conflict of interest, Registrars typically will not assist in the interpretation of the standard or provide guidance on how to fix nonconformances.

If compliant, the organization is registered as having met the requirements of the standard. This third-party audit process provides the customer with an independent review of the supplier's quality system, without the customer having to perform the audit.

Quality through consistency

The ISO 8402[12] definition of *quality* is "the totality of characteristics of an entity that bear on its ability to satisfy stated or implied needs." The fundamental premise underlying this definition, and upon which ISO 9001 is based, is the *reduction of variance*. Consistent processes should lead to consistent output. This premise contributes to the notion that once variations within a process can be stabilized to a degree that they are known, they can be managed and eventually reduced.

To achieve the delivery of quality products and services, the organization defines the (ISO 9001) system in which it will ensure and build that "totality of characteristics." A *quality system* is the "organizational structure, procedures, processes, and resources needed to implement quality management...as comprehensive[ly] as needed to meet quality objectives."[12] Those objectives are set by the customer in determining what it requires from its suppliers. The supplier, as a matter of business planning, determines its product base and

---

*Certification Body, Registration Body, Registrar are all terms that can be used interchangeably.

market segment, and targets to achieve its market share based on a combination of inputs into its business planning process.

When customers demand ISO 9001 as a demonstration of the supplier's quality strategy, they are essentially demanding that the organization incorporates into its business plan the management of quality as a "systematic way of guaranteeing that organized activities happen the way they are planned. [A quality management system] is a management discipline concerned with preventing problems from occurring by creating the attitudes and controls that make prevention possible."[12]

In the global community, with easier access to a greater number of suppliers, customers' expectations of the level of quality they receive from their suppliers will continue to increase. Once a customer has achieved registration for itself, one of the easiest ways to control the quality of product or service it receives from its suppliers is to demand conformance with the ISO 9001 standard as a condition of doing business. Within 4.6 *Purchasing*, paragraph 4.6.2 *Evaluation of subcontractors* requires a definition of "the type and extent of control exercised by the supplier over subcontractors." This type of control is strengthened by paragraph 4.6.3, which goes on to suggest that the supplier describes on its purchasing documents "the title, number, and issue of the quality system standard to be applied."

This "domino affect" of building quality into supplier systems promotes standardization by focusing suppliers' ability on meeting at least minimum requirements. Suppliers retain their ability to differentiate themselves from their competitors in terms of product characteristics, market segment, price, and so on, but commit to their customers that they will manage the business using a quality assurance model that is applied consistently within the organization.

To suppliers, the message is clear: customer demand for quality is increasing. Those organizations demonstrating a proactive approach to its achievement may benefit from being preferred in bidding situations.

ISO 9001's challenge as a generic model

ISO 9001 can be exceedingly complex for any organization to implement, especially if that organization lacks the rigor and discipline required by the quality model for easy compliance with the standard. Not only can compliance appear to be out of reach of both an organization's budget and resources, but often the requirements can appear to bear no resemblance to the manner in which work is being performed.

Originally targeted at manufacturers, ISO 9001 is intended to fit any type of industry and any size of company. The genericness designed into the standard to accomplish this objective is precisely why it often appears to be difficult to implement. The rationale underlying ISO 9001's lack of industry focus is because to specify such detail would deviate from the standard's need for applicability to all industry sectors.

As a result, ISO 9001 may often be implemented more easily in the following scenarios:

- in an industry that has either a high level of maturity based on history, from which it can draw for guidance on the interpretation of the standard as it applies the quality model to its processes
- in an organization that employs such simplicity and constancy of process that it can map its processes easily and simply to the requirements of the standard
- in a business that is so highly regulated and/or controlled that formally-documented procedures and audit trails are part of the fabric of the business.

Many industries have had to interpret ISO 9001 for their own use. Sector-specific guidelines (sometimes supplemented by industry requirements) in the consulting engineering,[13] transportation,[14] and aerospace industries have worked to overcome the interpretation gap and to assist in the implementation pragmatics. These guidelines often translate the experience of other, mature organizations, closer to mastering the management of their processes, thereby facilitating the understanding and interpretation of similar organizations that are just getting started. A measure of industry control is also introduced by such sector-specific guidelines: ISO 9001-registered companies set their own industry-specific baselines to ensure that others in the field comply in relatively the same way.

Yet, in spite of the prevalence of books, consultants, ISO 9000-specific publications, and shared experiences, few organizations in any sector find the task of becoming conformant to ISO 9001 an easy one.

The ISO 9001 software challenge

The institutionalization of a quality methodology and a quality system into an organization works well in most industries. This is especially true when the business processes are well-defined and the required controls for preventing problems from occurring can be well established according to industry benchmarks and techniques (such as statistical process control in manufacturing environments).

However, the software industry is unique. As a discipline, software engineering shares too few characteristics with other industry processes to learn by mimicry. In practical terms, the discipline most closely resembling software engineering is the traditional engineering industry. Even so, while certain parallels can be drawn, ultimately there remain significant enough differences in work practices and the product's development life cycle that software engineering remains unique unto itself.

Aside from being a relatively new discipline, the software industry has special challenges because it produces a unique product:

> Software demands different quality management emphases than 'traditional' products...Software is immaterial, intangible. Its flexibility is legendary but ultimately frustrating if not properly identified and controlled. Unlike other products, the production phase (replication) can be performed with arbitrarily high precision. On the other hand, the design phase calls for more discipline and insight than perhaps any other intellectual activity. Software doesn't wear out, so all failures are the result of faults injected during design...Software methodologies are based on a phased (often repetitious) progression through development. Design—not production—is a challenge.[15]

Unlike the benefit other, mature industries have gained by having a history from which to draw on, the complexities of rapidly-changing technology further compound software engineering's relative newness to industry. Especially in software organizations operating at a relatively low maturity level and which have yet to master the fundamentals of software process performance, the constantly-changing and evolving tools, methods, and technologies create a development environment in which the *variables* impacting the software process—the *how* of software development—often confound the organization's perception of the processes themselves—*what* to do to produce a product. The organization often experiences an inability to distinguish the variables (the *how*) from the process (the *what*).

A simple illustration of this phenomenon is an organization's transition from using a waterfall life cycle in a mainframe environment to rapid prototyping in a client/server environment (both instances of *how* a development process is performed). Since, for example, the use of object-oriented technology can facilitate the selection and sequence of activities being performed, developers often perceive that the life cycle processes themselves have changed. The waterfall model, as a sequential life cycle, incorporates discrete and discernible stages that produce independent and discernible work products (requirements, logical specifications, physical specifications, and so on). In an iterative life cycle, the results of the iterations continually evolve the work products, which in themselves fulfill the various phases of the life cycle processes. However, the perception is that the independent process stages of requirements, specifications, and coding appear to occur either simultaneously or not at all since the work product is almost finished before design is completed. The mechanisms for distinguishing between the processes and work products are perceived to become transparent and indistinguishable as a result of the development technology and environment in which they operate.

The software industry is so different in its practices that ISO published guidelines to assist in bridging the interpretation gap. In addition, the UK developed the TickIT[16] registration scheme to establish the common ground rules for auditors and registration bodies. In spite of the challenges, and with the assistance of such guidelines, to their credit many organizations have already, and are continuing to, become registered to ISO 9001. At the time this chapter was written, in North America alone, of the over 15,000 ISO 9001-registered companies, almost 1 percent are software organizations.[17]

Continuous improvement after ISO 9001 registration

While the use of guidelines can assist in interpreting the requirements of and in getting registered to the standard, the assistance ends there. The most critical challenge that awaits organizations registered to ISO 9001, as well as those still considering it, is what to do *after* compliance is achieved. While the objective clearly is to maximize the quality system structure to assure the software processes are continually improving, the question becomes one of *how* to do it.

ISO 9001 supports the establishment of a level of consistent process performance that, once baselined—upon registration—can be used to introduce and track incremental improvements that can be built permanently into the quality system as opportunities are discovered. However, the organization must discern its own process improvement strategy, based on the findings of 4.17 *Internal quality audits*, 4.14 *Corrective and preventive action*, and 4.1 *Management responsibility*. While the combination of these elements work together as building blocks to create a basis from which the quality system can be improved, the standard was not designed to provide a structured path toward optimum *software* process performance. Even with the guidance of ISO/IEC 12207[18] that has been built into the ISO/DIS 9000-3 guideline, an organization is still limited to its own definition of what a mature software development process should be.

The work involved in becoming compliant with ISO 9001 is often associated with intensive efforts to document processes. The documentation-based philosophy supports an approach that baselines and controls documented procedures as a means to control changes to those procedures *after* the quality system is implemented. However, implementing an ISO 9001 quality system often introduces such a delta of change between pre- and post-implementation that the organization, while not required to change, often does. That delta is often significant since the infrastructure that ISO 9001 requires usually demands formalization of practices where none existed before. Practices are rarely documented, and new procedures are often introduced to support compliance with the standard.

Yet changes to the system may not necessarily reflect best software engineering practices, particularly when the changes are either new and immature practices introduced as a result of the new system or in reaction to discovered problems (corrective actions).

One of the consequences of procedures that are introduced without adequate definition may be either stasis or breakdown of the software processes. While the introduction of ISO 9001 is intended to stabilize the organization, if the implementation approach is not appropriate to the organization's objectives, it can result in too much change too quickly and may become difficult to sustain. The stresses on the business can become overwhelming.[27]

The quality assurance model, properly implemented, provides the foundation with which an organization can improve its practices. However, when efforts are made to fix problems, potentially large investments of cost, time, and resources could be expended in research into best practices before any improvements can be realized.

During a quality initiative, all levels of management may welcome the opportunities for discipline and consistency that the philosophies of the ISO 9001 standard bring. Senior management driving this initiative forward may commit not only to its basic implementation but also to seek the real value of the quality system. Nevertheless, even with a solid plan and management commitment, the organization may discover that it is navigating a vague and nebulous course in its attempts to find the appropriate improvement path. While the experience would be invaluable (most experience usually is valuable), a cost-benefit analysis may reveal that the invested costs in productivity, resources, and customer satisfaction incurred en route to its improvement target have not provided the anticipated return.

Experienced managers want the benefits that continuous improvement bring, however, they often do not have the time to experiment. They want results. The organization will likely improve—slowly and eventually—the rate of which depends a number of factors, such as practitioner experience, knowledge, and understanding of good software engineering principles. However, it may find the cost of experimentation too tedious or too costly to continue, especially if having taken the wrong path means having to backtrack.

Within any process improvement program, senior management must decide what needs to change and what the effects will be on the organization.[20] Once committed, the reasons sustaining an improvement path may be influenced by whether or not there are sufficient resources to justify the risk of uncertainty in trying to maintain its focus on standardization. Measurable results are needed, either in terms of increased product quality or process effectiveness.

Irrespective of the organization's motivations, when process improvement is the ultimate means to attaining their objectives, the options available to the senior management of an organization are often limited by their awareness and understanding of the process improvement models that exist.

Speed is the essence of software development: speed to gain market share with new products, speed to keep up with changing technology, speed to market. To support ISO 9001's requirement to improve its quality system, and the organization's products, the organization must demonstrate, at a senior management level, its continuing "report on the performance of the quality system...as a basis for improvement of the quality system."[2] Given that "the quality of a software product is largely determined by the quality of the process used to develop and maintain it,"[19] the software organization concerned with improving its products and processes has two choices. It can either:

1. spend its resources and time to find its own way, via trial and error, to improve those processes, or

2. find an already-existing framework to provide the path to the best practices.

The latter offers speedier delivery of confident results.

Improvement as a continuous cycle is not a new concept, however the *confidence* of expecting to benefit as a result of the investments of cost, resources, and time clearly is.

The organization striving to improve may find that ISO 9001's focus on process performance and quality assurance a good start, but one that does not provide sufficient visibility into its processes *soon enough* for it to implement meaningful improvements. That organization may be looking for alternatives to help it leverage its strengths in a relatively short time, according to specific business objectives.

Using the SPICE framework as a basis for continuous process improvement

When the quality of a software product is a critical component of a customer's buying decision, and the need to know the strengths and weaknesses of the organization's capability to develop a product is paramount, leaving the customer with unanswered questions or doubts about just how capable the organization may be is not conducive to securing an advantage.

ISO 9001 is not a *process* model. It is a *quality assurance* model. Quality assurance institutionalized into an organization demonstrates that "all the planned and systematic activities [are] implemented within the quality system and demonstrated as needed to provide adequate confidence that an entity will fulfill requirements for quality."[12]

Depending on the organization's perspective and objectives, the institutionalization of a quality assurance model—and ISO 9001 registration—may be a primary or a secondary goal with respect to continuous process improvement. If registration is primary, incorporating the SPICE framework into the ISO 9000 quality system model may prove to be more suitable *after* registration has been achieved when a continuous process improvement is about to be launched. This approach would work to support the quality system's improvement requirements by providing the organization with a software process model that embodies best practices, a built-in improvement path, and the assessments to track progress.

If registration is a secondary consideration, with continuous process improvement as primary, the SPICE process model may prove to be more suitable as a *prerequisite* process model to ISO 9001 registration. Organizations may find that they fare better in their efforts to successfully integrate and maintain the quality system standard since an orthogonal model may provide specific focus and direction toward improving process capability and consequently product quality. This approach could reduce the inevitable stress that change inevitably brings. The flexibility to prioritize which processes to improve provides a balance to the entire system of processes since the organization exercises more direct control over how it is effecting change.

A model of best practices to which the organization can compare and emulate may illustrate a more intelligible process framework to the staff of the organization, thereby permitting a clearer map of its process improvement progress and growth. The SPICE document set has been designed specifically to provide the best-practice view of software process performance, with Parts 2[4] and 5[4] providing the reference model as the process dimension.

As with ISO 9001, the emerging standard is not prescriptive in specifying *how* the process should be defined or performed. It does, however, clearly identify *what* activities constitute best practices, as appropriate within the process context. Using the SPICE framework, the organization still has the flexibility to add or ignore any processes that, according to its organizational objectives, do not apply to its business. The framework offers guidance on how to ensure consistency in defining any new processes that may be unique to the business.

The dimensions of process performance

The SPICE process model, with its two-dimensional perspective of process performance *and* process capability, can help the organization focus on implementing only those practices in line with its organizational and quality objectives to ensure that it can cope with the inherent changes that result. The way in which the assessment is performed requires that the organization's objectives—and hence its quality objectives—are considered in an assessment of its capability.

When the organization attempts to improve its processes within the SPICE framework, it is first responsible for determining what its improvement goals and objectives are—its target capability. The assessment then measures actual capability. The qualified assessor first determines if the processes are actually performed according to the reference model. The establishment of process performance as a prerequisite of mapping the improvement path of the process is essential to assist the organization in understanding its deficiencies. Once the deficiencies become known, so do the opportunities. The process profile reveals whether any processes that should be performed are not being performed (meaning it would be at Level 0). If at Level 0, there would be no need to continue the assessment since without performing the basic processes, there would not be a capability to measure. The first task would be for the organization to establish an improvement plan that addresses initial performance of the software processes applicable to its organization.

Once a determination has been made that the processes are being performed, the qualified assessor can then measure how well the processes are performed using the process attributes of the capability dimension. The target capability is then compared to the current capability—how well the organization actually performs its processes.

The difference between the results of an ISO 9001 audit—which will also reveal deficiencies—and a SPICE-conformant assessment, is that the ISO 9001 results will only reveal conformance or nonconformance to the organization's own activities as it has defined them for itself. The organization's benchmark is against *its own practices*, whereas the SPICE assessment gives the organization an *external indication of best practices* and a determination of the level of performance of those practices. The opportunities that an ISO 9001 audit reveals would be limited by what the organization (or a third-party Registrar) can discover to be nonconformances against its own practices. The scope of the ISO 9001 audit may not review the quality system at the same depth that the SPICE qualified assessor would examine. In addition, the SPICE assessment is specific in the process instances the qualified assessor will examine. The ISO 9001 audit may or may not be. However, the key strength of the SPICE assessment is its output—*the process profile and its ratings*—in that it provides a software *process*-specific and industry-based benchmark—quantifiable and measurable—against which the organization can determine the rate at which it is performing:

> Without statistical control it is difficult to measure the effect of a change in the system.[28]

The assessment output, by providing a measure of capability, provides the organization with the data it needs to define for itself and its customers specific *quality criteria* with which to associate the measures of its products, processes, or both. The process profiles—specifically the ratings assigned at the end of an assessment—can be used to provide the quality system with the effectiveness indicators it requires. Measurable objectives are essential for determining whether or not the ISO 9001 quality system is improving in effectiveness. The SPICE framework does not attempt to measure the effectiveness of the process in achieving its goals since that determination can only be done in the context of the business objectives. However by measuring, during the assessment, the delta between the current and target capabilities on a per-process basis, the SPICE model can provide the quality system with such effectiveness measures.

The objectives of the SPICE assessment are to provide repeatable results, as long as the assessment is performed in a conformant manner according to the SPICE assessment requirements. The confidence in the data yielded by such the model essentially provides the software organization with closure of one iteration of its improvement cycle since it has reliable data with which to measure, track, and start the next cycle.

The SPICE ratings data can therefore become a usable and valuable metric of the quality system. The capability dimension can provide each of the organization's processes with attributes that indicate its capability level. It can do so with a degree of detail that specifies how closely the process met has its objectives (**N**ot adequate, **P**artially, **L**argely, **F**ully) thereby portraying a relatively accurate picture of its improvement opportunities.

The data can then be plotted against its target, and the improvements planned, implemented, tracked, verified, validated against the quality system objectives, and finally remeasured. Then the cycle starts over again. Since the intent is for the organization to create plan to implement a "redesign" of its quality system, the risk of misdirected experimentation—trial and error—is greatly minimized since the requirements for the quality system have been gathered in a systematic manner.

The SPICE capability levels provide the organization with specific and focused guidance. The "redesign" is specific, quantified, and capable of measurement against the organization's quality objectives.

The process of change

As illustrated in the previous section, the introduction of process change into any organization is essentially a modification of the design of its business processes. The best practices the organization is capable of achieving should be engineered to reflect its target level of capability, one that is practicable for the organization to achieve. For the design to be implemented effectively, the process of change should not only follow the discipline of a formal design process, with all the rigor of controlling, verifying, and validating those changes, but it should ensure *before* the change is committed that the organization's objectives are being met. This commitment can only be made if a clear path that delineates the engineering implementation of those objectives can be mapped along a path that the organization can follow. Just as customers present their requirements to their suppliers for fulfillment, in the design of a quality system or process improvement program, the software organization becomes its own customer, serving its own needs in the design of its system.

If left to a trial-and-error method, best practices may not ever be attained any more than quality software is developed if the requirements and design stages are bypassed. The attributes of the capability dimension can help the organization focus on and structure its internal mechanisms to ensure they are addressing customer needs. Since customer needs will be addressed by the quality system, the likelihood that the organization will be ensuring that its objectives are understood, addressed, and met is greatly enhanced. The reality of an effective system—effectiveness being determined by the organization's achievement of its business goals—*properly implemented* is in its ability to create a standardized environment that permits management to see, understand, and address the issues facing the business. Through ongoing reviews of the operational processes of the business, management arms itself with data reflecting the true process instantiations occurring within the organization. The value of such data lies in its ability to provide management with indicators that are clear enough to represent what in the quality system needs to be changed. Only then is management capable of ensuring that its requirements can be planned and managed.

The ability of staff to sustain the business through these self-imposed periods of change and improvement, in spite of the inconsistencies of process that occur during these changes, is dependent on the underlying management processes and direction. The commitment must be in place to see the improvement plan through its verification and validation stages. The work environment and the composition of the organization's staff can undergo radical modification. Changes in technology may erode the existing experience base until new skills can be developed. When problems are encountered they can serve to highlight management's responsibility to continue to implement a structure that controls the processes it manages, so that those processes can be allowed to mature. The capability dimension of the SPICE model provides the organization with an approach with which to institutionalize management processes that contain within it, as its basis, a process of controlled change.

In the Phase 1 Trials, a significant number respondents validated the assumption that the improvement path provided by the SPICE framework is one of its biggest advantages. When the statement *"The assessment provided valuable direction about the priorities for process improvement in the organization"* 93 percent of the sponsors (assessees) responded that they either "Strongly Agree" or "Agree."[21] When asked a similar question, 74 percent of the assessors agreed or strongly agreed. This empirical support will hopefully be validated by the results of the Phase 2 Trials.

Mapping ISO 9001 to the SPICE process model and base practices

This section provides one interpretation of how ISO 9001 and Part 5 of the SPICE document set can be mapped to one another. ISO 9001 and the SPICE process model are both interpretive models, depending on the context in which they are used, how the various elements and clauses are to be applied, and they objectives they are trying to achieve. The mapping provided here is only one interpretation. Others may differ and be equally valid.

The approach taken in formulating this mapping was to take each of the base practices contained in the Part 5 process model and map them to all 20 elements of ISO 9001. This mapping may not be applicable to every organization, especially if the any of the Part 5 processes do not have to be performed in the business. (For example, CUS.1 may not be applicable to every organization.)

The capability dimension process attributes were not mapped to ISO 9001 because the underlying assumption remains that the organization must first obtain the level of initially performing the processes. Once Level 1 has been achieved, the organization can then work toward instituting a program of process improvement that elevates the capability of each of its processes as needed.

Following the table is a very brief discussion to illustrate the rationale behind the selection of the processes and base practices for the most-commonly audited elements of ISO 9001 that relate to process improvement activities: 4.17 *Internal quality audits*, 4.14 *Corrective and preventive action*, and 4.1 *Management responsibility*.

SPICE	ISO 9001

SPICE	4.1	4.2	4.3	4.4	4.5	4.6	4.7	4.8	4.9	4.10	4.11	4.12	4.13	4.14	4.15	4.16	4.17	4.18	4.19	4.20
CUS.1–ACQUIRE SOFTWARE																				
CUS.1.1–Identify the need			X																	
CUS.1.2–Define the requirements			X			X														
CUS.1.3–Prepare acquisition strategy			X			X														
CUS.1.4–Prepare RFP						X														
CUS.1.5–Select SW product supplier			X			X														
CUS.1.6–Determine interfaces to independent agents & subcontractors			X																	
CUS.1.7–Negotiate contract						X														
CUS.1.8–Support contractor			X			X														
CUS.1.9–Accept supplied product		X					X			X										
CUS.2–MANAGE CUSTOMER NEEDS				X																
CUS.2.1–Obtain cust reqts & requests			X	X																
CUS.2.2–Agree on requirements			X	X																
CUS.2.3–Establish cust reqts baseline				X	X															
CUS.2.4–Manage cust reqts changes			X	X																
CUS.2.5–Understand customer expectations			X	X																
CUS.2.6–Keep customers informed				X																
CUS.3–SUPPLY SOFTWARE																				
CUS.3.1–Review before contract finalization			X						X											
CUS.3.2–Negotiate contract			X																	

SPICE	ISO 9001																			
	4.1	4.2	4.3	4.4	4.5	4.6	4.7	4.8	4.9	4.10	4.11	4.12	4.13	4.14	4.15	4.16	4.17	4.18	4.19	4.20
CUS.3.3–Determine interfaces to independent agents & subcontractors			X			X														
CUS.3.4–Develop system or software				X																
CUS.3.5–Review development with customer				X						X										
CUS.3.6–Provide customer feedback			X																	
CUS.3.7–Deliver & install software				X					X						X					
CUS.4–OPERATE SOFTWARE																			X	
CUS.4.1–Identify operational risks																			X	
CUS.4.2–Perform operational testing														X					X	
CUS.4.3–Operate the software																			X	
CUS.4.4–Resolve operational problems													X	X					X	
CUS.4.5–Handle user requests																			X	
CUS.4.6–Document temporary work–arounds														X					X	
CUS.4.7–Monitor system capacity & service																			X	
CUS.5–PROVIDE CUSTOMER SERVICE																				
CUS.5.1–Train customer																			X	
CUS.5.2–Establish product support																			X	
CUS.5.3–Monitor performance														X					X	
CUS.5.4–Determine customer satisfaction level														X						X
CUS.5.5–Compare with competitors														X						X

SPICE	4.1	4.2	4.3	4.4	4.5	4.6	4.7	4.8	4.9	4.10	4.11	4.12	4.13	4.14	4.15	4.16	4.17	4.18	4.19	4.20
											I S O 9 0 0 1									
CUS.5.6–Communicate customer satisfaction		X																		X
ENG.1–DEVELOP SYSTEM REQTS & DESIGN				X																
ENG.1.1–Identify system requirements				X																
ENG.1.2–Analyze system requirements				X																
ENG.1.3–Describe system architecture				X																
ENG.1.4–Allocate requirements				X																
ENG.1.5–Determine release strategy				X																
ENG.1.6–Communicate system requirements				X																
ENG.2–DEVELOP SOFTWARE REQTS				X																
ENG.2.1–Specify software requirements				X																
ENG.2.2–Determine operating environmt impact				X																
ENG.2.3–Evaluate requirements with customer				X																
ENG.2.4–Determine release strategy				X																
ENG.2.5–Update requirements for next iteration				X																
ENG.2.6–Communicate software requirements				X																
ENG.3–DEVELOP SOFTWARE DESIGN				X																
ENG.3.1–Develop software architectural design				X																
ENG.3.2–Design interfaces				X																

SPICE	4.1	4.2	4.3	4.4	4.5	4.6	4.7	4.8	4.9	4.10	4.11	4.12	4.13	4.14	4.15	4.16	4.17	4.18	4.19	4.20
ENG.3.3–Develop detailed design				X																
ENG.3.4–Establish traceability				X	X			X												
ENG.4–IMPLEMENT SOFTWARE DESIGN				X																
ENG.4.1–Develop software units				X																
ENG.4.2–Develop unit verification procedures				X						X										
ENG.4.3–Verify the software units				X				X		X		X								
ENG.5–INTEGRATE & TEST SOFTWARE										X			X							
ENG.5.1–Determine regression test strategy				X						X			X							
ENG.5.2–Build aggregates of software units				X						X			X							
ENG.5.3–Develop tests for aggregates				X						X	X		X							
ENG.5.4–Test software aggregates				X						X			X							
ENG.5.5–Integrate software aggregates				X						X			X							
ENG.5.6–Develop tests for software				X						X	X		X							
ENG.5.7–Test integrated software				X						X	X	X	X							
ENG.6–INTEGRATE AND TEST SYSTEM										X			X							
ENG.6.1–Build aggregates of system elements				X						X			X							
ENG.6.2–Develop tests for aggregates				X						X	X		X							
ENG.6.3–Test system aggregates				X						X	X	X	X							
ENG.6.4–Develop tests for system				X						X	X		X							

SPICE	4.1	4.2	4.3	4.4	4.5	4.6	4.7	4.8	4.9	4.10	4.11	4.12	4.13	4.14	4.15	4.16	4.17	4.18	4.19	4.20
ENG.6.5–Test integrated system				X						X		X	X							
ENG.7–MAINTAIN SYSTEM & SOFTWARE																				
ENG.7.1–Determine maintenance requirements				X																
ENG.7.2–Analyze user problems & enhancements				X										X						
ENG.7.3–Determine modifications for next upgrad				X																
ENG.7.4–Implement and test modifications					X			X		X	X	X								
ENG.7.5–Upgrade user system									X	X		X			X				X	
ENG.7.6–Retire user system															X				X	
SUP.1–DEVELOP DOCUMENTATION		X			X															
SUP.1.1–Determine documentation requirements		X			X															
SUP.1.2–Develop document		X			X															
SUP.1.3–Check document		X			X															
SUP.1.4–Distribute document		X			X															
SUP.1.5–Maintain document		X			X															
SUP.2–PERFORM CONFIGURATION MGMT					X			X				X								
SUP.2.1–Establish configuration management library system					X			X				X				X				
SUP.2.2–Identify configuration items					X		X	X				X				X				
SUP.2.3–Maintain configuration item descriptions					X		X	X				X				X				

SPICE	ISO 9001																			
	4.1	4.2	4.3	4.4	4.5	4.6	4.7	4.8	4.9	4.10	4.11	4.12	4.13	4.14	4.15	4.16	4.17	4.18	4.19	4.20
SUP.2.4–Manage change requests								X				X								
SUP.2.5–Control changes					X			X				X				X				
SUP.2.6–Build product releases					X		X	X				X								
SUP.2.7–Maintain configuration item history					X		X	X				X	X			X				
SUP.2.8–Report configuration status					X			X				X				X				
SUP.3–PERFORM QUALITY ASSURANCE																				
SUP.3.1–Select quality criteria	X																			
SUP.3.2–Define quality records																X				
SUP.3.3–Assure quality of SWE activities																	X			
SUP.3.4–Assure quality of work products																	X			
SUP.3.5–Report results	X																			
SUP.3.6–Handle deviations	X																X			
SUP.3.7–Produce independent QA resources& org	X																X			
SUP.4–PERFORM WORK PRODUCT VERIFCN				X	X				X	X			X							
SUP.4.1–Select work products				X	X				X	X			X							
SUP.4.2–Identify verification methods &techniques				X	X					X	X		X							
SUP.4.3–Establish completion criteria				X	X					X			X							
SUP.4.4–Conduct verification				X	X					X			X							
SUP.4.5–Document action items				X	X					X			X							

| | | | | | | | | I | S | O | | 9 | 0 | 0 | 1 | | | | | |
SPICE	4.1	4.2	4.3	4.4	4.5	4.6	4.7	4.8	4.9	4.10	4.11	4.12	4.13	4.14	4.15	4.16	4.17	4.18	4.19	4.20
SUP.4.6–Track action items				X	X					X			X							
SUP.5–PERFORM WORK PRODUCT VALIDN				X	X					X			X							
SUP.5.1–Identify work products subject to validatn				X	X					X			X							
SUP.5.2–Identify validation tasks & techniques				X	X					X	X		X							
SUP.5.3–Establish validation criteria				X	X					X			X							
SUP.5.4–Perform validation activities				X	X					X			X							
SUP.5.5–Document anomalies				X	X					X			X							
SUP.5.6–Track anomalies				X	X					X			X							
SUP.6–PERFORM JOINT REVIEWS				X																
SUP.6.1–Establish joint reviews				X																
SUP.6.2–Prepare for customer reviews				X																
SUP.6.3–Conduct joint management reviews				X																
SUP.6.4–Conduct joint technical reviews				X																
SUP.6.5–Support customer acceptance review				X																
SUP.6.6–Perform joint process assessment				X																
SUP.7–PERFORM AUDITS																	X			
SUP.7.1–Identify audit requirements																	X			
SUP.7.2–Prepare for audits																	X			
SUP.7.3–Conduct audits																	X			

SPICE	ISO 9001																			
	4.1	4.2	4.3	4.4	4.5	4.6	4.7	4.8	4.9	4.10	4.11	4.12	4.13	4.14	4.15	4.16	4.17	4.18	4.19	4.20
SUP.7.4–Perform corrective actions														X			X			
SUP.8–PERFORM PROBLEM RESOLUTION	X													X						
SUP.8.1–Report problem details	X													X						
SUP.8.2–Prioritize problems	X													X						
SUP.8.3–Determine resolution	X													X						
SUP.8.4–Track problem report to resolution	X													X						
SUP.8.5–Correct the defect	X													X						
SUP.8.6–Distribute the correction	X													X						
SUP.8.7–Analyze problem trends	X													X						
MAN.1–MANAGE THE PROJECT		X		X																
MAN.1.1–Define the scope of work		X		X																
MAN.1.2–Determine development strategy		X		X																
MAN.1.3–Select software life cycle model		X		X																
MAN.1.4–Develop project estimates		X		X																
MAN.1.5–Develop work breakdown structure		X		X																
MAN.1.6–Identify infrastructure requirements		X		X																
MAN.1.7–Establish project schedule		X		X																
MAN.1.8–Allocate responsibilities	X	X		X																
MAN.1.9–Establish project plans		X		X																

SPICE	ISO 9001																			
	4.1	4.2	4.3	4.4	4.5	4.6	4.7	4.8	4.9	4.10	4.11	4.12	4.13	4.14	4.15	4.16	4.17	4.18	4.19	4.20
MAN.1.10–Track progress against plans		X		X																
MAN.1.11–Evaluate project performance	X	X		X																X
MAN.2–MANAGE QUALITY	X	X		X																
MAN.2.1–Establish quality goals	X	X		X																
MAN.2.2–Define quality metrics		X		X																X
MAN.2.3–Identify quality activities	X	X		X																
MAN.2.4–Perform quality activities		X		X																
MAN.2.5–Assess quality		X		X													X			
MAN.2.6–Take corrective action		X		X										X						X
MAN.3–MANAGE RISKS	X			X																
MAN.3.1–Establish risk management scope	X			X																
MAN.3.2–Identify risks	X			X																
MAN.3.3–Analyze and prioritize risks	X			X																
MAN.3.4–Develop risk management strategies	X			X																
MAN.3.5–Define risk metrics	X			X																
MAN.3.6–Implement risk management strategies	X			X																
MAN.3.7–Assess results of risk mgmt strategies	X			X										X						
MAN.3.8–Take corrective action	X			X																

									ISO 9001											
SPICE	4.1	4.2	4.3	4.4	4.5	4.6	4.7	4.8	4.9	4.10	4.11	4.12	4.13	4.14	4.15	4.16	4.17	4.18	4.19	4.20
MAN.4–MANAGE SUBCONTRACTORS						X														
MAN.4.1–Establish statement of work						X														
MAN.4.2–Qualify potential subcontractors						X														
MAN.4.3–Select subcontractors						X														
MAN.4.4–Establish and manage commitments						X														
MAN.4.5–Maintain communications						X														
MAN.4.6–Assess compliance						X														
MAN.4.7–Assess subcontractor quality						X														
ORG.1–ENGINEER THE BUSINESS	X																			
ORG.1.1–Establish strategic vision	X																			
ORG.1.2–Deploy vision	X																			
ORG.1.3–Establish quality culture	X																			
ORG.1.4–Build integrated teams	X																			
ORG.1.5–Provide incentives	X																	X		
ORG.1.6–Define career plans	X																	X		
ORG.2–DEFINE THE PROCESS		X																		
ORG.2.1–Define goals	X	X																		
ORG.2.2–Identify current activitites, roles, authorities, & responsibilities	X	X																		
ORG.2.3–Identify inputs & outputs		X																		
ORG.2.4–Define entry & exit criteria		X																		
ORG.2.5–Define control points		X																		

SPICE	4.1	4.2	4.3	4.4	4.5	4.6	4.7	4.8	4.9	4.10	4.11	4.12	4.13	4.14	4.15	4.16	4.17	4.18	4.19	4.20
ORG.2.6–Identify external interfaces		X																		
ORG.2.7–Identify internal dependencies		X																		
ORG.2.8–Define process measures		X																		X
ORG.2.9–Document the standard process		X			X															
ORG.2.10—Establish policy	X	X																		
ORG.2.11–Establish performance expectations	X	X																		X
ORG.2.12–Deploy the process		X																X		
ORG.3–IMPROVE THE PROCESS														X						
ORG.3.1–Identify improvement opportunities														X						
ORG.3.2–Define scope of improvement activities														X						
ORG.3.3–Understand the process														X			X			
ORG.3.4–Identify improvements														X						
ORG.3.5–Prioritize improvements														X						
ORG.3.6–Define measures of impact														X						
ORG.3.7–Change the process														X						
ORG.3.8–Confirm the improvement														X						
ORG.3.9–Deploy improvement														X						
ORG.4–PROVIDE SKILLED HUMAN RESRCS																		X		
ORG.4.1–Identify human resource needs				X														X		

SPICE	ISO 9001																			
	4.1	4.2	4.3	4.4	4.5	4.6	4.7	4.8	4.9	4.10	4.11	4.12	4.13	4.14	4.15	4.16	4.17	4.18	4.19	4.20
ORG.4.2–Develop or acquire training				X														X		
ORG.4.3–Train personnel				X														X		
ORG.4.4–Recruit qualified staff																		X		
ORG.4.5–Evaluate staff performance																		X		
ORG.4.6–Provide feedback on performance																		X		
ORG.4.7–Maintain staff records																		X		
ORG.4.8–Define project teams	X			X														X		
ORG.4.9–Empower project reams	X			X														X		
ORG.4.10–Maintain project team interactions				X														X		
ORG.5–PROVIDE SWE INFRASTRUCTURE																				
ORG.5.1–Identify SWE environment requirements	X	X																		
ORG.5.2–Provide a SWE environment	X	X									X									
ORG.5.3–Provide support for developers	X	X																		
ORG.5.4–Maintain SWE environment	X	X									X					X				
ORG.5.5–Provide a workspace conducive to productive performance	X	X																		
ORG.5.6–Ensure data integrity and security					X			X				X								
ORG.5.7–Provide remote access facility	X	X			X															
ORG.5.8–Determine organizational reuse strategy	X	X			X			X												

SPICE	4.1	4.2	4.3	4.4	4.5	4.6	4.7	4.8	4.9	4.10	4.11	4.12	4.13	4.14	4.15	4.16	4.17	4.18	4.19	4.20
ORG.5.9–Establish a reuse library		X																		
ORG.5.10–Integrate reuse into life cycle	X	X																		

4.1 Management responsibility

The four base practices in the SUP.3 process were selected because of senior management's responsibility to define the quality criteria and to manage the results of the quality assurance function for not only projects but for the processes as well. These practices have a direct bearing on the quality system and on the organization's ability to define the role of quality within the organization. In these base practices, management is expected to fulfill similar responsibilities as outlined in ISO 9001's 4.1 element:

- to define the role quality assurance plays within the organization
- to understand the results of quality assurance activities
- to address deviations within the quality system
- to provide adequate resources for quality assurance to function properly.

SUP.8 and all of its base practices were selected because of management's requirement to be informed and to manage the results of the problem resolution process. Management may not be directly involved in actually resolving problems, but under ISO 9001, 4.1.3, reviews of such issues are required to ensure the ongoing effectiveness of the quality system.

MAN.1 base practices affect the allocation of resources (a management responsibility) and the overall evaluation of project performance as a gauge of the quality system.

MAN.2 was included because of the establishment of goals (policies) and activities that affect the health of the quality system.

MAN.3 affects the organization at an organizational level as well as at a project level. The risks inherent in projects must be identified and managed at a level senior enough to effect action, if required.

ORG.1 and ORG.2 are supportive of the intent of ISO 9001's 4.1 element in all the selected base practices.

ORG.4 and ORG.5 have a direct bearing on management's commitment and ability to sustain the business by provide resources at a personnel and environmental level.

4.14 Corrective and preventive action

CUS.4, CUS.4, and ENG.7, MAN.3 include base practices in which during testing, inspection, monitoring, or comparisons, opportunities for correction (via temporary workarounds) and or prevention may be implemented.

SUP.7 directly relates to the outcome of audits performed and their resulting opportunities for improvement.

SUP.8 is roughly the equivalent of the ISO 9001 element 4.14.2 corrective action.

MAN.2 relates directly to the correction of problems discovered within the quality system.

ORG.3 is roughly the equivalent of the ISO 9001 element 4.14.3 preventive action.

4.17 Internal quality audits

SUP.3 and MAN.2 involves activities performed by a quality assurance function within the organization, seeking to ensure that projects and process are followed consistently as required.

SUP.7 is roughly equivalent to the internal audit function of ISO 9001.

ORG.3 provides an assessment of the process in order to improve it.

ISO 12207: the common denominator in ISO/DIS 9000-3 and ISO/IEC PDTR 15504

The next version of ISO 9001 has been planned for the turn of the millennium in the year 2000. As a result of concerns expressed over the difficulty in cross-referencing ISO 9000-3 to ISO 9001, the interpretive guidelines are currently in the process of being realigned to directly correspond to the 20 elements.[5] This mapping should assist organizations in the translation of requirements for implementation of the standard in their own quality systems.

ISO/DIS 9000-3 in its current revision has referenced heavily ISO/IEC 12207 as the basis for its ISO 9001 interpretation for the software engineering industry in order to capture the essence of software processes as they should be performed within a two-party contractual relationship. As shown in other chapters in this book (see Chapters 3 and 4) the SPICE document set has also, and is continuing, to incorporate ISO/IEC 12207 as a process model. While the SPICE document set takes the process model beyond what is contained in ISO/IEC 12207, when considering it own software process improvement framework, the consistency between the three ISO documents lends credibility to the organization attempting to determine the approach it should adopt.

The Year 2000 ISO 9001 standard is expected to incorporate the principles behind the ISO 9000-3 guidelines and is expected to discontinue the publication of the software guideline. The Year 2000 Family[22] of ISO 9000-revised documents are targeted to be applicable to all industries without the use of such industry-specific ISO guidelines.[23]

ISO 9001 as it is written today is not a *process* model. It only states requirements for the quality system of an organization. The ISO 9000-3[25] guideline, however, discusses processes they relate to the life cycle model adopted by the organization in the development of its products. With the TC176 direction to incorporate the process principles contained within ISO 9000-4 into ISO 9001, the latter is targeted to become a process model[24] that will have even more applicability than the current standard has for software organizations today.

TC176's direction is also to blend ISO 9001 with ISO 9000-4 to provide consistency between the quality system and quality management models. The expected result of this combination will be to influence ISO 9001 to become a process-based model that more strongly supports continuous process improvement as one of its basic tenets.[24]

With ISO 9001 via ISO 9000-3, ISO/IEC 12207, and ISO/IEC PDTR 15504 sharing the same principles of process and process improvement, the organization seeking to determine its long-term improvement strategies may find the combination a particularly focused one that can provide a direction that will be sustainable and conducive to its business objectives.

Conclusions

Achievement of consistent software process performance alone is no longer sufficient to allow an organization to progress to a level of capability that permits changes to occur and to be managed effectively. ISO 9001 as a one-dimensional quality assurance model, the objective of which is to demonstrate consistent performance in the execution of its quality procedures, does not address what processes the organization should perform, only that it meets specific procedural requirements for the purposes of meeting quality system requirements. Hence, even for the organization that has identified process improvement opportunities as a result of its quality system structure, ISO 9001 is limited to presenting a one-dimensional paradigm of quality system requirements.

As customers' demands increase, software organizations will continue to seek a competitive edge. The increasing complexity of software technology—and the discriminating customers who buy it—will continue to demand more than consistent process performance. To remain competitive, software organizations must keep pace with the rapidity of technology's evolution, and the management of the organization must relentlessly focus its attention on the organization's ability to deal with that change.

In the business world, there is no such thing as "process nirvana." Every organization can find opportunities to improve. For those already registered to ISO 9001, they can use the SPICE model as a way to exercise the continuous improvement aspects of the standard (see Chapter 18).

For organizations seeking registration for the first time, SPICE can be used as a prerequisite model to simplify the effort of determining its target mode of operation by providing a path toward registration. The traditional gap analysis that is often used to help the organization determine its conformance level with ISO 9001 provides just that—the gap, but the organization must attempt to fill that gap with a conformant quality system. With its focus on conformance, it presents a pass/fail rating. The approach used to close that gap must be determined by the organization itself. While the results from the gap analysis usually are not a surprise to the organization, it often does not add any additional information to its knowledge level of where and how it its processes are deficient.

For organizations that must become registered to meet customer requirements, but that are also seeking a sound improvement path, the answer may be to blend the models. Used appropriately, SPICE can offer the next step in an evolution of software engineering standards that may provide organizations with specific guidance on how to achieve not only process performance but improved process capability.

Acknowledgments

Grateful appreciation and thanks should be extended to Jean-Martin Simon of Applied Quality Transfert (AQT) for his thorough review of this chapter and especially for his critical contribution in developing the ISO 9001—ISO/IEC PDTR 15505-5 mapping. He painstakingly reviewed the mapping and added many valuable insights for establishing this particular interpretation of how the two models could be used together.

Thanks should also go to the European Software Institute (ESI), and particularly to Bob Smith who made available early drafts of a Technical Report entitled *Driving process improvement with ISO 9000, Technical Baseline*, PIA97040[26] as a basis of comparison for the material discussed in this chapter.

Finally, thanks should also go to Khaled El Emam and Alec Dorling for their excellent comments and insights as to how this chapter could be improved.

Annex A: ISO 9001's 20 clauses

ISO 9001 clauses	
4.1	Management responsibility
4.2	Quality sysem
4.3	Contract review
4.4	Design control
4.5	Document and data control
4.6	Purchasing
4.7	Control of customer-supplied product
4.8	Production identification and traceability
4.9	Process control
4.10	Inspection and testing
4.11	Control of inspection, measuring, and test equipment
4.12	Inspection and test status
4.13	Confrol of nonconforming product
4.14	Corrective and preventive action
4.15	Handling, storage, packaging, preservation, and delivery
4.16	Control of quality records
4.17	Internal quality audits
4.18	Training
4.19	Servicing
4.20	Statistical techniques.

References

1. ISO 9001, *Quality Systems—Model for quality assurance in design, development, production, installation and servicing*, 2nd ed., July 1994.

2. ISO 9001, *Quality Systems—Model for quality assurance in design, development, production, installation and servicing*, paragraph 4.1.2.3.b, 2nd ed., July 1994.

3. Schmauch, C., *ISO 9000 for Software Developers*. ASQC Quality Press, Milwaukee, Wisconsin, 1995.

4. ISO/IEC/JTC1/SC7/WG10 15504-1—9, *Software Process Assessment— Parts 1—9*, Version 2.0, 1996.

5. Draft International Standard ISO/DIS 9000-3, *Quality management and quality assurance standards—Part 3: Guidelines for the application of ISO 9001:1994 to the development, supply, installation and maintenance of computer software*. 30 Aug. 1996.

6. ISO/IEC/JTC1/SC7/WG10, *Software Process Assessment—Part 5: An assessment model and indicator guidance*, Version 2.0, 1996.

7. Jenner, M.G., *Software Quality Management and ISO 9001*, John Wiley & Sons, Inc. 1995.

8. Vanguard Consulting Ltd., *BS5750 Implementation and Value Added,* Sept. 1993.

9. Vloeberghs, D. and J. Bellens., "Implementing the ISO 9000 Standards in Belgium," *Quality Progress*, ASQC, June 1996.

10. Weston Jr., F.C., "What do Managers Really Think of the ISO 9000 Registration Process," *Quality Progress*, ASQC, Oct. 1995.

11. Crosby, P.B., *Quality is Free*, Mentor, 1980.

12. ISO 8402. *Quality management and quality assurance—Vocabulary*. 1994.

13. CTA Quality Institute, *Interpretation of the ISO Standard for the Carrier Industry*, 1995.

14. FIDIC, *A Guide to the Interpretation and Application of the ISO 9001-1994 Standard for the Consulting Sector*, Draft for the London Seminar, (Unpublished), Jan. 1997.

15. Peach, R.W., *The ISO 9000 Handbook, 2nd ed.*, CEEM Information Services, Fairfax, VA, 1994.

16. Department of Trade & Industry and British Computer Society, *TickIT Guide to Software Quality Management System Construction and Certification using EN29001*, Feb. 1992.

17. Globus Information Systems, The ISO 9000 Universe, Aurora, Canada, Feb. 1997.

18. ISO/IEC 12207, *Information technology—Software life cycle processes*, 1ˢᵗ ed., Aug. 1995.

19. Carnegie Mellon University, Software Engineering Institute, *The Capability Maturity Model: Guidelines for Improving the Software Process*, Addison-Wesley Publishing Co. Inc., 1995.

20. Humphrey, W.S., *Managing the Software Process*, Addison-Wesley Publishing Co. Inc., 1990.

21. El Emam, K. and D. R. Goldenson, "An Empirical Evaluation of the Prospective International SPICE Standard," *Software Process Improvement and Practice*, Vol. 2, 1996, pp. 123–148.

22. ISO/TC 176/SC2/N243R2, *Year 2000 Family,* 8 Nov. 1996.

23. ISO/TC 176/SC2/N269, *Officers preliminary dispositioning of TC/176 documents/work items,* 9 Nov. 1996.

24. ISO/TC 176/SC2/N349. *Management Plan for the Development of a Consistent Pair of QA and QM Standards,* 14 Nov. 1996.

25. ISO 9000-3, *Quality management and quality assurance standards—Part 3: Guidelines for the application of ISO 9001 to the development, supply and maintenance of software,* 1st ed., June 1991.

26. European Software Institute, *Driving process improvement with ISO 9000, Technical Baseline*, PIA97040, July 1996.

27. Hermone, L. and L. McCoy, Hewlett-Packard, Golden Gate Service Center. "ISO 9000—Bureaucracy or Added Value?" in Canadian Standards Association, CSA Technical Committee on Quality Management (CAC/ISO/TC 176) *Plenary Meeting Minutes*. 4 Oct. 1996.

28. Deming, W.E., *Out of the Crisis,* Massachusetts Institute of Technology, 1986.

12

Introduction to the SPICE Trials

Fiona Maclennan[*]
Lloyd's Register, UK

Gary Ostrolenk
National Westminster Bank, UK

Mary Tobin
Lloyd's Register, UK

The software engineering community has produced a plethora of standards: by 1994, more than 250 software engineering standards had been produced by the world's major international and national standards bodies. However, there is considerable debate over the value of many of these standards. Over the last few years, a UK collaborative project, SMARTIE (Standards and Methods Assessment using Rigorous Techniques in Industrial Environments) has reviewed the content of software engineering standards as part of its work to

---

[*]Fiona Maclennan of Lloyd's Register was International Trials Coordinator for the SPICE Project during the first phase of the trials. She was supported by Gary Ostrolenk and Mary Tobin. In this capacity, they were representing the European Software Institute (ESI), of which Lloyd's Register was a founder member.

propose a procedure for the objective assessment of standards used in software development.[1] The project has made a number of observations about current software engineering standards:

- There is an imbalance, compared to other engineering standards, in the emphasis on process issues, relative to product and resource issues.

- The majority of software engineering standards are not really standards in the traditional sense of specifying mandatory requirements: most would better be described as guidelines.

- Even where requirements are specified, they are not normally stated in such a way as to enable an objective evaluation of compliance, nor does there tend to be any description of the method of compliance as found in standards from other disciplines.

- There is little, if any, objective evidence of the benefits of using software standards. Standards are devised and published without the use of case studies or experiments to demonstrate the benefits of using them and evaluating the costs relative to the benefits. Moreover, there is rarely a set of criteria that can be used to evaluate the use of a given standard.

As the SPICE Project is developing yet another software engineering standard, these issues are obviously of concern, particularly to the SPICE Trials program which was instigated at the beginning of 1994. Its primary aim is to obtain rapid feedback in the use of the SPICE documents to allow refinement before publication as a full international standard and thus ensure that the emerging standard satisfies the needs of its prospective users. The trials will validate the emerging standard against the goals and requirements defined at the start of the project and verify the consistency and usability of its component parts.

The first SMARTIE observation raises the question of whether a standard for Software Process Assessment (SPA) is needed. This question has already been addressed at the beginning of this book.

Regarding the second and third points, particular attention has been given, during the development of the SPICE documents, to separating out requirements from guidelines. The requirements relate to SPICE-conformant models and assessments. An important issue for the trials is whether these requirements can be complied with and whether or not compliance can be evaluated.

The last point is of most relevance to the SPICE Trials. The trials provide a unique opportunity to start to collect evidence of the benefits of conducting

SPICE-conformant SPAs (such as encouraging predictable quality products and optimum productivity), to look at cost-benefit issues, and to develop criteria for evaluating the use of the emerging standard. It will be the first such exercise for a software engineering standard. A fundamental issue is the validity and reliability—that is, the meaningfulness, repeatability, and comparability—of results from SPICE-conformant assessments.

The SPICE Trials program is now well advanced. Trials have been organized into three phases to coincide with key milestones in the standardization process, thereby maximizing the benefit of feedback. Phase 1 was concerned with the adequacy of the reference model for processes and process capability and for the assessment process. It was completed with a comprehensive report in October 1995. Phases 2 and 3 will evaluate the complete set of documents. Phase 2 started in the fourth quarter of 1996.

The rest of this chapter discusses the objectives of the overall trials program and the issues relating to the selection of a method for empirical validation before describing the approach adopted. It then describes how the Phase 1 Trials were organized and conducted and summarizes the conclusions drawn from them. Chapters 13 to 16 describe in some detail the different analyses that were conducted and their individual results.

Objectives

The overall trial objectives are to:

1. identify shortcomings in the SPICE products for resolution prior to standardization, particularly regarding coverage, usability, and applicability
2. seek evidence that the results of SPICE-conformant assessments are valid, repeatable, and comparable within defined parameters across organizational units (OUs) and organizations
3. initiate the collection of data regarding the benefits resulting from the use of the SPICE document set
4. validate that the SPICE products satisfy the requirements documented in the *Requirements Specification for a Software Process Assessment Standard.*[2]

The first three objectives relate to the key requirements for the SPICE documents as elaborated in the requirements (see chapter 3).

Coverage, usability, and applicability are of prime importance. The model is intended to include all important software engineering and management processes. The SPICE products must be usable (within reasonable time constraints, etc.) and applicable at the project and organizational levels, as well as across different application domains, criticality of products, sizes of organization, and so on.

These objectives, and the hypotheses derived from them (see Figure 12.1), recognize that data will have to be collected over a number of years before any convincing evidence can be established that a SPICE process profile reflects the "goodness" of a process. They also recognize that it can take a number of years for the benefits of process improvement to be realized or for capability to be demonstrated in the fulfillment of a contract.

Empirical validation method

Over the past few years, considerable attention has been given to the problems involved in the empirical validation of methods, tools, and standards for software engineering. The SMARTIE project developed a measurement-based approach to the assessment of software engineering standards.[1] The DESMET project developed a method for evaluating software engineering methods and tools.[3] Both projects successfully applied their results in actual evaluation exercises. Both approaches are concerned with evaluating the effectiveness of a given standard, method, or tool, either relative to some other standard, method, or tool, or compared with not using it, where the measure of effectiveness would be some combination of cost, timescale, and quality. Such approaches are suited most obviously to standards that prescribe *how* some process is to be performed. They are far more difficult to apply if the standard allows a wide range of alternative, compliant ways of working.

This was a particular issue for the SPICE Trials. The emerging standard specifies requirements for assessments, but it does not prescribe the conduct of assessments. Thus, any positive or negative results arising from the use of the emerging standard may be attributable not to the emerging standard, but to extraneous features of the assessment method used. Moreover, the target of the assessment itself is abstract: SPICE assesses processes and their capability, not the methods and tools used by those processes. The difficulty of the SPICE Trials is further compounded by the breadth of the objectives: to evaluate coverage, usability, applicability, and validity of assessment results, as well as the benefits resulting from the use of SPICE.

The following high-level hypotheses provide an overview of the claims that underlie the standard and that are to be tested by the trials:

1. Processes that implement software process best practice tend to be more effective than those that do not, all else being equal. (Effectiveness is to be judged informally, in terms of the ratio of value-to-cost for the organizational unit. It is recognized that different organizations have different process goals and therefore different measures of effectiveness.)

2. On the whole, the higher a process is rated by a SPICE-conformant assessment, the more it implements software process best practice. (Expert judgment shall be used to discriminate the extent of implementation of software best practice, independently of the standard.)

3. Similar ratings will be delivered of an organizational unit by different assessment teams, using any method and instrument, as long as:

   - both assessments are SPICE-conformant and use representative samples of process instances
   - both assessments are given the same assessment context
   - there have been no significant changes in process in the intervening period between the assessments.

4. Similar ratings will be delivered of two organizational units by different assessment teams using any method and instrument, as long as:

   - both organizational units are judged by independent experts to implement software process best practice more or less to the same extent in each of the processes assessed
   - both assessments are SPICE-conformant and therefore use representative samples of process instances
   - both assessments are given the same assessment context
   - The SPICE guidelines for process improvement are usable and useful.

5. The SPICE guidelines for process capability determination are usable and useful.

6. It is possible to tell from the output of an assessment whether or not it was SPICE-conformant.

Figure 12.1: Trials hypotheses.

Notwithstanding these issues, the terminology and guidelines developed by DESMET for the selection and design of empirical studies were useful in deciding the approach to be adopted for the SPICE Trials and recognizing its limitations.

There are three types of empirical study:

- A *formal experiment* is the most rigorous form of empirical investigation. It can be used to confirm conclusively a hypothesis, such as a statement about the benefit of the use of a method, tool, or standard, and usually generates results that demonstrate causal relationships, more strongly than those derived from other types of empirical study. In a formal experiment, a treatment (method/tool) is applied and varied in a controlled environment in the expectation that certain factors—response variables—will have related and predicted values. All variables that can affect the truth of a hypothesis, known as *state variables*, must be carefully controlled. The experimental sample must cover a sufficient range of possible values to establish that the treatment, and not some other state variable, caused the response. It must be possible to replicate the basic situation under investigation in order to confirm and generalize the effect of the treatment. For results to be conclusive, such replications are necessary.

- A *case study* is a way of conducting a trial evaluation in a realistic situation, in a complex environment, over which the investigator has little control. Because there is less control over state variables than in a formal experiment, it is much more difficult to draw causal conclusions from the results. Unless there is a clear baseline against which to judge the results, only anecdotal evidence can be provided for, or against, a hypothesis.

- A *survey* is a way of analyzing existing data available from a wide variety of sources in order to identify trends. Thus, surveys are only suitable when the object of investigation is already widely in use. Surveys can normally only identify an association, not a causal relationship. The data must be collected in the same way, with common data definitions. The analysis must be undertaken carefully to prevent extraneous factors from distorting evaluations.

All empirical studies should have:

- a well defined hypothesis
- response variables that are directly derivable from the hypothesis

- a full definition of all treatments to be applied
- a design that identifies and mitigates confounding effects that may affect the impact of the treatment
- a full description of the conditions of the study
- full definitions of the data to be collected and their method of collection that allows measurements of the response variables to be calculated
- valid statistical analysis techniques.

Consideration of the emerging SPICE standard within the above framework immediately made obvious the huge number of state variables involved in assessments. The requirements of the SPICE document set stipulate that it must be applicable irrespective of:

- current priority business objectives—in particular, the project is concerned with productivity, process turnaround time, and product quality attributes
- business sector and application domain
- size, complexity, and criticality of product or service
- size and structure of the assessed OU and of any wider organization, of which the OU is a part and whose management actions have a direct effect on the OU
- management philosophy/style
- software life-cycle model, development method, and technology
- national and linguistic culture.

During the trials, the intent is to test the emerging standard in as many different environments, covering as many values of these factors, as possible. There are other variables, such as the composition of the assessment team, that may also impact on the results of an assessment. To account for all these state variables, a formal experiment would require a vast sample, far bigger than is possible within the timescales and voluntary resources of the SPICE Trials. In addition, although mechanisms can be put in place to promote consistency across trials, the logistics of an international, voluntary exercise do not allow control over the environment in which they are undertaken. Therefore, the use of a formal experiment is not practical as the main method for the trials. Where it is possible to isolate and test particular aspects of the use of the emerging standard, formal experimental methods are being investigated.

The use of case studies is more appropriate given the environment in which a SPA is undertaken. There are many variables which are difficult to control and assessment objectives require the use of realistic scenarios.

Surveys would not be appropriate for testing many of the hypotheses as there will not be sufficient use of the documents nor data about their usage, especially early on in the trials.

The approach adopted for the trials is to employ indicative case studies to cover as much of the reference model and scenarios of use of the emerging standard as possible. The intention is also to cover as broad a range of values of the state variables (industries, cultures, development and organizational environments, and so on.) as possible. These case studies will be supplemented with more formal experimental methods where practicable, and by surveys where there has been sufficient usage to enable meaningful data to be gathered. Each empirical study is being used to gather data to support (or refute) one or more of the hypotheses given earlier. Data from these case studies, in the form of structured feedback, is being gathered through carefully-designed questionnaires.

As a consequence of using this approach, the trials will tend to provide anecdotal evidence to support the hypotheses rather than conclusive proof. The resource limitations of the trials and the size, complexity, and duration of the processes involved in software development, capability determination, and process improvement also constrain the extent to which objectively-measurable response variables can be specified in hypotheses. The trials rely extensively on expert human judgment and less on objective measures.

During the trials, data collection regarding the benefits of using the emerging assessment standard will be initiated. The mechanisms put in place to do this should support the long-term validation and continual improvement of the emerging standard.

Organization and infrastructure

A three-phase approach has been adopted for the trials (see Figure 12.2) in order to maximize the benefit from the trials during the development of the emerging standard and to fit in with the ISO review stages. Each phase has its own specific objectives and scope. Phase 1 focused on the early design decisions during the development of the emerging standard, while Phases 2 and 3 will focus on the integrity of the emerging standard as a whole, and on whether or not the original requirements have been satisfied. For each phase, the hypotheses to be tested are defined, as are the method, techniques, and scenarios to be used. An appropriate organization and infrastructure, including procedures and data collection mechanisms, has been established to support each phase, from selection and conduct of the trials through to analysis of trials data and reporting of results.

Phase 1	
Purpose:	Design decision and usability testing of the core products.
Scope:	Reference model for processes and process capability, requirements and guidance for process assessment, guidance on construction and use of assessment instruments and indicators.
Participants:	SPICE resources
Entry criteria:	Stable reference model and process assessment requirements and guidance.
Start date:	January 1995.
Completion:	October 1995.
Phase 2	
Purpose:	Product integration and repeatability testing.
Scope:	All SPICE products.
Participants:	Software engineering community.
Entry criteria:	Consolidated product set, following resolution of major problems discovered in Phase 1.
Start date:	September 1996
Completion:	September 1997[*] .
Phase 3	
Purpose:	Validation of SPICE goals and requirements.
Scope:	All SPICE products.
Participants:	Software engineering community.
Entry criteria:	Consolidated product set, following resolution of major problems discovered in Phase 2.
Provisional start date:	March 1998.
Expected completion:	March 2000.

Figure 12.2: Trials phases.

---

[*] At the time of writing, this deadline had been extended.

The trials are supported by an international trials team, set up in January 1994, responsible for planning the trials activities, designing questionnaires and forms, and analyzing and reporting the results.

All data collected from the trials is submitted to the RTCs who are responsible for removing any identifying information or confidential data before onward transmission to the trials team for analysis. Confidentiality of assessment data is paramount to securing participation in the trials.

The main customers of the trials are the SPICE product teams developing the emerging standard. They have been involved in the definition of objectives, hypotheses, questionnaires, and forms to ensure that the evaluation data from the trials satisfies their needs. The trials organization is depicted in Figure 12.3. The RTCs are responsible for soliciting trials participation and ensuring that the benefits and limitations are understood. For Phase 1, a *Call for Participation* was distributed across the technical regions that outlined the requirements,

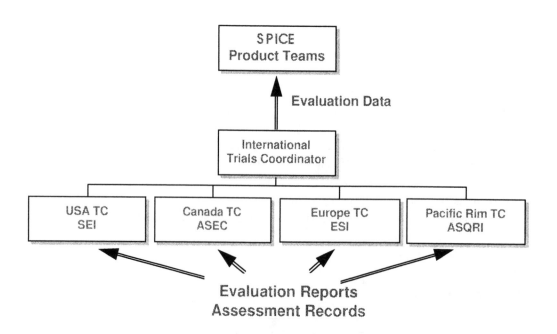

Figure 12.3: SPICE Trials organization.

benefits, and limitations of participation. Benefits offered to the participants included the ability to influence the emerging standard and gain early exposure to SPICE assessments, in addition to the benefits arising from the assessment itself. The limitations of participation related to the early stage of development of the emerging standard and the consequent possibility of encountering problems with it during the assessment.

To prepare those leading assessments during Phase 1, a number of briefing sessions were held, covering the SPICE products under trial, and the procedures to be followed with respect to questionnaires and forms. The briefing sessions were based on a set of briefing materials, including slides and case studies, to ensure consistency of approach between the qualified assessors in different case studies. They were also used to stress the limitations of the trials. The briefing sessions did not constitute any formal training in SPICE or process assessment in general. Experience in process assessment, and a background in the SPICE Project and document set were therefore prerequisites for participation in Phase 1 for the role of qualified assessor (as defined in the *Process Assessment Guide*).

As with the development of the emerging standard itself, resources for all the trials have been provided from around the world on a voluntary basis. The work of the trials team has been undertaken via quarterly meetings, teleconferences, and the extensive use of Internet servers and electronic email. The planning of Phase 1 Trials was dependent on the progress of the development of the emerging standard and analysis of the results on the submission of data from participating organizations. The successful completion of the Phase 1 Trials, more or less to schedule, required considerable commitment and dynamic risk management.

Phase 1

Objectives

The purpose of Phase 1 was to test the design decisions for the core products and their usability. At the time of Phase 1, these products were: the *Baseline Practices Guide* (BPG), the *Process Assessment Guide* (PAG), and the *Assessment Instrument* (AI). Assessments could be used in the context of process improvement or capability determination, although capability determination for supplier selection was discouraged at this early stage. However, use of the guidance material for process improvement and capability determination fell outside the scope of the Phase 1 Trials.

The objectives of Phase 1 were to:

1. evaluate the coverage, applicability, and usability of the BPG

2. evaluate the usability of the emerging standard and guidance parts of the PAG and the practicality of the assessment process defined in the PAG

3. evaluate the intuitive appeal, relevance, and feasibility of use of the measurement framework defined in the PAG, identifying the relative merits of the alternate scales for rating base practices

4. evaluate the coverage and usability of the AI, and the perceived necessity and benefits of using a conformant assessment instrument in assessments based on the BPG and the PAG

5. identify interface problems between the BPG, the PAG, and the AI

6. contribute to the improvement of the SPICE products

7. collect preliminary impressions of the benefits of SPICE-conformant assessments.

These objectives were refined into a set of hypotheses, shown in Figure 12.4.

Data sources

A preliminary questionnaire (Q1) was used to enable the selection of suitable cases, asking about the candidate assessor, the OU to be assessed, and the scope of the proposed assessment. Selection was guided by the need to optimize coverage of the software processes, capability levels, and organizational characteristics, and the need for qualified assessors to be sufficiently experienced to be able to apply the SPICE products.

The data employed by the trials team to validate the hypotheses came from the following sources:

- Trials Phase 1 questionnaire set (Q2-Q4)
- Trials Phase 1 context data and rating forms (TDR)
- Trials Phase 1 observation reports
- Trials Phase 1 problem reports.

1. A significant majority of assessed organizational units and assessors consider that SPICE-conformant assessments address the relevant and important aspects of the processes assessed.

2. No more than a small minority of assessed organizational units and assessors consider that SPICE-conformant assessments focus on unimportant aspects of the processes assessed.

3. No more than a small minority of assessed organizational units and assessors consider that relevant organizational unit processes cannot be mapped into the processes defined in the BPG.

4. A significant majority of assessors consider themselves (and/or are) able to use the PAG and the BPG to conduct assessments in a practical timescale.

5. A significant majority of assessors consider themselves (and/or are) able to use the PAG, the BPG, and the AI to conduct assessments in a practical timescale.

6. A significant majority of assessors who attempt to use the existence rating scale for base practices consider that it is usable within practical timescales and that it captures sufficient information for the assessment purpose.

7. A significant majority of assessors who attempt to use the adequacy rating scale for base practices consider that it is usable within practical timescales and that it captures sufficient information for the assessment purpose.

8. A significant majority of assessed organizational units and assessors consider that the profile output by a SPICE-conformant assessment is an accurate and fair representation of the degree to which the organizational unit implements software process best practice in the assessed processes.

9. A significant majority of assessors consider that the features required by the AI of a conformant assessment instrument make assessments more practical than would otherwise be the case.

10. A significant majority of assessors consider that the features required by the AI of a conformant assessment instrument are necessary to achieve repeatability of assessment results.

11. A significant majority of assessors who use only the PAG and the BPG in an assessment consider that a conformant assessment instrument would make assessment results more repeatable.

12. A significant majority of assessors who attempt to use the AI to develop a conformant assessment instrument consider that the AI contains sufficient clear and unambiguous information to enable the development of conformant assessment instruments.

13. A significant majority of assessors consider that the AI requires conformant assessment instruments to cover all the practices defined in the BPG for the assessed processes.

Figure 12.4: Trials Phase 1 hypotheses.

Assessor perspectives questionnaire (Q2a & Q2b)

Q2 was in two parts. Q2a was completed by the experienced assessor at the end of the trials assessment. The other assessment team members completed Q2b. Q2 sought:

- factual information about the assessment (sampling, resources, and process)
- judgments about the assessors' experience in using the SPICE products (usability, understandability, applicability, coverage, adequacy, and usefulness)
- judgments about the commitment, motivation, support, and understanding of the OU
- judgments about the value of the assessment results.

Assessee perspectives questionnaire (Q3a & Q3b)

Q3 was in two parts. Q3a was completed at the end of the assessment by the OU manager, acting as sponsor of the assessment. Other participants in the assessment from the OU were invited to complete Q3b, to ensure the representation of technical as well as management perspectives. Q3 sought:

- judgments about the understandability, relevance, usefulness, and practicality of the assessment process and its results
- judgments about the credibility and professionalism of the assessment team.

Assessment instrument questionnaire (Q4)

Since the AI was not ready for trials when Phase 1 began in January 1995, it was evaluated toward the end of Phase 1 by each individual who fulfilled the role of qualified assessor. Each qualified assessor provided feedback that was informed by the assessors' experiences of using other assessment instruments in the assessments or using the AI. Feedback was collected via questionnaire Q4.

Q4 was completed by the qualified assessor after completion of all assessments and after the AI had been baselined. Q4 asked qualified assessors either to review the AI in light of their experience of using an assessment instrument in the assessment or to report on their experiences using the AI.

Context data and rating forms (TDR)

These forms were used to record details of assessment output. This detail included information about the quality characteristics of the OU (as defined in ISO 9126), safety, economic, and environmental risks associated with the OU's software, as well as adequacy and existence assessment ratings of BPG practices.

Fields were provided for recording the BPG practice reference, the rating itself, and a free-text description of any evidence, observations, analysis, and so on that constituted the rationale for the rating.

Observation report form (F1)

F1 was intended for recording preliminary impressions of problems, positive points of note, and possible enhancements to the SPICE products as they were found during assessments. F1s were to be completed, as needed, by assessment team members and on occasion by OU participants.

Problem report form

This form was a SPICE Project-wide mechanism for recording problems. Its use was prescribed in the SPICE Project's Problem Reporting and Change Management Procedure. In the trials, the problem report form was intended to communicate conclusions drawn by the qualified assessor in an assessment concerning problems with, and possible enhancements to, the SPICE products. These conclusions were based on F1s filed during the assessment. The problem report form queried the nature of the problem or enhancement, its significance, and its location in the SPICE product set.

Trials data set

Trials were conducted in three of the four SPICE technical regions: Europe, Canada, and the Pacific Rim. None were conducted in the USA. The data used in the analysis was collected from 35 trials, 20 of which were conducted in Europe, 1 in Canada, and 14 in the Pacific Rim.

A complete trials data set was defined to be as follows:

- questionnaires Q2a, Q3a, Q4
- TDR context data and rating forms.

In addition, there may have been (one or more of) the following:

- questionnaires Q2b, Q3b
- observation and problem reports.

The data collected for the 35 trials was incomplete with regard to Q4 and TDR data. Two of the European trials were missing this data, as was the Canadian trial. Five of the Pacific Rim trials were missing Q4 data and 4 of these were also missing TDR data.

As a consequence, the context data and rating analysis was conducted on data from 28 trials (18 from Europe and 10 from Pacific Rim). A total of 48 projects and 324 process instances were included within the scope of these 28 trials.

All the data included in the questionnaire analysis came from Q2a, Q3a, and Q4. The "b" questionnaires were not analyzed, since they were not returned by comparable numbers of people in each assessment. However, a later analysis of this data has not been precluded.

One hundred observation and 128 problem reports were raised in total from 24 trials.

Two databases were used to collect the data and support analysis. The first contains the questionnaire, TDR, and observation report data. The second was used to analyze the problem reports. Delays in the provision of data impacted on the scheduling of analysis activities, with the effect that its scope had to be reduced. Although sufficient data was collected for the purposes of analysis, the incompleteness of the data did constrain the analysis activities.

Overall analysis approach

Two broad categories of analysis were conducted in Phase 1. The first, demographic analysis, included information on how many trials were conducted, the average duration of a trial, and the coverage and spread of adequacy ratings for the processes in the model for process management. This analysis was relatively simple and straightforward to design, process, and present. It provided a concise but informative summary of the Phase 1 Trials. As there were potentially a large number of demographics that could have been reported, the primary criterion for inclusion was to limit the report to those considered to be most relevant to the objectives of Phase 1 Trials.

The second category of analysis focused on extracting useful information from the commentary provided by trials participants. The extent to which Phase 1 hypotheses were satisfied was determined from the questionnaire responses.

Observation and problem reports were analyzed to identify common themes, recurring problems, and trends.

Details of the particular approach taken for each trial data source are provided in Chapters 13–16, where the results of the analyses and their individual conclusions and recommendations are presented.

Conclusions and recommendations

Despite some minor inconsistencies in the application of the data collection process across the trials, it has been possible to draw a number of useful conclusions and recommendations from the Phase 1 Trials.

The preliminary impressions gathered were generally positive about the SPICE document set, although a number of issues were highlighted for attention in the revision of the emerging standard for the Phase 2 Trials.

The SPICE model for process management generally was found to be relevant and applicable. However, major problems existed with the Phase 1 Trials version which have since been addressed, in a fundamental review and rework, for Phase 2.

Although assessments were generally easy to conduct, it was concluded that the SPICE document set needed to provide more direction and that the rating of processes needed to be reviewed. The results also indicated that attention should be given to reducing the time needed to undertake a SPICE assessment.

Although profiles generated using the proposed rating mechanism were generally considered to provide an accurate and fair representation of the degree to which an OU implements software process best practice, there was some difficulty in rating process management activities.

Conclusions about the guidance on the construction, selection, and use of assessment instruments and tools were more tentative. It was generally considered that:

- the guidance was useful for developing an assessment instrument
- the right instrument design characteristics were included
- the requirements for conformance were easy to understand
- the indicator set provided adequate coverage.

The indicators, which were provided to guide a qualified assessor in recognizing adequacy of software engineering or process management activities, were generally considered clear and easy to understand. Although the trials results were generally supportive of this part of the emerging standard, some substantial problems, regarding the size and organization of the indicator set, its complexity and maintainability, and the requirements for assessment instruments, were raised by a small number of trials participants.

The Phase 1 Trials were the first exercise of this kind. It is, therefore, not surprising that many lessons were learned from the experience. In retrospect, insufficient planning was undertaken for the trials to ensure that:

- the right, and only essential, data was collected

- a consistent approach was adopted across all trials, particularly with respect to the completion and submission of data in a timely manner

- problems with data entry were minimized

- the analyses tasks were consistent and focused.

In addition, insufficient time was allowed for the conduct of trials, for the collection and entry of data into the database for analysis, and for the analysis and report. A number of recommendations were made relating to the trials process to ensure that the same problems are not encountered in Phase 2.

In conclusion, the Phase 1 Trials have provided very useful feedback from the user community for the improvement of the emerging standard. Their successful completion is a major achievement and has demonstrated the feasibility of empirical validation of a full international standard. Any similar trials will require a similar approach and infrastructure to support them.

References

1. Lawrence, S. Pfleeger, N. Fenton, and S. Page, "Evaluating Software Engineering Standards," *Computer*, Sept. 1994, pp. 71–79.

2. ISO/IEC (1993), *Requirements Specification for a Software Process Assessment Standard*, JTC1/SC7/WG10 N017R, Issue 1.00, 3 June 1993.

3. DESMET (1994), *Guidelines for Evaluation Method Selection*, DES/WP2.2/7, Deliverable 2, Version 2.0, NCC Services Ltd, June 1994.

13

Empirical Evaluation of SPICE

Khaled El Emam
Fraunhofer—IESE, Germany

Dennis R. Goldenson
Software Engineering Institute, USA

This chapter presents some of the key results from studies conducted during Phase 1 of the SPICE Trials. These studies evaluated the Version 1.00 SPICE documents. The results indicate that the SPICE model and rating framework in general are sound and have been found to be useful and usable, but they also highlight some potential weaknesses. As of this writing, the weaknesses have been taken into consideration in developing Version 2.00 of the SPICE document set. More details of these results may be found in a published paper written on the subject.[5]

In the next section the research method that was used for data collection and data analysis is described. The detailed results are presented in the following section. Finally, conclusions are discussed at the end of this chapter.

Research Method

During each of the Phase 1 Trials assessments a set of questionnaires[*] were administered. For the purposes of this chapter, responses were obtained from two groups of people: (1) lead assessors who were in charge of the trials assessments and (2) the sponsors of the assessments in the organizational unit (OU). These responses gave us the assessors' and assessees' perspectives respectively. In total, questionnaire data from 35 assessments was collected before the response deadline.

The objectives of the analysis of the questionnaire responses as presented in this chapter are twofold:

1. to describe what actually happened during the Phase 1 assessments
2. to present an evaluation of some of the core SPICE Version 1.00 document set.

The evaluation results for the *Base Practices Guide* (BPG) and *Assessment Instrument Guide* (AIG) are also presented in this chapter.

The results given in this chapter provide the percentage of responses to various questions.[*] These results are shown in the form of histograms. To evaluate the SPICE document set, the team identified of the proportions of respondents who were supportive (as opposed to critical) of either the SPICE Project design decisions or the claim that the documents are usable. A supportive response was one that:

- said something positive about SPICE, and/or
- did *not* require any changes to the draft SPICE documents (Version 1.00 used during the Phase 1 Trials assessments)

A distinction was also made between *very supportive* and *moderately supportive* responses. This distinction helped make clear the extent of support for the SPICE document set. For example, assuming that a question asked the respondents to express their extent of agreement to the following statement:

> The assessment improved awareness of software process issues among the OU's software engineers.

---

[*]Copies of these questionnaires may be obtained directly from the authors.
[*]An inferential analysis of this data has been performed and is presented in a published paper[5].

and also assuming that the question had the following four response categories:

Strongly agree, Agree, Disagree, Strongly disagree

As shown in Figure 13.1, the *Strongly agree* and *Agree* responses would be considered supportive of the SPICE document set, and the *Disagree* and *Strongly disagree* responses would be considered critical of the SPICE documents. Furthermore, the *Strongly agree* response category would be considered to be very supportive of the SPICE document set and the *Agree* response category would be considered to be moderately supportive of the SPICE documents.

For the histograms presented in the results section of this chapter, the number of responses differ considerably. The reasons for the differences are mainly that: (1) for different questionnaires, a different number of responses were received and (2) for different questions, there were different numbers of missing data:

- the respondent did not answer the question at all

- responses to particular questions excluded the respondent from the analysis for other questions (for example, if the assessor did not use the *Assessment Instrument Guide* for preparing and/or during an assessment, the assessor was excluded from the analysis of certain questions that assume that the *Assessment Instrument Guide* was used).

It is important to remember that such an extensive empirical evaluation of a Software Process Assessment framework and/or model as was being conducted in the SPICE Trials had not been conducted before. Therefore, it was difficult to compare the trials' results to those from previous studies. In the few exceptional cases where precedents exist, this comparison was made in the presentation of our results.

Supportive Responses		Critical Responses
Very supportive responses	Moderately supportive responses	
Strongly agree	*Agree*	*Disagree strongly disagree*

Figure 13.1: Types and examples of response categories.

Results

Description of the assessments

The SPICE Version 1.00 documents provided general guidance for conducting assessments. The activities defined in the documents[*] are summarized in Figure 13.2. As seen in Figure 13.3, most of the assessment activities defined in the SPICE documents were performed during most of the assessments. However, in less than 70 percent of the assessments two processes were not performed: *Verify existence ratings* and *Determine derived ratings*. The former may be due to the fact that existence ratings were performed in a smaller number of assessments (when compared with adequacy ratings).

Activity	Brief Description[*]
Define and review the assessment inputs	The assessors review the assessment purpose, scope, and constraints to ensure that they are consistent and that the assessment purpose can be fulfilled; they also define responsibilities, and add any extended process definitions.
Select process instances	This activity involves mapping the OU's processes to the BPG model and then selecting instances in a manner that would satisfy the assessment purpose.
Identify assessment risk factors	Risk factors include changes in the commitment of the sponsor, unplanned changes to the structure of the assessment team, organizational changes, and lack of confidentiality.
Brief the OU's personnel	The briefing includes an overview of the assessment purpose, scope, and constraints, the conduct of the assessment, and how the assessment outputs can be used to provide the most benefit to the organization.
Verify ratings	Supporting documentation and records are collected to verify the ratings made.
Determine derived ratings	Derived ratings are based on an aggregation of actual ratings for process instances.
Validate the ratings	This validation includes comparing the results with those from previous assessments of the same OU, looking for inconsistencies in the ratings of related processes, and feedback sessions of preliminary findings to the OU.
Present the results to OU management	The assessment findings are presented to OU management and the sponsor.

Figure 13.2: Brief description of some assessment activities.

---

[*]*Collecting and verifying information* has been excluded because it is a basic activity that has to be performed in any assessment.

[*]These are only brief descriptions of the activities to aid the reader in interpreting the charts. More details of the activities can be found in the SPICE documents.

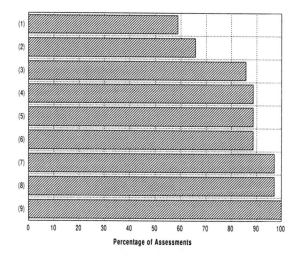

Percentage of Assessments

No.	Activity	Percentage of assessments
(1)	Verify existence ratings (existence is a two-point rating scale that can be used in an assessment)	(20/34) = 59%
(2)	Determine derived ratings	(23/35) = 66%
(3)	Identify assessment risk factors	(30/35) = 86%
(4)	Verify adequacy ratings (adequacy is a four-point rating scale that can be used in an assessment)	(31/35) = 89%
(5)	Present the assessment results to OU management	(31/35) = 89%
(6)	Validate the ratings	(31/35) = 89%
(7)	Select process instances	(34/35) = 97%
(8)	Brief OU personnel	(34/35) = 97%
(9)	Define and review the process inputs (purpose, scope, constraints, responsibilities, and extended process definitions)	(35/35) = 100%

Figure 13.3: The activities that were performed during the assessments.

During the assessments, the most commonly-used type of assessment instrument was a paper based checklist, followed next in frequency of use by a computerized spreadsheet (Figure 13.4). Apart from the spreadsheet, it was rare that any other form of computerized instrument was used. The instruments that were used were developed mostly by the qualified assessors themselves (Figure 13.5). Very few of the assessors (only 35 percent) used the exemplar instrument provided by the SPICE Project.

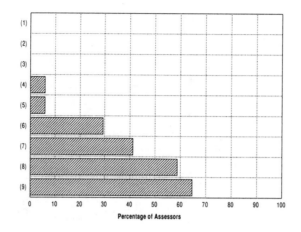

No.	Type of assessment instrument	Percentage of assessors
(1)	Computer-based flat file	(0/17) = 0%
(2)	Computerized checklist	(0/17) = 0%
(3)	Computerized Expert System	(0/17) = 0%
(4)	Computerized questionnaire	(1/17) = 6%
(5)	Computerized relational database	(1/17) = 6%
(6)	Computerized scoring	(5/17) = 29%
(7)	Paper-based questionnaire	(7/17) = 41%
(8)	Computerized spreadsheet	(10/17) = 59%
(9)	Paper-based checklist	(11/17) = 65%

Figure 13.4: Type of assessment instruments used by the assessors.

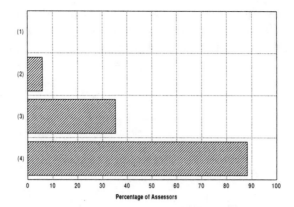

No.	Developer(s) of the assessment instruments used	Percentage of Assessors
(1)	OU representative(s)	(0/17) = 0%
(2)	Third party tool builders / vendors	(1/17) = 1%
(3)	Supplied as an exemplar from the SPICE Project	(6/17) = 35%
(4)	Experienced assessors(s)	(15/17) = 88%

Figure 13.5: The developer(s) of the assessment instruments used.

Most of the information that was collected during the assessments was through interviews, followed by the review of documents or interim work products (Figure 13.6). No qualified assessors used assessee self-reports, and very few collected data prior to the onsite visit (12 percent).

Overall Evaluation

The assessment sponsors' overall perceptions were generally quite positive towards SPICE. Almost *all* of them agreed that the benefits of their assessments were at least *on balance* worth the expense and time their organizations expended (Figure 13.7):

- Almost 40 percent said their assessments were *more than worth the expense*.
- Almost 80 percent of the assessment sponsors agreed that awareness, buy-in, and support for process improvement improved among their organizations' management as a result of their assessments.

- However, only 65 percent agreed to a similar question about their technical staffs, and relatively few chose the *strongly agree* response option to either question about commitment to software process improvement resulting from the assessments.

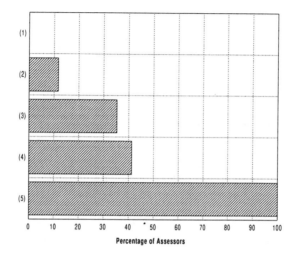

No.	Method for collecting information	Percentage of assessors
(1)	Assessee self reports	(0/17) = 0%
(2)	Data collection prior to onsite visits	(2/17) = 12%
(3)	Group feedback sessions	(6/17) = 35%
(4)	Document or interim work product reviews	(7/17) = 41%
(5)	Interviews	(17/17) = 100%

Figure 13.6: The method(s) the assessors used to collect information during the assessment.

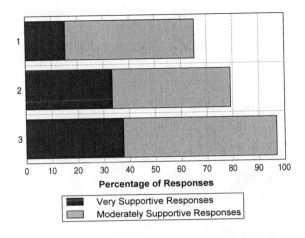

No.	Question	Supportive Response Categories	Critical Response Categories	Percentage Supportive
(1)	The assessment improved awareness, "buy-in," and support for process improvement among the organization's technical staff	• Strongly Agree • Agree	• Strongly Disagree • Disagree	(17/26) = 65%
(2)	The assessment improved awareness, "buy-in," and support for process improvement among the organization's management	• Strongly Agree • Agree	• Strongly Disagree • Disagree	(19/24) = 79%
(3)	Were the benefits of the assessment worth the expense and the time expended?	• More Than Worth the Expense • On Balance Worth the Expense	• Not Worth the Expense	(31/32) = 97%

Figure 13.7: Overall evaluation of the SPICE assessment by the assessees.

Overall, the experienced assessors were somewhat more positive toward the SPICE document set than were the assessees, but they too tended to qualify their responses (Figure 13.8)—indeed more so than did the assessees. Almost all the assessors said that the OU personnel were satisfied with the results of their assessments: over 80 percent thought that the assessments improved awareness of software process improvement issues among the engineers in the OUs that were assessed. Perhaps most pertinent from a SPICE document perspective, 85 percent of the experienced assessors characterized the SPICE approach as being at least somewhat better than other assessment methods* with which they were familiar. Once again, however, relatively few of their answers (less than 25 percent to all three questions) fall into what we have classified as responses that are *very supportive* of the SPICE document set and the Phase 1 Trial assessments.

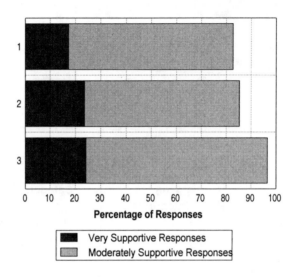

Figure 13.8: Overall evaluation of the SPICE assessment by the assessors.

No.	Question	Supportive Response Categories	Critical Response Categories	Percentage Supportive
(1)	The assessment improved awareness of software process issues among the OU's software engineers	• Strongly Agree • Agree	• Strongly Disagree • Disagree	(24/29) = 83%
(2)	Compared to other assessment methods with which you are familiar, how would you characterize the SPICE approach?	• SPICE Is Much Better • SPICE Is Better on Balance	• SPICE Is Much Worse • SPICE Is Worse on Balance • SPICE Is Neither Better Nor Worse	(29/34) = 85%
(3)	The OU's personnel were satisfied with the results of the assessment	• Strongly Agree • Agree	• Strongly Disagree • Disagree	(28/29) = 97%

*SPICE does not define a complete process for conducting an assessment. It does provide guidance however.

Accuracy of assessment results

As seen in Figure 13.9, the assessment sponsors were generally quite satisfied with the accuracy and actionability of their assessment results. Over 90 percent of the assessors reported that their assessments provided valuable direction for process improvement in their organizations, characterized their organizations' strong points at least *reasonably well*, and that their SPICE process profiles accurately described their organizations' major problems. Once again, however, the assessees did express some reservations. Over 20 percent said that the process profiles were only *generally accurate* within the scope of their assessments. Well over 30 percent of the assessment sponsors reported inappropriately identified *problems* in their process profiles. A similar proportion said that their profiles *failed* to identify problems in the scope of their assessments.**

Some of the results obtained for the SPICE document set can be compared with those obtained in another survey*** of users of the CMM.[6] When asked about how well the CMM assessment described the organization's major problems with the software process, 98 percent responded with the *very accurately* or *generally accurately* categories. This is comparable to the 91 percent obtained from the assesees in the SPICE Trials. In addition, when asked how well the assessment characterized the organization's strong points, 92 percent of the respondents to the CMM survey chose the *very well* or *reasonably well* response categories. This percentage is comparable to the 93 percent obtained from the SPICE questionnaires. Therefore, at least by these two criteria, the results from the Phase 1 assessments are comparable to those obtained from a previous process assessment model survey.

Here, the assessment sponsors are more supportive of SPICE in its Phase 1 incarnation than are the assessors. Figure 13.10 summarizes the assessors' responses to two general questions about the accuracy and actionability of the Phase 1 assessments. The *supportive* responses approach 80 percent in both instances. However, rather few of the assessors chose the unequivocal response option *strongly agree*.

**There may be question wording problems though. "Any" problems and "anything" are quite unrestrictive modifiers.

***This survey was done at least one year after the assessment was conducted.

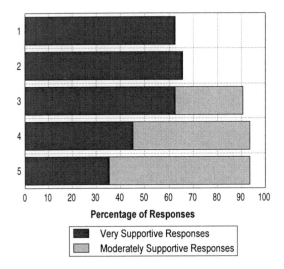

Percentage of Responses

■ Very Supportive Responses
▨ Moderately Supportive Responses

No.	Question	Supportive Response Categories	Critical Response Categories	Percentage Supportive
(1)	Did the software process profile inappropriately identify anything as a problem(s)?	• No	• Yes	(20/32) = 62%
(2)	Did the software process profile fail to identify any problems within the scope of the assessment?	• No	• Yes	(21/32) = 66%
(3)	To the best of your knowledge, how accurately did the software process profile describe the organization's major problems within the scope of the assessment?	• Very Accurately • Generally Accurately	• Not Very Accurately	(29/32) = 91%
(4)	How well did the assessment characterize the organization's strong points?	• Very Well • Reasonably Well	• Not Very Well	(29/31) = 93%
(5)	The assessment provided valuable direction about the priorities for process improvement in the organization	• Strongly Agree • Agree	• Strongly Disagree • Disagree	(29/31) = 93%

Figure 13.9: Assessees' impressions about the accuracy of the assessment results.

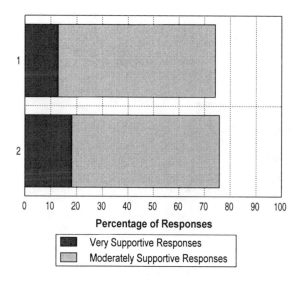

Percentage of Responses

■ Very Supportive Responses
▒ Moderately Supportive Responses

No.	Question	Supportive Response Categories	Critical Response Categories	Percentage Supportive
(1)	The assessment provided valuable direction about priorities for process improvement in the OU	• Strongly Agree • Agree	• Strongly Disagree • Disagree	(23/31) = 74%
(2)	The assessment helped management identify important strengths and weaknesses in their OU	• Strongly Agree • Agree	• Strongly Disagree • Disagree	(25/33) = 76%

Figure 13.10: Assessors' impressions about the accuracy of the assessment results.

General evaluation of the Base Practices Guide

The experienced assessors expressed reservations about this version of the BPG after having used it in their Phase 1 assessments (Figure 13.11). *All* of them did agree that the BPG was in fact useful for the assessments about which were queried. However fewer than half of them chose the more strongly worded response alternative. Two-thirds of the assessors said that additional processes

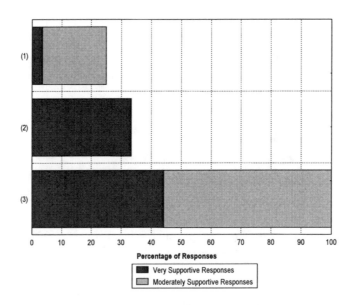

Figure 13.11: Assessors' overall evaluation of the BPG.

No.	Question	Supportive Response Categories	Critical Response Categories	Percentage Supportive
(1)	The BPG provides sufficient direction for scoring the practices	• Strongly Agree • Agree	• Strongly Disagree • Disagree	(7/28) = 25%
(2)	In your opinion, are there any processes or common features which are not covered in the *Baseline Practices Guide* and should be?	• No	• Yes	(8/24) = 33%
(3)	Overall, the BPG was useful for this assessment	• Strongly Agree • Agree	• Strongly Disagree • Disagree	(34/34) = 100%

or common features should be included in the BPG. Very few agreed that the BPG provided sufficient direction for scoring the practices.*

The assessees tended to have generally positive attitudes toward the BPG (Figure 13.12) although they would not have used it as extensively as the

---

*This question may overstate dissatisfaction with the BPG. It could be interpreted to mean that the BPG does not adequately define the practices. It could also mean that scoring is the domain of another SPICE document: the Process Assessment Guide, which explains how to rate practices. Therefore, this result does not necessarily indicate that the BPG was not achieving its purpose.

assessors. Almost 70 percent of the assessees stated that there were no important missing areas in the BPG (question 1). The BPG did allow for extending the practices through the generation of application/sector specific practice guides. The majority of assessees felt that the process improvement order implied in the SPICE framework was valuable. Almost all of the assessees (92 percent) felt that the BPG provided real hope for long term process improvement.

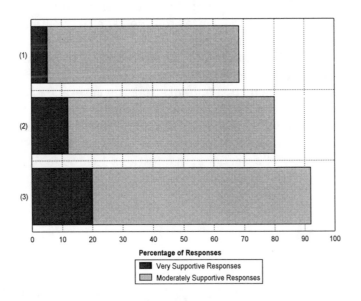

No.	Question	Supportive Response Categories	Critical Response Categories	Percentage Supportive
(1)	There are important areas that the BPG does not address	• Strongly Disagree • Disagree	• Strongly Agree • Agree	(13/19) = 68%
(2)	The SPICE *Baseline Practices Guide* provides valuable direction about the order in which process improvements should be made	• Strongly Agree • Agree	• Strongly Disagree • Disagree	(20/25) = 80%
(3)	Because of its comprehensive nature, the BPG provides real hope for long term process improvement	• Strongly Agree • Agree	• Strongly Disagree • Disagree	(23/25) = 92%

Figure 13.12: Assessees' overall evaluation of the BPG.

Evaluation of the *Assessment Instrument Guide*

Much of the analyses presented so far were based on questionnaires meant to be collected at the end of each of the Phase 1 assessments. The AIG was not available throughout most of Phase 1, and there was concern about overtaxing the goodwill of the assessors. Hence the following analyses are based on a single questionnaire that was created for distribution to each experienced assessor after the completion of all of his or her Phase 1 assessments.

The experienced assessors' responses to nine general questions about the AIG are summarized in Figure 13.13. Their reviews are somewhat mixed. First of all, notice that large majorities agreed that the AIG met its most basic requirements (questions 7, 8, and 9). They agreed that the AIG did in fact provide useful help for developing an assessment instrument, that the coverage of the indicator set was adequate, and that the AIG was compatible with the other two core SPICE documents. However, fewer (71 percent) thought that the guide was helpful in selecting an existing assessment instrument (question 6), and fewer than two-thirds agreed to a series of assertions (in questions 1 through 5) about the clarity and usability of the AIG.

Conclusions

The SPICE Trials do show that it is possible to provide empirical evidence that can inform decision making for an evolving, emerging International Standard. In the spirit of continuous improvement, the Phase 1 Trials identified a number of areas in need of modification in Version 1.00 of the SPICE documents. As planned, the Phase 1 of the SPICE Trials was completed in time for a critical decision point in the standardization process of the SPICE document suite. This decision point was a ballot by the member national bodies on the documents. The results from Phase 1 of the SPICE Trials were used as input into this process, whereby the Phase 1 Trials report was made available to all member bodies prior to the ballot deadline. The team is aware of at least two bodies that made explicit reference to the results of the trials in their comments.

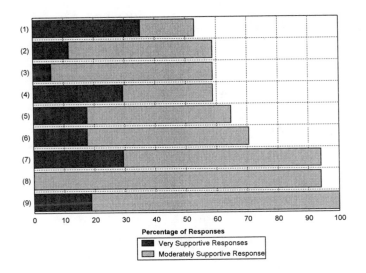

Percentage of Responses

▪ Very Supportive Responses
▦ Moderately Supportive Response

No	Question	Supportive Response Categories	Critical Response Categories	Percentage Supportive
(1)	Without the availability of an AIG an assessment is/would be more difficult to conduct	• Strongly Agree • Agree	• Strongly Disagree • Disagree	(9/17) = 53%
(2)	The AIG is/would be usable in terms of time scale and effort for developing a new assessment instrument	• Strongly Agree • Agree	• Strongly Disagree • Disagree	(10/17) = 59%
(3)	The AIG is/would be usable in terms of time scale and effort for selecting an assessment instrument	• Strongly Agree • Agree	• Strongly Disagree • Disagree	(10/17) = 59%
(4)	Without the availability of an AIG an assessment is/would be more difficult to prepare for	• Strongly Agree • Agree	• Strongly Disagree • Disagree	(10/17) = 59%
(5)	The AIG is clear and easy to understand	• Strongly Agree • Agree	• Strongly Disagree • Disagree	(11/17) = 65%
(6)	The AIG is/would be helpful in selecting an Assessment Instrument	• Strongly Agree • Agree	• Strongly Disagree • Disagree	(12/17) = 71%
(7)	The AI/Guide is/would be helpful in developing and assessment instrument	• Strongly Agree • Agree	• Strongly Disagree • Disagree	(16/17) = 94%
(8)	The coverage of the indicator set in the AIG is adequate	• Strongly Agree • Agree	• Strongly Disagree • Disagree	(16/17) = 94%
(9)	The AIG is compatible with the BPG and the Process Assessment Guide	• Strongly Agree • Agree	• Strongly Disagree • Disagree	(16/16) = 100%

Figure 13.13: Evaluations of the AIG overall by the assessors.

Acknowledgments

Many individuals have contributed their time to the SPICE Trials, however, they are too numerous to thank them individually. However, we would like to acknowledge the key contributions to the Phase 1 Trials of Fiona Maclennan, Mary Tobin, Gary Ostrolenk, Robin Hunter, Ian Woodman, Peter Krauth, Peter Marshall, Terry Rout, Greg Jenkins, Jerome Pesant, Dave Kitson, and Inigo Garro.

References

1. A. Dorling, "SPICE: Software Process Improvement and Capability dEtermination," *Information and Software Technology*, Vol. 35, Nos. 6/7, June/July 1993, pp. 404–406.

2. J-N Drouin, "Software Quality—An International Concern," *Software Process, Quality & ISO 9000*, Vol. 3, No. 8, Aug. 1994, pp. 1–4.

3. J-N Drouin, "The SPICE Project: An Overview," *Software Process Newsletter*, IEEE Computer Society, No. 2, Winter 1995, pp. 8–9.

4. K. El Emam and D.R. Goldenson, "SPICE: An Empiricist's Perspective," *Proc. 2nd IEEE Int'l Software Engineering Standards Symp.*, IEEE Computer Society Press, Los Alamitos, Calif., 1995, pp. 84–97.

5. K. El Emam and D.R. Goldenson, "An Empirical Evaluation of the Prospective International SPICE Standard," *Software Process Improvement and Practice*, Vol. 2, No. 2, 1996, pp. 123–148.

6. D. Goldenson and J. Herbsleb, *After the Appraisal: A Systematic Survey of Process Improvement, Its Benefits, and Factors that Influence Success*, Technical Report CMU/SEI-95-TR-009, Software Engineering Institute, 1995.

7. M. Konrad, "On the Horizon: An International Standard for Software Process Improvement," *Software Process Improvement Forum*, Sept./Oct. 1994, pp. 6–8.

8. F. Maclennan and G. Ostrolenk, "The SPICE Trials: Validating the Framework," *Proc. 2nd Int'l SPICE Symp.*, Australian Software Quality Research Institute, Brisbane, Australia, 1995.

9. M. Paulk and M. Konrad, "Measuring Process Capability Versus Organizational Process Maturity," *Proc. 4th Int'l Conf. Software Quality*, ASQC Quality Press, Milwaukee, Wisconsin, 1994.

10. T. Rout, "SPICE: A Framework for Software Process Assessment," *Software Process Improvement and Practice J.*, Pilot Issue, Aug. 1995, pp. 57–66.

11. The SPICE Project, *SPICE Phase 1 Trials.*

14

Analysis of Assessment Ratings from the Trials

Ian Woodman and Robin Hunter
University of Strathclyde, Scotland

This chapter describes the analysis performed on the process ratings and associated data gathered during Phase 1 of the SPICE Trials.

The analysis of this data consisted of three stages:

- demographic summary—an overview of the context, coverage, and duration of the trials

- profile analysis—analysis of the process data collected on trial assessments

- conclusions and recommendations resulting from the analysis.

Since the Phase 1 Trials used an earlier version of the SPICE document set, a brief description of the ratings framework is included here to put the analysis into context. This description complements that which is provided in Chapter 3.[*] As part of the analysis exercise, a prototype tool for viewing ratings data from one or several assessments was built to assist with the exploratory analysis of the data. The functionality of this tool is also described. This tool is a precursor to the one included with this book.

---

[*]A complete specification of the rating scheme used in Version 1.00 of the SPICE document set may be found in the electronic Version 1.00 documents included with this book.

Thirty five trials were conducted during Phase 1. However, complete sets of ratings were only returned for 28 trials, which represented the data set for this part of the analysis. Eighteen of these trials were conducted in Europe and 10 in the Pacific Rim. A total of 49 projects were included within the scope of these trials, yielding 324 process instances in total.

Phase 1 assessments

As well as assessing the capability of individual processes, the extent to which the processes were actually *performed* was determined. To achieve this determination, base practices can be rated using either the same four-point ordinal scale for adequacy as the generic practices or a binary scale for existence (or otherwise). By examining the base practices of a process, the team assessed the extent to which the process was actually implemented. If a process is barely implemented, applying the concepts embodied by the generic practices will have little effect. To determine capability, a rating for adequacy was assigned to a particular generic practice in the context of a particular process.

First, if the same process or set of processes has been assessed on several different projects, the process instance ratings can be aggregated to give an overall rating for the *generic process*. Second, the ratings for processes within a process category can be aggregated to provide an overall capability for that category. In practice, some aggregations may not make sense.

These aggregations can be combined in various ways and the combinations allowed the team to view the data at different levels of abstraction and from different perspectives. This approach provided a powerful means to understand and inspect the overall process.

When aggregated in any direction, the information that tells which ratings are associated with which process instance is lost. Instead, the data is represented by a vector of percentages of the four ratings. For example, the rating for common feature 2.2, with respect to process instance A of CUS.2, is:

CUS.2;2.2 [A] = [50, 50, 0, 0]

That is, 50 percent of the generic practices of the common feature 2.2 were rated Fully adequate and 50 percent were rated Largely adequate. This structure is known as a *tuple*.

As another example, if three instances (A, B, and C) of the same generic practice (for example, 3.1.1, *Standardize the process*) are rated, the ratings can be aggregated as follows:

PRO.5;[A];3.1.1 = L

PRO.5;[B];3.1.1 = P

PRO.5;[C];3.1.1 = L

The aggregated ratings are [0,67,33,0].

Generic practice ratings only form part of the output of an assessment. Other information is also recorded to characterize the assessment and the organizational unit (OU), the scope and limitations of the assessment, and the base practice ratings for each process instance. However, the generic practice ratings alone are used to characterize the capability of the processes assessed.

Exploring the data

In Version 1.00, there were 35 processes and 26 generic practices in total. The actual data may be somewhat less than this suggests. For example, all processes need not be assessed and processes may be assessed at only some of the capability levels. However, even the smallest assessment will generate a large amount of data, and manual interpretation and aggregation quickly becomes impractical.

The nature of the data and its various transformations made the task ripe for automation via a statistical package or specialized tool. To this end, a tool was developed at Strathclyde University with the following capabilities:

- to show and summarize the coverage and context of individual projects within an assessment

- to select ratings from individual projects, whole assessments, or sets of assessments

- to summarize this data in terms of process category and capability level

- to browse through the data interactively, moving from one view to another, following the various rules for aggregation.

The tool was developed to interface with the SPICE database that holds the complete trials data. The tool is described in Appendix A of this chapter.

Demographic summaries

To give an overall summary of the Phase 1 Trials, various demographics were collected and used to determine the context, coverage, and duration of assessments.

Types of organization assessed

An integral part of a SPICE-conformant assessment is the collection of information regarding the characteristics of the OU being assessed and the nature of the software it develops. This *process context* is used to provide a frame of reference for assessing the capability of the OU and for comparing the results of assessments of different OUs. The process context includes such things as the application domains and business sectors for which the OU develops software, the development techniques used, and information concerning the size, criticality, complexity, and quality characteristics of software products. Also collected is general information about the OU, such as the number of software personnel.

In the Phase 1 Trials, process context information was collected at the level of individual development projects within OUs. The graphs in Figure 14.1 and Figure 14.2 relate to the set of assessment data at this level. Owing to the fact that a nonexclusive set of categories was used to collect application domain and business sector information, multiple responses were received for several projects. Rather than count them more than once, which would have given them more weight, these responses were assigned to the *Other* category in the following graphs.

This factor suggested that in later phases of the trials, an exclusive set of categories should be formulated to enable unique classification of assessments. It is recognized that different types of software will require a different emphasis on development in terms of, for example, desired quality characteristics, criticality, and time to market. The software processes that exist within organizations developing software for different domains, therefore, will have different emphases and objectives. It is important to be able to classify types of software unambiguously so that process assessment results can be compared in a meaningful way. Many large organizations have developed taxonomies for categorizing their own software products[3] and work is underway to produce an international standard for classification.[5]

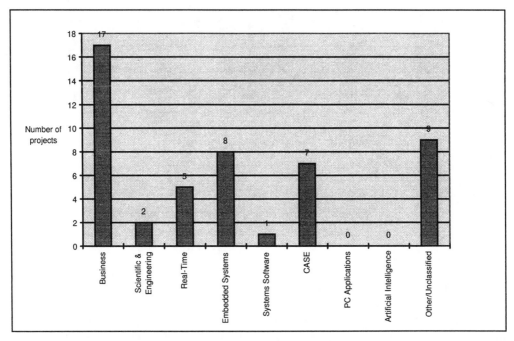

Figure 14.1: Coverage of application domains.

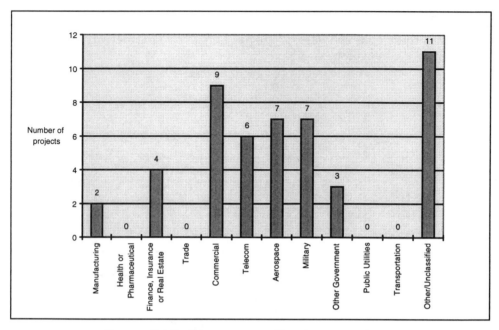

Figure 14.2: Coverage of business sectors.

Sample size

The number of projects in which individual processes are observed during the course of an assessment may have some bearing on the confidence that can be placed in the results of that assessment. For example, if a process is observed in only one project, that project may or may not be representative of the average project in the OU. By sampling across several projects, a more representative profile of capability is obtained.

Figure 14.3 shows the number of projects from which process instances were selected for assessment. As can be readily seen, the majority of assessments were based on a single project.

Coverage of process categories by trials

Figure 14.4 shows the number of process instances that were assessed in each of the process categories. The process categories from which the majority of the process instances were chosen were the Engineering and Project categories.

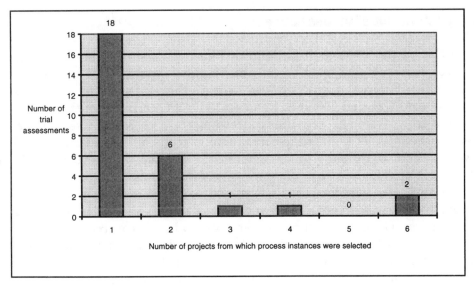

Figure 14.3: Sample size.

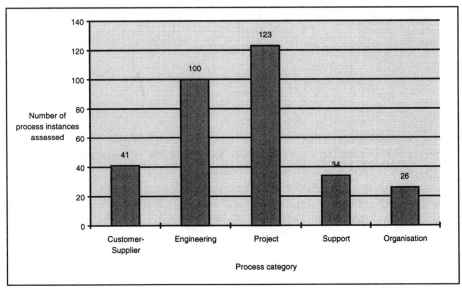

Figure 14.4: Coverage of process categories.

Average duration of an assessment

In calculating the average duration of a Phase 1 Trial, the number of process instances assessed was used as an approximate indication of the scale of an assessment. Figures were derived from the information supplied in questionnaires Q2a and Q3a (see Chapter 12 for a description of these). The raw data for a trial covered all activities concerning the assessment itself. It excluded assessor briefings, as well as the completion of trials questionnaires and forms. However, there were many other factors that affected the duration and these factors were merely used as a reference point for normalization.

The times calculated for both assessment teams and assessees were based on the same set of assessments. However, four of the 28 had to be omitted due to missing data. Three significant outliers were also discovered. These outliers were not included in the calculations since they deviated from the mean quite substantially and were not considered representative. In the case of the assessment teams, there were two outliers of 45 and 100 hours per process instance. In the case of the assessees, there was one outlier with a duration of 40 hours per process instance.

Average duration of trial— assessment teams	10.11 person hours per process instance
Average duration of trial— assessees	8.52 person hours per process instance

As well as the missing values and outliers, several anomalies in the data were noticed. For example, in one instance the number of employees on the assessment team exceeded the total size of the team. This anomaly could have been a result of a problem with the interpretation of questionnaires or with data entry, but was most likely due to the fact that the questions were not asked until after the assessment had taken place. Perhaps the best solution to this problem would be to record this kind of data at the time of the assessment.

Profile analysis

The actual assessment data collected by trial assessments was analyzed to provide an overall summary of capability and to elicit information about the SPICE framework and its underlying concepts.

Overview of profile data

To give an overall picture of the data from the Phase 1 Trials, all profile data was aggregated as illustrated in Figure 14.5 and Figure 14.6. Two high-level summaries of the data are provided. The first summary is from the perspective of the five process categories, while the second provides an orthogonal perspective from the five capability levels. The y-axis represents the percentage of adequacy ratings (of Fully, Largely, and Partially adequate) over all the trials. The graphs do not distinguish between Not adequate and Not rated ratings. Not applicable ratings were omitted from the aggregation. There is a certain redundancy in the data, in that each view can be inferred from the other, but it serves to illustrate the general trends in the data from the differing perspectives.

Bearing in mind the size of the data set, this view is simply a summary of the data and should not be considered to be a representative profile of capability or other such concept. It served as a control for a comparison of the data from the coherent subsets described later. The number of process instances assessed in each of the process categories is shown in Figure 14.5.

Note that the 80 percent rating for the SUP process category at the Performed-informally level was caused by a single assessment that had seven Not adequate ratings for SUP process instances at all levels.

Clusters of profile data

The next stage in summarizing the assessment results was to identify coherent subsets of process data that would allow meaningful and valid comparisons to be made.

Part 3 of the SPICE product set[6] states that to make comparisons between assessment outputs, their process contexts should be similar. In particular, the product-related factors affect comparability. In Phase 1 of the trials, data was collected about the application domain, business sector, criticality, and quality characteristics of the software product. This data was used to identify coherent subsets of assessments, in the sense that they had similar values of the above parameters. Also collected was the size of the individual project teams, but this was deemed to be less important in comparing profiles.

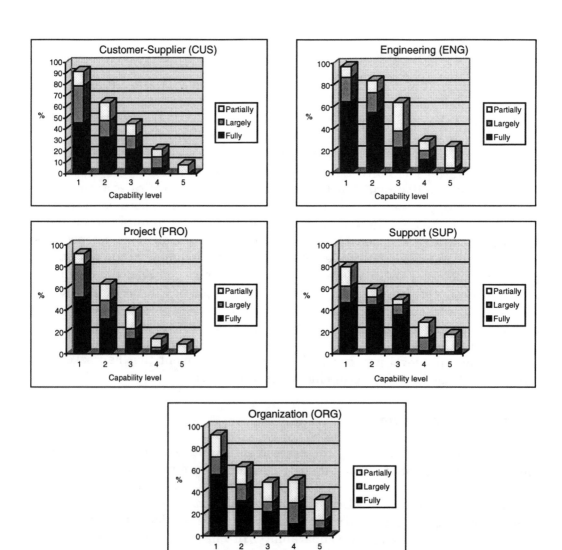

Figure 14.5: High level summary by process category.

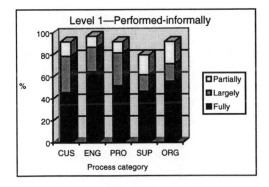

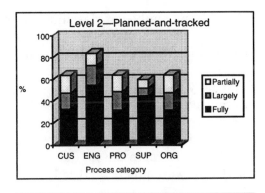

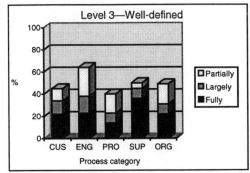

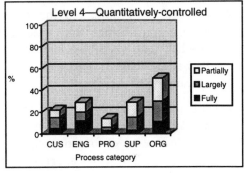

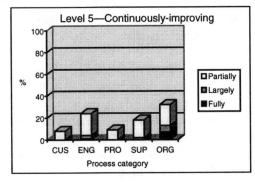

Figure 14.6: High level summary by capability level.

Originally, context information was collected for each OU as a whole. In order to classify the process data that was actually collected, however, the process context was later collected for each project assessed within an OU. In this way, each project effectively was treated as an individual assessment for this part of the analysis. When averaging was performed across projects, those assessments with more projects were given greater weight. Inasmuch as the projects were being considered to be independent observations, this approach seemed reasonable.

An obvious method of classification was to identify clusters on primarily the application domain information. This method should provide a logical grouping since products from similar application domains were expected to exhibit similar characteristics. However, as mentioned previously, several values were occasionally recorded for the application domain since the categories used were not exclusive. As a result, this classification became impractical.

Instead, a hierarchical cluster analysis was used to identify projects that had relatively similar process contexts. The clustering was based on the ten ordinal variables that represented the quality characteristics and criticality of the project's software products. Briefly, these variables comprised:

- ratings of importance for functionality, reliability, usability, efficiency, maintainability, and portability of the product being developed. These variables are the six product quality characteristics of ISO/IEC 9126.[4] Importance was rated Essential, Substantial, Moderate, or Little if any.

- ratings concerning the criticality of the software product in terms of safety, economic, security, and environmental risks. Each category of risk had a set of four descriptive levels, ranging from no risk to high criticality. These categories were based on those developed by the SCOPE project[1] to identify the stringency of techniques needed to assess a particular software product.[2] Descriptions of individual levels are used in the cluster summaries that follow.

The clustering method used, known as *Within-Groups Linkage*.[1] aimed to minimize the distance between the members of individual clusters and hence identify projects with similar contexts. For the purposes of the cluster analysis, it was assumed that the distance between adjacent values of the variables was equal. For example, the distance from essential to substantial was the same as substantial to moderate. Instances with missing process context information (six) had to be omitted from the clustering process.

Analyses of the profile data from the individual projects within each cluster were conducted for the three largest clusters. Clusters 4—6 contained too few projects to be considered significant. Several patterns emerged from this analysis, although they proved to be general in nature, rather than specific-to-single clusters. These patterns are described later in this chapter.

In comparing capability levels between an individual cluster and the average,

---

[1] This was a European ESPRIT project that, amongst other things, defined general characteristics of software products.

it was necessary to introduce a weighting scheme to determine if one profile was of a higher capability than another. By attaching a weight to the derived ratings for adequacy, a single value is provided rather than the vector form of the tuples.

The weighting scheme from Part 4 of the SPICE product set[7] was used. This scheme suggested the following weights for ratings:

Fully 100%	Largely 75%	Partially 25%	Not 0%

There is a greater gap between Partially and Largely than between other neighboring ratings. The weighting scheme was somewhat arbitrary, but was used for summary purposes only.

Each cluster is described below along with, where appropriate, summaries in terms of the average capability of each process category at each level, capability as compared with the overall average, and some general observations.

The descriptions include application domain information since it was observed that clusters contained projects from mostly similar domains.

Cluster 1 (18 projects)

The Support and Organization process categories comprised too small a sample size to be considered meaningful.

Context Variable	Rating	%
Application Domain	Mainly Business and CASE tool development	78
Functionality	Essential	89
Reliability	Essential	72
Usability	Essential or Substantial	72
Efficiency	Essential or Substantial	83
Maintainability	Substantial or Moderate	78
Portability	Moderate or Little if any	89
Safety Risks	Small damage to property—no risk to people	94
Economic Risks	Significant economic loss (company affected)	83
Security Risks	Protection against error risk or Protection of critical data or services	83
Environmental Risks	No environmental risk	94

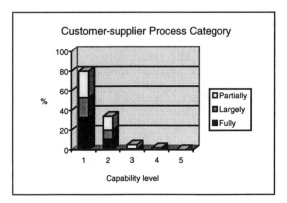

Capability Level	% Difference from Overall Aggregation
1	-26
2	-56
3	-95
4	-97
5	-100

CLUSTER 1: CUS—15 process instances. All processes except CUS.6 assessed.

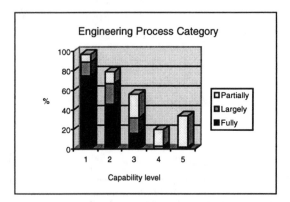

Capability Level	% Difference from Overall Aggregation
1	+4
2	-10
3	-17
4	-68
5	+30

Cluster 1: ENG—36 process instances. All processes assessed.

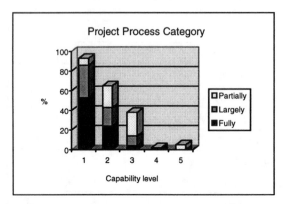

Capability Level	% Difference from Overall Aggregation
1	+3
2	-10
3	-30
4	-86
5	-44

Cluster 1: PRO—40 process instances. All processes assessed.

Cluster 2 (11 projects)

Again, the Organization process category comprised too small a sample to warrant analysis.

Context Variable	Rating	%
Application Domain	Mainly Business and Other	73
Functionality	Essential or Substantial	100
Reliability	Essential or Substantial	100
Usability	Substantial	91
Efficiency	Substantial	91
Maintainability	Essential or Substantial	91
Portability	Substantial or Moderate	73
Safety Risks	Small damage to property—no risk to people	100
Economic Risks	Negligible economic loss	73
Security Risks	No specific risk identified	73
Environmental Risks	No environmental risk	100

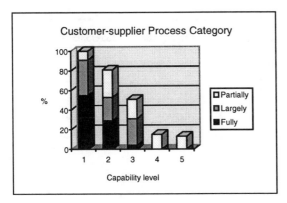

Capability Level	% Difference from Overall Aggregation
1	+14
2	+12
3	-13
4	-74
5	+63

Cluster 2: CUS—11 process instances. CUS.2—CUS.5 assessed.

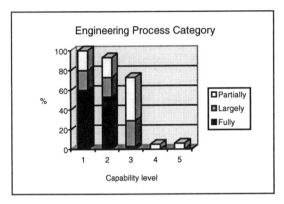

Capability Level	% Difference from Overall Aggregation
1	-5
2	+1
3	-18
4	-94
5	-80

Cluster 2: ENG—25 process instances. All processes except ENG.6 assessed.

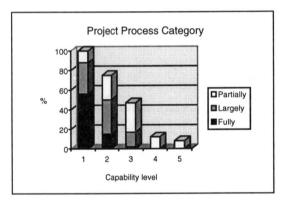

Capability Level	% Difference from Overall Aggregation
1	+8
2	-2
3	-17
4	-59
5	-11

Cluster 2: PRO—25 process instances. All processes assessed.

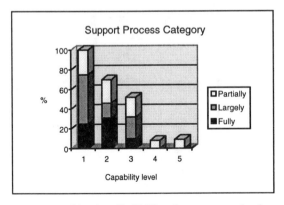

Capability Level	% Difference from Overall Aggregation
1	+10
2	-10
3	-28
4	-87
5	-59

Cluster 2: SUP—8 process instances. All processes assessed.

Cluster 3 (8 projects)

Here, high capability was found at Levels 1 and 2, with less at Level 3 but little above this. This cluster was the largest that covered a single application domain.

Reliability was high, while usability and portability were low for the embedded systems. Criticality was higher, which generally would be expected. Neither the Customer-Supplier nor the Project process categories were analyzed, but the single processes that had been sampled in the Support and Organization categories were examined.

Context Variable	Rating	%
Application Domain	Embedded Systems	100
Functionality	Essential	88
Reliability	Essential	100
Usability	Little if any	100
Efficiency	Substantial	88
Maintainability	Substantial	75
Portability	Little if any	100
Safety Risks	Many people killed	75
Economic Risks	Significant economic loss (company affected)	100
Security Risks	Protection against error risk	100
Environmental Risks	Recoverable environmental damage	75

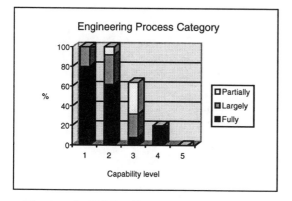

Capability Level	% Difference from Overall Aggregation
1	+13
2	+20
3	-17
4	-2
5	-100

Cluster 3: ENG—5 process instances. ENG.3, ENG.4, and ENG.6 assessed.

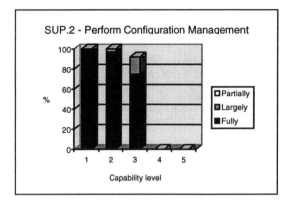

Cluster 3: SUP—3 process instances. Only SUP.2 assessed.

Capability Level	% Difference from Overall Aggregation
1	+60
2	+90
3	+99
4	-100
5	-100

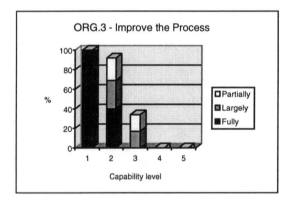

Cluster 3: ORG—3 process instances. Only ORG.3 assessed.

Capability Level	% Difference from Overall Aggregation
1	+38
2	+41
3	-51
4	-100
5	-100

There were three more small clusters (only two projects each). While these clusters were considered too small for their assessment results to be considered significant in any way, the contexts of the three clusters are described in the tables below, principally to provide further evidence of how the clustering algorithm worked. In each of these clusters, the two projects concerned came from the same assessment.

Cluster 4 (2 projects)

Context Variable	Rating	%
Application Domain	Real-Time Applications	100
Functionality	Substantial	100
Reliability	Essential	100
Usability	Substantial	100
Efficiency	Essential	100
Maintainability	Substantial	100
Portability	Essential	100
Safety Risks	Damage to property—few people injured	100
Economic Risks	Significant economic loss (company affected)	100
Security Risks	Protection of strategic data and services	100
Environmental Risks	Recoverable environmental damage	100

Cluster 5 (2 projects)

Context Variable	Rating	%
Application Domain	Business	100
Functionality	Moderate or Little if any	100
Reliability	Essential	100
Usability	Substantial or Moderate	100
Efficiency	Essential	100
Maintainability	Moderate or Little if any	100
Portability	Moderate or Little if any	100
Safety Risks	Small damage to property—no risk to people	100
Economic Risks	Significant economic loss (company affected)	100
Security Risks	No specific risk identified	100
Environmental Risks	No environmental risk	100

Cluster 6 (2 projects)

Context Variable	Rating	%
Application Domain	Business or Real-Time applications	100
Functionality	Substantial	100
Reliability	Moderate	100
Usability	Moderate	100
Efficiency	Moderate	100
Maintainability	Little if any	100
Portability	Little if any	100
Safety Risks	Small damage to property—no risk to people	100
Economic Risks	Significant economic loss (company affected)	100
Security Risks	Protection of critical data and services or Protection of strategic data and services	100
Environmental Risks	No environmental risk	100

Trends in the data

In observing the profile data from the Phase 1 Trials, generally the team found the expected trends. For example, the adequacy of a process usually decreased as the capability levels moved up. Also, some process categories were frequently observed to be stronger than others. For example, the Engineering and Project categories usually had the most capability. However, during analysis of the results of individual assessment profiles, the team observed several recurring trends in the data. The team believes these trends highlight interesting aspects of the results.

Some of these trends are described below, along with example profiles from the data set that illustrate them.

Greater adequacy at the Continuously-improving level than at the Quantitatively-controlled level

As Figure 14.7 illustrates, a process (ENG.2 in this case) was sometimes observed to have greater adequacy at Level 5 than at Level 4. Of the 14 assessments that had ratings beyond the Well-defined level, nine exhibited this trend. Possible interpretations include:

- The practices at the Continuously-improving level were less stringent than those at the Quantitatively-controlled level—an architectural problem.
- There were problems with interpretation of the practices.

The team observed that when this trend occurred, the practice most frequently rated Partially adequate or above at the Continuously-improving level was 5.1.2—*Continuously improve the standard process*. Perhaps the fact that an organization is participating in a SPICE Trial assessment shows at least partial fulfillment of this practice.

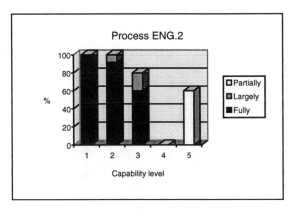

Figure 14.7: Greater adequacy at Level 5 than at Level 4.

Practices that were frequently rated Not adequate

Figure 14.8 shows the number of occasions (expressed as a percentage) that each generic practice was rated Not adequate. Most noticeable was the jump in the number of practices rated Not adequate from the Planned-and-tracked level to the Well-defined level (except for generic practice 3.1.1). Also, the relatively low number of Not adequate ratings for generic practice 5.1.2 correlates with the findings discussed previously, concerning higher adequacy at the Continuously-improving level than at the Quantitatively-controlled level. Generic practice 5.1.2 was the most common practice being rated when this trend occurred.

Practices that were frequently rated Not applicable

Figure 14.9 shows (as a percentage) the number of instances in which each generic practice was considered Not applicable. Perhaps of significance were the particular generic practices that were rated Not applicable the most often, such as 2.1.4 *Provide tools*, 2.1.5 *Ensure training*, 2.4.1 *Track with measurement*, and 2.4.2 *Take corrective action*. The provision of tools may have been interpreted only as an engineering activity, for example.

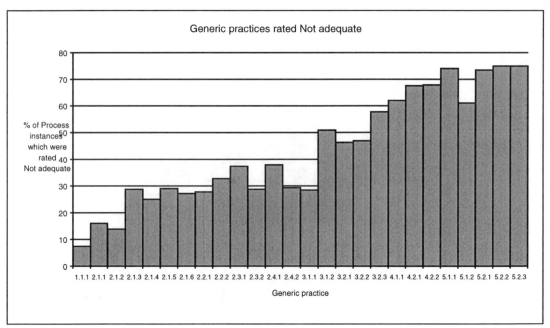

Figure 14.8: Generic practices rated Not adequate.

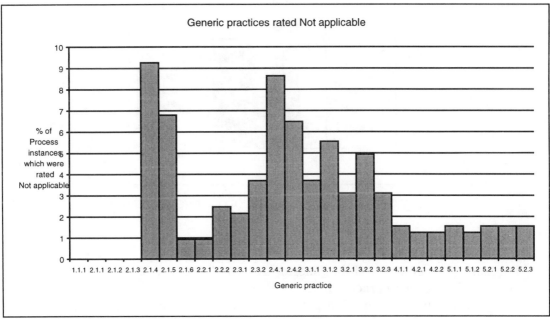

Figure 14.9: Generic practices rated Not applicable.

At the higher capability levels, the team noted that there may have been some confusion between the Not rated and Not applicable ratings that may be the cause of these values. There were no significant patterns found in a similar analysis of the base practice ratings.

Significant difference between base practice ratings and generic practice 1.1.1

Figure 14.10 illustrates a trend observed in the data indicating a lack of correlation between base practice ratings and ratings for generic practice 1.1.1. Although generic practice 1.1.1 is not explicitly derived from the base practice ratings, a reasonable level of correlation between them was expected. The trend is illustrated in the graph (which represents a single process instance of CUS.3—*Identify customer needs*).

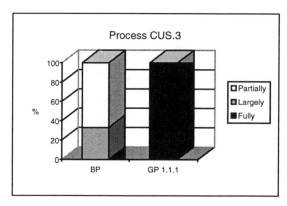

Figure 14.10: Low correlation between ratings.

The base practices of CUS.3 have been rated Largely (33 percent) and Partially (67 percent), while generic practice 1.1.1 has been rated Fully (100 percent) for the same process instance.

Two hundred and fifty-five process instances had adequacy ratings for both base practices and generic practice 1.1.1. Comparing the single rating for generic practice 1.1.1 with the aggregated rating for the base practices, and applying the same weighting scheme used for the profile analysis, it was observed that 12.16 percent of these process instances had a difference of 25 percent or more between the two values. This comparison may have indicated a misinterpretation of the emerging standard or a misunderstanding about the relationship between the base practices and generic practice 1.1.1.

Mappings from existence to adequacy

Forty-five process instances from seven trials employed both the existence (Y, N) and adequacy (F, L, P, N) measurement scales for rating base practices. Altogether, these instances contained 225 base practice ratings that had values recorded for both scales. The three likeliest mappings between existence and adequacy were applied to the data from these assessments and the percentage of consistent and inconsistent mappings observed. These mappings are detailed in the table below. A completely-consistent mapping was not found between existence and adequacy ratings. However, the first mapping in the table, where a base practice that is at least Partially adequate is deemed to be Existent, had the least and very few inconsistencies.

Adequacy ratings mapped to Y	Adequacy ratings mapped to N	Percentage Consistent	Percentage Inconsistent
F, L, P	N	98.22	1.78
F, L	P, N	88.89	11.11
F	L, P, N	66.67	33.33

Variability across a process

One of the fundamental concepts behind software process assessment (SPA) is the notion that the generic process used in an organization can be captured by observing instantiations of that process in individual projects. The variability across these projects affects the confidence that can be placed in this identification. The data set contained several assessments that had observed the same process across more than one project. Consequently, it was possible to perform some initial, if uncontrolled, studies of variability. The two processes with largest sample size were chosen for investigation. Each was observed in four independent assessments.

What the team began to find, although there was limited evidence, was that *as the overall capability of a process increases, the variability of its capability on individual projects decreases.* This finding was most apparent at the Planned-and-Tracked level. This issue was regarded as an important candidate for future investigation during the later phases of the trials since it has the potential to give insight into the basic premise of process assessment through observation of process instances.

In the graphs shown in Figure 14.11 and Figure 14.12, each vertical line of points represents the selected process as observed in one assessment. The y-axis denotes the capability of the individual process instances, while the x-axis denotes the aggregated capability of the process derived from these instances. The numbers next to the points represent the number of process instances assessed with equal capability, on top of which one is plotted over another. Again, the weighting scheme from the emerging standard was used to order the data. The fact that, in these examples at least, *the variability in capability across process instances is less at the higher capability levels, is supportive of the notion that SPICE-conformant assessments are indeed measures of process maturity.* The evidence also supports the notion of the existence of a generic process belonging to the OU.

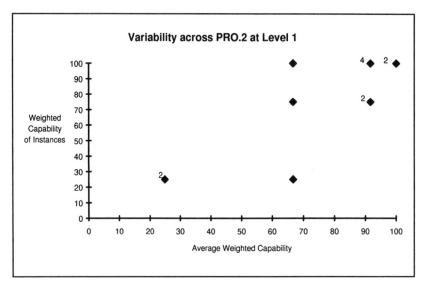

Figure 14.11: PRO.2—Establish project plan.

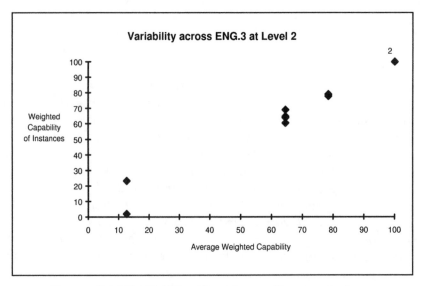

Figure 14.12: ENG.3—Develop software design.

Some lessons learned

Not rated and Not applicable ratings

As well as the existence and adequacy ratings, a further two ratings were required when performing assessments:

- **Not applicable**—When a practice was considered out of the scope of the project, for example because of the project size, it was recorded as Not applicable and did not contribute to determining the capability.

- **Not rated**—During some assessments, when low capability was observed at a particular capability level, capability at higher levels was not recorded. In these cases, the omitted practices were recorded as Not rated.

In analyzing profiles, practices that were rated Not applicable were omitted and did not affect derived ratings. Practices that were Not rated were considered different but indistinguishable from those that were rated Not adequate or Not existent.

The team observed that there may have been some confusion in rating practices as one of Not adequate, Not rated, or Not applicable. This confusion suggested that perhaps proper definition of the Not rated and Not applicable ratings should be added to the emerging standard.

Data collection

Generally, in later phases of the trials, a more rigorous approach to data collection needs to be adopted. The nature of some of the questions relating to this part of the analysis left them open to differing interpretations and requiring subjective responses. Context information especially would be better collected as part of the assessment in a predefined, uniform manner rather than in a retrospective questionnaire.

Conclusions and recommendations

In forming conclusions and recommendations from this part of the trials analysis, three main audiences were identified:

1. the Trials Core Team

2. the SPICE Project

3. the software engineering community in general.

Conclusions and recommendations for the Trials Core Team

These comments were distributed to the Trials Core Team to improve the planning for future phases of the trials.

The following data collection and analysis issues were distributed:

- Parts of the questionnaires need to be more carefully defined since the nature of some of the questions relating to this part of the analysis leaves them open to differing interpretations

- Context data, in particular, needs to be better defined. Further investigation into exclusive classification of application domains and business sectors is needed.

- If standards such as ISO/IEC 9126 are to be used, which seems to be a good idea, there needs to be at least a short explanation of the relevant terms to avoid different interpretations.

- Data, such as that concerning the process context and duration of assessments, should be collected objectively as the assessment takes place, rather than in a retrospective questionnaire.

- It may be possible to use the Phase 1 assessment data in future trials, for example, if the same OU or project is reassessed. If the framework, structure, and conduct of assessments do not change dramatically, the data potentially could be used for more general comparisons between assessments.

- The use of tools proved to be very helpful in analyzing the profile data.

- Tools need to be developed to identify anomalies in the database.

Possible future investigations include:

- Studies should be repeated on data from future trials, such as those that highlight potential anomalies in the model (for example, more adequacy at the Continuously-improving level than at the Quantitatively-controlled level). These studies, in conjunction with other analyses, hopefully will help pinpoint specific reasons for such trends.
- Other studies, such as those of variability across processes and process categories, should be further investigated in larger data sets since they may provide evidence, supportive or otherwise, about the framework.
- The clustering of assessments and projects provides a meaningful context in which to make comparisons between assessment results.

Conclusions and recommendations for the SPICE Project

These comments were distributed to the SPICE Project as a whole to provide feedback about the trials and to recommend changes to the emerging standard:

- The Phase 1 assessments provided reasonable coverage of the model for process management, application domains, and business sectors. All processes were rated at least once. However, many assessments included only one project in the scope of the assessment.
- The general trends observed in the individual and summary assessments are as expected, which is encouraging in terms of the overall structure of the model.
- Trends, such as the large jump from the Well-defined level to the Quantitatively-controlled level, may be due to inherent characteristics of the process rather than problems with the model.
- Trends that perhaps highlight anomalies in the model warrant future investigation since they may feed back into the SPICE product set.
- There is a need to define or explain the Not applicable and Not rated ratings in SPICE to avoid future confusion.
- Within the SPICE product set, there is a need to suggest or reference standards or other documents that can be used to define the process context. Otherwise, future comparability will be difficult. This information may arise from investigation in later stages of the trials.

Conclusions and recommendations for the software engineering community

For the software engineering community in general:

- Studies such as those concerning the variability of processes provide us with valuable results in terms of the underlying concepts behind SPA.
- The SPICE Trials provide a valuable vehicle for validating the emerging standard, as well as for collecting empirical information regarding the validity of SPA in general.

Although limited assessment data was collected during Phase 1, the team was able to conduct interesting analyses and gain useful experience. It is hoped that parts of the analysis will be repeated in future studies.

Many lessons have been learned regarding the SPICE framework, data collection, and assessment conduct. These lessons will help in the planning of later trials as well as feeding back useful information into the documents themselves.

Appendix A: Assessment visualization tool

The data visualization and analysis tool developed at the University of Strathclyde in connection with the SPICE Trials is described in this appendix and its use illustrated with the aid of screen shots produced by the tool.

The tool may be used to select data from one or more projects within one or more assessments. (The structure of the database in Phase 1 was such that process instance ratings were identified by the project in which they were assessed.)

Figure 14.13 to Figure 14.16 show the tool displaying data that was selected from several projects within a single trial assessment. Having selected the data, the user is presented with a high-level summary of overall capability from the perspective of the five process categories as shown in Figure 14.13. Within each

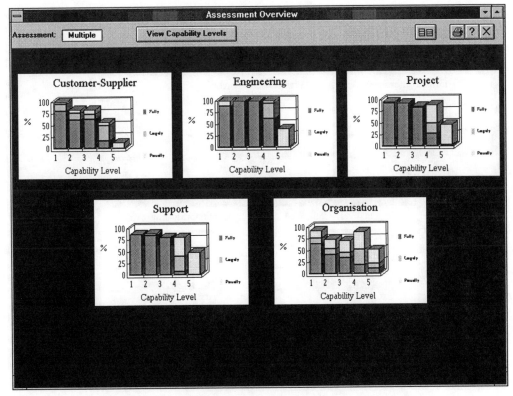

Figure 14.13: Overview of process categories.

category, the data from all processes assessed on all projects selected is aggregated at each of the five capability levels. At this stage, general comparisons can be made between capability levels, within and across process categories. For example, the Engineering process category has a rather high capability up to Level 4, but drops dramatically at Level 5. Also, the Engineering and Project categories show the strongest capability overall.

Clicking on the button labeled *View Capability Levels,* the view of the data changes to the perspective of the five capability levels, shown in Figure 14.14. This time, the five bars on each graph represent the derived ratings for each process category at the appropriate capability level.

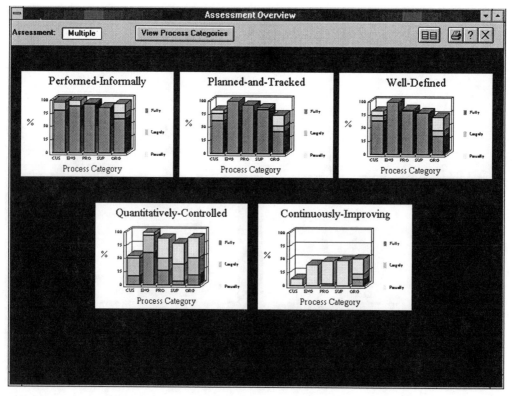

Figure 14.14: Overview of capability levels.

These two overall views represent the highest level of abstraction possible since it does not make sense to aggregate either process categories or capability levels. From either of the two views, the user can select either a particular process category or a capability level to explore simply by clicking on the relevant graph. The result is a display of the screen shown in Figure 14.15. In this instance, the user has opted to examine the Support process category. The form provides an enlarged version of the graph selected, along with three separate methods of changing the current view of the data. These screens represent the main part of the navigation system.

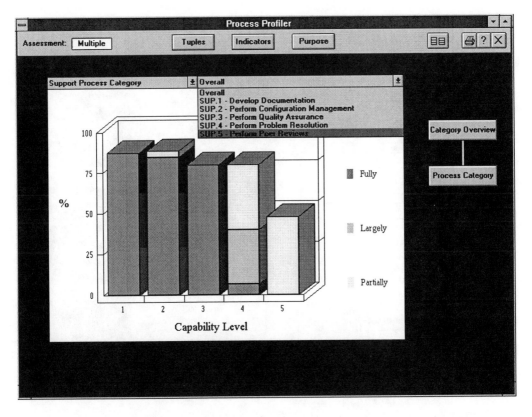

Figure 14.15: Choosing a process within the process category.

First, the two list boxes directly above the graph allow the user to change the current process category or to select an individual process from within the category. In the former case, the data on the graph is replaced by that of the new category. In the latter, the graph data is replaced by that for the single process selected rather than all processes in the category. This method allows the user to inspect all process categories and the processes within them in terms of relative capability. The user clicks on the button on the right of the relevant listbox. A list of options drops down and the user clicks on the desired one. Depending on what view of data is displayed, the listboxes contain different options.

The second method of navigation is contained within the graph itself. Looking at the overall view of the Support process category in Figure 14.16, by clicking on one of the five bars in the graph, the user can select a particular capability level to examine. For example, if the first bar is selected, the tool will display derived ratings for all the processes of the Support process category at Level 1, the Performed-informally level. This method is used to delve deeper into the data.

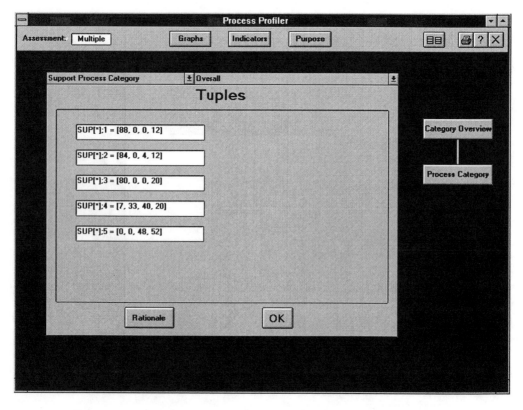

Figure 14.16: Tuple data for Support process category.

The final method of navigation involves the hierarchy of buttons to the right of the graphs. When first selecting a category to view, only two buttons were displayed, *Category Overview* and *Process Category*. Moving further down into the data, more buttons are added to represent the level of detail being viewed. The user can return to a previous, higher level of detail by clicking the appropriate button in the hierarchy.

At any stage in the navigation process, the user can switch to the tuple view by clicking on the *Tuples* button. Whatever the current view of the data, the actual values being plotted on the graph are shown in the form proposed in the SPICE product set. For example, in Figure 14.16 the data behind the graph of overall ratings for the Support process category from Figure 14.15 is shown.

Initially, the visualization tool was envisaged to operate as part of an assessment instrument, complementing data collection mechanisms and supporting the qualified assessor in the field. To enable its use in the analysis activity, the basic tool was tailored and extended in various ways to provide additional functionality, such as:

- the option to select multiple projects from several different assessments: originally, it was possible to select only single assessments and all projects from the assessment were included automatically
- a grid to show automatically the individual processes assessed
- a grid to display the process context of each project and to order them in terms of the various parameters involved
- graphs depicting the distribution of trials by geographical region, application domain, and business sector
- overall summaries in terms of process category and capability level
- mechanisms to retrieve the ratings for generic practice 1.1.1: the tool uses ratings for base practices to represent the Performed-informally level which was inappropriate for the analysis activity
- forms to show the ratings data in tabular form to help detect anomalies in the database before analysis.

References

1. Anderberg, M.R., *Cluster Analysis for Applications*, Academic Press, New York, N.Y., 1973.

2. Bache, R. and G. Bazzana, *Software Metrics for Product Assessment*, McGraw Hill, New York, N.Y., 1994.

3. Glass, R.L. and I. Vessey, "Contemporary Application—Domain Taxonomies," *IEEE Software*, July 1995, pp. 63–76.

4. ISO/IEC 9126, *Information Technology—Software Product Evaluation—Quality Characteristics and Guidelines for their Use*, 1991.

5. ISO/IEC DIS 12182—*Classification of Software*, Draft International Standard, ISO/IEC JTC1/SC7/WG9, 1995.

6. SPICE Project, *Software Process Assessment,—Part 3: Rating Processes*, Consolidated Product—Version 1.00, June 1995.

7. SPICE Project, *Software Process Assessment—Part 4: Guide to Conducting Assessments*, Consolidated Product—Version 1.00, June 1995.

15

Analysis of Observation and Problem Reports

Peter Marshall
Defence Evaluation Research Agency, UK

Fiona Maclennan and Mary Tobin
Lloyd's Register, UK

In defining the data to be collected during Phase 1 of the SPICE Trials, it was decided by the trials team to distinguish between *observations* and *problems*. Observation reports were designed for Phase 1 assessors and assessees to record preliminary impressions, whether positive or negative, on any aspect of the assessment or SPICE framework. Problem reports were a project-wide mechanism used for recording and tracking the resolution of problems.

Following the Phase 1 assessments, the qualified assessors reviewed the observation reports raised during their assessment and distilled the negative observations and criticisms into a number of problem reports. This reporting mechanism allowed the qualified assessors to use their understanding of the assessment method and the SPICE framework to link symptoms together and identify higher-order problems that required resolution.

A check was in place, at a regional level, to ensure that for each assessment, the set of resulting problem reports fully captured all the negative points noted in observation reports during the assessment.

This chapter is divided into five parts:

- The results from the analysis of the observation reports are presented.
- The analysis of the problem reports follows.
- A description of the actions taken, based on these analyses, is then provided.
- A description of the recommendations made about the SPICE document set.
- The chapter concludes with the subsequent progress achieved in addressing these recommendations.

Observation reports

This section describes the analysis of the observation reports raised as a result of the Phase 1 Trials.

Observation report distribution

Details of 100 observation reports were received by the analysis team: 78 from Europe and 22 from the Pacific Rim. None were received from Canada. Within Europe and the Pacific Rim, observation reports were raised in only half of all trial assessments conducted in Phase 1.

Observation reports were raised during assessments to record preliminary impressions, positive and negative points of note, and possible enhancements to the SPICE document set. The observation was classified on the observation report form as either a positive aspect or a problem, the latter including possible enhancements. Although most observation reports received were classified as one or the other, in four cases, both or neither classifications were selected.

Most of the observation reports that were received concerned problems with the SPICE document set and are covered in the next section, in the analysis of problem reports. Only approximately 10 percent of the observation reports were classified as positive aspects. These reports are considered below.

Summary of positive aspects

Given the small number of responses, it is not possible to generalize the observations made. Instead, the following summary should be read as anecdotal information, presented by one or more trials participants. These observations are broadly in line with the findings of the questionnaire analysis, described in Chapter 13:

- Conducting trials of the SPICE document set before standardization was considered a very good idea.

- Benchmarking was considered to be potentially one of the most useful aspects of the trials.

- One organization that performed a SPICE self-assessment identified a number of benefits: project managers found the experience useful in identifying improvement opportunities in their particular projects, while at the organizational level, management expressed interest in the SPICE document set for the purpose of recognizing the organization's current profile and improving it to meet business objectives. The key element contributing to the success of the assessment was the effectiveness of the data collection mechanism—in particular the specially-designed questionnaires used.

- The SPICE model was considered easy to understand, learn, and use. The structure and power of the model and its documentation were appreciated. The graphical presentation of results was considered helpful.

- The mappings in Part 2 from the SPICE document set to ISO/IEC 12207 and ISO 9001 were found to be useful.

- The application domain must be carefully considered when choosing process instances. It has been acknowledged that the use of the SPICE document set requires a high level of experience in software engineering, as well as judgment and understanding of the assessment environment.

The only conclusion that was drawn from these positive reports was that their low number indicated a problem with the reporting process used, rather than with the SPICE document set.

Problem reports

This section describes the demographic distribution of problem reports raised as a result of the Phase 1 Trial assessments. It then describes the overall approach taken in analyzing the problems and deciding on what action to take. The section concludes with a description of the classification of problems by severity and cause.

Problem report distribution

Figure 15.1 and Figure 15.2 provide details of the number of trials in each region and the number of problem reports from each region.

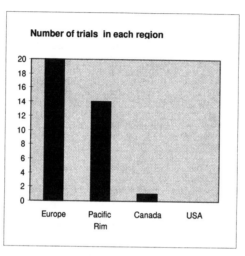

Figure 15.1: Distribution of trials by region.

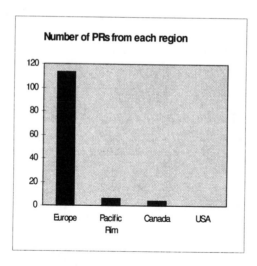

Figure 15.2: Number of problem reports from each region.

In total, 118 problem reports were raised in the 20 European trials conducted, six from the 14 Pacific Rim trials, and four from the single Canadian trial. The number of problem reports from each region appears disproportionate to the number of trials in each region, meaning that significantly fewer problem reports were raised per trial in the Pacific Rim region than in either of the other two regions in which trials were conducted. This finding was identified as being due to a difference in approach to raising problem reports in the Pacific Rim region.

Analysis approach

The primary purpose of conducting an analysis of problem reports raised in the Phase 1 Trials was to address objective 6 of the Phase 1 Trials, namely "to contribute to the improvement of the SPICE products." Clearly the problem report analysis also contributed to other objectives of evaluation and identification of the interface problems between Parts 2—5 of the document set.

When the Phase 1 Trials commenced in January 1995, the trials participants had available to them an initial version of the SPICE document set. Subsequently, the SPICE documents were consolidated into an ISO/IEC set and reissued. Because problem reports were raised by qualified assessors against the earlier version of the SPICE document set, the analysis of problem reports had to include a stage to investigate if problems raised by assessors were still applicable against the consolidated set of ISO/IEC documents. In one case, a problem had been resolved in the process of generating the consolidated set.

A number of factors were considered when analyzing the problem reports raised, including the following:

- Was the problem with the SPICE document set or did it concern something else—for example, the trials process itself or the level of assessor expertise and familiarity with the SPICE process and products?
- Was the problem really a symptom of a larger problem?
- What was the cause of the problem and how might it be addressed?
- Had the problem already been addressed?
- Was the problem widespread and perceived by many people across different trials or had the problem been encountered by only a few people? Account was taken of a conscious decision, made in a number of cases, to avoid duplication of problem reports: for example, the case of an assessment team who conducted more than one assessment.

- Was something that was perceived as a problem by one person perceived as being entirely adequate by others?
- How did the problem relate to other Phase 1 analysis findings: for example, trials coverage, rating scales used, and use of assessment instruments (Part 5)?

Analysis of the problem reports that were received was undertaken to answer the type of questions on which the above elaborated and to provide a mechanism whereby a coherent set of actions could be identified.

This analysis consisted of a number of stages:

- Every problem report was reviewed to establish the symptom, effect, and probable cause, and then assigned one or more classifications.
- Each classification was then analyzed for commonality of, and conflict between, problems. Grouping problems by classification enabled patterns to emerge and supported the identification of underlying problems.
- Finally, actions for resolution of the problems were derived.

Classification of problem reports

Each problem report was classified against two classification schema, for the purpose of an initial analysis. The first classification schema indicated the severity of the problem, as judged by the analysis team, while the second indicated the probable cause(s) of the problem.

Problem reports received by the analysis team had already had a severity rating allocated by the originator of the problem report. This allocated rating captured the severity of the problem from the point of view of the assessment team during a trial assessment. The motivation behind allocating an additional severity rating during analysis was to ensure that a consistent approach was taken across the teams and to allow cross-verification of the severity ratings.

Problem reports indicated the probable cause of the problem, but this information was variable in content and presentation. It was therefore considered appropriate to identify a number of *cause categories* for each part of the SPICE document set and to classify problem reports accordingly. Many problem reports were given more than one cause classification, indicating the likely scope and extent of the problem, and thus reflecting the relationships between different parts of the SPICE document set. This classification of the causes of problems raised allowed an analysis of commonality and overlap between problem reports and the identification of underlying problems.

Actions

Having classified all problem reports by severity and probable cause, and having conducted an analysis of commonality and conflict, the next stage was to consider the appropriate action for each problem report. Three possibilities were identified:

1. *Requests for change* (RFC) were raised where changes to one or more SPICE documents were both required and justified by weight of evidence.

2. A *project issue report* (PIR) was raised when a procedural, rather than document set, difficulty was identified, or when problems were identified, but without sufficient information, or evidence, to warrant raising a *request for change*.

3. *No action* was taken when neither of the above was applicable: for example, the problem had already been addressed or the problem was perceived to be due to a misunderstanding.

The problem reports were analyzed and allocated one of the above actions. In the case of (a few) problem reports identifying multiple problems, more than one of the above actions were allocated.

Subsequent inspection of the problem reports and their actions resulted in the grouping together of related actions. This practice allowed a structured approach to the final identification actions to be taken, so that more than one problem report could be addressed by the same action, resulting in a reduced number of actions and simplifying the process of addressing them.

Requests for change

The approach taken with *requests for change* was to structure them so that each consisted of a high-level statement of change, supplemented by details corresponding more closely with the problems detailed in individual problem reports.

Six requests were identified and are outlined below:

1. Undertake a fundamental review and rework, as necessary, of the model for process management—Part 2 of the document set—to address problems regarding the relationships between generic practices and processes and the interpretation and organization of generic

practices. Particular issues included the need to ensure consistent capability meaning and applicability across capability levels, irrespective of the process, and restructuring of the model into capability levels of similar sizes, with more even *delivered capability* between the levels.

2. Make amendments to the processes in the model for process management to address the problems identified with individual processes and with the relationships between processes.

3. Make amendments to the generic practices in the model for process management to address the problems identified with individual practices.

4. Provide further clarification and guidance on interpreting the model for process management to address the problems encountered.

5. Provide further guidance and clarification in conducting assessments to address the problems encountered.

6. Provide clarification and guidance on the functionality requirements of assessment instruments and tools.

Project issue reports

Eight issues were identified, as outlined below:

1. It was acknowledged that it was easier to assess processes that are documented (more mature) than *ad hoc* (immature) processes. This issue was seen as unavoidable, given the nature of team-based process assessment.

2. One problem report was received concerning the adequacy rating scale. It was decided that further evidence of the problem was needed to justify changing the rating scale.

3. A number of problem reports were raised against the indicator set: too verbose, unmaintainable, and the level of detail was misplaced. The whole issue of indicators had to be reexamined, based upon the Phase 1 Q4 analysis (see Chapter 13).

4. One problem report claimed that using the SPICE document set may be too expensive to cost justify for a small organization. If this was the case, one of the SPICE requirements had not been met.

5. One problem report stated that the benchmarking of SPICE results—comparability—was jeopardized because extended processes were al-

lowed. If true, this finding would have adversely affected the ability of the SPICE Project to meet its requirements.

6. The issue of *Not applicable* ratings needed to be examined in detail, based on more than just the data from the Phase 1 Trials problem reports.

7. The issue of whether an existence rating scale was needed was raised in a single problem report. This issue needed to be examined in detail, based upon more evidence.

8. Single instances of minor problems were found where more evidence was necessary to justify any change.

No action

No action was recommended for a number of issues raised in problem reports. These issues were grouped into four types, as outlined below:

1. Interpretation confirmed: no changes were necessary.

2. Problem was outside the scope of the SPICE document set: application to non-software projects, inclusion of template confidentiality agreement, interpretation of the SPICE framework as a process model rather than as a model for process management and assessment method issues.

3. Issue already known, and documented, as a constraint on the use of the SPICE document set.

4. Problem already fixed during consolidation of the document set. (See "Analysis approach" above.)

Distribution of problem reports by action

Figure 15.3 shows the number of problem reports allocated to each action. All problem reports were allocated at least one action. All actions were traceable to problem reports.

Note that RFC #1 refers to the first *request for change*, PIR #1 the first *project issue report*, and No Action #1 the first *no action*.

Figure 15.4 shows the distribution, by trial of problem reports, allocated to the first request for change. There was clearly widespread reporting of this problem: 12 of the 18 trials raised problems concerning this change. Such problems were raised in all three regions in which the trials were conducted.

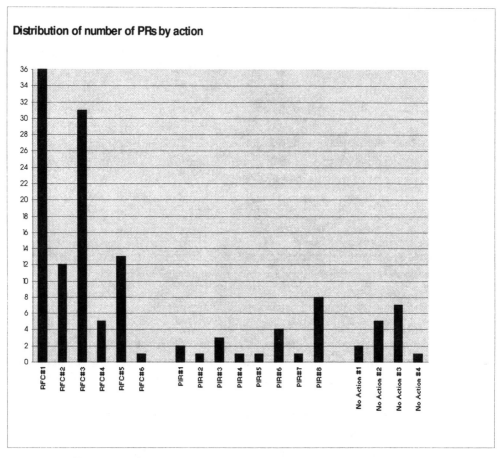

Figure 15.3: Distribution of problem reports by action.

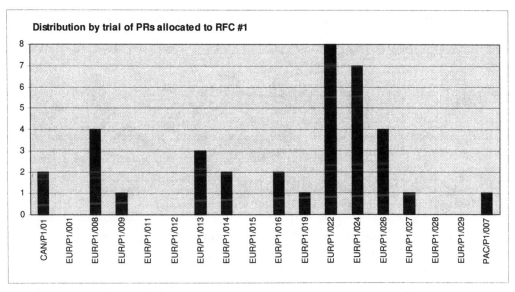

Figure 15.4: Distribution by trial of problem reports allocated to RFC #1.

Recommendations

The following recommendations were made at the time, in light of the actions identified:

1. RFC #1 was expected to necessitate a fundamental review and rework of the model and a revision of Part 2 of the SPICE document set. Resolution of this problem was considered essential before commencement of Phase 2 Trials.

2. The remaining five requests were considered to be less critical, in that the Phase 2 Trials could commence without the changes being reflected in the document set. However, it was strongly recommended that these changes were at least documented as clarification, interpretation, and guidance for use in conjunction with the document set. This recommendation should encourage the adoption of a consistent approach by qualified assessors in the trials. In addition to promoting repeatability, a key issue for Phase 2, it should also minimize the repetition of reporting in Phase 2 of problems already raised in Phase 1 and allow the qualified assessors to focus, in Phase 2, on other, as yet unreported, problems.

3. Account should be taken of the problems identified in project issue reports.

Progress on recommendations

At the time of writing (August 1996), the following progress had been made against each of the above recommendations:

1. This recommendation, and the underlying RFC #1, resulted in the formation, in late 1995, of an *Other Working Group* (OWG) within the project (see also Chapter 3). This group was tasked, among other things, with the revisions of Parts 2, 3, and 5 to encompass a revised capability dimension. This effort resulted in a change of terminology—from *generic practices and common features* to *attributes*—and a vastly-reduced set of more orthogonal measures that are taken of every process assessed. All changes were incorporated into the SPICE Version 2.00 document set.

2. All the specific trials group RFCs were input into the formal ISO ballot process via a *C liaison* body—the European Software Institute. All changes were incorporated into the SPICE Version 2.00 document set. More specifically:

   - RFC #2: The Part 2 working group was tasked with incorporating specific comments into the document set to address the problems with individual processes and with the relationships between processes in the model.
   - RFC #3 and RFC #4: These requests for change were implemented by the Part 2 working group in conjunction with the OWG.
   - RFC #5: This request for change was implemented by the Part 4 working group.
   - RFC #6: This request for change was implemented by the Parts 4 and 5 working groups.

3. Specific action on each PIR was as follows:

   - PIR #1: No action has been taken on this PIR. In hindsight, this PIR perhaps should have been classified as a *No action*.

- PIR #2: Following further review of the Phase 1 results, a decision was taken to search for further evidence regarding the rating scale during Phase 2 Trials.

- PIR #3: The Phase 1 Q4 analysis (see Chapter 13) in conjunction with the work of the OWG showed that major work was needed on Part 5 and on the indicator set. This work was dealt with by the Parts 5 and 2 working groups. All changes were incorporated into the ISO/IEC Version 2.00 document set.

- PIR #4 & PIR #8: These project issue reports are still open, pending resolution by the SPICE Project Management Board.

- PIR #5: The concept of extended processes was examined and refined as part of the work on Parts 2 and 3, Version 2.00.

- PIR #6 & PIR #7: These issues were addressed as part of the fundamental reviews of Parts 2 and 3, and included in the release of the Version 2.00 document set. The new framework requires the achievement scale to be used to rate *attributes*, while leaving the indicator rating scales outside the scope of the normative parts of the emerging standard.

16

Interrater Agreement in Assessment Ratings

Khaled El Emam
Fraunhofer - IESE, Germany

Peter Marshall
Defence Evaluation Research Agency, UK

This chapter is concerned with the reliability of assessments using the SPICE framework. Reliability is defined as *the extent to which there exists random measurement error in assessment ratings*. Random measurement error exists whenever a subjective measurement procedure is used. Process assessments are a subjective measurement procedure since they rely on the judgment of qualified assessors in making ratings.

There are different types of reliability that can be studied. A review of different types of reliability is given in *SPICE: An Empiricist's Perspective.*[2] The focus in this chapter is on *interrater agreement*.

Interrater agreement is concerned with *the extent of agreement on the ratings given by independent, qualified assessors to the same organizational practices after being presented with the same evidence*. If interrater agreement is low, then that is an indicator that assessment ratings are too dependent on the qualified assessor(s) conducting the assessment and that it is likely that a different qualified assessor or assessment team will produce a markedly different set of ratings. Given that assessment ratings are used as the basis for decision making in many assessment approaches, including those based on the SPICE framework, it is desirable that interrater agreement is high.

In this chapter, the results of evaluating the interrater agreement is presented, based on data collected from a single assessment conducted in the UK. This assessment used the SPICE Version 1.00 document set. This study is a follow-up study to that described in *Interrater Agreement in SPICE-Based Assessments: Some Preliminary Results.*[3] In the initial study reported in this paper, independent ratings were made by two assessment teams. In the current study, independent ratings were made by *three* assessors. It is also necessary to replicate previous studies to have confidence in and confirm the original findings.

We evaluated the interrater agreement for two processes: ENG.3—*Develop software design* and PRO.7—*Manage resources and schedule.* Our results indicate that interrater agreement is indeed high, hence confirming the earlier findings.[3]

The next section provides a general overview of how to conduct interrater agreement studies and how to calculate and interpret an interrater agreement coefficient. This overview is followed by a description of the data collection process and the organization that was assessed. The results are then presented their implications and limitations are discussed.

Research Method

Data Collection

To evaluate interrater agreement, an assessment must be conducted in a manner that provides the appropriate data. A suitable approach is to divide the assessment team into two groups. It is assumed that each group's qualified assessors are equally competent in making practice-adequacy judgments. Ideally, the division into groups would be achieved through random assignment or matching. The qualified assessor(s) in each group would be provided with the same information—for example, all would be present in the same interviews and provided with the same documentation to inspect—and then they would perform their ratings independently. Subsequent to the independent ratings, the two groups would meet to reach a consensus or final assessment team rating. General guidelines for conducting interrater-agreement studies are given in Figure 16.1.

Instructions for Conducting Interrater Agreement Studies

- For each SPICE process, divide the assessment team into two groups, with at least one person per group.
- The two groups should be selected so that they are as closely matched as possible with respect to training, background, and experience.
- The two groups should use the same evidence (For example, attend the same interviews, inspect the same documents, and so on), assessment method, and tools.
- The first group examining any physical artifacts should leave them as close as possible (organized/marked/sorted) to the state that the assessees delivered them.
- If evidence is judged to be insufficient, more evidence should be gathered and both groups should inspect this new evidence before making ratings.
- The two groups independently rate the same process instances.
- After the independent ratings, the two groups then meet to reach consensus and harmonize their ratings for the final SPICE profile.
- There should be no discussion between the two groups about rating judgment prior to consensus building and harmonization.[**]

Figure 16.1: Guidelines for conducting interrater-agreement studies.

The organization in which the current assessment was conducted used the classic waterfall life cycle for system development. The methods used for design were JSD and Yourdon, with a mix of Ada and C++ as programming languages. The project that was assessed was to develop a real-time simulation and training system with high usability requirements. The project had 57 software personnel working on it and was expected to take 40 person/years of effort.

The three qualified assessors who took part in this study examined all the documented evidence together and each heard the answers to the questions asked by the other qualified assessors during the interviews.[*] They followed an

---

[**]This requirement needs special attention when the assessment method stipulates having multiple consolidation activities throughout an assessment (for example, at the end of each day in an assessment). Observations that are discussed during such sessions can be judged as organizational strengths or weaknesses, and therefore the ratings of the two groups would no longer be independent. This factor can be addressed if consolidation is performed independently by the two groups. Then, before the presentation of draft findings to the organization, independent ratings are given followed by consensus building and harmonization of ratings by both groups.

[*]Even though each qualified assessor may not ask the same questions as the other assessors if s/he was alone with the interviewees, it would be necessary for the assessors to attend the same interviews to ensure that they have the same evidence. This approach is the specification of our interrater-agreement study.

early version of a commercial software assessment method based on the SPICE framework. Two of the assessors had substantial experience in software assessment and audit (six years each), and the third assessor had more than 10 years of software engineering management experience, but little experience in process assessment. All assessors had considerable knowledge of the SPICE framework. For both processes, the ratings were made only up to the Level 3 generic practices.

Evaluating interrater agreement

To evaluate interrater agreement, the SPICE adequacy ratings are treated as being on a nominal scale. Cohen's paper *A Coefficient of Agreement for Nominal Scales*[1] has defined the coefficient Kappa (κ) as an index of agreement that takes into account agreement that could have occurred by chance. The value of Kappa is the ratio of observed excess over chance agreement to the maximum possible excess over chance agreement. Cohen's statistic, however, is applicable when there are two raters. In the case when there are more than two raters, Fleiss[4] has presented an alternative version of Kappa. See *Nonparametric Statistics for the Behavioral Science*[6] for the details of calculating Kappa and its variance for more than two raters.

If there is complete agreement, then $\kappa=1$. If observed agreement is greater than chance, then $\kappa>0$. If observed agreement is less than would be expected by chance, then $\kappa<0$. The minimum value of κ depends upon the marginal proportions. However, since the purpose is evaluating agreement, the lower limit of κ is not of interest.

Using the variance of Kappa for more than two raters[6], it is possible to test the null hypothesis that $\kappa=0$ against the alternative hypothesis $\kappa\neq0$. Using a one-tailed test, a test can be made against the alternative hypothesis $\kappa>0$, which is more useful. This test means testing whether or not a value of Kappa bigger than zero, as large as the value obtained, could have occurred by chance.

Interpreting interrater agreement

After calculating the value of Kappa, the next question is "how can it be interpreted"? One approach is to use the guidelines developed and accepted within other disciplines. To this end, Landis and Koch[5] have presented a table that is useful and commonly applied for benchmarking the obtained values of

Kappa. This table is shown in Figure 16.2. Another approach is to compare the current values of Kappa with those obtained in the previous study reported[3] since these values can serve as a reasonable baseline.

Results

The results of the Kappa evaluation are shown in Figure 16.3. These results indicate that the Kappa values are statistically significant at a one-tailed alpha level of 0.05. These values of Kappa can be categorized as *moderate* according to the earlier interpretation guidelines. For ENG.3, which was also evaluated in the previous study, the values of Kappa are very similar (0.59 vs. 0.61). For the PRO.7 process, the values obtained from the current study are less than those obtained in the previous study in general, but not markedly so. As a preliminary observation, however, the PRO.7 process ought to be studied further to determine whether it exhibits consistently lower interrater agreement compared to other SPICE processes.

The above results indicate a generally high interrater-agreement level for SPICE processes. When combined with the results from the previous study, it is seen that interrater agreement for the SPICE processes evaluated is above what would be expected by chance (if the ratings were made randomly). A criterion of better than chance agreement is perhaps not a completely satisfactory one to evaluate the reliability of process assessments. More research would be necessary to determine a more appropriate threshold based on the evaluation of the impact interrater agreement could have on actual decisions made.

Kappa Statistic	Strength of Agreement
<0.00	Poor
0.00-0.20	Slight
0.21-0.40	Fair
0.41-0.60	Moderate
0.61-0.80	Substantial
0.81-1.00	Almost Perfect

Figure 16.2: The interpretation of the values of Kappa.

	Average Proportion Agreement	Kappa	Interpretation
ENG.3	78 percent	0.61*	Moderate
PRO.7	74 percent	0.54*	Moderate

Figure 16.3: Results of Kappa evaluation (* indicates statistical significance at an α-level of 0.05).

It must be noted that the study reported in this chapter is a small-scale study, where only two processes were evaluated. There may be factors that did not vary in the current study but that may show an influence on interrater agreement in a larger study. At the time of writing, larger-scale investigations are being planned to evaluate further the interrater agreement of assessments based on the SPICE framework.

References

1. J. Cohen, "A Coefficient of Agreement for Nominal Scales," *Educational and Psychological Measurement*, Vol. XX, No. 1, 1960, pp. 37–46.

2. K. El Emam and D.R. Goldenson, "SPICE: An Empiricist's Perspective," *Proc. 2nd IEEE Int'l Software Engineering Standards Symp.*, IEEE Computer Soc. Press, Los Alamitos, Calif., 1995, pp. 84–97.

3. K. El Emam et al., "Interrater Agreement in SPICE Based Assessments: Some Preliminary Results," *Proc. 4th Int'l Conf. on the Software Process*, IEEE Computer Soc. Press, Los Alamitos, Calif., 1996, pp. 149–156.

4. J. Fleiss, "Measuring Nominal Scale Agreement Among Many Raters," *Psychological Bulletin*, Vol. 76, No. 5, 1971, pp. 378–382.

5. J. Landis and G. Koch, "The Measurement of Observer Agreement for Categorical Data," *Biometrics*, Vol. 33, Mar. 1977, pp. 159–174.

6. S. Siegel and J. Castellan, *Nonparametric Statistics for the Behavioral Sciences*, McGraw Hill, New York, N.Y., 1988.

17

Using SPICE as a Framework for Software Engineering Education: A Case Study

Val E. Veraart and Sid L. Wright
Murdoch University, Australia

There has been a great deal of healthy debate on the topic of whether or not software engineering process concepts and skills can be taught to undergraduate students with little or no industry experience. As academics, we have a tendency to take for granted the implicit, discipline-based framework within which we develop software. We understand, with the benefit of hindsight that comes from having experienced and internalized the whole process—how all the pieces fit together. However, the majority of students fail to see the forest since they're too busy worrying about the trees. They need a visible framework that illustrates the interrelationships between skills they learn from the various, discrete courses they take.

Many courses that teach software engineering topics either adopt a theoretical, teach-from-the-book approach that gives students little practical experience of the many, varied topics normally included in those courses, or they use a team-based project to try to convey the practical aspects of the discipline, but allot very little time for studying and understanding the underlying concepts and their rationale. In our opinion, neither of these approaches can give students a realistic experience of the processes by which software is developed that will help them with their careers in the software development industry. Nor do they provide the necessary framework for a conceptual understanding of the process issues that allow them to develop, extend, and evolve their skills in an industry undergoing such rapid change.

Working with the initial documents for the emerging standard for Software Process Assessment demonstrated that a coherent framework for describing and measuring the software process was possible. We recognized that this framework might be a suitable structure on which to focus our curriculum and, indeed, our educational processes in the teaching and assessment of students. To investigate these possibilities, a case study investigation was carried out as described in this chapter.

The result was a set of curricula for three software engineering courses that will educate and train students in the knowledge and skills necessary to work within an organization that is executing its software engineering processes at a SPICE Level 2 capability. This curricula will also provide educators with a greater understanding of the process of curriculum development, educational delivery and student performance assessment within a standards framework.

Context

Software Engineering Project is the final course in our university's three-year, undergraduate program in Computer Science. Its main objective is to give students an opportunity to work in teams to produce a software product, starting from the initial software requirements phase and taking it right through to a final product, giving them a taste of the complete software development process they might experience in industry. Unfortunately, prior to 1995, the structure of the degree program did not allow the teaching of *basic* software engineering principles and practice to be delivered prior to the project course, although the students had already experienced all the product-related activities of analysis, design, and implementation. In 1994, it was decided to incorporate a software engineering stream into the degree program, providing us with two courses dedicated to software engineering topics, in addition to the project course.

The first of these courses, *Software Engineering I* (SE I), was timetabled for the penultimate semester, to be taken concurrently with the course *Software Architectures*. The second, *Software Engineering II* (SE II), was to be taken in the final semester, concurrent with the revised *Software Engineering Project* (SEP) course. Each course was timetabled for 13 weeks and typically involved two or three lectures, a laboratory, and a tutorial session. A student normally takes four courses per semester.

Our task was to define the content of these additional courses, revise the project course to take advantage of the preceding software engineering course, and present an integrated view of a modern approach to software engineering. Many members of the software engineering community strongly believe that, as applications become more complex, the knowledge and understanding of the software engineering processes that guide development are as important as the skills necessary to develop the product. For this reason, it was incumbent upon us to ensure that the courses presented a strong process focus.

Unfortunately, at the time, there were few software engineering textbooks that present a unifying framework for software engineering that integrates process with product. Many are considerably out of date in areas related to software process, process engineering, and process improvement. The lack of adequate reference information makes curriculum development using a single-textbook approach, common in practical courses with well-defined technical content, difficult for software engineering. This difficulty was compounded by a lack of published, up-to-date curriculum models for software engineering.

One of the authors (Veraart) had considerable involvement in reviewing the evolving set of SPICE documents in 1994–1995 and believed that the explicit structure of the SPICE reference model could be translated into a curriculum framework. Our decision to use the SPICE document set[*] was based on the consistency, completeness, and level of detail it provided when compared with other capability models.

Case study focus

In considering the philosophies of process assessment and process improvement that underpin SPICE, we had an ideal opportunity to apply these concepts to both the development of the course curricula and to the educational outcomes. We adopted a research focus for our work, in addition to the primary educational focus, and defined an exploratory case study with three clear objectives in its information gathering process. We looked to determine whether:

---

[*]All references in this chapter are either to the SPICE Version 2.00 documents or to drafts of these documents before they were issued as Version 2.00. The terminology used may therefore be slightly different from the current Version 2.00 documents.

1. the SPICE document set could yield a curriculum framework
2. the emerging SPICE standard was tailorable, and then applicable, to small-group projects, undertaken by relatively inexperienced software engineering practitioners
3. group projects, undertaken by our third-year students, could be improved (relative to those of the previous year) by mandating a specific SPICE-capability level for selected processes.

The success of the case study in achieving these objectives could be determined by:

- the existence and survival of a software engineering curriculum that would be used again in one or more subsequent academic years
- a curriculum that would be useful to other educational institutions requiring similar courses
- a curriculum that is publishable and that could withstand the scrutiny of our educational peers
- via tailoring the SPICE model, our ability to derive standards that students undertaking project work would be able to understand and with which they could comply
- an assessment of the current and previous year's projects, using an appropriate assessment framework that would show improvement—in this case, using process documentation, product documentation, and execution.

Rationale for using the SPICE document set

In defining the educational content of courses, consideration must be given to both the academic background of the students and the needs of the industry they aspire to join. Consequently, it is a fundamental requirement that any software engineering curriculum addresses the concepts of both the software engineering process *and* the software engineering product for the following reasons:

1. If our graduates enter organizations that are committed to software process management and improvement, they will have an understanding of, some experience in, and be comfortable with the process practices involved.

2. If our graduates enter organizations that are not committed to software process management and/or improvement, they may identify opportunities, as they progress through the organizational structure, to introduce and/or support these concepts while maintaining an individual commitment to personal process improvement.

Since we wanted to emphasize the process aspects of software engineering, it was important to identify the relevant concepts of the software engineering process and to justify their relevance to students in terms of their future careers. It was also necessary to identify clear educational objectives that would be acceptable to the relevant university educational committee. The emerging SPICE standard appeared to be a suitable vehicle for identifying the concepts since it is process oriented and details the activities and outcomes that form the foundation of a rational software development process.

Curriculum development

The SPICE reference and assessment models provided us with a framework that contained both processes and maturity levels, forming the basis for capability assessment. Our first step was to translate the processes in that framework into a viable, teachable curriculum.

Orthogonal to the processes and base practices are the capability attributes and their associated indicators, the *management practices*.

Deriving essential processes from base practices

The use of base practices to assess an organization's capability to develop software indicated to us that, according to the worldwide SPICE Project software community, these practices are important to the development of software, providing us with a strong motivation to include them in our software engineering courses.

Our first activity in defining the detailed curricula for the software engineering courses was to examine the list of processes within each process category and elide any processes we considered to irrelevant within an educational context. This categorization effort did *not* imply that the excluded processes would not be covered within the courses, but rather that they would be taught within a *guidance* context, rather than within the *prescriptive* context. Prescriptive processes were those we expected to be adopted by all project teams, whereas guidance processes were those we felt the students should be familiar with upon entering into employment, but that were inappropriate or not essential for student projects.

Our approach was, to some extent, tempered by pragmatism: in the first version of the SPICE documents we used (December 1994), there were too many base practices to cover adequately in the limited time available to us. (This conclusion was substantiated by some Phase 1 Trials assessors and has since been addressed by the current release of the SPICE reference model.)

The processes in the *Customer-Supplier* process category that we defined to be within a guidance context related to the dealings with independent suppliers in tendering, contract negotiation, and interfacing with subcontractors. These areas would be very difficult to teach to undergraduates with little or no work experience. However, within the curriculum of a post-graduate course, we thought they should be considered for inclusion with the prescriptive processes.

The *Engineering* and *Support* process categories were adopted with one exclusion: the Engineering process *Maintain system and software*. It was felt that this process could not be applied in a prescriptive manner since all the project work the students would be undertaking would be based on green-field development and the short timeframe for development would preclude any realistic maintenance efforts.

Within the *Management* process *category*, the single exclusion was the process *Manage subcontractors*, for the same reason as that of the *Customer-Supplier* process.

The most exclusions were made in the *Organization* process category, since we believed that the majority of these processes would be outside the sphere of control of student project teams since they lie within the overall domain of management and their responsibility for projects and their resourcing.

Deriving capability goals from management practices

The capability goal for our student projects was Level 2 *Managed*. Since our SE I course was the predecessor of the SEP course, we again used the exemplar model to define the capability level at which the course would address the process material. A Level 2 *Managed* process is capable of delivering work products of defined quality within defined timescales and resource needs.

This capability is achieved by managing the performance of the process and its resulting work products. Applicable practices are:

1. **Performance management** attribute:
   - assign responsibilities for developing work products

- document the approach to performing the process in standards and/or procedures
- allocate resources for performing the process
- provide support tools to perform the process
- ensure training for those who perform the process
- plan the performance of the process
- use plans, standards, and procedures
- verify compliance of the process to applicable standards and/or procedures
- track the status of the project against the plan with measurement
- take corrective action as appropriate when progress varies significantly from that planned.

2. **Work product management** attribute:
   - use configuration management
   - verify compliance of work products with the applicable standards and procedures
   - perform peer reviews of appropriate work products of the process.

Once we had defined both the processes to be covered and the capability indicators, we had, in essence, a two-dimensional framework for our curriculum. This information was incorporated into a spreadsheet format and the intersection cells would eventually contain the topic number in which the material was to be presented.

The final stage was to populate the framework with teaching materials. We were not limited by the usual constraints that arise from the single textbook approach, so we were able to draw these materials from quite diverse sources. The teaching materials we gathered together for SE I (taught in first semester) covered all the prescriptive processes so that the students would be capable of executing their project processes at Level 2 during the second semester.

Our major objective for SE II was to add depth to the treatment of particular areas—such as software process, process improvement, verification, validation, and maintenance—described earlier as guidance rather than prescriptive processes. A minor but still important objective was to extend the treatment of some processes to consider Levels 3 and 4 process capability, namely the *Established* and *Predictable* capability attributes. Consequently, within the three courses, we were able to achieve the following:

- address all the concept and problem areas described in the previous section
- provide a spiral approach to learning
- provide a strong, practical emphasis on real-world activities within the project
- emphasize communication and teamwork skills.

Some of the activities had been carried out in earlier projects; however, our ultimate objective is to make the included activities a mandatory part of the development process in future projects. Their usage could be measured objectively since, in all cases, they produce identifiable artifacts, such as documents. The result of their inclusion will be a subjective judgment, by us as educators, as to whether or not they have made each project more controllable and managed as compared to previous projects. We anticipate that it will take several years to define and put into place all the necessary policies and procedures, and that this process will be cumulative, as we create a baseline set of curricula to benchmark using the concept of current best practice within the projects.

Developing course content

The content matrix we were able to derive from the SPICE documents identified the desired capability for students at the conclusion of the SE stream courses. By reviewing the curricula for the preceding courses the students had completed, we were able to define the capabilities we could expect the students to have acquired: previously-completed courses represented their entry capability into the SE stream courses. Once we had compared the current and desired capabilities, we could identify the shortfall, or gap, that represented the material we would use to populate the framework.

Educational objectives

We believe that our educational responsibility is to ensure that the software engineering process activities students are taught become ingrained as part of their own personal process models. By imprinting these activities upon students, the software engineering processes become as normal and familiar as any of the more *product*-related activities they have been taught to consider as essential to software development. Our goal is to provide our students with an education in software engineering process that will:

- imbue the concepts of specific responsibilities and roles to be part of an organizational unit (OU) such as a project team, rather than having them adopt a pure, self-survival attitude
- illustrate that active team work and communication goes beyond the activity of programming as a group
- explain, using practical examples, that although process models (or frameworks) may be defined, the reality is that these models cannot be mandated: development processes have to be adapted to fit the tasks at hand, rather than attempting to mold the project requirements to fit a conceptual model
- illustrate that while it is relatively easy to create process models for the traditional life-cycle methods (such as waterfall), software development is dynamic and the process models must be able to handle this aspect of software development—however, this dynamism does not imply a descent into chaos, as deadlines approach and schedules tighten.

We used this goal as a focus for structuring the material content and practical work for the two-theory and one-project courses that formed the SE stream.

Project objectives

The *Software Engineering Project* (SEP) course has, since its inception in 1988, been recognized as important in that it has become a capstone course that ties together much of the technical content that students had been taught over the previous two and a half years of their studies. In addition, it provides experience with the realities of working as part of a development team under the constraint of hard deadlines. With the inclusion of the software engineering process concepts in the theory courses, we expected to see both qualitative and quantitative outcomes from this course. The outcomes we were looking for—as a result of adopting explicitly-taught process activities in the projects, rather than relying on some implicitly-acquired knowledge of them—included:

- **improved scheduling and planning**—resulting from task identification activities, identification of roles and responsibilities, understanding of critical activities, and better estimation techniques

- **decreased time pressure**—resulting from better scheduling, planning, risk management, and progress-monitoring activities
- **improved quality of deliverables**—resulting from identification of quality factors appropriate to the projects and the use of standards, procedures, acceptance test plans, reviews, and inspections using the quality factors as guidelines
- **improved identification and control of development artifacts**—resulting from active use of configuration management, version control, and change management activities.

Sequencing of material content

With our curriculum framework in place, our material and practical content decided, and our educational goals defined, the final, essential development activity was to sequence the material into 12–14 topics for each course. With the SPICE-derived framework already in place, the sequencing was a relatively simple task. Initially, we grouped related concepts into 13 topics and defined *concept* and *practical* objectives for each topic. The next step was to define what prerequisite knowledge was essential for a student to successfully undertake studies in that topic: we sought to determine what the *entry criteria* for the course was in terms of the content of preceding courses as well as the other topics within the software engineering courses themselves. Sequencing the topics on the basis of this prerequisite knowledge provided us with the final topic sequence for each of the theory courses. Sequencing the material in the project course was based on a *just-in-time* approach that ensured students would get the material appropriate for their current project-related activities.

Software Engineering I (SE I)

This course is the first identifiable, full software engineering course in the undergraduate degree structure. The goal of this course is to present the fundamentals of the software development process to students so that they are prepared for the work necessary to achieve a SPICE Level 2 process capability for the identified processes in their project work. We presented the material by varied means, including traditional lectures, large-group workshops, interactive tutorials, and a set of readings. The latter comprises about 60 recent (1990-onward) articles and papers in the literature, from journals such as the *IEEE Software*, *Software Development*, and *Software Engineering Journal*. Some examples of the type of readings provided are given in Appendix B. The material is organized into 14 topics as follows:

1. an overview of software engineering
2. life cycles and process models—the synergy and interactions between them
3. project management—major tasks, resource identification, and building teams
4. estimation techniques—applying and adapting common methods and capturing appropriate data to improve future estimating efforts
5. risk management—identification, definition of mitigation strategies, and continuous assessment
6. configuration management—including policy definitions, versioning using common tools, and change management
7. standards and templates—consideration of accepted standards AS3563, ISO 9001, and ISO 9000-3, and development of project-specific standards
8. software development environments (SDE)
9. proposal ↔ requirement ↔ specification and iterative pathways
10. acceptance test plans—relationship to requirements, specifications, and implementation
11. quality assurance—definition of quality factors, using factors during development
12. software maintenance—existing problems and building in maintainability from the analysis phase
13. documentation and technical writing—future-proof documentation of both the process and the product
14. reuse and reengineering—planning for the former and adapting the process for the latter.

The practical work has two sample projects, of different scales, as its process foci. The first, an image visualization application, would be implementable by a two-person team with a one-month timeframe. This application is amenable to a simple, phased approach with some user interface prototyping. Working on this application does not take students too far away from the material they learned about development in previous courses. However, it includes solution-domain concepts about which they have little or no expert knowledge, such as X-Windows programming and an unfamiliar interpretive language tcl/tk. We find that this unfamiliarity helps students to concentrate on process issues rather than starting to solve the problem. Practical work based on this project is undertaken either individually or in pairs of students.

The second process project is a much larger-scale application that we estimated would require an 18-month to two-year timeframe for a small development team (approximately five people). Its requirements exhibit a number of attributes, making it obvious that adopting the waterfall paradigm will not be an effective solution strategy. This larger project provides the foundation for practical group work (approximately four students). We designed the products that students acquire in working on this project, such as standards, procedures, and essential process activities, to be reused at the commencement of the projects in the following semester. The practical exercises include:

- working on task and deliverable definitions for real tasks, beyond the simple analysis and development tasks
- identifying the risks associated with using tools and languages with which they are unfamiliar
- applying function points and three alternative estimating techniques, illustrating the differences in estimates that can arise when the techniques are applied to their own projects
- developing policies and procedures to support the needs of different process models
- developing configuration management and version control policies and procedures for the two projects, based on the experience students gain with the tools available and the control required to manage a prototyping development process.

Important practical aspects stressed are visibility, lack of fear of criticism, and the realization that different ideas and approaches are not necessarily mistakes. We have visibility areas on the walls in our purpose-designed, discussion room, where work is displayed along with comment sheets. We actively encourage students to critique other people's ideas and proposals, often allocating time during a practical session to do a "wall walk." They gain from the experience of looking over other people's work (inspections and review experience) and they pick up ideas from others and apply them to their own work (process improvement). Students recognize that when they are required to complete work on blue paper, it is for public consumption. Comments go on pink paper and are returned to the owner of the original work. After the first such experience, they become quite comfortable with the idea.

In addition to the practical work based on the two projects mentioned above, reviews are also carried out on various process artifacts from the previous year's project documentation. These projects are also subjected to critical examination of the process activities. By including these discussions and reviews, we encourage a culture of process improvement. The current students have already identified a number of process deficiencies and proposed changes to the policies and procedures to those used in the last year.

Software Engineering II (SE II)

In line with the SPICE-based capability approach taken in SE I, the topics in SE II cover activities that are necessary to execute projects at capability Levels 3 and 4 of the SPICE model. A detailed treatment of process models allow us to define the *Established* process capability of Level 3. Tailoring such processes includes a strong emphasis on maintenance or *software evolution* as we prefer to call it. A focus on software quality assurance (SQA), metrics, and verification and validation(V&V)—including reviews, inspections, and testing—allows us to cover Level 4 of the model, a *Predictable* process capability.

A further goal of SE II is to revisit certain aspects of process activities, previously covered in SE I, in more depth, such as verification and validation. There is a paucity of textbooks covering this material in depth, so the material presented in lectures is supported by a set of approximately 60 articles from the current literature. An extensive set of local Web pages—recently becoming known as an Intranet—provides information about the topics, practical work, and other information related to the course (such as assignment work). The use of the Web allows students to grasp the whole structure of the course and how it relates to SE I (via extensive links back to the SE I Web).[7]

SE II addresses the following topics:

1. maturity models—SPICE capability Levels 3, 4, and 5, associated management practices, and the relationship to the Capability Maturity Model (CMM)
2. principles of software quality—client-defined quality, Quality Function Deployment (QFD), and metrics
3. process descriptions, process models, and process enactments
4. requirements verification, rapid application development (RAD), Formal Methods, and Z-notation
5. verification and validation overviews
6. reviews, inspections, walkthroughs, and audits

7. testing, reliability, robustness, problem resolution, and defect tracking
8. document engineering, traceability matrices, and issue management
9. maintenance—taxonomy, life cycle, management, and techniques
10. tools—taxonomy, evaluation, and selection
11. software development environments and issues related to tool integration
12. professional, legal, and ethical issues in the software industry.

Much of the practical work in this course is linked with the project work being carried out concurrently. The tutorial groups are arranged to contain complete project teams and most practical exercises are done in project team groups. The SE II work is scheduled so that a topic and related practical work are covered just before the students need to perform that task in their project. Therefore, issues relating to quality factors, requirements analysis, and specification are dealt with before the students are required to submit their project specification document.

The QFD exercise is performed on their actual project and many teams include the SE II QFD analysis in their project documentation. The practical exercises on the inspection process are carried out in time for them to perform an inspection on their project's design document. Other exercise formats include, for example, examining how the Level 2 work they are doing in their project could be modified to conform to a Level 3 or 4 process or examining the relevant IEEE standards to help them with their project documentation.

Software Engineering Project (SEP)

The objective of this course is for students, in teams, to undertake a full software development project from its initial inception to a delivered application. Each team is required to achieve within their project a Level 2 *Managed* process capability, as defined in the SPICE model. To achieve this capability, the following process-related activities were identified as being essential:

- **task identification**—responsibilities, input and output products, and entry and exit criteria
- **software estimation**—based on functionality or alternative estimation techniques
- **project scheduling**—critical tasks, task dependencies, task status, and resource allocation
- **risk management**—identification, analysis, mitigation, and monitoring

- identification, definition, and use of **project standards, policies, and procedures**
- **software quality assurance**—identification of quality factors to be addressed during the life cycle
- **acceptance test plans**—the concept of testing as a life cycle activity, rather than a phase
- **progress monitoring**—plan revision and personnel resource tracking
- **configuration management**—baselines, change management, and version control
- **reviews and inspections**—of specified process and product artifacts.

Students commit most of their time during this course to the actual project work. However, there are two scheduled workshops each week that are related to the current work in the project: "Questions on notice" are addressed, current project activities are discussed, and inspection results and software quality assurance activities are presented by individual students. Minor areas not covered in SE I, but essential in effectively undertaking a number of necessary process activities, are also addressed. These areas include:

- teams, meetings, minutes, and agendas
- package/tool evaluation strategies
- HTML and web document structures
- preparation of a software distribution package
- presentations—preparation and delivery.

The students also view recent videos on software engineering material of topical interest. The prescribed "textbook" is the set of ESA standards.[2] In addition, students have access to the IEEE software engineering standards. A range of supporting material is also available on a software engineering Intranet. An in-house *Policy and Procedures Manual* is also available, having been developed by drawing information from the SPICE assessment model about work products and their characteristics as success indicators.[3,4]

Synergy between SE II, SE I, and SEP

SE II material builds very naturally on the content covered in SE I. Connections between the two courses have been made explicit, via the Intranet, by mapping links from the SE II Web pages back to the SE I Web pages. This connection is further enhanced by carrying forward the same case studies from SE I to SE II, having been supplemented by material from previous projects and other exercises. The issues are explored at a level of detail more appropriate to the higher SPICE process levels. This emphasis on providing linkages gives the students a strong sense of continuity.

As discussed previously, many exercises in the tutorials require the students to discuss or use techniques in the context of their ongoing projects. In an early tutorial, students examine additional activities that they would have to undertake if their project processes were to be assessed at capability Levels 3 and 4. They then modify the Level 2 project development processes they are actually using to include these extra activities and develop a potential Level 3 or 4 process. Later in the course, the students actively develop more comprehensive software verification and validation plans that complement the Level 2 software development plans that are in actual use within their projects.

This interaction—applying new techniques to their current project work—has been working very well and has been well received by the students. The synergy also works the other way, with the better teams choosing to include additional activities in their project development processes. The material within, and the timing of, the videos shown in the project course both supports and reinforces the applicability of the SE II material. As students encounter practical problems in their projects, they are given cause to reflect on the possible application of SE II methods and techniques to solve them.

Case study results

At the conclusion of the first year in which these courses were presented, we evaluated the outcomes of our case study. In this section, we revisit the objectives we defined for the case study earlier in this chapter and discuss the results of this exploratory work.

Objective 1—To determine whether or not the SPICE document set can yield a curriculum framework

Success criterion 1: the existence and survival of a software engineering curriculum that would be used again in one or more subsequent academic years

Evidence: In the first semester 1996, the SE I course curriculum that resulted from the original work with the SPICE documents has been reused with no change in its material content. Changes have been confined to the practical exercises undertaken during the tutorials. These exercises have been edited to remove ambiguities and to help clarify misconceptions. The requirements for the major assignments have been revised in line with records of the time expended on them by the 1995 student cohort.

Neither of the authors will be available to teach the SE II course in the second semester 1996 and an industry-based consultant, specializing in the area of quality assessment and certification, has been contracted to deliver the course. He has assessed the curriculum developed by us and will use it with little or no adaptation.

The second semester 1996 project course has a more doubtful outlook. In our absence, a staff member with a strong Computer Science background will be delivering lectures in the project course and managing the student projects. He has admitted to having a weak background in software engineering process and does not feel confident in applying this approach and communicating it effectively to the students. It appears that he is inclined to resile from the process issues and return the project emphasis to more technical (programming) and product-driven issues. Unfortunately, for this reason, we cannot use this course to support our claim to success in this objective.

Success criterion 2: a curriculum that would be useful to other educational institutions requiring similar courses

Evidence: Since this work was undertaken throughout 1995, knowledge of the curricula is not yet widespread enough to draw any conclusions.

Success criterion 3: a curriculum that is publishable and that could withstand the scrutiny of our educational peers

Evidence: We have been successful in publishing several conference papers relating to the work undertaken in the first half of the year.[5,6] Discussions with peers at these conferences have been very positive and have reinforced our beliefs in the merits of this approach. This preliminary anecdotal evidence supports our conclusion, but further evidence is required to have more confidence in our assessment of success in this objective.

Objective 2—To determine whether or not the SPICE emerging standard is tailorable, and then applicable, to small-group projects, undertaken by relatively inexperienced software engineering practitioners

Success criterion: via tailoring the SPICE model, our ability to derive standards that students undertaking project work would be able to understand and with which they could comply

Evidence: Based on a subset of the SPICE base practices, we developed a *Policy and Procedures Manual* that was used by all project teams during the project course. The successful production of many process and product artifacts complying with the manual supports our claim for success in this criterion. This positive conclusion was reinforced during the project presentations—at which students present their projects to their peers, faculty members, and a number of industry representatives—when the majority of teams included explanations of the SPICE document set and its use in evaluation of process capability.

The successful development of working products, together with documentation of the product and the process by which it was produced, gives encouragement to the belief that such standards can be successfully used by small project teams.

Objective 3—To determine whether or not group projects, undertaken by our third-year students, could be improved (relative to those of the previous year) by mandating a specific SPICE-capability level for selected processes

Success criterion: an assessment of the current and previous year's projects, using an appropriate assessment framework that would show improvement—in this case, using process documentation, product documentation, and execution

Evidence: To undertake the comparison, we used the SPICE assessment model to assess the capability levels of the 1994 and 1995 student projects. Using the same spreadsheet format that was created during our curriculum design work, we checked for the existence of appropriate work products as evidence of base practices. Once we had established the base practices undertaken by each project team, we assessed the process capability levels of the practices using the SPICE assessment model-suggested ratings of **N**ot adequate, **P**artially, **L**argely, **F**ully. These ratings were entered as cell values in the spreadsheet. The work products chosen for the assessment were drawn from the Project Development Folders (PDF)—containing process documentation and product deliverables—that every team was required to submit. Further, quantitative information was drawn from the software development managers logbooks to corroborate our findings.

Our assessment concluded that a majority of the 1994 projects (n=7) exhibited a Level 1 *Performed* capability overall, with some projects exhibiting higher process capabilities than some of the base practices, notably those from the Engineering process category. The weakest team was rated at Level 0 *Incomplete process*, which, in our assessment, meant that we could find little or no evidence of any formalized processes other than those of the Engineering process category.

In contrast, the majority of 1995 projects (n=6) exhibited a Level 2 *Managed* capability. The weakest team was rated at a strong Level 1 *Performed* capability, missing out only on a few Support process category base practices. Three of the strongest teams rated as very strong Level 2s, approaching Level 3 capability. Their achievements resulted from taking the *Policy and Procedures Manual*, extending it together as a group, and then tailoring it to the needs of their individual projects. Although our evidence is purely anecdotal, it appears that this cooperative effort arose from the practical work undertaken in the SE II course. It would have been very enlightening to compare various quality factors, such as measured defect rates, between the products from the two years. However, since the first year did not have a process in place to consistently capture the required data, this comparison is not possible.

Other computer science staff have provided anecdotal evidence stating that *perceived* product quality factors, such as completeness and reliability of the delivered software products, had improved from 1994 to 1995. This perception is supported by the higher success rate in meeting acceptance test plans by 1995 project groups relative to those of 1994. We believe that this objective measure of product functionality and user acceptance is indicative of a generally-improved product quality in 1995. Whether this factor is due to the improved processes used by the 1995 teams or to other factors (such as greater innate ability of the teams, improved product development tools, and so on) can only be determined by further data gathering and analysis in future years. Given the very large number of factors, many of which are outside our control, it will be difficult to perform such experiments. However, case studies, similar to the one described here, can still be very useful in gaining some understanding of the role of process in product development and in the education of students. Based on this study, what we can say is that other data, such as grade-point averages in other courses of the degree, do not indicate that the 1995 students were very different to previous student cohorts, nor that the development environments or methods were significantly better.

Case study result conclusions

Of the information available to us to date, it appears that a number of the case study objectives have been met. We are further encouraged by the reactions of several local employers. These organizations have process and quality group employees attending the local SPIN (Software Process Improvement Network). After reviewing our curricula and examining the students' PDFs, they are actively recruiting our graduates since they believe our students have skills and knowledge that will prove to be useful in their organizations' process and quality endeavors.

Effect of SPICE on our software engineering educational process

Using the SPICE documents has provided us with an opportunity to evaluate the educational processes we use to teach the software engineering material and to consider whether or not they are, in fact, amenable to the same type of capability determination. If we compare the characteristics of our education process with their equivalents in the software development process we can conclude that we are operating at a Level 2 process capability. Of course, many concepts are not directly applicable, so we need to develop a better educational process capability model. However, we have based our conclusions on the following evidence:

1. **Performance management attribute**
    *   Resources from the teaching budget are allocated for our educational process.
    *   Responsibilities for developing course materials, presentation methods, and so on are assigned to the lecturers and tutors, as appropriate.
    *   We have documented the way in which we have derived and are performing the process.
    *   Tools for supporting the educational process have been provided, including material preparation tools, presentation tools and facilities, Web site, labs for student practical work, and so on.
    *   We currently are self-training for the process, but consider it highly likely that we can train others in this approach to software engineering education.
    *   All material content for topics, teaching schedules, timetables, and practical activities are planned in advance.
    *   We use the teaching plans, documentation standards, and teaching procedures that we have developed.
    *   Our students and various university bodies verify compliance with our process.
    *   Our progress through the process is tracked by both our work products (such as the topic outlines) and those of our students' (such as tutorial and assignment work).
    *   We take corrective action when the course progress varies significantly from that planned, such as too much or too little material for lectures or taking too long to present material.

2. **Work product management attribute**

- All our work products are under configuration management and version control.
- Our students verify compliance of work products with our standards and procedures.
- Peer review is a standard process within the tertiary education environment, both by colleagues and through publication.

We currently meet the majority of the Performance Management management practices through the standardization of documentation templates for topic materials and lecture overheads. We have documented most of our procedures for producing and delivering lectures, tutorials, and so on. It is not clear how applicable the compliance verification aspects might be, but our students are quick to tell us if we deviate from *our* standards and procedures.

Tracking is more difficult. We have informal tracking for the number and types of questions that students ask about such items as the material and assignment marks, but we really need finer-grained quantitative measures. In 1996, we were using short quizzes at the conclusion of each topic as quantitative exit criteria. This practice allowed both us and our students to evaluate their understanding of the material and allowed us to determine the effectiveness of our teaching process.

In the Work Product Management management practices, all materials are under explicit, visible configuration and version control systems. Again, our students are quick to indicate if we fail to comply with this practice.

We believe our educational process also displays some evidence of higher capability levels. We have standardized on an organizational process model for these three courses (Level 3 capability). Some continuous process improvements (Level 5 capability) have already taken place between SE I, SE II, and SEP including, for example:

- improved documentation templates for topic materials and lecture overheads
- improvements in the structure of the Web pages
- improvement in the process of updating the Web pages.

Notwithstanding our desire to improve the process itself, it is important not to lose sight of the ultimate goal of most development processes: to deliver high quality products. We believe that our product quality—the students—shows an improvement. They are capable of, and have had experience in, running projects at a Level 2 capability level of the SPICE model. However, to ensure that the process is achieving its ultimate goal, we will need to establish metrics to track student quality and, as necessary, adjust our process (Level 4 and 5 capabilities).

Future directions

At the conclusion of our case study, we identified several major directions for the future work in the areas of software engineering education and improving the capability level of our education process. These directions encompassed such educational activities as:

- to develop our *Policy and Procedures Manual* into a full set of software process documentation that students can tailor for use in their projects—allowing the best project groups to aim for a Level 4 *Predictable* process
- to develop a set of metrics for use in quantitatively measuring properties of the educational process—to enable assessment and improvement of the process we were using
- beginning with the undergraduate program, convince our colleagues to integrate software engineering concepts into all our courses rather than include a few, isolated topics in various courses, with the majority of the material being presented in third year. The ideas based upon a Personal Software Process[1] should feature strongly in any such revised structure.

Both authors of this work have left the tertiary education sector and are now employed in a large, public-sector, scientific, and industrial research organization. The major thrust of our work will be to provide software engineering support and training to a number of small software development groups, some of which are involved in developing software of strategic importance to the organization. Using the experience gained in this case study, we are exploring whether or not we can package the SPICE-derived software engineering topics we have developed and use them to provide on-the-job training for practitioners with strong technical (programming), skills but with little or no knowledge of current software engineering practice.

In this context, we are intending to use our experience, both past and future, to determine if it is both possible and feasible to adapt the *Organization* base practices ORG 4.2 *Develop and acquire training* and ORG 4.3 *Train personnel* into a full **Education Process Category** for the particular needs of our organization. In undertaking this aspect of the case study, we will consider the implications of the Software Engineering Institute's People Capability Maturity Model on our work.

In the context of the SPICE model and our educational curricula, we postulate the following hypotheses:

1. that our curricula can be used to educate technically-competent software developers in current software engineering processes and practices
2. that a set of educational base practices can be defined that in turn can define an additional process category in the SPICE model and that the existing generic practices can be used to derive an organization's training capability level (in the context of software engineering).

The objectives for our next case study are to:

1. determine whether or not the educational curricula, derived from the SPICE documents, is applicable to the task of training software developers, *in situ*
2. develop and refine an educational process category (in terms of base practices and work products) and assess whether or not the existing management practices and success indicators used for the existing SPICE process categories are appropriate to define its capability levels.

The success criteria will be:

1. the successful use of the curricula within areas of the proposed organization
2. successful application of the derived educational process category to assess the capability of an organization's software engineering training capability.

Evaluation of the latter will be performed by interviews, historical documents, and skill and competency reviews.

Conclusions

When we started the work described here we believed that the teaching of essential software engineering skills would be achievable if the material was presented within the context of an explicit, unifying framework that tied all the software engineering concepts together *and* placed them in the context of the technical skills the students had already acquired in previous courses. Drawing from the SPICE process categories and their base practices provided the first dimension of our skills' matrix.

Extending this dimension orthogonally against the capability levels and their associated management practices provided us with the second dimension of the matrix. Finally, examining the work product indicators, their characteristics, and the process capability indicators provided us with the breadth and depth of material content for each cell within the matrix. The end result was a set of curricula for the three software engineering courses that educated and trained students with the knowledge and skills essential to work within an organization as it executed its software engineering processes at a SPICE Level 2 *Managed* capability. The resulting matrix was also used to evaluate the 1994 and 1995 student projects to determine the process capability levels of the 13 teams working on the projects. Part of this matrix is shown in Appendix A.

We have found the resulting curricula to be highly successful both in molding our teaching strategies and in guiding the students throughout their project work. Our belief in the goodness and appropriateness of the curricula has been reinforced by the responses we received from a number of local software engineering organizations that employ graduate students. The project results tend to suggest that students educated with this curricula are capable of running projects with Level 2 process capability. Potentially, they could work at Level 3 if we were to extend the *Policy and Procedures Manual* to encompass a full organizational process model document that could be tailored to meet the needs of their particular projects. This view is supported by the efforts in this direction of several 1995 project teams.

A final and unexpected benefit of working with the SPICE model was that it caused us to think about the educational process itself and our potential to improve our capability in this area. In conclusion, we both found the curriculum development work and the teaching associated with these courses to be the most satisfying of our tertiary education careers (10 and 12 years). There was a strong feeling of ownership of the courses that we had not experienced when using the more common textbook or professional body of knowledge approach to curricula development.

Appendix A—Sample SPICE to software engineering course topic matrix

		Topic (Course)	1. Performance management attribute			
			allocate resources for performing the process	document the approach to performing the process in standards and/or procedures		provide support tools to perform the process
CUS	2	Identify customer needs	9	4	7	8
ENG	2	Develop software requirements	9+10	4	9, 2 (II)	8
	3	Develop software design	9	4	9, 4 (II)	8, 10 (II)
	5	Integrate and test software	10, 5(II)*	4	7(II)	8
	7	Maintain software	12	12, 9(II)	9+10(II)	9(II)
SUP	1	Develop documentation	13, 8(II)	4	7,13,8(II)	13, 8(II)
	2	Perform configuration management	6	4	6	8, 10(II)
	3	Perform quality assurance	10+11, 2 (II)	4	6	2+4(II)
	4	Perform work product verification	5(II)	4	5 (II)	10(II)
	5	Perform work product validation	5 (II)	4	5 (II)	10(II)
MAN	1	Manage project	3	4	3	8
	2	Manage quality	11, 2(II)	4	5+6+7(II)	5+6+7(II)
	3	Manage risks	5	4	5	8
ORG	1	Define the process	2, 1+3(II)	4	2+3(II)	11+3(II)

*The references notation used with the topics reflects the structure of the spreadsheet. The references refer to the cell that forms the intersection between a management attribute and a process category. If no roman numeral appears, the cell contains references to SE I topics. The topic numbers after a comma refer to SE II for that cell only. If there is either a single number followed by *II* or *n+n* followed by *II*, the notation indicates that this cell refers to SE II topics only.

1. Performance management attribute

			plan the performance of the process	use plans, standards and procedures	track the status of the project against the plan with measurement	take corrective action as appropriate when progress varies significantly from that planned
CUS	2	Identify customer needs	2, 1+3 (II)	7	3, 2+7(II)	5
ENG	2	Develop software requirements	2, 8 (II)	7	3	5
	3	Develop software design	9	7	3	5
	5	Integrate and test software	7(II)	10,7(II)	3, 2+7(II)	5+7(II)
	7	Maintain software	7	7	9(II)	5
SUP	1	Develop documentation	8(II)	7	3	5
	2	Perform configuration management	2	7	3	5
	3	Perform quality assurance	2	7, 6(II)	2(II)	5
	4	Perform work product verification	3(II)	5(II)	3	5
	5	Perform work product validation	3(II)	10, 5(II)	3	5
MAN	1	Manage project	3	7	3	5
	2	Manage quality	2+5+6+7(II)	7	3	5
	3	Manage risks	5	7	3	5
ORG	1	Define the process	3(II)	7	3	5

2. Work prod mgmt attr

			use configuration management	perform peer reviews of appropriate work products of the process
CUS	2	Identify customer needs	6	6 (II)
ENG	2	Develop software requirements	6	6(II)
	3	Develop software design	6	6(II)
	5	Integrate and test software	6	6(II)
	7	Maintain software	6	6(II)
SUP	1	Develop documentation	6	6(II)
	2	Perform configuration management	6	6(II)
	3	Perform quality assurance	6	6(II)
	4	Perform work product verification	6	6(II)
	5	Perform work product validation	6	6(II)
MAN	1	Manage project	6	6(II)
	2	Manage quality	6	6(II)
	3	Manage risks	6	6(II)
ORG	1	Define the process	6	6(II)

Topic References—SE I

1. Overview of software engineering
2. Life cycles and process models
3. Project management
4. Estimation techniques
5. Risk management
6. Configuration management
7. Standards and templates
8. Software development environments
9. Proposals, requirements, and specifications
10. Acceptance test plans
11. Quality assurance
12. Software maintenance
13. Documentation and technical writing
14. Reuse and reengineering.

Topic References—SE II

1. Maturity models
2. Principles of software quality
3. Process models and enactment
4. Requirements verification
5. Verification and validation overview
6. Reviews, inspections, and audits
7. Testing, reliability, and defect tracking
8. Documentation, traceability, and issue management
9. Maintenance—taxonomy and life cycle
10. Tools—taxonomy, evaluation, and selection
11. Software development environments
12. Professional, legal, and ethical issues

Appendix B—Sample References

SE I Sample References

Reference	T	Citation
[EloA94]	4	Elo, A., "An Algorithm for Estimating Development Costs," *Software Development*, May 1994, pp. 73–76.
[FaiR94]	5	Fairley, R., "Risk Management for Software Projects," *IEEE Software*, May 1994, pp. 57–66.
[LinD93]	5	Lindstrom, D.R. "Five Ways to Destroy a Development Project," *IEEE Software*, Sept. 1993, pp. 55–58.
[KeuW92a]	6	Keuffel, W., "Configuration Management," *Computer Language*, Nov. 1992, pp. 31–34.
[KeuW93b]	6	Keuffel, W., "Making Sense of make," *Computer Language*, Mar. 1993, pp. 31–38.
[BD91]	6	Bersoff, E.H. and A.M. Davis, "Impacts of Life Cycle Models on Software Configuration Management," *Comm. ACM*, Aug. 1991, pp. 104–117.
[WalJ93]	11	Walsh, J., "Determining Software Quality," *Computer Language*, Apr. 1993, pp. 57–65.
[BiaR91]	11	Bias, R., "Walkthroughs: Efficient Collaborative Testing," *IEEE Software*, Sept. 1991, pp. 94–95.

Appendix B—Sample References

SE I Sample References

Reference	T	Citation
[EloA94]	4	Elo, A., "An Algorithm for Estimating Development Costs," *Software Development*, May 1994, pp. 73–76.
[FaiR94]	5	Fairley, R., "Risk Management for Software Projects," *IEEE Software*, May 1994, pp. 57–66.
[LinD93]	5	Lindstrom, D.R. "Five Ways to Destroy a Development Project," *IEEE Software*, Sept. 1993, pp. 55–58.
[KeuW92a]	6	Keuffel, W., "Configuration Management," *Computer Language*, Nov. 1992, pp. 31–34.
[KeuW93b]	6	Keuffel, W., "Making Sense of make," *Computer Language*, Mar. 1993, pp. 31–38.
[BD91]	6	Bersoff, E.H. and A.M. Davis, "Impacts of Life Cycle Models on Software Configuration Management," *Comm. ACM*, Aug. 1991, pp. 104–117.
[WalJ93]	11	Walsh, J., "Determining Software Quality," *Computer Language*, Apr. 1993, pp. 57–65.
[BiaR91]	11	Bias, R., "Walkthroughs: Efficient Collaborative Testing," *IEEE Software*, Sept. 1991, pp. 94–95.

References

1. Humphrey, W.S., *A Discipline for Software Engineering*, Addison-Wesley, Reading, Mass., 1995.

2. Mazza, C. et al., *Software Engineering Standards*, Prentice Hall, London, 1994.

3. Veraart, V.E., *Policy and Procedures Manual, V1.0*, Murdoch University Computer Science Department, 1995.

4. Veraart, V.E., *Baseline Practices Definitions*, Murdoch University Computer Science Department, 1995.

5. Veraart, V.E. and S.L. Wright, "Software Engineering Education—Adding Process to Projects: Theory, Practice and Experience," *APSEC 95, Proc. Asia-Pacific Software Engineering Conf.*, 1995.

6. Veraart, V.E. and S.L. Wright, "Experience with a Process-driven Approach to Software Engineering Education," *SE:E&P'96, Conference Abstracts of the 6th Working Conf. Software Engineering: Education and Practice*, 1996 pp. 419–426.

7. Veraart, V.E. and S.L. Wright, "Supporting Software Engineering Education with a Local Web Site," *Symp. Computer Science Education—96*, 1996, pp. 275–279.

18

Assessment Using SPICE: A Case Study

Jean-Martin Simon
CISI, France

A software organization with a strong quality background and an ISO 9001 registration needs to maintain the efficiency of its Quality Management System (QMS) over time. The registration program will have consumed much effort, cost, and individual investment. Once this goal has been reached, a major quality challenge will have been met and completed. However, the QMS must be maintained to support the (often new) business goals of the organization.

A common practice to check the applicability and use of the QMS' procedures is to perform internal quality audits. This basic action for quality assurance is required by the ISO 9001 standard and provides good results. Nevertheless, it is usually considered by the software practitioners of the organization to be a *control* action, rather than an opportunity to participate in the improvement of the practices and procedures.

It was for this reason that we decided to consider the Software Process Assessment (SPA) emerging standard as a new way to involve software personnel in the evolution of internal software best practices. We felt that the performance of assessments dedicated to process improvement should contribute to the overall quality of the software development activities and should provide inputs to the evolution of the QMS' procedures.

This chapter presents the results of a standalone-assessment case study using the SPICE framework. The study had been conducted during the PEACE project (ProcEss Assessment for Certification) in the context of the European Systems and Software Initiative (ESSI) June 95 call. The goals of the project were to experiment with the latest deliverables of the SPICE document set and to consider the software assessment method as a tool for quality management. This chapter also provides some practical recommendations and advice to the reader wanting to use the SPICE documents. The preparation and performance of the assessment as required by the SPICE documents in Part 3[5] and guided by Part 4[6] is explained.

Version 2.00 of the SPICE assessment model was used during the project. The results show that in the new SPICE model the *capability dimension* is more usable and the *process dimension* is more coherent. We now have an efficient model for SPA that can be used to complement internal quality audits to maintain and improve the QMS of an organization.

The PEACE project's goals

This section presents the global context of the PEACE project and discusses specific issues, mainly related to the purpose—the *assessment goals*—of the case study.

The 1995 ESSI call that was dedicated to Standalone Assessment Tasks was the perfect opportunity to evaluate the usability of a new assessment framework. At the same time, the SPICE Project had just completed the Phase 1 Trials based on Version 1.00, the results of which had been used as input to the development of Version 2.00. With a new version available, the PEACE project decided to experiment with the new version to evaluate how the assessment technique could be used to maintain a registered QMS. The assessment clearly had two goals:

1. to experiment with the new version of the SPICE software process model and assessment framework
    Since we had participated in the Phase 1 Trials,[1, 9, 12, 13, 14] we easily could compare the added value of Version 2.00 to Version 1.00.
2. to add the assessment technique to the tool set available to quality managers and quality engineers to assist them in maintaining and improving the QMS procedures.

The next section shows how these two goals influence the assessment preparation.

Performing the assessment

The following description illustrates one possible way to perform a SPICE assessment. Some of the requirements expressed in Part 3, as well as the tasks achieved in each step of the assessment, are illustrated below.

Even though the case study was not dedicated to an actual process improvement or capability determination initiative, we decided to follow the rules of assessment to perform a SPICE-conformant assessment. These rules are:

- use a model compatible with the reference model—Part 5[7] was selected
- review the defined inputs and record and document the justification of the assessment results
- satisfy the requirements of the Part 2 document[4]
- plan the expected outputs (process profiles, improvement orientations, and so on)
- include in the assessment team a qualified assessor: the author had acted as qualified assessor during the Phase 1 Trials and for other SPICE assessments.[12]

How to use the SPICE documents

Figure 18.1 shows how the different documents are combined together for use in assessing process capability and to either improve capability or consider how to determine capability using the results of the assessment.

When preparing for an assessment, the requirements of Parts 2[4] and 3[5] must be considered if the assessment is to be SPICE-conformant. Part 2 describes the two dimensions of the reference model: the process dimension and the capability dimension with its six levels. It gives a reference framework for the existing assessment methods so that the assessment results can be input into the SPICE framework and be compared. The SPICE document set also provides an assessment model in Part 5[6] that can be used for the assessment, independent of other models. The PEACE project used Part 5 as the assessment model. Chapter 7 of this book describes how the reference model in Part 2 is embedded within the Part 5 assessment model. Finally, helpful guidance is given to the qualified assessor in Part 4[6] to organize the assessment and develop the assessment plan.

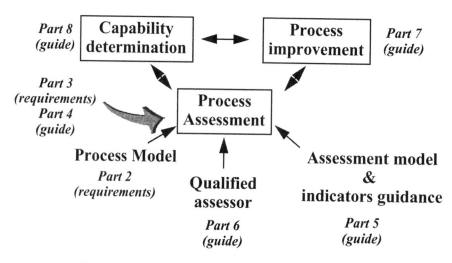

Figure 18.1: Using the SPICE document set.

The document set might be read in the following sequence:

1. the introduction in Part 1, with the help of the *Vocabulary* in Part 9 (these documents are not shown in Figure 18.1)
2. an overview of the SPICE reference model in Part 2
3. Parts 7 or 8 according to the organizational unit's (OU) assessment goals
4. Part 3 requirements and Part 4 guidance to prepare the assessment and develop the assessment strategy, with the help of Part 5 if the experiment is planned in a full SPICE context.

Assessment organization and planning

The PEACE project lasted over two and one-half months and included:

*   a phase for project initialization to establish a detailed plan, to determine the requirements for the output documents, and to write the assessment plan

    During this phase, the first goal required the development of documents and forms to support the assessment process itself. To contribute to the achievement of the second goal, a preliminary analysis of the SPICE framework with the QMS of the organization was undertaken.

- an assessment phase to assess the process instances of the process within the assessment scope (see below)
- a phase to analyze the assessment output data and write the assessment and PEACE project experiment reports

At this phase of the project, a strategy was suggested for using the results of the SPICE assessments.

For the case study, the assessment tasks had been planned over a period of four weeks according to the plan presented in Figure 18.2. The assessment scope included nine processes at the project level and five processes addressing the OU. Two process instances were selected (as described in "Selecting the processes" below).

This type of planning usually provides only a high-level view and should be completed as part of the assessment plan in more detail, indicating precisely when (date and time) the meetings and interviews will be performed. The detailed schedule should be established in collaboration with the OU facilitator to guarantee the availability of each individual involved in the assessment. To define the detailed schedule, the following points must be identified clearly:

- assessment tasks to be performed—inspections of documents, meetings, interviews, feedback sessions, and so on

- assessment scope, according to the assessment purpose

- process instances, according to the assessment scope

- time allocated for each interview or meeting, according to the resources and infrastructure availability and considering the assessment budget

- project team and individuals involved

- availability of documents—*assessment inputs*

- expectations of the assessment sponsor.

A draft version of the detailed schedule should be given to the OU as soon as possible to establish the final schedule, encouraging a collaborative approach between the assessment team and the OU.

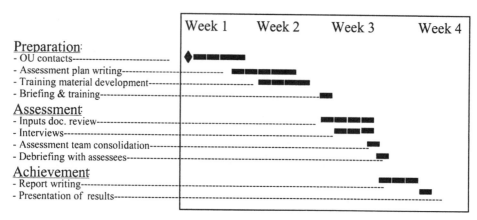

Figure 18.2: Assessment planning.

Assessment inputs

The assessment team must identify and describe in the assessment plan all the inputs to be used during the assessment, including:

- **assessment goals/purpose:** a very clear understanding of the assessment goals as defined by the sponsor is a key prerequisite for the success of the assessment

  For example, the assessment may be to assess process improvement, however, the improvement strategy will impact the assessment scope. If the experiment is based on using an assessment technique and/or participation in the SPICE Trials, the approach would be different.

- **process context:** guidance for the SPICE assessment method requires the assessment team to consider the process environment when making its judgments and determining the process attribute ratings and process capability level(s)

  As an example of specific processes, consider that ENG.3 *Develop software design* or MAN.3 *Manage risks* might have different requirements if the process is instantiated for a real-time embedded system or a client-server application lasting only three person-months.

- **level to be assessed:** indicates the investigation coverage of either the six capability levels or only a subset

- **selected processes:** the processes to be assessed are identified according to the inputs described above (see also Reference 11)

  A mapping between the SPICE standard processes and the processes of the OU might be necessary. This mapping might be the occasion to develop *extended processes* that do not exist in the standard model.[4]

- **process instances/projects:** the selected processes are assessed with *process instances* at the level of the project and/or the organization (units, department, teams, and so on)

- constraints: any constraint to be considered during the assessment must be identified, such as resource availability, confidentiality issues, sponsor requirements, assessment output data collection, and so on

- principles: a brief explanation of what the SPICE assessment philosophy is to those (such as executives) who receive the assessment plan and may not attend the training sessions, interviews, or debriefings

- **additional information to be collected:** by means of interviews (if this basic assessment technique is used), the assessment gives the opportunity to collect additional data such as improvement actions to be conducted and difficulties identified in performing project tasks or implementing internal standards and procedures.

Assessment plan

The assessment process is described in an assessment plan written by the qualified assessor, checked by the coassessor, and approved by the sponsor. For the PEACE project, the assessment plan contained the items in Figure 18.3. Some of these items are described later in this chapter.

The plan is used as a roadmap throughout the assessment. Part 4[6] gives other guidance to organize an assessment and write an assessment plan.

1. Introduction—Context
2. Terminology
3. Reference documents
4. Confidentiality agreement
5. Assessment inputs
   Assessment goals
   Assessment scope
     Process context
     Selected processes
     Levels to be assessed
     OU's units concerned
     Process instances/projects
   Constraints
   Principles
6. Assessment outputs
   Process capability profiles
   Process capability levels
   Assessment report
   Experiment report
7. Role and responsibilities
   Assessment sponsor
   Qualified assessor
   Coassessors
   OU facilitator
   Participants
8. Progress tracking and quality control
9. Assessment performance
   Planning
   Briefing and training
   Assessment technique and tools
   Resources—Infrastructure—Logistics
   Document inputs
   Data collection
   Data validation
   Debriefing
   Results presentation
   Next action
10. Detailed planning

Figure 18.3: Contents of an assessment plan.

Responsibilities

The roles and responsibilities of the participants involved in the assessment process are described in the assessment plan (see Part 4). Some specific issues described are:

- **assessment sponsor:** has a strong influence on the attitude of the assessment participants—the assessees—to have (or not have) a positive and collaborative approach during the interviews
- **qualified assessor:** the assessment success depends on knowledge of the SPICE framework and assessment techniques
- **coassessors:** provides assistance and support of the qualified assessor by sharing their expertise of the processes and establishing their own judgment and ratings to compare and validate against the qualified assessor's
- **OU facilitator:** very useful when the assessment team does not know the business sector of the assessed OU, acting, in some cases, as a moderator in the event of a conflicting situation during an interview with a participant
- **participants:** require a briefing about the assessment before the interviews.

Selecting the processes

The two goals of the project, as well as the availability of internal resources for the assessment phase, determined the project's assessment scope. Nine processes addressing the software projects and five processes concerning the organization were selected:

Goal #1 suggested considering some uncommon processes from the process dimension of the model to try them out during this assessment—for example, ORG.1 *Engineer the business*. We also included in the scope processes that were not assessed during our Phase 1 Trials participation.

Goal #2 suggested considering processes that would fit closely with some of the QMS procedures—for example, the ENG process category.

Table 18.1 and Table 18.2 contain, for each assessed process, the reference to its process category and a comment to explain why it was selected. A process is supposed to contribute to the achievement of one or both of the assessment goals (see Goals #1 or #2 indicated in the tables).

One instance of each process was assessed for the organization and two instances at the project level.

Table 18.1: Processes addressing the OU.

CUS	CUSTOMER SUPPLIER PROCESS CATEGORY
CUS.5	**Provide customer service—Goal #2** The QMS and ISO 9001 are strongly oriented to the customers' satisfaction. One of the OU's business goals is to guarantee the customers' satisfaction. This satisfaction is a key issue of the QMS and should be correlated to the capability of this process.
SUP	**SUPPORT PROCESS CATEGORY**
SUP.5	**Perform work product validation—Goal #2** The validation activities are performed throughout the software life cycle. A global assessment of this process should give information on the mean capability of the validation practices inside the OU.
MAN	**MANAGEMENT PROCESS CATEGORY**
MAN.3	**Manage risks—Goal #1** This process is considered important because it might have an influence on project achievement and the satisfaction of quality requirements. The process corresponds to a recent evolution of the QMS by means of an additional procedure. This process had not been assessed before.
ORG	**ORGANIZATION PROCESS CATEGORY**
ORG.1	**Engineer the business—Goal #1** This process addresses any kind of business and is not specific to software engineering activities. It is close to the TQM approach and contributes to the global efficiency of the OU which impacts customer satisfaction. It also allows an assessment of how the internal culture is spread inside the company. This process was not assessed before.
ORG.4	**Provide skilled human resources—Goal #2** This process is also dependent on the kind of business the OU is in. Its capability reflects how management considers individuals with respect to the strategic goals of the company.

Table 18.2: Processes at the software project level.

CUS	CUSTOMER-SUPPLIER PROCESS CATEGORY
CUS.2	**Manage customer needs—Goal #1** This process was selected to determine the scope of the *needs* that are not exclusively functional and because of the impact of its capability on the relationship with the customer.
CUS.5	**Provide customer service—Goal #2** This process was selected to determine the instantiation of the process at the project level.
ENG	ENGINEERING PROCESS CATEGORY
ENG.3 ENG.5	**Develop software design—Goal #2** **Integrate and test software** These two processes are supported by internal procedures that should be covered by the SPICE processes.
SUP	SUPPORT PROCESS CATEGORY
SUP.3	**Perform quality assurance—Goal #2** This process was selected to estimate how the model covers the quality assurance and quality control activities as they are implemented in the organization according to its internal culture. The process, with MAN.2 *Manage quality* (see below), gives complementary data about quality management.
SUP.4	**Perform work product verification—Goal #2** This process was selected because the verification activities are widely addressed by the QMS procedures.
MAN	MANAGEMENT PROCESS CATEGORY
MAN.1	**Manage the project** This process was selected to have a global overview of the project management of the instantiated processes.
MAN.2	**Manage quality—Goal #2** See SUP.3 *Perform quality assurance.*
MAN.3	**Manage risks—Goal #1** This process was included in the assessment scope, first to evaluate how the standard procedure for risk management is implemented, and second to experiment with its assessment at the project level.

Assessment techniques

The assessment can be based on one of the following techniques:

- interviews
- individual discussions

- group discussions
- closed-team sessions where the assessment team discusses findings among themselves
- documentation inspections
- feedback sessions where the assessment team discusses findings with OU representatives
- questionnaires

Interviews are considered the most efficient means with which to collect the output data because of the interactiveness of this approach. This technique also minimizes the validation activities: the assessment plan includes a step to validate the data collected during the interviews. Feedback from a previous assessment[12] influenced the choice of interviews as the main assessment technique. The assessment team interviewed the process owners, referring (if needed) to paper-based SPICE documents and collected the assessment data online with a PC laptop. Because validated assessment tools, specific files, forms, and documents were unavailable, they were developed during the initialization phase to support the assessment.

Performance and capability rating

The process rating is made by the assessment team, using *indicators* described in Part 5[7]). Two kinds of *process performance indicators* exist:

- *base practices* corresponding to software engineering or management activities that address the purpose of a particular process: a process has between 3–12 base practices
- *work products*: process inputs and outputs—data and documents.

The *process capability indicators* are:

- *management practice*: a management activity or task that addresses the implementation or institutionalization of a specified process attribute
- *management practice characteristics*: objective attributes or characteristics dedicated to the management practice's performance, resources, and infrastructure that validate the judgment of the assessment team as to the extent of achievement of a specified process attribute.

The process performance estimations, as well as the process capability evaluations, are made using a specific *rating* scale. For each assessed process instance, the ***first step*** is to estimate the base practice's *existence* by using the following rating scale:

- *Nonexistent*: the base practice is either not implemented or does not produce any identifiable work products
- *Existent*: The implemented base practice produces identifiable work products.

The base practice adequacy is evaluated by the assessment team using a four-point adequacy rating scale (see Figure 18.4 and Figure 18.5 for the Level 1 rating).

The ***second step*** when assessing a process instance is to estimate and rate the adequacy of the management practices, using the management practice adequacy rating scale:

- ***Not adequate:*** the management practice is either not implemented or does not to any degree satisfy its purpose
- ***Partially adequate***: the implemented management practice does little to satisfy its purpose
- ***Largely adequate***: the implemented management practice largely satisfies its purpose
- ***Fully adequate***: the implemented management practice fully satisfies its purpose.

This scale is very practical to assist qualified assessors in making their judgments. Instead of answering only Yes/No questions, the assessment team must consider the assessment context to estimate the adequacies with respect to the requirements of the SPICE model. All the members of the team are involved, must have a good knowledge of the SPICE process model, and also must have a fair understanding of the rating principles.

Assessment team preparation

The assessment team usually includes a qualified assessor and a coassessor. The qualified assessor has a deep understanding of the SPICE framework: the main items of concern are the process dimension of the model, the capability dimension, the assessment requirements, and the rating principles. The coassessor is experienced in software quality, software engineering, and has a good knowledge of SPICE. This assessment team in the PEACE project had already performed SPICE assessments before.

MAN.3   Manage risks ◄

The purpose of the Manage risks process is to continuously identi̶ project risks throughout the life cycle of a project. The process involv̶ cus on management of risks at both ̶t̶h̶e̶ ̶p̶r̶o̶j̶e̶c̶t̶ ̶a̶n̶d̶ ̶o̶r̶g̶a̶n̶i̶z̶a̶t̶i̶o̶n̶a̶l̶ ̶l̶e̶v̶e̶l̶s̶.̶ ̶A̶s̶ ̶a̶ result of successful implementation o̶f̶ ̶t̶h̶e̶ ̶p̶r̶o̶c̶

| Process name |

| Process goal description |

◊   the scope of the risk managem̶e̶n̶t̶ ̶t̶o̶ ̶b̶e̶ ̶p̶e̶r̶f̶o̶r̶m̶e̶d̶ ̶f̶o̶r̶ ̶t̶h̶e̶ ̶p̶r̶o̶j̶e̶c̶t̶ ̶w̶i̶l̶l̶ ̶b̶e̶ ̶d̶e̶termined;

◊   ....

◊   corrective action

| Base practice (= Process performance indicator) |

MAN.3.1   **Establish risk management scope.** Determine the scope of risk management to be performed for this project.

Note: Issues to be considered include the sev̶e̶r̶i̶t̶y̶,̶ ̶p̶o̶s̶s̶i̶b̶i̶l̶i̶t̶y̶,̶ ̶a̶n̶d̶ ̶t̶y̶p̶e̶ ̶o̶f̶ ̶r̶i̶s̶k̶s̶ to identify and manage.

| Assessment data |

Existence: Adequacy:

No ☐   Yes ☑   Not ☐   Partially ☐ Largely ☑ Fully ☐

Notes: Le champ de la gestion des risques concerne au niveau RSO, les risques de type coûts, délai et qualité associés à la réalisation de prestations forfaitaires. RSO a établi une méthodologie nommée MARS pour l'analyse et la diminution des risques. Cette dernière est en c̶o̶u̶r̶s̶ ̶d̶'̶e̶x̶p̶é̶r̶i̶m̶e̶n̶t̶a̶t̶i̶o̶n̶ ̶à̶ ̶l̶'̶é̶c̶h̶e̶l̶l̶e̶ sur un projet.
Proof of conforman̶

| Base practice |

MAN.3.2   **Identify risks. Identify risks to the project as they develop.**

Note: Risks include cost, schedule, effort, resource, and technical risks.

Existence: Adequacy:

No ☐   Yes ☑   Not ☐   Partially ☐   Largely ☐   Fully ☑

Notes: Réalisé, dans le champ défini en MAN3.1.
Proof of conformance:

Figure 18.4: Form to collect assessment outputs (extract).

Level	Processes Attribute	Management Practices	Result. (NPLF)	Rating (NPLF)
1	1.1 Process performance	Ensure base practice performance	/	F
2	2.1 Performance management	Design/Document the	I	L
	2.2 Work management			P
3	3.1 Process definition			L
	3.2 Process resource			L
4	4.1 Process measurement			P
	4.2 Process control	Analyze metrics & deviations	P	P
		Ensure that corrective	P	
5	5.1 Process change		N	N
			N	
	5.2 Continuous improvement	Establish improvement product quality goals	N	N
		Establish improvement process effectiveness goals	N	
	Capability level:		**1**	

LEVEL 1: This rating is the result of the process performance evaluation, according to the process's base practices, using the adequacy scale:

◊ *Not adequate:* The base practice is either not implemented or does not to any degree contribute to satisfying the process purpose,

◊ *Partially adequate*: The implemented base practice does little to contribute to satisfying the process purpose,

◊ *Largely adequate*: The implemented base practice largely contributes to satisfying the process purpose,

◊ *Fully adequate*: The implemented base practice fully contributes to satisfying the process purpose.

LEVELS 2-5: These ratings are the results of the process capability evaluation

Figure 18.5: Form for recording ratings.

A minimum of two people is usually needed for the assessment team. Depending on their experience and approach, a single qualified assessor might feel uncomfortable in having to manage the interview, listen to and record the answers and proofs of conformance, prepare the next question, and refer to SPICE documents.

The assessment team must be cohesive and knowledgeable about the parts of the SPICE model within the assessment scope (rating scheme, concept of achievement of attributes, and so on). All members of the team must be aware of the assessment: its purpose, scope, constraints, approach, planning, schedule, and so on. If possible, the assessment team members should be involved in writing and/or verifying the assessment plan.

Assessment goal #2 also suggests establishing a draft of the mapping between the scope of the QMS procedures and the processes of the SPICE model.

Preparing the OU

The preparation of the OU's members is also very important. Basically, at least two meetings should be organized:

1. a meeting to present the assessment (+/- 1 hour), conducted by the sponsor and the qualified assessor: both present to the OU staff the assessment purpose, scope, constraints, how the assessment will be conducted, the benefits of assessment results, and the principles for confidentiality and ownership
2. a training session (a ½ day is a minimum) for the assessment participants, in particular those who will be interviewed: members of the assessment team explain the SPICE assessment approach and method they will use.

   During the half-day course for the PEACE project, the following items were presented:

   1. process improvement for software quality improvement
   2. software process concepts: the ISO 12207[2] standard
   3. software process capability concepts
   4. other models for assessing software process capability
   5. the ISO/SPICE Project
   6. the ISO/SPICE Part 2 reference model—rating rules
   7. the assessment technique and method

8. the SPICE Part 5 assessment model
9. assessment performance and output examples.

To provide a short overview of the SPICE framework, Part 1[3,] the introduction document, might also be distributed to the participants.

Risk analysis

When preparing the assessment, a risk analysis should be done to guarantee the achievement of the assessment goals. Potential risks include unavailability of documentation, OU individuals' availability, resistance from the OU to provide information, changes to the purpose or scope of the assessment, and lack of confidentiality.

Assessment results

Assessment report

The assessment outputs, shown below as graphical representations, are useful to provide a global overview of process capability. Nevertheless, it is essential to write a full assessment report and to record all the collected data. Depending on the assessment goals, other documents might be necessary, such as an improvement plan and an assessment experiment report. Table 18.3 is an example of an assessment report that includes comments for each process instance—typically improvement opportunities—as well as feedback about the assessment process itself.

The assessment report is dedicated mainly to the assessment sponsor, but it also should be distributed to those who have collaborated in the assessment: we observed that the people interviewed had a strong expectation of feedback as a result of their collaboration.

The capability of each process instance was included in the assessment report to represent graphically (Figure 18.6) the detailed achievement of the different attributes.

This representation gives a detailed view of process capability, compared to Figure 18.8 which shows only the global process capability level.

Table 18.3: Elements of an assessment report.

1. Introduction—Context
2. Terminology
3. Reference documents
4. Confidentiality agreement
5. Assessment inputs overview
   Assessment goals
   Assessment scope
   Process context
   Selected processes
6. Assessment results
   Process capability profiles
   Process capability levels
7. Comments per process instances
   Process instances from project 1
   Process instances from project n
   Process instances from Organization 1
   Process instances from Organization n
8. Assessment feedback
   Resources—Infrastructure—Logistics
   Assessment technique and performance
   Meeting—Training—Presentation
   Planning—Schedule
9. Further actions
10. Quality control records
11. Annexes:
    A1: Assessment records
    A2: SPICE process dimension
    A3: SPICE capability dimension

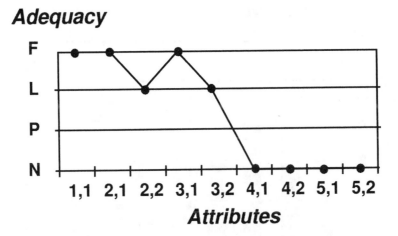

Figure 18.6: Example of process capability profile (Level = 2).

The attributes achievement represented in Figure 18.6 is useful for revealing the strength and weakness in the process capability and also to compare two processes capabilities (see Figure 18.10).

By combining the attribute ratings of different instances of the *same process,* we obtained derived ratings showing the attribute rating distribution (Figure 18.7). This representation highlights the global process capability.

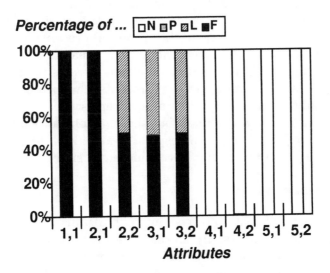

Figure 18.7: Attribute rating distribution.

Capability Level

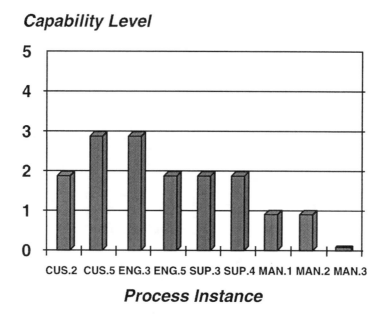

Process Instance

Figure 18.8: Process capability level.

Process capability level

The reference model for process assessment[4] indicates how to determine the capability level for a process instance by using the attribute ratings (also see chapter 6). Complementing the capability profile represented in Figure 18.6, the capability level gives a global value of the process capability.

By combining the capability levels from all the process instances, we obtained another derived rating. Figure 18.9 represents the process capability level distribution for all processes within the assessment scope:

Other representations can be used, but these graphical results are based only on assessment records and do not correspond to any absolute measurements: any variation of +/- 10 percent must not be considered as significant.

Improvement opportunities

An assessment is (almost) always an opportunity to identify potential suggestions for improvements. In the case of PEACE, the assessment report contained a mean value of two significant improvement actions per process instance. This assessment output was not expected initially to satisfy any of the goals, but provided added value to the experiment.

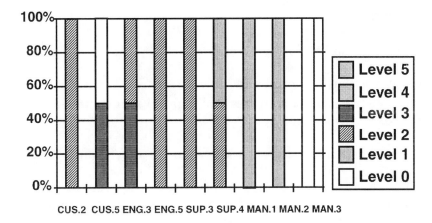

CUS.2 CUS.5 ENG.3 ENG.5 SUP.3 SUP.4 MAN.1 MAN.2 MAN.3

Figure 18.9: Process capability distribution.

Participants' feedback

Whenever an assessment has been performed within an organization or project that initially had no awareness of the SPA philosophy, we have observed a high degree of interest from participants, even if they already had a quality-oriented culture. The assessment is a good opportunity to introduce new concepts for managing the processes. During the PEACE project, everyone collaborated very positively and we did not have any problem collecting the data. Other experiences show an average of 4 percent of participants have a negative attitude against the assessment approach and the SPICE framework.

From the assessment sponsor's point of view, we have always been able to provide a satisfying appreciation of the assessment performance and results.

Case study results

This section describes some of the problems and remarks made during the assessment about the process and capability dimensions of the model described in Part 5, Version 1.00. At the end of 1996, the SPICE Project had integrated changes into the model for assessment to establish Version 2.00. Nevertheless, some problems are still significant, even for the reference model in Part 2 and should be tracked during the Phase 2 SPICE Trials.

Process dimension

The major changes in Version 2.00 were:

- changes or clarification of some areas
- a new distribution of activities and a global reduction of the number of processes from 35 to 29.

Below are examples of comments concerning the assessed processes:

- CUS.2 *Manage customer needs*: this process requires the OU to manage all types of requirements, functional and nonfunctional. Its assessment interferes with process ENG.2 concerning software requirements.

- CUS.5 *Provide customer service*: the constitutive base practices make it difficult to assess an instance at the level of the organization

- ENG.5 *Integrate and test software*: the distribution of the base practices are not clear enough: the tasks for integration testing, validation testing, and qualification should be more explicit

- SUP.3 *Perform quality assurance*: the base practices are not coherent enough: the process should be more specific, such as "Define the project quality framework"

- SUP.5 *Perform work product validation*: the process description addresses any kind of validation, but the base practices only address code validation and overlap with the ENG.5 process for *Integration and test*.

- MAN.1 *Manage the project*: the process description should include *effective project tracking* (see the base practice MAN.1.11). The base practice MAN.1.10 could be removed

- MAN.2 *Manage Quality*: the process has a strong quality goals orientation that is barely implemented in actual situations and anticipates the state-of-the art

- MAN.3 *Manage risks*: the process description should contain actions at the organizational level since the process is not implemented at only the project level. The base practice MAN.3.5 *Define risk metrics* belongs in Level 4. An adaptation could be made with the notion of risk tracking indicators.

Capability dimension

The evolution of this dimension corresponds to a major change in the SPICE software process model architecture. The Part 2 reference model used during the case study has a six-level capability dimension, each of which has two attributes (except for Levels 0 and 1).

For level determination, the rule to apply to determine the capability of a process makes it possible to give the same capability to two processes with strong differences in the achievements of the attributes. For example, see Figure 18.10.

The process instance A presents a higher capability than the instance B because the attributes 2.2, 3.1, 4.1, and 4.2 have attained a higher achievement. This aspect of the level's determination is not a real problem if the mechanism is clearly known and understood by those using the assessment results. On the other hand, the new concept of process capability level is useful for global comparison or improvement tracking.

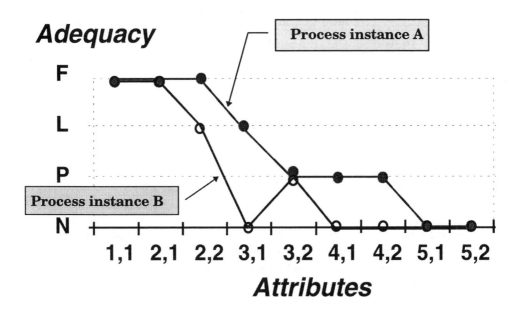

Figure 18.10: Two processes A and B at Level 2.

- *attribute 1.1 rating*: The attribute 1.1 indicates process performance and by using Part 5, Version 1.00, indicators are available: base practices and work products' input/output. There is no formal rule to determine the attribute rating after having estimated the existence and adequacy of the base practices.

- *ratings of the attributes 2.1 to 5.2*: Similarly, the principle to determine the rating of these attributes from their two management practices is not defined

- *attribute 3.1 process definition*: This attribute stipulates that the business goals are defined: they should be adapted. Also, 3.1 interacts with ORG.1

Using SPICE for managing quality

The second goal of the assessment was to consider the SPICE assessment to support the implementation and evolution of standard procedures. The assessment allowed us to estimate the implementation of a specific procedure's scope as covered by some processes of the model—*project management* in the case of the experiment. Using this approach, we mapped the whole set of procedures included in the QMS to the SPICE process model so that assessments could be performed during the quality assurance actions that had been planned to maintain the QMS. The mapping also has the benefit of being a complementary analysis of the ISO 9001 requirements.[10]

Project statistics

The two months of the project were divided roughly into

- Phase 1—initialization: one month
- Phase 2—assessments: two weeks
- Phase 3—assessment results and experiment analysis: one additional month.

The initial estimations for costs and effort were followed closely and were adequate. The overall method for the assessment preparation, planning, data collection, and validation was satisfactory because it was based on experience gained in previous assessments.

Nevertheless, this kind of experience might be improved upon with a less-conflicting selection of the assessment goals: Goal #1 suggested selecting some processes with which to experiment with the SPICE model, some specific or new processes of SPICE available only in Version 2.00. However, Goal #2 involved selecting some processes covering clearly some of the QMS procedures.

Conclusion

The PEACE project allowed us to experiment with the new version of the SPICE framework for process assessment. The case study confirmed that the SPICE documents are an operational tool for managing software quality. Both the process model that gives a reference framework for SPA and the assessment model are operational.

One of the most efficient approaches to using the assessment technique for internal quality improvement is to tailor the process assessment model to the specifics of the QMS, with the result being a customized model. This activity would involve changing and adapting base practices, work products, or even adding specific processes, called *extended processes*. All these actions can be performed by keeping compliance with the assessment reference model. Further action should also include adding new processes to the QMS and planning assessments to occur at the same time as the internal quality audits.

References

1. El Emam, K. and D.R. Goldenson, "Some Initial Results from the International SPICE Trials," *IEEE TCSE Software Process Newsletter*, No. 6, Spring 1996.

2. ISO/IEC 12207, *Information technology—Software Life Cycle Processes*, 1st Ed., Aug. 1995.

3. ISO/IEC/JTC1/SC7/WG10/N101, *Software Process Assessment—Part 1: Concepts and Introductory Guide*, July 1996

4. ISO/IEC/JTC1/SC7/WG10 WD N102, *Software Process Assessment—Part 2: A Reference for Process and Process Capability*, July 1996.

5. ISO/IEC/JTC1/SC7/WG10 WD N103, *Software Process Assessment—Part 3: Performing an Assessment*, July 1996.

6. ISO/IEC/JTC1/SC7/WG10 WD N104, *Software Process Assessment—Part 4: Guide to Performing an Assessment*, July 1996.

7. ISO/IEC/JTC1/SC7/WG10/OWG WD N103, *Software Process Assessment—Part 5: An Assessment Model and Indicator Guidance*, Version 1.006, 18 Aug. 1996.

8. ISO/IEC/JTC!/SC7/WG10, *Software Process Assessment—Part 5: An Assessment Model and Indicator Guidance*, Version 2.00, 1996.

9. Marshall, P., F. Maclennan, and M. Tobin, "Analysis of Observation and Problem Reports from Phase 1 of the SPICE Trials," *IEEE TCSE Software Process Newsletter*, No. 6, Spring 1996.

10. Radice, R.D., *ISO 9001 Interpreted for Software Organizations*, Paradoxicon Publishing, 1995.

11. Simon, J.M., "Choosing the Process for the Assessment Scope: A Key Factor for SPICE Assessment Success," *Proc. European Conf. Software Process Improvement — SPI95*, 1995.

12. Simon, J.M., "Experiences in the Phase 1 SPICE Trials," *IEEE TCSE Software Process Newsletter*, No. 8, Winter 1996.

13. SPICE Project. *Phase 1 Trials Report*, Version 1.00, Oct. 1995.

14. Woodman, I. and R. Hunter, "Analysis of Assessment Data from Phase 1 of the SPICE Trials," *IEEE TCSE Software Process Newsletter*, No°6, Spring 1996.

19

The Future of the SPICE Trials

Robert Smith

European Software Institute, Spain

Following the success of the SPICE Phase 1 Trials, and the subsequent publication of their results, there has been a significantly higher level of interest in SPICE and the SPICE Trials. The Phase 2 Trials have a number of important differences that raise new challenges for the trials team and the SPICE Project, the most significant of which are:

- Phase 2 is open to the entire worldwide software engineering community and many countries that had not participated before are now involved in SPICE
- the scope of Phase 2 is all nine products of the document set
- the document set now introduces a reference model for software process assessment.

Since one of the goals of the SPICE Project is to promote the use of SPICE, it was decided by the project that, whereas the Phase 1 Trials participation was restricted to those organizations already involved in the project, Phase 2 will be open to any organization wishing to participate. This decision has a number of implications for the Phase 2 Trials and the development of the trials materials and infrastructure. In Phase 1, 35 trials were conducted. A conservative estimate for Phase 2 is that there will be five times that number. In addition, since many countries will be participating that had not before, the Phase 2 Trials coordination structure has been revised to manage this increased scope.

With many new participants unfamiliar with the original version of SPICE, and the significant changes to the document set following the Phase 1 Trials, it is critical that the Phase 2 participants obtain a good understanding of what the document set contains, especially Part 2 containing the reference model, Part 5 for the SPICE assessment model, and Part 3 for the requirements for conducting an assessment.

For the Phase 1 Trials, a briefing session was sufficient to provide the required familiarity because all participants had already been part of the SPICE Project. For Phase 2, full training courses have been developed, covering introductions to both the document set and its use for assessment. These training courses have been developed separately from the trials team activities.

With the Phase 2 Trials evaluating all nine products of the document set, and with an expected five-fold increase in the number of trials to be performed, there will be a significantly greater amount of data that will collected. The data collection issue is one of the major development tasks for the trials team and new ideas, based on the recommendations provided in the *SPICE Phase 1 Trials Report*, have been investigated. The data collection approaches and issues surrounding the Phase 2 Trials are described in this chapter.

The Phase 2 Trials will evaluate the full document set from a number of perspectives. Emphasis will be placed on two major aspects: (1) the repeatability of assessment results and (2) the use of both the reference model defined in Part 2 and the SPICE assessment model defined in Part 5, in conjunction with the relationship between the two models.

Trials team organization for Phase 2

A SPICE Trials team is responsible for the following activities:

- planning the trials activities
- designing the necessary questionnaires and forms to support the trials assessments
- developing a trials database to store the results of the assessments
- collecting and analyzing the data to report the results.

The trials team is headed by the International Trials Coordinator (ITC) who reports directly to the SPICE Project Manager on all aspects relating to the trials. Figure 19.1 shows the trials organization chart. The conduct of the trials is managed by the five designated SPICE Technical Centers (TC) of the SPICE Project: Europe, USA, Canada, Southern Asia-Pacific, and Northern Asia-Pacific.[*] Each Technical Center has a nominated Regional Trials Coordinator (RTC), who is a member of the trials team. Each RTC is responsible for coordinating all trials activities in their region to ensure that all the necessary information is available and that all the trials assessment data is collected and included in the database.

A new feature for the Phase 2 Trials is the introduction of a Local Trials Coordinator (LTC). For Phase 2, a significant increase in the number of trials assessments is expected. The Local Trials Coordinator will work with the RTC to:

- deal with the increased workload in supporting organizations and assessors
- collect and process the trials results
- ensure that all participants receive quick and efficient responses to questions and solutions to their problems.

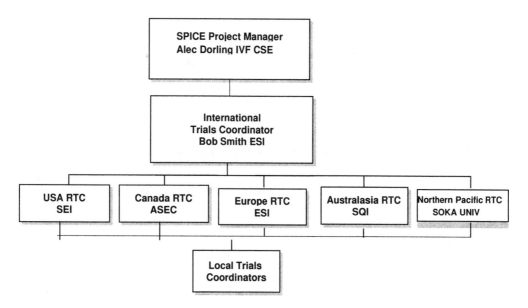

Figure 19.1: The organization of the Phase 2 SPICE Trials.

·Note that one new technical center was added for the Phase 2 Trials.·

Local Trials Coordinators will be established at a national level, organizational level, or through model/method providers. Each LTC is expected to coordinate a minimum of five trials.

Phase 2 requirements

The technical requirements for Phase 2 are in three forms:

- objectives
- trials studies
- trials types.

These three types of requirements enable the trials team to define the type of data to be collected, develop the questionnaires to capture specific data, and create the trials specifications and procedures. The trials studies also help to specify the questionnaire content and the data analysis to be performed on the trials results. These requirements are discussed in more detail below.

Phase 2 objectives

The objectives of the SPICE Phase 2 Trials are to evaluate:

1. the reference model as a basis for Software Process Assessment
2. the adequacy of the SPICE requirements for conducting a Software Process Assessment
3. the usefulness of the SPICE guidelines for conducting a Software Process Assessment
4. the usefulness of the SPICE guidelines for software process improvement
5. the usefulness of the SPICE guidelines for process capability determination
6. the usefulness of the assessment model to support Software Process Assessment and to evaluate the usability of the assessment indicators of the assessment model
7. the usefulness of the SPICE guidelines for assessor qualification and training.

These objectives are based on the purpose of each of the documents contained in the emerging standard. To be able to achieve these objectives, it is necessary to design a number of different types of trials. It is also necessary to specify the type of information that should be collected during a trial so that a number of data analysis studies can be performed to demonstrate whether or not the objectives have been achieved.

Phase 2 studies

The Phase 2 Trials are exploring simultaneously a number of issues, including:

- evaluation of the nine-part document set
- reliability of assessments
- harmonization of compatible models and comparability of assessment results from these models
- validity of the SPICE framework.

In addition, the trials are also aiming to collect information on the contexts in which the SPICE document set is being used to validate its applicability. Many of these issues are complex and currently there is little understanding of what the influencing factors are (for example, factors influencing the reliability of assessments). Therefore, much of the empirical work in Phase 2 is exploratory. For example, data will be collected to identify the critical factors that affect issues such as the reliability, comparability, and validity of the SPICE framework. Therefore, the aim is to have the results provide a greater understanding of these important issues, with a view to encouraging future work.

The overall approach being taken in Phase 2 differs from Phase 1 in that precise hypotheses have not been established *a priori* because not enough is understood of the issues to be able to define hypotheses that would be precise, realistic, and that would provide valid results.

This approach has already been adopted in some preliminary reliability trials conducted prior to the start of Phase 2. Five trials were conducted that collected reliability assessor-rating data. Initial analysis of the data provided very valuable information about the factors that could influence the reliability of assessment results. These preliminary trials improved understanding of the topics being explored in Phase 2 and confirmed that the approach being adopted for Phase 2 of the trials is valid.

Repeatability studies

The repeatability studies are essential to understanding the extent to which the results of a SPICE-conformant assessment are reliable and can be recognized as such. The studies focus on the extent to which different assessment teams, or individual assessors, agree in their ratings when they independently rate the same processes.

The results of these studies will identify the features of the reference model and SPICE-compatible assessment models that either aid or increase the difficulty of obtaining repeatable assessment results. Specifically, the reference model rating scheme, processes, and process attributes will be evaluated.

The composition of the assessment teams and the experience of each individual assessor will also be important factors that will be analyzed for their effects on the repeatability results. These studies will also support the testing of the assessor qualification and training guidelines defined in Part 6. (A fuller description of the issues related to these studies can be found in Chapter 16.)

Comparability studies

The comparability studies consider the comparability of assessment results produced by different SPICE-compatible assessment models. They focus on the results produced by using various assessment models to compare levels of repeatability, accuracy, and benefit of results achieved amongst these models. They will investigate areas of commonality or significant difference to establish the extent to which the reference model enables the use of SPICE-compatible models. The characteristics of SPICE-compatible assessment models, such as the rating scheme, indicator sets, and capability framework will be evaluated to identify any common aspects affecting the repeatability of results.

Harmonization studies

The harmonization studies will determine the extent to which the reference model provides a clear route for the harmonization of SPICE-compatible assessment models. The studies will consider the model purpose; the model scope including the processes and process attributes; the model elements and indicators; mapping of the model elements to the processes and process attributes of the reference model; and the translation of assessment data into process attribute ratings.

Business benefit studies

The business benefit studies are aimed at investigating the relationship between the process ratings and the critical software development success factors of cost, schedule, and quality. The primary goal of the study is to determine if there is a relationship between higher levels of process maturity and improved performance. The study will examine the process ratings of ISO 9001-approved organizational units (OU) to determine whether or not there are any preliminary relationships between SPICE and ISO 9001.

Assessment conduct studies

Part 3 of the document set contains the requirements for conducting an assessment. These are the requirements according to which a SPICE-conformant assessment will be performed. They are applicable to process assessments using models that are compatible with the SPICE reference model. The assessment conduct studies aim to verify the relevance, usefulness, and understandability of these requirements for the purpose of conducting an assessment.

Four main aspects will be evaluated:

1. preparing for the assessment and defining the assessment input
2. conducting the assessment (the assessment process)
3. recording the assessment output
4. definition and allocation of responsibilities.

In addition, the costs of conducting process assessments will be analyzed, including:

- the costs of using an external assessor
- the costs of the OU staff participating in different aspects of the assessment
- the costs of the various tasks of the assessment process.

Applicability studies

The applicability studies intend to demonstrate in what type of environments the SPICE document set has been used in Phase 2 of the trials. The categories of use include:

- country
- organization size, both in terms of total number of staff and number of software staff
- primary business sector of the organization and the business sectors of its customers
- product size
- product type
- product criticality factors, including safety, economic, security, and environmental
- product quality characteristics as defined by ISO 9126
- product development methods
- product hardware/technical environment.

Assessment model studies

The assessment model studies examine the level of consistency between all parts of the reference model and the assessment model of Part 5. The structure of the assessment model will be examined, as will its various elements. The usability of the model for assessment and process attribute repeatability will be analyzed. The adequacy of the process dimension in terms of understandability, scope, and completeness will be evaluated. The capability dimension will be investigated for:

- general applicability across all processes
- understandability
- ordering of attributes
- distance between attributes
- completeness.

Coverage analysis of the model elements will also be conducted.

Assessment result studies

The assessment studies are designed to evaluate a number of aspects including:

- the understandability and appropriateness of SPICE assessment results

- the accuracy of the assessment results compared to the OU view of their process capability
- the usability of the results for process improvement.

The variability of assessment results between processes, process categories, and business benefits will also be explored.

Process capability determination studies

The process capability determination studies are directed at the specific guidance material developed by the SPICE Project. Participants will be required to test concepts such as setting a target SPICE profile for an Invitation-To-Tender Document, identifying gaps between a target and an assessed profile to quantify potential risk, and evaluating the guide to process capability determination.

Process improvement studies

These studies are aimed at testing the specific guidance material developed by the SPICE Project for software process improvement. Participants will be required to test concepts such as:

- developing a process improvement plan to meet a required assessment profile
- using the proposed measurement framework as a roadmap for process improvement
- evaluating the proposed process improvement guidance.

Assessment follow-up studies

One of the first studies to be performed as part of Phase 2 is a Phase 1 assessment follow up. This study will be executed by means of a questionnaire to be distributed to all the OUs that participated in Phase 1. The questionnaire is designed to investigate what process improvement activities have occurred in the organization since the Phase 1 assessment.

Three specific aspects will be considered:

- usefulness of the assessment findings for initiating a process improvement activity

- features of the process improvement implementation program
- OU characteristics that may have an influence on process improvement.

The results of this study will provide valuable information on whether or not SPICE results are a useful aid to process improvement initiatives within an organization. The results will also identify the most important organizational and human factors that can have an influence on the success of a process improvement activity. This information will be used in the short term to provide guidance to Phase 2 Trials assessors to inform them of the environments in which they will be working so that they can present assessment results more effectively. In the long term, the information can be used to update and supplement the process improvement guidelines contained in Part 7 of the document set.

Phase 2 Trial types

Trials participants can select from a number of different trial types. At a minimum they can select from:

- assessments using the assessment model contained in Part 5 of the document set
- assessments using other SPICE-compatible assessment models
- a process improvement trial using the guidelines in Part 7 of the document set
- a capability determination trial using the guidelines in Part 8 of the document set
- an assessment follow-up survey on process improvement

Part 5 assessment model trial

This type of trial involves the use of the assessment model contained in Part 5. The trials assessor is required to conduct an assessment on the OU using the Part 5 assessment model and the trials instructions prepared by the SPICE Trials team. The trials assessor is required to meet the requirements of Part 3, which define the requirements for conducting an assessment. Briefly, these requirements address defining the assessment input, the assessment process, recording the assessment output, and the definition of responsibilities.

The trials instructions provide support to the trials assessor to meet these requirements.

SPICE-compatible assessment model trial

This type of trial can be conducted using an assessment model that claims to be SPICE-compatible against the requirements for a model, as defined in Part 2. SPICE-compatible assessment models, in general, will be made available for use by each model provider, together with the description of how it is compatible. Trials participants who conduct such a trial will have unique requirements to meet, as defined by the model provider. In general, these requirements will address the mapping of the compatible assessment model to the Part 2 reference model and will describe how the assessment results, obtained using the compatible model rating system, are to be translated into the Part 2 reference model rating system.

This trial type will be of particular interest to those organizations already having made investments into particular assessment models since it will give them an early indication as to how the compatible model fits into SPICE. These trials are essential to the comparability and harmonization studies to determine whether or not the reference model requirements are relevant and usable.

Assessment follow-up survey

This trial type consists of completing a short questionnaire that captures information on post-assessment activity on software process improvement. It asks for information about the results of the assessment, the OU, and any process improvement activity. Initially, this questionnaire will be distributed to Phase 1 Trials participants to provide early feedback.

Subsequently, it will be provided to all Phase 2 Trials participants at a suitable period after their trial assessment to obtain a comprehensive set of data aimed at identifying the critical success factors of a process improvement program.

Process improvement guideline trial

Part 7 contains guidelines for implementing a process improvement program. This type of trial intends to allow participants to follow these guidelines for a process improvement exercise within the context of SPICE. Depending on the context, this type of trial may include conducting an assessment using one of the assessment trial types. Alternatively, an assessment does not need to be conducted as part of the trial.

Either an assessment may already have been conducted by the OU prior to Phase 2 Trials, for example in Phase 1, or an exercise can be performed where a simulated set of assessment results is provided with the aim of developing a process improvement plan based on the guidelines contained in Part 7.

This type of exercise will provide an OU with experience in developing an improvement plan that can be critically reviewed in the context of a trial rather than in the normal working environment. It will also provide feedback on the process improvement guidelines so that they can be combined with the results of the trial assessment follow-up survey to provide valuable insights into the implementation of software process improvement.

Process capability determination trial

Part 8 contains guidelines for conducting a software capability determination activity. This type of trial aims to verify that the guidelines are useful, provide usable results, and define an understandable and well-defined approach to capability determination. As with the process improvement guideline trial, it is not necessary to conduct a trial assessment to participate in this type of trial. Again, the results of a previous assessment can be used or a simulated set of assessment results can be used that will be provided by the SPICE Trials team.

A process capability determination can be performed by a customer on a supplier to verify that the supplier has or will have the capability to deliver the required product and service specified by contract requirements. Equally, a supplier may wish to perform a self-capability determination as a risk management exercise, for example, at the bid stage of a contract or at specific periods within the course of development.

This type of trial will be of particular interest to acquirers of software-intensive systems wanting to gain more confidence in the ability of their suppliers. They may also prefer to have a well-defined approach that provides them with relevant and understandable results.

It will also be of interest to managers responsible for software development who would like to improve their program's risk management activities. The trial will simply consist of following trials instructions and the Part 8 guidelines to provide feedback in the form of questionnaires to capture information on the usefulness, applicability, and understandability of the guidelines.

Phase 2 Trials data management

Data management is critical to the success of the Phase 2 Trials. There will be a significant amount of data collected from all parts of the world that will need to be processed very quickly so that it can be used in the trials analysis studies. The data will be used to provide essential user feedback into the review process of the Proposed Draft Technical Report (PDTR) documents. It will also be used to publicize the results of the trials and show how the SPICE document set can be used.

Data collection in Phase 2 has a number of goals, based on recommendations made in the *SPICE Phase 1 Trials Report*:

- to reduce the number of data input errors
- to reduce the inconsistency and incompleteness of the data sets received from trials participants
- to make trials data readily available to the trials analysis teams to improve the timeliness of trials analysis reports
- to increase the use of trials data in analysis by verifying its relevance to the analysis studies
- to improve the design of the data being collected to ease its analysis.

A further goal is to provide the baseline for a database that can continue to expand and be used in the Phase 3 Trials and beyond. The database will be able to record the long-term benefits of SPICE and provide a repository for storing SPICE assessment results and experiences.

Responsibility for the data collection and data input lies with the Local Trials Coordinator. The LTC will ensure that all the relevant data collection forms have been completed and will then ensure that the data is in the specified Trials Data Record (TDR) format. The data can then be transmitted to the main trials database. This distribution of responsibilities will ensure that there is no bottleneck in data input and will make the data available more quickly for analysis.

All trials data to be stored will be managed in accordance with the requirements of the SPICE Data Management Policy. These requirements will ensure confidentiality to all trials participants. It is recognized that many participants will be concerned about the use of sensitive data. To support the implementation of this Data Management Policy, a trials confidentiality agreement will be signed for each trial by all relevant parties (the trials assessor, the Local Trials Coordinator for the trial, and the OU). In addition, a

Trials Identification Scheme will have been defined and incorporated into a TDR so that only trials identifiers are stored in the trials database. *There is no information stored that identifies any of the trials participants.* This is an important safeguard to respect the confidentiality of the trials results and was designed to enable trials participants to submit their trials data with confidence.

As in Phase 1, a separate Trials Observation Report form will be used to capture additional information from trials participants. This form will enable the collection of a wide range of comments to be used as input to the trials analysis studies. The observation reports will be used both to verify the results of trials analysis and to highlight where further analysis may be required. These reports will also be an important input into the formal ISO review cycle. The observation reports themselves will be analyzed, categorized, and summarized to provide direct trials participant feedback.

Requirements to participate in Phase 2

To participate, all Phase 2 Trials participants are expected to meet the following minimum requirements:

- Participate in one of the defined trial types.
- Provide the ratings of the trial assessment to the SPICE Trials team for inclusion into the trials database and to support the trials analysis studies.
- Answer and return the trials questionnaires associated with the type of trial to be conducted.
- Each registered trials assessor must be able to demonstrate relevant knowledge of the SPICE reference model and of the document set.
- Each registered trials assessor should have had some previous experience of conducting assessments or should have had relevant training.
- When a trial assessment is conducted, a model compatible to the SPICE reference model must be used. The compatible model contained in Part 5 of the document set or any other model that claims compatibility may be used.
- All trial assessments shall satisfy the requirements for the conduct of assessments as defined in Part 3 of the document set.
- All trial participants should adhere to the instructions provided for the conduct of the trial.

Spice Trials following Phase 2

On completion of Phase 2 a significant amount of process assessment experience will have been gained. Knowledge and expertise will have been acquired by assessors; organizations who have been assessed, assessment model and method providers, and organizations involved in promoting software process improvement where process assessment is an essential feature. A trials database will have been established containing data on assessment practice and experience.

As the document set continues on its standardization route, it will be essential to maintain the momentum established during Phase 2 to ensure that the adoption of process assessment grows and is successful. Phase 3 of the SPICE Trials is being planned to evaluate a subsequent version of the document set. Phase 2 of the trials will lead to the introduction of a number of new services aimed at supporting the adoption of the SPICE framework. New methods of assessment may be developed using SPICE-compatible models that are tailored for specific environments. New services may include SPICE practice and experience repositories aimed at improving the rate of process improvement. The role of assessment in process improvement with respect to the benefits it provides and how it should be used may also be better understood.

The use of process assessment will not only be seen as a means to deliver a capability rating. Process assessment will be used as a diagnosis tool to accurately understand performance and risk. It will also be used as a tool to transfer the objectives and understanding of improvement models to organizations through the practical application of assessment. All of these market factors will have a role to play in the subsequent trials and industrial adoption of the emerging standard.

Appendix A:
SEAL of Quality
SPICE Assessment Tool

Alastair Walker, Richard Him Lok, Linhong Li, and
Jim Knight

University of the Witwatersrand, South Africa

The SEAL of Quality SPICE Assessment Tool supports the assessment of software processes and the determination of process capability in organizations developing and implementing software products or systems. The tool is aimed at determining the levels of process capability and at supporting process improvement within one or more projects.

The development of the SEAL SPICE tool

The SEAL of Quality SPICE Assessment Tool (SEAL OQ) has its origins in a Master of Science degree registered in January 1995. The topic sought to explore quality practices in a sample of South African software companies. Early in the research project, the emerging SPICE standard was selected as the framework for capturing suitable metrics to perform this evaluation. Richard Him Lok, the MSc candidate, rapidly concluded that paper-based methods for collecting assessment data would prove to be too cumbersome for serious studies and set out to prototype a tool for performing SPICE-conformant assessments. As a consequence of his considerable experience in developing client-server applications in a Microsoft Windows[*] environment, a beta version of the project

---

[*]*Microsoft, Windows, Windows/95, and Microsoft Excel* are all trademarks or registered trademarks of Microsoft Corporation.

(Rev 0.70) was released to the SPICE Project in March 1996. This version of the tool was based on the SPICE document set Version 1.00, released in July 1995. Version 2.00 of the SPICE documents provide the baseline for SEAL OQ revision 0.80 and the minor releases in this series (the version included on the CD-ROM is 0.82).

With regard to future product development, Revision 0.90 of the SEAL SPICE tool is planned to be released once the SPICE document set Version 3.00 is released. The SEAL OQ tool Version 1.00 will be released following ISO approval of the SPICE document set as a Technical Report. Registered product users will be advised of new product releases as the SPICE emerging standard is revised and consolidated.

Current product features

Features of the SEAL of Quality Software Assessment Tool include:

1. A *SPICE-compatible assessment instrument application* running under Microsoft Windows* 3.1 or Windows/95,* with a fully-graphical user interface and online help.

   Fast manipulation of data and speedy generation of colorful reports can be created via a local database built into the program.

2. The ability to *create multiple projects*—one for each organization or company.

   Single or multiple process instance assessments can be created within each project for evaluations of different software systems or products or of successive versions of a product. Full assessment details are stored for each project and process instance, with security ensured by password protection on projects. Assessor information and background experience records are maintained within the system. Many system settings allow the operation of the SEAL of Quality application to be customized to the user's preference.

3. *Presentation of processes on full GUI-interactive screens* for assessing the ratings and existence of base practices, management practices, work products, and process management indicators.

   Interactive assessment screens allow the user to input adequacy ratings and flag warnings easily via point-and-click, as well as to enter comments and justifications on each practice or process attribute.

Automatic aggregation of base and management practices are performed for process attributes. Capability levels of processes are automatically determined.

4. Conduct of an assessment with the *complete SPICE process model stored online for instant referencing* of descriptions of processes, practices, work products, and indicators.

Each project is created with a separate copy of the SPICE model, and its processes can be edited and maintained on the system to form a framework tailored to an organization's specific needs, procedures, or rules. Add, delete, or change any aspect of the SPICE model, including process categories, management practices, base practices, and work products. Users can also associate work products and indicator evidence to processes and process attributes.

5. Twenty-two attractive, *displayable and printable report views on assessment results*—process capability rating profiles with automatic adequacy rating aggregation, drill-down summary graphs, as well as process or capability rating distribution profiling.

Context-sensitive pop-up menus are present on report views for capturing, printing, and saving the data contained in the view. Graphs allow for on-the-fly change of the type (pie charts, bar graphs, line graphs, and so on) and reorientation (zoom, rotate) of the graph on a 3D axis.

6. *Transfer (import/export) of the project framework or process instance assessment data between projects or systems.*

The tool supports team-based assessments by allowing more than one assessor of a process instance assessment to work independently and to consolidate data at the end of the assessment.

7. *Sample data files* of a process instance assessment example for the user to experiment with and to evaluate the tool as quickly and as easily as possible.

The sample data allows the user to simply load up the data and to evaluate the full range of features and reports without having to enter large amounts of data by trial and error.

8. *Complete set of supporting products and service.*

Fill in and edit the complete set of SPICE Trials questionnaires and forms from within the tool and Microsoft Excel*. The tool is accompanied by comprehensive user reference manual documentation, international product support, a troubleshooting help line via the Internet, as well as a dedicated Internet mailing list and news server for the tool.

System support requirements

The SEAL of Quality Software Assessment SPICE Tool software was developed using the PowerBuilder application development platform. In view of this technology, the PowerBuilder run-time files and Watcom ODBC database must be installed in order to run the application, as well as to install the SEAL of Quality application itself.

The total installation will require approximately 25 MB of space on the hard drive, along with Microsoft Windows 3.1 or Windows/95. A minimum of 8 megabytes of memory on a 486 or higher machine is recommended.

Up to date information can be downloaded from the SEAL server via anonymous FTP at the following site:

"seal.ee.wits.ac.za" in the "ftp/pub/sealoq/install" directory.

Use of the SEAL OQ

The user is licensed to:

- review the Shareware version of the software for a 21-day evaluation period
- make as many copies of the Shareware version of this software and documentation as required
- give exact copies of the original Shareware version to anyone
- distribute the Shareware version of the software and documentation in its unmodified form via electronic means.

There is no charge for any of the above.

The user is specifically prohibited from charging, or requesting donations, for any such copies, however made and from distributing the software and/or documentation with other products (commercial or otherwise) without prior written permission, with one exception: Disk vendors approved by the Association of Shareware Professionals are permitted to redistribute the SEAL of Quality tool, subject to the conditions in this license, without specific written permission.

Evaluation and registration

1. **Prior to the emerging standard being recognized as a Technical Report Type 2:**

   This license allows the user to evaluate this software for a period of 21 days. If you use this software after the 21-day evaluation period, registration is required.

   Following the submission of registration details, the user will be supplied with a registration key that will provide access to all the package facilities.

2. **Once the emerging standard is released as a Technical Report Type 2:**

   This tool is not free software. This license will allow you to use this software for evaluation purposes without charge for a period of 21 days. If you use this software after the 21-day evaluation period, a registration fee is required. Credit card ordering and quantity discounts are available.

Disclaimer of warranty

This software and the accompanying files are sold *as is* and without warranties as to performance of merchantability or any other warranties, whether expressed or implied. In particular, there is no warranty for the optional virus-scanning feature. (The SEAL of Quality SPICE Assessment Tool does not scan for viruses.) Because of the various hardware and software environments into which the SEAL of Quality may be installed, no warranty of fitness for a particular purpose is offered.

Good data processing procedures dictates that any program be thoroughly tested with noncritical data before relying on it. The user must assume the entire risk of using the program. Any liability of the seller will be limited exclusively to product replacement or refund of the purchase price.

Inquiries

All inquiries should be directed to:
    The Product Manager
    SEAL of Quality SPICE Assessment Tool
    Software Engineering Applications Laboratory
    PO Box 278
    WITS
    2050
    South Africa
    Phone: +27 11 716-5469
    Mobile: +27 82 452-0933
    Facsimile: +27 11 403-1929
    email: walker@odie.ee.wits.ac.za

Appendix B: Strathclyde Process Visualization Tools

Robin Hunter

University of Strathclyde, Scotland

The tools described in this appendix were developed as part of the final year project by a fourth-year honors Computer Science student (Gordon Robinson) at the University of Strathclyde in Glasgow, Scotland. The tools were based on an earlier tool, also developed at the University of Strathclyde by Ian Woodman. It is this original tool that is referred to in Chapter 14 of the text. The current toolset is fully compatible with the Version 2.00 of the SPICE document set described in the text.

Although the emphasis is at present on data visualization, the tools could also form the basis of powerful data analysis tools.

Purpose of the tools

The main purpose of the tools are to allow the user to visualize the result of a SPICE software process assessment (SPA) or set of assessments in a number of complementary ways. Histograms are the main method used to display the data, and the viewer can see summaries of the complete data, subsets of the data, summaries of subset, and so on, as well as being able to move from a capability-oriented view to a process-category oriented view, and vice versa. The tools have been implemented in Microsoft Visual BASIC with an interface to a Microsoft Access database.

SPICEMAKE is a program for creating and storing data about SPICE assessments. The program creates random, but realistic, data that is then stored in the Access database. The database created by this program can then be analyzed by the program *SPICEANALYSE*.

SPICEANALYSE is a visualization tool for browsing through the results of a SPICE assessment that have been stored in the database created by *SPICEMAKE*.

The user can view and move easily between histograms and pie charts showing the results for different capability levels, process categories, individual processes, and individual process attributes.

Installation procedure

The tool *SPICEMAKE* is installed by running the *setup* program in the directory *SPICEM* on the CD-ROM.

The tool *SPICEANAYSE* is installed by running the *setup* program in the directory *SPICEA* on the CD-ROM.

There are two versions of these tools: *versionA* and *versionB*. Use versionA if the version of your Windows/95 operating system is either 4.00.950 or 4.00.950a. Use versionB if the version of your Windows/95 operating system is 4.00.950B You can determine the version of your operating system by going to *Control Panel / System*.

System requirements

The minimum requirements for running the tools are:

- Windows/95
- 75 MHz Pentium Processor (recommended)
- 8 MB of RAM
- 15 MB hard disk space (8 MB for *SPICEANALYSE*), 7 MB for *SPICEMAKE*)

Inquiries

Questions and comments regarding the tools should be addressed to Robin Hunter at the University of Strathclyde, "rbh@cs.strath.ac.uk".

Glossary

The definitions provided here are based on a number of sources, including:

- SPICE Project. *Software process assessment—Part 9: Vocabulary*. Version 1.00, June 1995.
- ISO/IEC/JTC1/SC7/WG10. *Software Process Assessment—Part 9: Vocabulary*, Document WG10/N119, Version 2.00, Oct. 1996.
- ISO/IEC 12207. *Information technology—Software life cycle processes*. First edition, Aug. 1995.

actual rating: A rating that has been determined by assessing a specific process instance.

artifact: A tangible output, such as a work product, produced from the execution of an implemented process.

assessed capability: The output of one or more recent, relevant process assessments conducted in accordance with the provisions of the prospective International Standard.

assessment: See *process assessment*.

assessment constraints: Restrictions placed on the freedom of choice of the assessment team regarding the conduct of the assessment and the use of the assessment outputs. Such restrictions may be positive (for example, requiring that a specific group or individual provides information) or negative (such as requiring that a specific group or individual be excluded from providing information). These restrictions may include:

- specific process instances to be included or excluded from the assessment
- the minimum, maximum or specific sample size or coverage that is required for the assessment
- ownership of the assessment outputs and restrictions on how they may be used
- controls on information resulting from a confidentiality agreement.

assessment indicator: An objective attribute or characteristic of a practice or work product that supports the judgment of the performance of, or capability of, an implemented process.

assessment input: The collection of information required before a process assessment can commence. This information includes:

- the assessment purpose
- the assessment scope
- the assessment constraints
- the assessment responsibilities, including at a minimum the identity of the qualified assessor
- the definition of any extended processes identified in the assessment scope
- the identification of any additional information required to be collected to support process improvement or process capability determination.

assessment instrument: A tool or set of tools that is used throughout an assessment to assist the assessor in evaluating the performance or capability of processes and in handling assessment data and recording the assessment results.

assessment output: All of the tangible results from an assessment (see *assessment record*).

(assessment) owner: The management role that takes ownership of the assessment and the assessment output and has the authority to make the assessment happen.

assessment purpose: A statement, provided as part of the assessment input, that defines the reason for performing the assessment. The purpose may include:

- promotion of an understanding of the software process
- support of process improvement
- support of a process capability determination.

assessment record: An orderly, documented collection of that information that is pertinent to the assessment and adds to the understanding and verification of the process profiles (*quod vide*) generated by the assessment. This information usually includes:

- the assessment input
- the assessment approach
- the assessment instrument used
- the base practice ratings for each process instance assessed
- the date of the assessment
- the names of team members conducting the assessment
- any additional information required that was identified in the assessment input to support process improvement or process capability determination
- any assessment assumptions and limitations.

assessment scope: A definition of the boundaries of the assessment, provided as part of the assessment input, encompassing the organizational limits of the assessment, the processes to be included, and the context within which the processes operate (see *process context*).

(assessment) sponsor: The individual, internal or external to the organization being assessed, who requires the assessment to be performed and provides financial or other resources to carry it out.

attribute: See *process attribute*.

attribute rating: See *process attribute rating*.

base practice adequacy: A judgment, within the process context, of the extent to which the implemented base practice contributes to satisfying the process purpose.

base practice existence: A judgment, within the process context, of whether a base practice is implemented and produces some output.

base practice: A software engineering or management activity that directly addresses the purpose of a particular process and contributes to the creation of its output. A base practice is an essential activity of a particular process.

capability: See *process capability*.

capability determination: See *process capability determination*.

capability determination sponsor: See *(process capability determination) sponsor*.

capability level: See *process capability level*.

capability level rating: See *process capability determination rating*.

common feature: A set of generic practices that address an aspect of process implementation or management.

compatible (assessment) model: An operational model, used for performing assessments, that meets the defined requirements (for model purpose, scope, elements and indicators, mapping to the reference model, and translation of results) for conformance to the reference model in the prospective International Standard.

competence: The work performance that results from effectively applying skills, knowledge, and personal attributes.

competency: The skills, knowledge and personal attributes that enable effective work performance.

constructed capability: A capability constructed from existing organizational elements plus subcontractors, consultants, partners, and so on.

defined process: The operational definition of a set of activities for achieving a specific purpose. A defined process may be characterized by standards, procedures, training, tools, and methods. See also *standard process* and *well-defined process*.

derived rating: A rating that has been determined by aggregating two or more actual ratings to derive an aggregate or average rating.

enhanced capability: A capability greater than current assessed capability, justified by a credible process improvement program.

extended process: A process that differs from any process contained in Part 2 of the prospective International Standard, by either having additional base practices defined for an existing process or being an entirely new process. An extended process should conform to the requirements for laid down in Annex A in Part 2 of the prospective International Standard.

generic practice: A process management activity that enhances the capability to perform a process. A generic practice supports the implementation or management of a process and may be applied to any process.

generic practice adequacy: A judgment, within the process context, of the extent to which the implemented generic practice satisfies its purpose.

indicator: See *process indicator*.

organizational unit (OU): That part of an organization that is the subject of an assessment. An organizational unit deploys one or more processes that have a coherent process context (*quod vide*) and operates within a coherent set of business goals. An organizational unit is typically part of a larger organization, although in a small organization, the organizational unit may be the whole organization. An organizational unit may be, for example:

- a specific project or set of (related) projects
- a unit within an organization focused on a specific life-cycle phase (or phases) such as acquisition, development, maintenance, or support
- a part of an organization responsible for all aspects of a particular product or product set.

owner: See *(assessment) owner*.

practice: A software engineering or management activity that contributes to the creation of the output (work products) of a process or enhances the capability of a process.

process: See also *software process*.

1. A set of interrelated activities, which transform inputs into outputs (Note: the term "activities" covers the use of resources. (See ISO 8402:1994, 1.2) [ISO/IEC 12207:1995]
2. In the prospective International Standard, a statement of purpose and an essential set of practices (activities) that address that purpose. The processes described in Part 2 of the prospective International Standard are not full, formal process definitions. Rather, the statements express high level, abstract concepts without constraining how a process may be implemented.

process assessment: A disciplined evaluation of an organization's software processes against a model compatible with the reference model in the prospective International Standard.

process attribute: A measurable characteristic of process capability applicable to any process.

process attribute rating: A judgment of the level of achievement of the defined capability of the process attribute for the assessed process instance made using the defined attribute rating scale (Not, Partially, Largely, Fully achieved).

process capability:

1. The ability of a process to achieve a required goal.

2. The range of expected results that can be achieved by following a process. (See *process performance* for contrast.) [CMM Version 1.1 - CMU/SEI-93-TR-25].

process capability determination: A systematic assessment and analysis of selected software processes within an organization against a target capability, carried out with the aim of identifying the strengths, weaknesses, and risks associated with deploying the processes to meet a particular specified requirement.

(process capability determination) sponsor: The organization, part of an organization, or person initiating a process capability determination.

(process) capability level: A point on the six-point ordinal scale (of process capability) that represents the increasing capability of the performed process. Each level builds on the capability of the level below.

process capability level rating: A representation of the achieved process capability level derived from the attribute ratings for an assessed process instance according to the process capability level model defined in the prospective International Standard.

process category: A set of processes addressing the same general area of activity. The process categories address five general areas of activity: customer-supplier, engineering, project, support, and organization.

process context: The set of factors, documented in the assessment input, that influence the judgment, comprehension and comparability of process attribute ratings. These factors include:

- the application domain of the products or services
- the size, criticality and complexity of the products or services
- the quality characteristics of the products or services (see, for example, ISO 9126)
- the size of the organizational unit
- the demographics of the organization unit.

process improvement: Action taken to change an organization's processes so that they meet the organization's business needs and achieve its business goals more effectively.

process improvement action: An action planned and executed to improve all or part of the software process. A process improvement action can contribute to the achievement of more than one process goal.

process improvement program: All the strategies, policies, goals, responsibilities and activities concerned with the achievement of specified improvement goals. A process improvement program can span more than one complete cycle of process improvement.

process improvement project: Any subset of the process improvement program that forms a coherent set of actions to achieve a specific improvement.

process indicator: An assessment indicator that highlights base practices or work product characteristics. Process indicators help in substantiating the rating of base practice adequacy or base practice existence and are associated with the performance of a process.

process instance: A single instantiation of a process, where its purpose is fulfilled in terms of taking the process inputs, performing a set of practices and producing a set of process outputs.

process management indicator: An assessment indicator that highlights characteristics of a particular generic practice. Process management indicators help in substantiating the rating of generic practice adequacy and are associated with the organization's ability to manage a process.

process performance:

1. The extent to which the execution of a process achieves its purpose.
2. A measure of the actual results achieved by following a process. (See *process capability* for contrast.) [CMM Version 1.1—CMU/SEI-93-TR-25].

process profile: The set of nine process attributes ratings for an assessed process instance.

process purpose: The high level measurable objectives of performing the process and the likely outcomes of effective implementation of the process.

proposed capability: The process capability that the organization proposes to bring to bear in meeting the specified requirement. For core process capability determination, the proposed capability is the organization's current assessed capability, whereas for extended process capability determination, the proposed capability is either an enhanced capability or a constructed capability. See also *target capability*.

provisional assessor: A person who is competent to carry out assessments under the guidance and supervision of a qualified assessor.

qualified assessor: An individual who has attained the qualifications for carrying out process assessments, as defined in Part 6 of the prospective International Standard.

software process: The process or set of processes used by an organization or project to plan, manage, execute, monitor, control, and improve its software related activities. See also *process*.

SPICE resource: A person or organization that has committed time and/or funds to the SPICE project.

sponsor: See *(assessment) sponsor* and *(process capability determination) sponsor*.

standard process: The operational definition of the basic process that guides the establishment of a common process in an organization. It describes the fundamental process elements that are expected to be incorporated into any defined process. It also describes the relationships (for example, ordering and interfaces) between these process elements. See also *defined process* and *well-defined process*.

target capability: That process capability that the process capability determination sponsor judges will represent an acceptable process risk to the successful implementation of the specified requirement. See also *proposed capability*.

Technical Report Type 2: A prospective International Standard can be published initially as a Technical Report Type 2 to enable the developing standard to stabilize during a period of the user trials, prior to its issue as a full International Standard. ISO/IEC Directives state that a Technical Report Type 2 may be used to publish a prospective standard for provisional application so that information and experience of its practical use may be gathered.

well-defined process: A process with inputs, entry criteria, tasks, validation, outputs, and exit criteria that are documented, consistent, and complete. See also *defined process* and *standard process*.

work product: An artifact associated with the execution of a practice (for example, a test case, a requirement specification, code, or a work breakdown structure). The existence of the work product indicates that the practice is performed.

work product characteristic: An attribute of a type of work product that indicates the adequacy of an implementation of a practice.

SPICE Bibliography

The following is a list of articles on SPICE that have been published by the time of writing. These articles provide further details of the prospective standard and its application (for example, comparisons with existing models and practical experiences of its application). Furthermore, this list indicates where SPICE related articles tend to be published. In particular, three good places where SPICE related articles tend to appear are the proceedings of the SPICE series of conferences, the Wiley *Software Process Improvement and Practice Journal*, and the *IEEE TCSE Software Process Newsletter* (issues available for downloading from "http:\\www-se.cs.mcgill.ca\process\spn.html").

An electronic version of this list is maintained by the SPICE User Group. The electronic list of references will be updated as the literature on the SPICE documents and their application expands. The web site of the User Group is "http://www.iese.fhg.de/SPICE."

1. C. Buchman, "Assessment Instruments in Support of SPICE," *Proc. Conf. Software Quality*, South African Soc. for Quality, 1995.

2. M. Campbell, "Tool Support for Software Process Improvement and Capability Determination: Changing the Paradigm of Assessment," *Software Process Newsletter*, IEEE TCSE, No. 4, Fall 1995, pp. 12–15.

3. A. Dorling, "SPICE: Software Process Improvement and Capability dEtermination," *Information and Software Technology*, Vol. 35, Nos. 6/7, June/July 1993, pp. 404–406.

4. A. Dorling, "SPICE: Software Process Improvement and Capability dEterminaton," *Software Quality J.*, Vol. 2, 1993, pp. 209–224.

5. A. Dorling: "SPICE Spotlight," *Software Process Newsletter*, IEEE TCSE, No. 7, Fall 1996, pp. 14–16.

6. A. Dorling, "SPICE Spotlight," *Software Process Newsletter*, IEEE TCSE, No. 8, Winter 1997, pp. 14–15.

7. A. Dorling, "SPICE Spotlight," *Software Process Newsletter*, IEEE TCSE, No. 9, Spring 1997, pp. 14–16.

8. A. Dorling, "Perfect Partners: ISO9001 and SPICE," Keynote, *Proc. SQM96*, British Computer Soc., 1996.

9. J-N Drouin, "Software Quality—An International Concern," *Software Process, Quality & ISO 9000*, Vol. 3, No. 8, Aug. 1994, pp. 1–4.

10. J-N Drouin, "The SPICE project: An Overview," *Software Process Newsletter*, IEEE TCSE, No. 2, Winter 1995, pp. 8–9.

11. K. El Emam and D.R. Goldenson, "SPICE: An Empiricist's Perspective," *Proc. 2nd Int'l Software Engineering Standards Symp.*, IEEE Computer Soc. Press, Los Alamitos, Calif., 1995, pp. 84–97.

12. K. El Emam and D.R. Goldenson, "Some Initial Results from the International SPICE Trials," *Software Process Newsletter*, IEEE TCSE, No. 6, Spring 1996, pp. 1–5.

13. K. El Emam and D.R. Goldenson, "An Empirical Evaluation of the Prospective International SPICE Standard," *Software Process Improvement and Practice J.*, Vol. 2, No. 2, 1996, pp. 121–148.

14. K. El Emam and D.R. Goldenson, "Some Initial Results from the International SPICE Trials," *IEEE TCSE Software Process Newsletter*, No. 6, Spring 1996, pp. 1–5.

15. K. El Emam et al., "Interrater Agreement in SPICE-Based Assessments: Some Preliminary Results," *Proc. 4th Int'l Conf. on the Software Process*, IEEE Computer Soc. Press, Los Alamitos, Calif., 1996, pp. 149–156.

16. K. El Emam and D.R. Goldenson, "Description and Evaluation of the SPICE Phase One Trials Assessments," *Proc. ISCN'96 Conf.*, 1996.

17. K. El Emam, R. Smith, and P. Fusaro, "Modelling the Reliability of SPICE Based Assessments," *Proc. 3rd Int'l Software Engineering Standards Symp.*, IEEE Computer Soc. Press, Los Alamitos, Calif., 1997, pp. 69–82.

18. K. El Emam, L. Briand, and R. Smith, "Assessor Agreement in Rating SPICE Processes," To appear in *Software Process Improvement and Practice J.*, 1997.

19. European Software Institute, "First Feedback from SPICE Trials Gives Encouraging Results," *Improve—The Newsletter of the European Software Institute*, Issue 3, 1995, pp. 4–5.

20. P. Fusaro, K. El Emam, and R. Smith, "The Internal Consistencies of the 1987 SEI Maturity Questionnaire and the SPICE Capability Dimension," International Software Engineering Research Network technical report ISERN-97-01 (revised), 1997.

21. S. Garcia, "Relationships between CMMs & SPICE," *Proc. SPICE '96*, 1996, pp. 29–38.

22. M. Konrad, M. Paulk, and A. Graydon, "An Overview of SPICE's Model for Process Management," *Proc. 5th Int'l Conf. on Software Quality*, 1995, pp. 291–301.

23. M. Konrad, "On the Horizon: An International Standard for Software Process Improvement," *Software Process Improvement Forum*, Sept./Oct. 1994, pp. 6–8.

24. M. Konrad, M. Paulk, and A. Graydon, "An Overview of SPICE's Model for Process Management," *Proc. 5th Int'l Conf. on Software Quality*, 1995, pp. 291–301.

25. P. Kuvaja, A. Bicego, and A. Dorling, "SPICE: The software process assessment model," *Proc. ESI-ISCN Conf. on Practical Improvement of Software Processes and Products*, 1995.

26. P Kuvaja, A Bicego, and P Jansen, "The SPICE Model for Software Process Improvement," *Proc. Software Quality Management '95*, South African Soc. for Quality, 1995, pp. 13.1–13.14.

27. A. Lemire, "Process Improvement at Hydro-Quebec's Automatic Systems Department," *Proc. SPICE '96*, 1996, pp. 65–70.

28. F. Maclennan and G. Ostrolenk, "The SPICE Trials: Validating the Framework," *Proc. 2nd Int'l SPICE Symp.*, 1995.

29. P. Marshall, F. Maclennan, and M. Tobin, "Analysis of Observation and Problem Reports from Phase 1 of the SPICE Trials," *Software Process Newsletter*, IEEE TCSE, No. 6, Spring 1996.

30. R. Messnarz, "How the BOOTSTRAP Principles Can be Applied in SPICE," *Software Process Newsletter*, IEEE TCSE, No. 8, Winter 1997.

31. T. Miyoshi, "Early Experiences with Software Process Assessment Using SPICE Framework at Software Research Associates, Inc." *Software Process Improvement and Practice J.*, Vol. 2, 1996, pp. 211–235.

32. M. Morel-Chevillet and A. Kuntzman-Combelles, "Using the ami Method to Target Improvements Following a SPICE Assessment," *Proc. SPICE '96*, 1996, pp. 39–43.

33. M. Paulk, "A Perspective on the Issues Facing SPICE," *Proc. 5th Int'l Conf. on Software Quality*, 1995, pp. 415–424.

34. M. Paulk, M. Konrad, and S. Garcia, "CMM versus SPICE architectures," *Software Process Newsletter*, IEEE TCSE, No. 3, Spring 1995, pp. 7–11.

35. M. Paulk and M. Konrad, "Measuring Process Capability versus Organizational Process Maturity," *Proc. 4th Int'l Conf. on Software Quality*, 1994.

36. M. Paulk and M. Konrad, "ISO Seeks to Harmonize Numerous Global Efforts in Software Process Management," *Computer*, Vol. 27, No. 4, Apr. 1994, pp. 68–70.

37. J.G. Phippen, "Auditor and Assessor Training and Qualification," *Software Quality Management '95*, South African Soc. for Quality, 1995, pp. 8.1–8.4.

38. P. Rogoway: "Transitioning to SPICE," *Proc. SPICE '96*, 1996, pages 17–18.

39. T.P. Rout, "SPICE: A Framework for Software Process Assessment," *Software Process Improvement and Practice J.*, Pilot Issue, Aug. 1995, pp. 57-66.

40. T.P. Rout, ed., *Proc. 2nd Int'l SPICE Symp.*, published by the Australian Software Quality Research Institute, 1995.

41. T.P. Rout, "Moving Toward an International Software Quality Standard," *IS Audit & Control J.*, Jan. 1995.

42. T.P. Rout, "Determination of Software Process Capability and the Management of Risk in the Evolution of Federated Distributed Database Systems," *ICIS/University of Essex Symp.: Software Technology for Information Infrastructure*, 1995.

43. T.P. Rout, "The SPICE Project—Past, Present and Future," *Proc. SPICE '96*, 1996, pp. 5–15.

44. J-M. Simon, "Practical Tips on SPICE Structure and Guide for Use," *Proc. ISCN'96 Conf.*, 1996.

45. J-M. Simon and M. Anglade, "ProcEss Assessment for Certification (PEACE): An ESSI Project Experience," *Proc. SPICE '96*, 1996, pp. 57–63.

46. J-M. Simon, "Experiences in the Phase 1 SPICE Trials," *Software Process Newsletter*, IEEE TCSE, No. 8, Winter 1996.

47. J-M. Simon, "Choosing the Process for the Assessment Scope: A Key Factor for SPICE Assessment Success," *Proc. European Conf. on Software Process Improvement—SPI'95*, 1995.

48. R. Smith and K. El Emam, "Transitioning to Phase 2 of the SPICE Trials," *Proc. SPICE '96*, 1996, pp. 45–55.

49. R. Smith, "The SPICE Trials," *Software Process Newsletter*, IEEE TCSE, No. 8, Winter 1997.

50. V.E. Veraart and S.L. Wright, "Software Engineering Education—Adding Process to Projects: Theory, Practice and Experience," *APSEC 95, Proc. Asia-Pacific Software Engineering Conference*, 1995.

51. V.E. Veraart and S.L. Wright, "Experience with a Process-driven Approach to Software Engineering Education," *SE:E&P'96, Conference Abstracts of the 6th*

Working Conference on Software Engineering: Education and Practice, 1996, pp. 419–426.

52. V.E. Veraart and S.L. Wright. "Supporting Software Engineering Education with a Local Web Site," *Proc. Symp. Computer Science Education '96*, 1996, pp. 275–279.

53. A. Walker and R. Him Lok, "SPICE Assessments Using the SEAL Assessment Tool," *Proc. SPICE '96*, 1996, pp. 19-27.

54. I. Woodman and R. Hunter, "Analysis of Assessment Data from Phase One of the SPICE Trials," *Software Process Newsletter*, IEEE TCSE, No. 6, Spring 1996, pp. 5–10.

55. S.L. Wright and Veraart, V.E., "Software Process Improvement within the APSRU Group: Our Experience using SPICE," To appear in *Proc. 8th Int'l Conf. Information Resources Management Association*, 1997.

Index

T

About the Authors

Azuma, Motoei

Motoei Azuma is a professor at the Department of Industrial and Management Systems Engineering, School of Science and Engineering, Waseda University. He spent his sabbatical as a visiting professor at Center for Systems and Software Engineering, South Bank University in London 1991—92. He is a member of IEEE, ACM, IPSJ (Information Processing Society of Japan), JIMA (Japan Industrial Management Association), and JASMIN (The Japan Society for Management Informatics). He is a Golden Core Member of the IEEE Computer Society.

His research fields include software engineering such as software quality management and measurement, requirement analysis, software process support, and software engineering tools. He is also interested in office information systems, such as human computer interface, hyper media, and groupware.

He also has been very active in many committees for international conferences and magazines including: IEEE/Computer Society's COMPSAC steering Committee Member, IEEE/Computer Society's COMPSAC'89 Program Committee Cochairperson, IEEE/Computer Society's COMPSAC'91 Program Committee Chairperson, IEEE/Computer Society Asia Pacific Activity Committee Member, ISESS '95 (International Software Engineering Standards Symposium)—Committee Member, AQuIS'96 (Achieving Quality In Software) Program Committee Cochairperson, OOIS'96 (Object Oriented Information Systems) Program Committee, ISESS '97—Program Committee Member, ICSE'98 (International Conference on Software Engineering 98)—Subcommittee Chairperson, Interacting With Computers (Butterworth)—Editorial Board, *Journal of Computer and Software Engineering* (Ablex Publishing)—Editorial Board, and *Empirical Software Engineering: An International Journal* (Kluwer)—Editorial Board.

Barker, Harry

Harry Barker is employed as the SPICE Assignment Manager by the Defence Evaluation Research Agency (DERA), Command and Information Systems,

Systems Engineering, Software Engineering Group. He has managed the assignment since its inception in 1990 and is a founder member of the SPICE Project which was created in January 1993. The DERA is sponsored by the United Kingdom Ministry of Defence to create a method for supplier selection that is acceptable to industry.

Harry is also the Business Manager for the DERA *Process Professional Portfolio* products which are the DERA approaches to the application of ISO 15504 (SPICE).

Harry is the European Technical Centre Manager coordinating the resources donated for product development and the European Chairman of the SPICE Management Board. He is a founder member of the SPICE Executive Management Board.

Harry has been employed in the UK Ministry of Defence since 1964, engaged in assurance of the quality of military platforms and their equipment during the procurement and repair cycle. Since 1986 he has managed a team of software quality specialists who provided technical support to Project Managers during procurement and development of platforms containing software. These activities have involved: (a) acting as a team leader during the assessment of the suitability of the Quality Management Systems of prospective and current defence contractors to the requirements of the Defence Standard 05-21, followed by Allied Quality Assurance Procedures AQAP 1 and AQAP 13, now ISO 9001 and 9000-3 and (b) managing a team of software quality specialists providing advice and carrying out audits during procurement and development phases of most weapon systems life cycles and advising the Project Manager of unsatisfactory situations and their possible resolutions.

Buchman, Carrie

Mrs. Buchman is an engineering manager at the AlliedSignal Center for Process Improvement, an arm of corporate engineering. She is the chief architect of AlliedSignal's Software Process Improvement Program and is the leader of the AlliedSignal Software Technology Council. Mrs. Buchman led a cross-functional and cross-business unit team in designing a one-company software process and is a core team member on the ISO Software Assessment Standard effort. Similarly she is also responsible for systems engineering processes. Prior to employment at AlliedSignal, Mrs. Buchman was employed by Eaton Corporation to supporting manufacturing/engineering interface software, and by Bolt Beranek and Newman to generate simulation models of submarine acoustics. Mrs. Buchman graduated from Smith College with a Bachelor of Arts degree in Physics and Mathematics. She received her Master of Science in Computer Science from Fairleigh Dickinson University.

Coallier, François

François Coallier is General Manager—IT Procurement & Supplier Quality at Bell Canada. He is responsible for the procurement of Bell Canada IT products as well as for the standards and process used by Bell for assessing and managing Supplier Quality. He also leads the team that assesses and manages the risks associated with the procurement of software products. François is the International Secretary of the Joint ISO and IEC subcommittee responsible for the elaboration of Software Engineering Standards (ISO/IEC JTCS/SC7). Coauthor of numerous IEEE Software Engineering Standards, he has been a member of numerous Software Engineering conference program committees. In 1992 François chaired the International Workshop on computer-aided Software Engineering (CASE 92). He is the architect of the TRILLIUM model. François has a BSc in Biology from McGill University and a BEng in Engineering Physics and an MASc in Electrical Engineering from Montreal's Ecole Polytechnique. He is also a "Certified Quality Analyst" (CQA) from the Quality Assurance Institute.

Colleta, Antonio

Antonio Coletta is currently employed at Tecnopolis, a Science and Technology Park located in Southern Italy, with the position of Manager of Software Process Quality Services. He graduated from the University of Toronto (Canada) with a Bachelor's degree in Computer Science. After graduation, he worked extensively in the field of Database Management Systems, holding a position in the Italian subsidiary of Cullinet Software Inc. He also worked for many years with Olivetti as a Lead Software Engineer. In Olivetti he led a project for the development of a CASE (Computer-Aided Software Engineering) environment. He is a qualified ISO 9000 auditor and has extensive experience in helping software small and medium-sized enterprises (SME) in implementing process improvement plans. He participates actively in international standardization activities and has been part of the SPICE Project team since the project kick-off. He has contributed to the development of the parts concerning the Process Assessment activities, the Rating Framework and Assessment Instruments and has also conducted several experimental assessments with the early version of the SPICE documents. He currently acts as the Italian National coordinator in the SPICE/WG10 project.

Craigmyle, Mac

Mac Craigmyle is the architect of the Process Professional Model and Process Professional Assessment method, part of the Process Professional Portfolio of products and services. He is a principal UK expert for the SPICE Project. In the last year, Mac has participated in assessments conducted by some of the largest companies in the UK, extending the Process Professional Model to match their business requirements. These assessments have involved incorporating additional systems and hardware processes into the Process Professional Model.

Davies, Alan

Alan Davies (M Sc, C Eng., Eur Ing., QAI) is a Director of QAI Europe, Member of TC1/SC7/WG10,Lead TickIT & ISO9001 auditor and an Independent Software Consultant. He has 30 years in the Aerospace field with Westlands, MOD(PE) and British Aerospace, with tasks and projects relating to Software Engineering.

Dorling, Alec

Alec Dorling is the international SPICE Project Manager. He is currently resident at IVF's Centre for Software Engineering in Sweden. Previously he was the International and Strategic Projects Manager at the European Software Institute (ESI) in Spain.

Alec is a Chartered Engineer with 25 years experience in the software industry gained both in real-time and commercial systems environments. He is an internationally-recognized expert in the field of Software Quality Management and Process Improvement.

Alec has been involved with most of the UK Government's initiatives in software engineering and software quality over the years, including the STARTS program, the Software Tools Demonstration Centre, the Software Engineering Solutions program, the Quality Management Library, and TickIT. He has also been consultant to the Software Quality Unit of the UK Department of Trade and Industry providing advise on priorities for government action on Software Quality, Standards, and Certification. He carried out the initial studies for the UK Ministry of Defence which were a precursor to the launch of the SPICE Project.

Drouin, Jean-Normand

Jean-Normand Drouin has more than 12 years experience as a software engineer at Bell Canada, the largest Telecom company in Canada. He is a Trillium author and assessor (Trillium is Bell Canada's own Software Process Assessment method for the Telecommunications industry). He is also the SPICE Technical Center Manager for Canada, Central and South America, as well as one of the first SPICE assessors.

El Emam, Khaled

Khaled El Emam obtained his PhD from the Department of Electrical and Electronics Engineering, King's College, the University of London (UK) in 1994. He was previously a research scientist at the Centre de recherche informatique de Montreal (CRIM) in Canada. Currently he is the head of the Quantitative Methods Group at the Fraunhofer Institute for Experimental Software Engineering in Germany. El Emam is also the founding and current editor of the *IEEE TCSE Software Process Newsletter*.

He is a member of the Core Trials Team of ISO's SPICE Project, which is empirically evaluating the emerging International Standard. He has previously worked in both small and large software research and development projects for organizations such as Toshiba International Company and Honeywell Control Systems. He has published more than forty articles on software engineering measurement, empirical evaluation in software engineering, software process improvement, and requirements engineering.

Graydon, Alan

Allan Graydon is currently working at Nortel (Northern Telecom) as a manager of Process Evolution in its Public Carrier Networks division. Allan's education is in Computer Science. He received his BS in Mathematics—Computer Science from the University of Waterloo located in Waterloo, Ontario. Allan is located at Nortel in Ottawa, Canada and his responsibilities span the continuous improvement of the processes, procedures, and methods used in the design, development, and support of the Nortel Telecommunications products and services. He has over 20 years of software development, process and software quality experience, fifteen of those years at Nortel. Allan was one of the authors of the Bell Canada/Nortel Trillium Software Assessment standard which is the current *defacto* standard for telecommunications Software Process Assessments. Allan is also the Product Manager of Part 2.

Goldenson, Dennis

Dennis Goldenson is a member of the technical staff at the Software Engineering Institute (SEI) in Pittsburgh, Pennsylvania, USA. His interests focus on software engineering measurement and analysis. Goldenson came to the SEI over six years ago, after teaching at Carnegie Mellon University since 1982. He is the author of many published papers and professional presentations. A coauthor of a recent SEI technical report on the benefits of software process improvement and of several papers on the SPICE Trials, he was a lead developer of the SEI's Software Process Maturity Questionnaire and was part of the development team for the Interim Profile appraisal method. Currently he is an active member of the SPICE Project's Core Trials Team.

Hailey, Victoria

Victoria has over 17 years experience in the software and service industries (including 4 years at IBM Canada Software Laboratory in Quality Assurance and Information Development). She is a SPICE Lead Assessor, an ISO 9000 Lead Assessor, a trained SEI/CMM Software Capability Evaluator (SCE), and a Certified Management Consultant (CMC) with the Institute of Certified Management Consultants of Canada. She contributes to several projects, including ISO/IEC /JTC1/SC7/WG10, WG7, and ISO TC 176/SC2 for ISO 9000. She received her Bachelor's degree from the University of Toronto, Canada.

She is currently president of The Victoria Hailey Group Corporation, a management consultancy providing process improvement consultancy services in the software and service industries, using models such as the SPICE model, ISO 9000, ISO 9000-3, TickIT, and CMM. Their mandate is to help businesses, through process assessment, develop process-improvement, quality management, and workplace performance improvement programs. Clients include Sony of Canada, Bell Canada, Ontario Hydro, Canadian Tire Acceptance, Microsoft Canada, IBM Canada Limited, and Delcan Corporation. Victoria has published and presented papers at ACM conferences (1992, 1993) as well as at numerous international and national trade shows and conventions, including: COMDEX'95, Client/Server World'95, Canadian Information Processing Society CIPS'95.

She is a member ACM, IEEE, CIPS, and the SPICE Trials team and is the technical editor of the *IEEE TCSE Software Process Newsletter*. She is also a Local Trials Coordinator for SPICE Trials in Canada.

Hamilton, John

John Hamilton has been a key member of the international SPICE Project since it began in 1993. He has contributed directly to five of the nine parts of the draft standard and is technical editor of the SPICE guide for determining supplier process capability. John has developed and delivered training material on the SPICE document set throughout the world and has participated extensively in the international SPICE Trials. He is a qualified PPA (Process Professional) Assessor, a trained Software Capability Evaluation (SCE) team leader, and has participated in a number of SCEs on behalf of the UK Ministry of Defence.

Hunter, Robin

Robin Hunter has an honours BSc in Mathematics and Astronomy and a PhD in Astronomy (Celestial Mechanics), both from the University of Glasgow. He has been on the teaching staffs of the Universities of Glasgow, Newcastle upon Tyne, and Strathclyde and is currently a Senior Lecturer in the Department of Computer Science at the University of Strathclyde. He is a Member of the British Computer Society and the ACM. His research interests are in Software Engineering, particularly Software Assessment and the Implementation of Programming Languages. He was Grant Holder for the University of Strathclyde's contribution to the SCOPE (ESPRIT) project and, over the last two years, has been contributing to the ISO SPICE Project, particularly in the areas of Software Process Capability Determination and analysis of the results of the SPICE Trials. He is adviser to the Brazilian Government's TAQS project on Technology for Software Quality and is currently collaborating with colleagues in the Russian Academy of Sciences on issues concerned with Language-Based approaches to the definition and collection of software metrics.

Jansen, Pascal

Pascal Jansen received an engineering degree in Computer Science from the Swiss Federal Institute of Technology of Lausanne in 1987 and a Master of Science in Management from Boston University in 1993. He has been working as a project leader and software engineering consultant in Finsiel, Italy since 1988. He has been participating in the SPICE Project since 1993. His current interests and activities are related to audits and assessments, quality system management, and improvement program management.

Maclennan, Fiona

Fiona Maclennan was sponsored through an Electronics Engineering degree at the University of Southampton by Marconi Space and Defence Systems Limited. She has worked in the software industry since 1984. Her experience covers a range of software development projects for the software tools and electronic design automation markets, including the development of tools for static analysis of software and the development of programming language subsets for safety-critical applications. In 1990 she joined Lloyd's Register. She has been largely responsible for the development of Lloyd's Register's software assessment services and is currently manager of the software assurance service. She has managed and undertaken a variety of software system assessment and consultancy projects in a range of industries. She is a registered ISO 9001

(TickIT) assessor and has undertaken over 30 TickIT certification audits. At the time of writing, she has undertaken three assessments using the SPICE document set. In January 1994 she was appointed International Trials Coordinator for the SPICE Project, a role she undertook on behalf of the European Software Institute (ESI). In this role, she was responsible for the planning, coordination, monitoring, analysis, and reporting of the first phase of SPICE Trials.

Marshall, Peter

Not available at time of printing.

Nevalainen, Risto

Risto Nevalainen (Tech.Lich., Computer Science) is the founder and director of Software Technology Transfer Finland Ltd, a company specializing in software process assessment and effectiveness analysis. During 1989–1995 he was director of the Information Technology Development Center and Finnish Data Communication Association. He has been project manager of the Finnish Information Society Strategy and many other national IT-related projects in Finland. In 1996 he worked as a Senior Fellow in the European Software Institute ESI, participating in SPICE development and trials projects. He has been one of the original developers of the SPICE product set.

Ostrolenk, Gary

Gary Ostrolenk began his career in IT at Lloyd's Register, where he pursued research interests in reliability prediction, software measurement, reverse engineering, and repositories. He conducted TickIT audits & SPICE assessments, and coordinated international SPICE Trials on behalf of the European Software Institute ESI). More recently, Gary has led the definition and implementation of a standard Systems Development Process for NatWest UK, integrating business and IT activities. He is now developing project and program management processes for NatWest Retail Banking Services.

Rout, Terry

Terry Rout is a Senior Lecturer in the School of Computing and Information Technology at Griffith University, Queensland and is associated with the Software Quality Institute at the University. He is Chair of Committee IT/15 of

Standards Australia, dealing with Software Engineering Standards and has been a member of the Australian delegation to the International Committee on Software Engineering Standards from 1992 to 1996. He has been a member of the international Management Board for the SPICE Project since its inception, working toward the development and validation of an International Standard for Software Process Assessment. He is Manager of the Australian Software Process Assessment Centre, established to provide a regional focus for this work and is the editor of two of the components of the SPICE document suite. He was heavily involved in the redevelopment of Version 2.0 of the document set. In 1996, he was a visiting fellow at the European Software Institute (ESI).

Sanders, Joc

Joc Sanders is a senior consultant at the Centre for Software Engineering, Dublin, Ireland, where he manages quality and software process improvement programs, and provides consultancy, ISO 9000 audit, and training services to the Irish software community. He has contributed to several EU software best practice projects and is currently the European coordinator for the SPIRE project. He is actively involved in developing international software engineering standards, and in particular, contributes to the SPICE Software Process Assessment project through ISO/IEC JTC1/SC7/WG10.

He has more than 25 years experience in software and management information systems, as a freelance consultant and as a developer and manager, much of it gained with British Telecom in the United Kingdom.

He holds an MSc in Computer Science from London University, is a Member of both the Irish Computer Society (currently on Council with responsibility for development of a professional development scheme) and the British Computer Society, and is a Chartered Engineer.

He is the coauthor of *Software Quality—a Framework for Success in Software Development and Support*, Addison-Wesley, 1994.

Simms, Peter

Peter Simms is the Technical Architect and Project Editor within the international SPICE Project. As Director of the Process Management Programme at CITI Limited in the UK, he is a specialist in the assessment, management, design, and improvement of software processes, providing consultancy and research services to government and commercial organizations. He is also an experienced lecturer and teaches within CITI's core Project Management Education Programme and other short courses.

Simon, Jean-Martin

Jean-Martin Simon has over 14 years of professional experience, including project management and software engineering activities for real-time and industrial systems and software. He had been working since 1993 as a Quality Manager for CISI/France. His experience in software process management is based on feedback from operational practices conducted during project development. He also takes benefits from an involvement in standardization related to software engineering. Working for AFNOR (French national body) he contributes as an expert with working groups about the software life-cycle processes series standards (ISO 12207) and the assessment and improvement for software engineering processes standards (ISO 15504). He contributes to the SPICE Project within ISO/IEC JTC1/SC7/WG10 and did SPICE assessment during the Phase 1 Trials as Lead Assessor. He managed internal quality improvement programs and is involved in external consulting about Software Process Assessment and improvement strategies and techniques. He has recently founded the company Applied Quality Transfert (AQT).

Smith, Robert

Robert Smith is a Project Manager at the European Software Institute (ESI) in Bilbao, Spain where he is responsible for product management. He has over 13 years of experience in the development and management of embedded software systems in the avionics industry. He is the SPICE International and European Trials Coordinator for Phase 2 of the SPICE Trials. He is an instructor of the ESI SPICE Training course and is also an SEI-qualified instructor of the Introduction to CMM. He has a degree in Computer Science from Strathclyde University and is a Chartered Engineer through membership of the British Computer Society.

Thomson, Helen

Helen's career in industrial software development has been extensive, including time spent with CERN in Geneva, Logica in London, Spacelab in Bremen, Tornado in Munich, Airbus in Freiburg, and Metier Management in Ipswich. She is now a director of her own firm Faxbase Limited in Suffolk UK as well as leading research into Software Process Improvement at the University of East Anglia. Helen has made major contributions to the development of the SPICE assessment instrument and brings a perspective of applying Software Process Assessment to small business enterprises.

Tobin, Mary

Mary Tobin read Mathematical Sciences at Trinity College Dublin. She has worked in the software industry since 1984. During this period, she spent nine years in software development, covering a range of applications and technologies, in both a technical and managerial capacity. This time included the development of reverse engineering tools, as well as flight test and data take-on software. Experience was gained initially in a software house and, since 1989, at Lloyd's Register. She is now quality representative for the System Integrity and Risk Management Department, responsible for the development, implementation, and audit of its ISO 9001 Quality System. She is also involved in conducting SPICE Software Process Assessments and ISO 9001/TickIT audits.

Veraart, Val

Val Veraart was a partner in a computing consultancy company in the early 1980s at a time when personal computers were finding their way into small business. She joined the Computer Science Program teaching staff in 1986. During her ten years at Murdoch University, Val designed and taught courses in Systems Analysis and Design and, with Sid Wright, in Software Engineering. She also supervised a number of student Software Engineering projects that developed and built a range of software engineering tools suitable for use by small project teams. Val is currently with CSIRO Tropical Agriculture as the software engineering manager for the APSIM project and undertakes research in Software Engineering and Software Process Engineering

Walker, Alastair

Alastair Walker is presently an associate professor in the Department of Electrical Engineering, University of the Witwatersrand. He was responsible for establishing the Software Engineering Applications Laboratory in 1988. Since that time, the SEAL has become known as the leading provider of advanced professional courses on topics in Software Engineering, particularly in the areas of application of object-oriented design methodology in industrial applications and in software quality systems management. SEAL was the first academic enterprise internationally to receive an ISO 9001 certification for software development. He is a Certified Quality Analyst and a Certified Software Quality Systems Auditor. He is the Chairman of the SABS work group involved in the development of the emerging International Standard for Software Process Assessment and for the upgrade of the 1991 version of ISO 9000-3. He is the South African representative on the ISO/IEC JTC1/SC7 Advisory Board.

Woodman, Ian

After receiving an honors BSc degree in Computer Science from the University of Strathclyde in 1994, Ian Woodman worked as a Graduate Teaching Assistant in the Department of Computer Science in the University while studying for an M.Phil. degree in the area of Software Process Assessment. His research interests lie in the area of Software Process Assessment, in particular in the visualisation and analysis of assessment results and their use in the prediction, control, and evaluation of Software Process Improvement. He is also interested in Software Product Quality and the relationship between Software Process and Product. He was a member of the Core Trials Team for the SPICE Project.

Wright, Sid

Sid Wright started out as an astrophysicist and migrated to building software development environments and computer management with the Starlink Project in the UK. He then emigrated to Australia to become the foundation lecturer in the Computer Science Program at Murdoch University. After 12 years of teaching, research, and building the software engineering program at Murdoch, it was time for a change. He is now with the CSIRO's Outreach project as a software process engineer attached to the APSIM project in CSIRO Tropical Agriculture helping to improve their software development process.

IEEE Computer Society Publications

The world-renowned Computer Society publishes, promotes, and distributes a wide variety of authoritative computer science and engineering texts. These books are available in two formats: 100 percent original material by authors preeminent in their field who focus on relevant topics and cutting-edge research, and reprint collections consisting of carefully selected groups of previously published papers with accompanying original introductory and explanatory text.

Submission of proposals: For guidelines and information on Computer Society books, send e-mail to cs.books@computer.org or write to the Acquisitions Editor, IEEE Computer Society, P.O. Box 3014, 10662 Los Vaqueros Circle, Los Alamitos, CA 90720-1314. Telephone +1 714-821-8380. FAX +1 714-761-1784.

IEEE Computer Society Proceedings

The Computer Society also produces and actively promotes the proceedings of more than 130 acclaimed international conferences each year in multimedia formats that include hard and softcover books, CD-ROMs, videos, and on-line publications.

For information on Computer Society proceedings, send e-mail to cs.books@computer.org or write to Proceedings, IEEE Computer Society, P.O. Box 3014, 10662 Los Vaqueros Circle, Los Alamitos, CA 90720-1314. Telephone +1 714-821-8380. FAX +1 714-761-1784.

Additional information regarding the Computer Society, conferences and proceedings, CD-ROMs, videos, and books can also be accessed from our web site at http://computer.org/cspress

4/15/97